Immaculate
& Powerful

Immaculate & Powerful

The Female in Sacred Image and Social Reality

Edited by
Clarissa W. Atkinson
Constance H. Buchanan
and Margaret R. Miles

The Harvard Women's Studies in Religion Series

Beacon Press
25 Beacon Street
Boston, Massachusetts 02108

Beacon Press books are published under the auspices
of the Unitarian Universalist Association
of Congregations in North America.

Printed in the United States of America

92 91 90 89 88 87   8 7 6 5 4 3 2

Library of Congress Cataloging in Publication Data

Main entry under title:

Immaculate and powerful.
    Bibliography: p.
    Includes index.
    1. Women and religion—Addresses, essays, lectures.
2. Feminism—Religion aspects—Addresses, essays,
lectures.   3. Woman (Theology)—Addresses, essays,
lectures.   I. Atkinson, Clarissa W.   II. Buchanan,
Constance H.   III. Miles, Margaret Ruth.
BL458.I46   1985   291.1′78344   85–70448
ISBN 0–8070–1004–9

Contents

Contents

Preface

In the last decade, feminist scholars have begun to redefine central methodological problems and approaches in religion and history. One of these is the relationship between religious images and social reality. Religious images play a powerful role in shaping cultural patterns and social structures, but the precise nature of that role has not been well understood; it was not often examined directly by historians and theologians until scholars began to take gender as a primary category of analysis. When women's religious experience is placed at the center of scholarly attention, it becomes obvious that religious images cannot be usefully explored in isolation from social roles and institutions. Traditional disciplines must often be disrupted when the dynamics of these crucial relationships are explored, and particularly when they are explored across cultures and with attention to gender.

Since 1973, a community of international feminist scholars has assembled at Harvard Divinity School each year to pursue a wide variety of questions about women and religion. For this volume, the first in a series of Harvard Women's Studies in Religion, we have invited scholars from the program to address issues of image and reality from the perspective of their own interests and disciplines. A characteristic of this volume, as of the program itself, is its attention to gender in relation to other variables such as race, culture, and class. Diversity of perspective has made possible the exploration of vital questions too frequently overlooked when "fields" are narrowly construed in terms of the interests of one group. Future volumes in the series, while consistent with the commitment of the program to seek out and support scholarship centered on the richness and diversity of women's experience, will focus on various themes in the investigation of the relationships of gender, culture, and religion.

This volume, as well as the series of which it is the first, represents one aspect of the intellectual and educational endeavor of the Women's Studies in Religion Program at the Harvard Divinity School. At a time when the presence of women in academia is sometimes construed as a "simple" question of access for women to disciplines defined and dominated by men, the generous support of the Ford, Rockefeller, and Merrill foundations has allowed Harvard Divinity School to pursue the intellectual implications of women's presence in religion and religious studies. The support of these foundations undergirds the work and vision of students, faculty, and visiting scholars at the Divinity School and of the Advisory Committee, which helps to shape the research goals of the program. This volume is published in recognition of the achievements of the decade past and in anticipation of the work to come; our intention has been to convey the importance and excitement of this innovative research.

CLARISSA W. ATKINSON
CONSTANCE H. BUCHANAN
MARGARET R. MILES

Cambridge, Massachusetts, 1985

Immaculate & Powerful

One

Introduction

Margaret R. Miles

Scholars of women's experience have discovered the problems and satisfactions of attempting to reconstruct an accurate account of historical and contemporary people who have been excluded from setting the values, style, and momentum of their cultures. A crucial part of the task of recovering the stories of those who have neither defined their cultures nor played dominant roles in them is the development of new methodologies. When women's historical and contemporary experience is taken as the focus of study, not only do new stories come to light to be added to the store of humanistic learning already in hand, but our understanding of historical and contemporary societies itself changes; a whole new picture of these societies emerges. Taking seriously the different values, concerns, and interests of women often alters dramatically our sense of the achievements of the intellectual, political, and cultural elites traditionally viewed as the only members of their societies worthy of scholarly inquiry.

All explorations of women's lives are historical studies, in a sense; the cultural matrix and life situation of the women we study —whether these women are historical or contemporary—are integrally related, and form the ground of their ideas and symbols. The authors whose work is presented here find the interface of religious symbols and social situations decisive for understanding both the oppression and the creativity of women; they show that without attention to the religious ideas and symbols accessible to women, an account of their experience is seriously incomplete. On the other hand, without consideration of the social and cultural arrangements supported by religions, the practical effect of religious symbols cannot be discerned. Neither religion nor culture

1

in isolation from the other yields a basis for analysis of women's experience. Seen together, they enable us to form educated hypotheses about women's energies and activities.

Let us first examine the specific thesis of this volume, namely, that the area of intersection of religion and culture provides a fruitful nexus for exploring women's lives. The essays included here reveal that religion can provide women with a critical perspective on and alternatives to the conditioning they receive as members of their societies. In addition, the ambiguity of this relation between women and religion also becomes apparent. Not only can religion make available tools with which women may create a degree of spiritual, political, and personal autonomy not provided by secular culture, but it also inevitably forms part of women's cultural conditioning.

The relative activity with which religious ideas and images are critically appropriated or the passivity with which they are introjected seems to be crucial. The religious myth of the Christian West insists that Eve, the innovator, can lead her followers only to evil; Mary, the passive, submissive, obedient woman, is urged as the model and goal of women who aspire to the acceptance and appreciation of their families and communities. Yet our essays indicate that when women dare to reject the religious ideas and images that inhibit and enervate them, when they begin to weave new patterns with the religious ideas and images conducive to personal transformation and social change, religion can become a powerful positive factor in their lives. In this volume, Clarissa Atkinson, Dorothy Bass, Jo Ann Hackett, Nancy Jay, Delores Williams, and Judith Van Herik deal poignantly with the ambiguity of religious ideals, symbols, and practices for the women they discuss. In using the religious ideas and images offered within their cultures, women must choose carefully the religious symbols that effectively challenge and empower them rather than those that oppress and render them passive. Again and again our essays demonstrate the danger and opportunity simultaneously contained in religious symbols for women.

Perhaps Judith Van Herik's discussion of Simone Weil gives the strongest description of any in this volume of the ambiguous role of religion in a woman's life. Simone Weil violently rejected the roles available to women in her culture, and created an alternative drawn partly from resistance to political and ecclesiastical institutions and partly from critical appropriation of religous ideals. Religious ideas both empowered Weil's life and ultimately destroyed it. The ambiguous power of religious symbols for creativity and danger is revealed in Weil's story with an intensity not found when religion plays a less central role in the life of a woman.

As Elisabeth Schüssler Fiorenza demonstrated in her recent book, *In Memory of Her*, it is not sufficient simply to identify in any particular society the forms of oppression of women.[1] An accurate sense of women's experience can come only from detecting *both* the ideologies and institutions that oppress and the struggle of women to create active and fulfilling lives for themselves and their daughters. If we look only for oppression we will miss the creativity with which women—never the primary shapers of their cultures— have foraged in their cultural environments for the tools with which to make their lives.

The essay by Dorothy Bass illustrates the subtlety with which "presumably restrictive views of womanhood" must be interpreted in particular cultural contexts. A historian who is looking only for the ideas and institutions that oppressed women in nineteenth-century New England would be likely to identify distinctions between men's public sphere of action and influence and women's restricted private sphere as one of the sources of women's oppression. Yet Bass describes how religious perfectionism originating in the "private sphere" gave a social action group, the Garrisonians, and in particular two members of that group, the Grimké sisters, a perspective on Victorian gender arrangements that enabled them to campaign vigorously for social change. The clear cultural identification of "woman's virtue" became the basis for the Garrisonians' choice of a single moral standard—that of women's nonviolent ethical sensitivity—as their religious and political ideal.

What emerges when we look for women's creativity within their cultures as well as the cultural forms of their oppression is a growing awareness of a process by which women receive and create the patterns of their lives. The process is always a blend of identifying, adapting, and rejecting fragments of the cultural fabric that contribute to, or detract from, their lives. While men have frequently envisioned and described the task of culture making as one of creation *ex nihilo,* women's creativity in predominantly male cultures has proceeded more on the model of quilt making. Women have selected and arranged in new configurations pieces of the cultural tapestry and in so doing have created strong and unique new patterns, patterns that display the vivid colors of their experience.[2]

Men also rearrange rather than create the material of cultural products, but they do not often acknowledge that this is the process by which they create. In our own time, the pejorative use of the word *patchwork* expresses scorn for the activity of repatterning already existing pieces. Yet patchwork is what all human beings do in their most creative moments. Oppression and creativity, both found in the interface of religion and culture, appear simultaneously in the design of women's lives. Thus these essays identify religion not only as a form of women's oppression, though this is one of the common threads in the very different social and religious situations discussed, but also as one of the primary tools of women's creativity.

Anne Klein discusses the religious tools available to women in Tibetan Buddhism, a religion in which women's bodies and birth-giving capacity symbolize the creative emptiness from which all living beings are generated. Despite the potentially honorific implications for women in this symbolism, however, "religious egalitarianism fails to translate into social egalitarianism." Klein distinguishes between acceptance of an "outer" religion, that is, fitting oneself to the behavioral and attitudinal requirements of a particular religion, and "inner" appropriation of aspects of religion that tend toward personal and social transformation. As her study shows, even the existence of a generous array of female imagery at the heart of a religious tradition does not guarantee that women will automatically achieve ecclesiastical and social roles congruent with this imagery. Klein suggests some reasons for this "failure of religious vision," finding the lack of a vibrant "appropriation of inner religion" a decisive factor in separating positive female symbolism from full social equality for women. Her essay shows that even strong female symbols can lose their potential for social change by ritualized expression in male institutions.

Several of the other essays also discuss the distinction between religion passively accepted and religion critically appropriated. Barbara Corrado Pope discusses nineteenth-century Marian devotion, distinguishing between religion as personal and communal energy and the appropriation of this energy by a powerful ecclesiastical hierarchy. She gives a vivid account of the use of a female symbol by the Roman Catholic church to reinforce established

4

political and ecclesiastical power. A reinterpretation of the Virgin Mary by Roman Catholic officials at the end of the nineteenth century acted as a powerful counterattack to modernism and rationalism. Klein, Van Herik, Jay, Hackett, and Brooten, in the contexts of their different studies, also distinguish between the fruitfulness for women of critically appropriated religion and religion governed by ecclesiastical structures. These writers describe situations in which informal popular religion was amalgamated into ecclesiastical organizations in order to provide much needed resources of strong religious commitment and affective energy for spiritually impoverished or threatened institutions. The losses for women resulting from this incorporation are often dramatic.

Clarissa Atkinson describes the other side of this coin; instead of ecclesiastical appropriation of women's religious energy and vitality, she shows how a female symbol was used as a vehicle by a male clergy to communicate to women how they should think and act. The story and visual images of Saint Monica, Saint Augustine's mother, were repeatedly used "to show mothers how to be good, as good was variously defined by the clerical men who held up her image and exhorted women to follow." Atkinson's essay gives a fascinating example of the multivalence of the saints as religious symbols. These symbols can be used "at different times by different persons for totally different ends." The essay illuminates the process of the "saint making" of a fourth-century woman, a process in which men's notions and fantasies of the "good mother" defined Monica's cult and image.

If women's religiousness is not, in some form, preserved in institutions, it is not available for the support and inspiration of other women. On the other hand, in those instances in which women's religious creativity has been gathered into ecclesiastical institutions, its specificity and particular beauty has been dissipated in its use for institutional renewal. In a crude but expressive phrase, women's religious creativity and commitment has frequently been "sucked up" for the support of male religious institutions in which women have neither leadership roles nor direct influence. In the major religions of the world, women have not created institutions that effectively preserve, communicate, and transmit across generations women's specific religious syntheses. Rather, women's religious insights and practices have either been ignored or discounted by male hierarchies, or they have been incorporated without bringing about structural or axiological change in these institutions. None of our essays presents a positive picture of women's experience in relation to ecclesiastical institutions.

The question of women's access to formal and informal power recurs throughout this volume. Issues of power and empowerment form one of the fundamental categories of analysis. Do religions provide women with tools for self-actualization? Where do such tools come from in particular societies, and exactly what are they? How can we determine whether and when religious tools are more likely to support the suppression of women? Under what conditions can women use religious symbols as support or challenge for growth, initiative, and creativity? Under what circumstances can religions offer women possibilities for transcending the social and ecclesiastical arrangements of their societies? Do the same religious symbols act on women differently according to whether a woman lives in a conventional family situation or, as in the case of women religious, has left the family for a community of women? Do the multivalent messages of visual religious images affect a woman differently in direct relation to her life situation so that, for example, the image of the Virgin and Child might reinforce docility, submissiveness, and passivity in one woman while communicating to another woman her potential for participation in the Virgin's power? These and other questions relating to power and empowerment occur frequently in our essays.

Questions concerning women's sexuality also emerge in several of the essays. Who controls a woman's sexual identity? Here the political dimensions of sexuality are the major focus of attention. Williams's critique of most feminist theology from the perspective of the literature by and about black women identifies a woman's ability to determine her sexuality and its expression as essential to her autonomy and energy. This is an aspect of self-realization and transformation on which many white feminists are silent.

The political and theological dimensions of women's sexuality are raised in Bernadette Brooten's essay on late classical and early Christian attitudes to female homoeroticism. She demonstrates the close link in the minds of male writers between male control of women's sexuality and women's sexuality as a theological issue. Heterosexuality and male control of women's sexuality is treated, in the writings of the Apostle Paul, as the reflection of an eternal cosmic order, a link in a long chain of interconnected reflections of cosmic hierarchy. Thus, female acceptance of the "passive, sub-

6

ordinate role accorded to them by nature" was promoted on the basis of woman's position in the "order of creation." Brooten shows that politics and theology were firmly interwoven in Paul's exhortations to patriarchal order. Clearly, the control of women's sexuality is an issue our authors find pivotal in the attempt to understand the interface of women and religion.

Several of our essays are not primarily about women, but treat male use of female symbols or male formulations of gender ideology and women's roles in society. Nancy Jay explores the relationship between the ritual practice of orthodox Christianity and the exclusively male hierarchy of the Roman Catholic church as features of each other. She describes the alternative and conflicting patterns of descent from females and from males, finding in the Christian Eucharist a ritual of blood sacrifice structurally parallel to ceremonies in which descent from males is established. Apostolic succession, the "male descent" of the Roman Catholic ecclesiastical hierarchy, underlies the claim of this male clergy to control life-giving salvation, an alternative to the "death through birth from women." In Jay's discussion, the Christian eucharistic ritual, seen from an anthropological perspective, claims to be "birth done better," intentionally, and on a spiritual rather than physical level. Jay describes the structural parallel and conflicting alternative to women's birth giving in the Christian Eucharist.

Sheila Briggs's essay discusses male use of gender analysis. Briggs finds in nineteenth-century descriptions of gender as destiny the model on which can be posited, in the twentieth century, the belief in race and nationality as destiny. An "order of creation" in which women were seen as "naturally" suited to a private sphere of marriage and motherhood supplied the basis for a "theology of orders"; a theology of orders based firmly on created order, in turn, attributes the formulations of female character by nineteenth-century theologians to the Jews, thereby defining them "out of the male Christian sphere." Briggs sees this intricate concatenation of ideas originally constructed around gender issues as crucial for rationalizations of the anti-Semitism of Hitler's regime.

Methodological issues are also raised by examining women's history. What constitutes trustworthy evidence for women's lives and how are we to interpret this evidence? The first difficulty facing the historian of women stems from the limitation of material evidence that directly reveals women's longings, fears, and everyday lives. Material that was often ignored by historians of ideas, however, now plays an important role in the reconstruction of women's history. Popular devotional texts and visual images, letters and journals, demographic studies, studies of food supply patterns, and sexually differentiated laws: all these are used to understand the daily lives of those members of particular cultures who have had little part in defining the social arrangements and values of their cultures. In this volume, essays by Anne C. Klein, Frédérique Apffel Marglin, and Barbara Corrado Pope make effective use of popular visual images that played central roles in forming religious orientations. Clarissa W. Atkinson also examines the visual content and ecclesiastical uses of paintings of Saint Monica, Saint Augustine's mother, in order to understand Monica's cult and its continuing popularity. Instead of assuming that verbal communications were decisive in determining beliefs and pious practice, these authors examine the devotional pictures owned and treasured by large numbers of people for clues to the religious ideas widely available in the society.

Even though we have new kinds of evidence, the person who seeks to understand women of a particular time and place must inevitably use evidence provided by men. How can a vivid and nuanced picture of the lives of women be constructed on the basis of texts written by male authors? Are the expectations, descriptions of women's roles, and the value of these roles in the community expressed in such writings to be understood as normative for women in that culture? Would the women we study have recognized themselves and their own lives in these statements about what women should and should not say, feel, and do?

From the opinions of an educated male contemporary, we can learn about one facet of a culture in which women lived. But as social historians have realized for some time, the significance of this information should not be overestimated. Although they claim to speak universally, the men who wrote the normative texts of the major world religions in fact represent an atypical perspective in relation to most people of their cultures. Literate, educated, and culturally privileged, these authors cannot provide trustworthy descriptions of women's self-esteem and their esteem in communities.

Even so, these texts can be explored for what they *reveal* rather than for what they *intend* to communicate. Understood as prescriptive rather than descriptive, these texts often indicate, by their objections, what practices were current. In this volume Bernadette Brooten, by turning over the text, discusses an intricate matrix of male assumptions, attitudes, and fears revealed by the Apostle Paul's emphatic denunciation of female homoeroticism. She concludes that same-sex sexuality was prevalent because of continuous objections to it in the classical and late classical world. The more emphatic and vitriolic the condemnation of active sexual roles for women was in classical and biblical texts, the more prevalent these activities are likely to have been. Thus, even though they cannot speak directly of women's experience, male authors reveal both the existence of certain activities or attitudes and the opinion of a literate male toward the social situation.

Until recently, most historians of ideas have not recognized that the particular perspective they bring to historical study determines the history they write. Claims to the universality of ideas have effectively diverted historians of ideas from asking rigorous questions about the particular circumstances, sex, and social class of the authors of historical texts. Until recently, the conflicts and values of a particular author have usually been accepted by historians as characteristic of that author's culture, or at least as the most interesting and important information about that culture—the only information worth studying.

Even when historians have acknowledged that the construction they present is simply one plausible picture—at best a picture that cannot be disproved by any of the available evidence—there is a more or less explicit claim for the historian's ability to understand a variety of perspectives presented by the evidence, to evaluate the validity of each, and to coordinate these perspectives in a God's-eye view. Our essayists work more respectfully with their evidence. Delores Williams stays close to the narrative form of her sources in order to retain the strong sense of black women's lives that comes with their own style of speech. In Anne Klein's essay, analysis of Tibetan Buddhist female symbolism of the Great Bliss Queen begins with and develops from a recounting of the life of one woman who appropriated the symbols.

Another aspect of the relationship between a historian's presuppositions, approach, methodology, and evidence is the question of women's personal and cultural contexts. Recovering the history of persons who have played major parts in determining the cultural values and commitments of their societies is a far easier job than understanding the lives of those who have not been makers of their cultures. If one seeks to understand Augustine one can—and must —study the matrix of philosophical and theological ideas and problems of late Roman culture, the intellectual heritage from which he received both his problems and his tools. Every late classical author studied will be likely to help us understand Augustine's projects more adequately and accurately. One assumes, and tries to reconstruct in detail, a discourse participated in by a group of similarly educated men, a discourse on which one can draw in seeking to understand that part of the conversation which bears Augustine's name. The more we understand about the culture as a whole, the more easily we can identify the precise role of any particular voice in the cultural conversation.

However, if we set about to understand a person—for example, Augustine's contemporary, the nun Egeria—who did not participate in the intellectual, philosophical, or theological discussion of her time, we cannot assume that her activities and writings will become more comprehensible to us if we understand the voices of her powerful male political and ecclesiastical contemporaries in greater depth. We do not know whether or to what extent Egeria's interests, values, and experience reflect the dominant ideas and concerns of her culture. She was not a participant in the discourse of men. Nevertheless, to understand Egeria's delight in her freedom from the legal and emotional dominance of males, her avid desire to see with her own eyes the holy places of Christian faith, and her outspoken love for the community of women that was her emotional home is to recognize the voice of a person engaged in a lively discourse.

What is the relationship of the two contemporary but different clusters of energy and excitement represented by Augustine and Egeria? We cannot know without painstaking examination of each; we certainly cannot assume that they are functions of each other so that learning something about the philosophical and theological ideas of the dominant culture will help us understand Egeria's zest for experience. Moreover, our study of Egeria's travels, her personal commitments, loyalties, and interests will have sensitized us to the need to take into account aspects of Augustine's life that we had formerly overlooked. We will begin to ask how his ideas were influenced or determined by his personal experience, the concrete realities of his daily life and pastoral duties, his health and age.

This new path can pose its own problems. The historian who studies people who did not participate in the dominant intellectual interests of their cultures often does not have the material that would contextualize her evidence. To understand Egeria, we need to determine *her* intellectual and emotional partners in discourse. We know they existed; Egeria addressed her travel journals to them. But we do not know who received and answered Egeria's letters; the other side of the correspondence has been lost. We cannot base our interpretation of Egeria on anything more solid than an assumed discourse, and this lack of corroborating evidence produces a feeling of risk and insecurity in historians, whose training has led them to expect a gratifying sense of gradual but cumulative discovery from a variety of evidence. Information central to accurate interpretation of Egeria cannot now be gleaned from the women who shared her perspective and conversed with her.

This problem is even more pronounced in the case of a woman like Monica, Augustine's mother, from whom we have no words of her own, but only her son's descriptions of her words and actions. Atkinson's essay deals with the lack of Monica's own speech by discussing what Hans-Georg Gadamer calls the effective history of Monica, the history of Monica's influence as a symbol.

The historian of women's experience often finds that the conventions of traditional historiography are at odds with her findings. The problem of periodization identified by Joan Kelly about ten years ago illustrates the failure of historiographical conventions to illuminate women's history. Kelly argued that the Renaissance, a time of cultural achievement and innovation for educated or artistically talented males, was emphatically *not* a time of advance for women. Quite the opposite: men advanced at the immediate expense of women. Women who lived during the Italian Renaissance experienced a truncation of their freedom of self-definition and social opportunities in the several categories explored by Kelly. A completely different schema of historical periodization would result, Kelly argued, if women's advances became the criteria of cultural achievement.

Jo Ann Hackett's essay in this volume analyzes women's participation and power in ancient Israel in light of contemporary feminist questions and hypotheses. Issues of social and economic class, of rural or urban life styles, and of political structures featuring local or centralized institutions inform her discussion of the life of ancient Israelite women as it is described in a passage from the Hebrew Scriptures, Judges 3:12 to 16:31. She found that when institutions were hierarchically structured and centralized, women were less likely to play central roles. In agreement with Kelly's thesis, Hackett found in her study of a vastly different culture that male power appears to be in conflict with women's participation in the decision making of the community. Yet historians have traditionally identified male institutions and leadership with cultural strength. Anne Klein also explores the hypothesis that male power may be antithetical rather than complementary to women's power and authority. In Tibetan Buddhism, although spiritual power is accessible to women, when spirituality is strongly institutionalized by males, women are excluded from power in these institutions.

Methodologically, the essays included in this volume do not work within the framework of traditional histories of ideas in that they do not understand their subjects as informed by or congruent with the dominant ideas of the societies in which they exist. Rather, the essays identify contextual pressures and look for the tools women found for creating their lives. They do this by illuminating the cultures they discuss from a perspective outside the mainstream, by sketching, as vividly as possible on the basis of the available evidence, the lives of members of the cultures who did not determine large cultural syntheses but nevertheless lived rich and creative lives. Although the authors do not approach their material with traditional questions concerning the relation of their evidence to the philosophical or theological discussions contemporaneous with them, they nevertheless contribute to the reconstruction of a comprehensive picture of the motivating and energizing ideas of a particular culture, which is the primary task of intellectual history.

The history of ideas, in confining its interest to the writings of philosophers and theologians, implicitly suggests that the proper context of ideas is other ideas, not the human lives within which they appeared attractive or compelling. Traditional histories of ideas define the historian's task as that of discovering and rethinking the ideas that motivated or supported the decisions by which political and intellectual history was shaped. In looking to the juncture of religion and culture for information about women's lives, our essayists infer that ideas must be interpreted in the context of the lives in which they occur. They demonstrate that people's daily lives, their relationships, and the commitments and pressures with which they lived and died constitute the only accurate context for understanding their religious ideals and symbols.

Frédérique Apffel Marglin discusses religious symbols relating to women's sexuality in India. Using both rituals she has observed and textual interpretation to understand what attitudes and values are communicated to women in popular Hinduism, Marglin finds either textual data or observation of rituals incomplete without attention to the other. Together, ritual, "the poetry of everyday practice," and texts dealing with Hindu goddesses provide data for a sensitive and nuanced analysis of Hindu attitudes toward female sexuality.

The essays in this volume present comparative as well as historical analysis. The Judeo-Christian tradition is well represented, but essays on women whose religious symbols were Hindu and Buddhist are also included, and the essential perspective of cross-cultural analysis is brought to bear on the formulation of hypotheses about women and religion. Only by serious attention to the broadest possible range of situations in which women live can our hypotheses hope to escape a culture-bound provincialism. Since there is no absolute or universal perspective from which accurate generalizations can be made, contributions from a variety of perspectives are *necessary*—not merely helpful. Finally, the authors of this volume do not approach their analysis from a parochially committed position. They do not attempt to defend the religious traditions they discuss, nor do they try to establish the orthodoxy within their traditions of the women they discuss.

The painstaking reconstruction of a perspective neither valued nor honored in traditional historiography carries with it the joy of discovery and a sense of support for the "patchwork" of our own lives. The student of women's lives, in piecing together from the evidence she can find a picture of the lives of historical women and women of other cultures, recapitulates the methods of the women she studies. She does not think of herself as surveying from the castle of an academic institution the quaint customs and superstitions of the "peasants." Rather, because she is engaged with the women she studies, her work enriches, reinforces, and illuminates her own life. The process of patchwork, of stitching one's life together with the lives of the women one studies, requires asking new questions, questions that express one's own most pressing and intimate problems and that still allow one's partners in discourse to respond on their own terms.

Examining the relationship of religion and cultural arrangements as it affected the lives of historical women and women of other cultures reveals the extent to which the problem of finding the pieces of available material that extend and enhance the design of women's lives is not only related to the women who are the "objects" of our study. The problem is also related to contemporary women and men; it is our problem. The present poverty of Western religious and cultural institutions—of educational institutions and churches—points to men's need to find new, egalitarian ways to think, labor, and live in relationship. Even women who have rejected religious ideas and affiliations are not exempt from the need to find fruitful life-orienting ideas and images. Contemporary North American secular culture offers a daily diet of ideas, values, and images, many of which inhibit rather than promote personal and social transformation. Where can *we* find the symbols that challenge, support, and comfort us? From the study of historical women and women of other cultures we can begin to gather questions and support, ideas and energy, and a sense of the discipline, daring, and delight with which a new design can be cut and stitched from the seamless garments of religion and culture.

Notes

1. Elisabeth Schüssler Fiorenza, *In Memory of Her: A Feminist Theological Reconstruction of Christian Origins* (New York: Crossroads, 1983).

2. See also Mary Daly, *Pure Lust: Elemental Feminist Philosophy* (Boston: Beacon Press, 1984), p. 399: "Metamorphosis is not creation 'out of nothing' but rather transformation of whatever materials are at hand."

Two

In the Days of Jael:
Reclaiming the History of Women
in Ancient Israel*

Jo Ann Hackett

In the past fifteen years there has been a movement toward a new
kind of women's history.[1] This new effort aims to portray women's
lives in a different way from that of the earlier "compensatory"
women's histories. Compensatory histories attempted to fill in traditional history with information about women whose contributions
were clearly on a scale acceptable to traditional historians, but who
had not been included in their histories.[2] By contrast, the new
women's history, like the larger social history movement, demonstrates that traditional historiography is too narrow because it
focuses upon elite power groups (the events precipitated by them
and affecting them, and their responses to those events) to the exclusion of most of humanity. In other words, traditional history
does not give a history of the world, but only of a small part of it.
This narrowness results largely from the nature of traditional historiography, which is viewed as inappropriately limited from the
perspective of the new social history.[3]

Examination of data about women in various places and time
periods has given rise to theories about women's status in specific
societies. I have attempted to determine what in these theories and
general trends is applicable to understanding the status of women

* An earlier version of this paper was read at the 1983 annual meeting of the Society of Biblical Literature, and excerpts from it at the
Third Conversation in Biblical Studies in April 1984. Besides the participants in those meetings, several people have read and commented
upon this paper in its various incarnations. I would particularly like to
thank Barbara Corrado Pope, John Huehnergard, and Marcia Homiak
for their time and their valuable contributions.

in ancient Israel. Approaching the Bible in terms of women's status as portrayed in the texts is a departure from the usual biblical scholarship. In all the centuries and volumes of interpretation of the Hebrew Bible, women have seldom been at the center of a theologian's or scholar's interest, even to the present day. Furthermore, perspectives and tools gained from the new women's history allow us to go beyond those few scholars who have concentrated on biblical women, just as women's history in general has now gone beyond compensatory women's histories. It is also important to note the converse. Historians of women often do not see religious status as an important component of status in general.[4] In that light, the application of women's studies tools to a religious text is a departure not only from biblical scholarship but also from most recent studies of women.

The following brief discussion is intended to outline the directions of women's history within historiography. Many of the suggestions are pure common sense; many are derived from work done by anthropologists in recent years; and many are developed from painstaking collections of data from various times and places. Not all will be useful to Bible scholars, but the growing mesh of observations and methods does make it possible for us to look at the old texts from a new perspective. Sheila Ryan Johansson has lamented that there is as yet

> almost . . . no thorough discussion of what the status of women means. "Status" is used as if it were a perfectly self-evident concept. . . . The status of women is a composite of many details about the rights, duties, privileges, disabilities, options, and restrictions that the women of a specific group experience as they move through an inevitable progression of age-group and social roles.[5]

I know of no more precise definition of women's status, and it is this composite that the work presented in this article aims to achieve for women in ancient Israel. My goals are simple: first, to employ recent understandings of women's lives in order to give us new insight into the status of Israelite women; second, since there are analogies between Israel and other societies, to add our knowledge of women in ancient Israel, on a historical and sociological level, to the growing body of research about women the world over.

16

The New Women's History

Recent histories of women pay attention to the day-to-day lives of women of all classes and explore women's responses to societal upheavals and changes. In some cases, they even redefine the turning points of history as they appear from women's points of view.[6] Women are not, and have not been, dominant in any known society.[7] Their subordination and their relationships among themselves and with the dominant males in their societies should be important features of any study of the women in a society. As Joan Kelly explained,

> We have made of sex a category as fundamental to our analysis of the social order as other classifications, such as class and race. And we consider the relation of the sexes, as those of class and race, to be socially rather than naturally constituted, to have its own development, varying with changes in social organization. Embedded in and shaped by the social order, the relation of the sexes must be integral to any study of it.[8]

Within this broad understanding of sex as a category of analysis, scholars have used many other categories to describe and illuminate the position of women of various classes within a given society. These categories are based upon societal features that serve as accurate indicators of status. For instance, it appears that hierarchical and centrally structured institutions have been less open to participation by women than have local and nonhierarchical institutions. (Note that centralization already implies structuring and probably hierarchical decisions.) As with many other categories, this exclusion need not occur, but in fact, when institutions develop structure and specific standards, women seem to be excluded.[9] This means that an increase in the centralization of a society's institutions will often coincide with a decline in participation by women within those institutions.

A similar indicator involves the amount of decision making done within a domestic context, as opposed to decision making removed from the domestic sphere and placed in a "public" or "political" sphere. The "public" sphere can be defined as the level of organization that links and regulates several private or domestic units. Studies have shown that women tend to have more status within a society when the public and domestic spheres are not widely separated, that is, when important decision making is done within or near the home.[10]

Use of the public-domestic category assumes certain domestic responsibilities for most women in a given society because of the amount of time spent bearing, nursing, and raising children. (Although the last is not necessarily done by women rather than by men, the norm in most societies is that most of the childraising is done by women.)[11] Because of these responsibilities, women are less mobile, and may have less freedom to pursue extra-family, "political" (or "public") activities, when those activities are clearly separated from the domestic sphere.[12] Consequently, the political sphere becomes a male sphere insofar as it is separated from the domestic, that is, when decisions are not made within but outside the family unit, in groups that link several family units.

Michelle Zimbalist Rosaldo, one of the scholars who best articulated the consequences of a division into public and private spheres, later suggested that the public-private category has been misused in writing about women.[13] She pointed out that such a model invariably portrays women as primarily responsible for the domestic sphere, and so "assumes—where it should rather help illuminate and explain—too much about how gender really works." [14] Her point is well taken. Although the degree of separation between domestic and public spheres in a given society is a useful indicator, we must not see this separation as the *origin* of women's subordinate status. Realizing, as Rosaldo pointed out, that such a simple oppositional category may obscure the actual workings of gender within a society, we must take care to explicate the position of gender as a category in itself within that society.

The Marxist concept of social labor is another significant category. Marx and Engels argued that work takes on prestige according to its value to the entire community; work done for the society in general, as opposed to work done only for one's family, is "social" work and the basis of social worth.[15] "Social labor" is comparable to "political" or "public" activities, whereas labor done strictly for one's family generally falls within the "domestic" sphere.

All historians deal with social and economic classes. It is clear that one cannot compare by the same criteria a queen and a peasant widow. But evidence of classes within a society has further implications for the analysis of women's status within that society.[16] For instance, upper-class women have often fared better than middle-class and lower-class women, not only in terms of the obvious material advantages, but also in terms of their status within their own class. Class (and consequently ownership of property) may supersede sex as a qualification for leadership roles among traditional elites, so that if a ruling man is absent, or if an elite couple fails to produce a male heir, a woman may take over the duties of ruling and the economic responsibilities involved in the family's estate.

Interestingly, and perhaps not surprisingly, periods of what has been termed social dysfunction are actually periods when women's status is relatively higher than in settled times.[17] This phenomenon follows from some of the points presented above. In times of war or other crises, hierarchical structures may break down, and oppressed groups (particularly women) often take the opportunity to exert more power. As Hilda Smith points out, even when they have little public power, women are usually close to the center of power, by virtue of their relationships with men, so that although they were previously not allowed into the inner circle of those who exercise power, they are often the obvious choices to attempt to deal with a crisis.[18] Furthermore, men are often absent in these periods, particularly in times of war, so that women are called upon to perform the work men left behind. Finally, in periods of severe dysfunction, centralized institutions might give way to more local handling of affairs, a situation we have already seen to be often conducive to women's participation.

A discussion of women's status in a society should include whatever information is available about the degree of urbanization within that society, for the obvious reason that people's lives are lived in substantially different ways in the country and in the city. Furthermore, the differences between the lives of rural and urban women will not be the same as the differences among their male counterparts, especially if in each case women are responsible for the domestic sphere, whatever that sphere's definition in their culture.

The kinship system operative in a given society has implications for the status of women within that society. For example, whether inheritance and group identity are matrilineal or patrilineal, and whether settlement is matrilocal or patrilocal, will have an obvious effect on the amount of contact and influence allowed the wife's family and support group as opposed to the husband's.[19] Evidence

19

of the practice of polygyny or polyandry is important in determining sources of the influence a woman or man may exert in a society. (For example, must co-spouses compete for the attention of and influence over their mate? Does multiple marriage imply a lowering of status for the first spouse? Is inheritance affected?) Other factors that must be considered include the position of people outside the major kinship system (men and women not yet married, widows and widowers, prostitutes) and the degree of their dependence on a family system, and the issue of an individual's sexual preference.

There are, further, many questions the historian asks about women within the structure of a given society. Typical questions are these: What kinds of occupations are available to women? To what degree are women responsible for the raising and socialization of children? Who supplies most of the food? How is it distributed? Do women (and men) cooperate with each other or do they compete? [20] Is there societal propaganda designed to subjugate women to men, and if so, how does it operate? What is the average age of death for women? for men? Do women have their own systems of rank and value separate from that of the society as a whole? Is the system of pollution fears (biblical *ṭāmē* and *ṭāhôr*) restrictive for women (or men), and if so, are these restrictions a source of bonding? [21] Who controls a woman's sexuality? Is a woman's status dependent upon her social class? Is it affected by age?

The legal status of women is not always easy to describe because so many systems of law, including those in the Hebrew Bible, are written by and for the men in a society.[22] It may be difficult to determine how many and which laws were actually meant to apply to women and to affect their behavior.

Religious status is particularly difficult to define for women in ancient Israel, since many features of people's lives in Israel that were seen, or at least reported to us, as "religious" might be classified today as legal or societal. One must decide, for instance, whether fears of pollution are "religious" or "social" features. At any rate, certain questions arise: To what extent are women considered part of the covenant community? What theological attitudes toward women are evident in the various writings? Are there female cult personnel? Are women involved in the religions considered non-orthodox by the biblical authors? more involved than men? If so, what are the possible reasons for this involvement?

Finally, one must attempt to identify the sources of power available to women in the various societal strata and time periods in question. Here it is necessary to make a distinction between power and authority. Power is simply the ability to achieve one's goals; authority is power that is legitimated by the structures of a society. To paraphrase Lamphere, when one has the "right" to use one's power, one has authority.[23] It may be that a woman's power in a given society comes to her primarily through a man or men (husband, father, brother, son) and not through her own status. That is, she can get what she wants by convincing a man or men that she should have it, by a variety of means. She can assert or reserve her sexuality; she can call upon family bonds or set family members against each other; she can socialize her sons in such a way as to accomplish her ends; she can refuse to perform domestic chores.[24] Kinship relationships are important here: An extended family with a structured hierarchy increases the complexity of the sexual politics, the struggle to influence men in the group. In such a family, a mother's influence over her son is threatened when the son marries; if the hierarchy gives the mother power over the daughters-in-law, then the mother is likely to use that power to assure her dominance over her son, a situation of obvious friction.[25] If polygyny is practiced, co-wives may become a threat to each other in that no one wife can hope to influence her husband exclusively, and such means as withholding sexual privileges would clearly not be as effective.[26]

Nevertheless, we would expect a woman to have her own sources of power. Even if most of her power comes from her relations to various men in the group, we must determine the extent of her ability to accomplish her goals in her own undertakings without using those relationships.[27] Such power sources might include her position in (probably local) institutions; her ability to limit family size; her control over child socialization; role revolts and marriage resistance—she can vow virginity or another state that leaves her outside the usual marriage and childbearing system—even prostitution, if it is the woman's choice;[28] her control of the society's food resources (in many societies the major source of food is not hunting but pastoralism and agriculture, and it is often the women who are in charge of producing this food);[29] certain occupations, which give women freedom from dependence on males because of mobility or economic independence (in some societies women are the long-distance traders, for instance).[30] Furthermore, elite women (as was pointed out above) may receive training and be expected to take over, even in a patriarchal society, when the usual men are not available.[31] Finally, there are always the "great women" in a society, the ones who become famous in spite of their sex. Are they merely out of step with the rest of society, or did most of them live in periods when many women had more power than usual, and what remains of this situation is the fame of a few women? [32]

Women in Judges 3–16

An examination of women in Israel as seen in the stories of Judges 3:12–16:31,[33] from approximately the twelfth and eleventh centuries B.C.E.,[34] suggests new categories for discussing both the roles women play in these narratives and their status in Israel at that time. One's first impression on reading these stories is that we meet here several strong women; more significantly, we learn about them without a negative judgment on the part of the narrators. Deborah is the obvious example. We are introduced to Deborah in Judges 4:4, where she is described as a prophetess, and is said to be "judging" Israel. In the context of the Book of Judges, the phrase "judging Israel" means that Deborah was one of Israel's chief executive officers. Within her story we see her acting as judge when she calls on Barak, her military man, to organize Israelite troops in a divinely ordained battle against the Canaanites, who were led by their general, Sisera. It is because she is judge that Barak would only agree to go to battle if she accompanied him: Her presence would reassure him that Yahweh was with him in the battle. Deborah tells him that she will go with him, but warns him not to expect the glory from the victory, because Sisera will actually be conquered by a woman. The reader assumes that Deborah is speaking of herself, and only at the end of the story finds that it is another woman, Jael, who kills Sisera with a tent peg after he has fled to her tent expecting hospitality and refuge.

Jael's act, too, is described without surprise or negative judgment by the narrators. Further, in the ancient poem in Judges 5, Israel in this period is described as equally "the days of Shamgar" and "the days of Jael." We know of Shamgar from Judges 3:31, where he is said to have delivered Israel. In Judges 5:6, the names Shamgar and Jael are used together to evoke their unstable era, implying that the two, a male and a female, shared a reputation as Israelites who had delivered their people from a serious threat. The story suggests a question: What features of the society of Israel at that period encouraged such active participation by women?

Israelite society in this era was generally rural and agrarian. At the beginning of Gideon's story in Judges 6, for instance, we are told that the Midianites were destroying Israel's agricultural yield during their raids. When we first see Gideon himself, he is beating out grain in secret, to keep it from the notice of the Midianites. Agriculture is the background for Jotham's fable in Judges 9, where the olive tree, the fig tree, and the vine decline the kingship, and the bramble accepts, and for Gideon's quick answer to the Ephraimites, who were angry for being called to the battle against the Midianites only at the last minute: "Isn't the gleaning of Ephraim better than the vintage of Abiezer?" (Judg. 8:2.)

One of the notable features of the social organization of this period is its lack of centralization. In this premonarchical phase of Israel's history, the cry for participation in war, for example, did not come from a standing, centralized, hierarchical "government," but rather from a covenantal agreement that there would be occasions when concerted action was necessary and, in Israelite terms, demanded by Yahweh.

Where such information is available, these stories portray a public sphere that does not seem to be widely separated from the private. For instance, the description of Deborah's duties as judge at the beginning of her story, Judges 4:4–5, allows us to assume she could perform those duties while still resident in her own area (whether that was "under the palm of Deborah, between Ramah and Bethel," as 4:5 would have it, or, more likely, within the tribal territory of Issachar, as 5:15 implies). Her public life as judge need not have interfered with her domestic life. Except when he was at war, Gideon is described (8:29) as residing in his own house, in Ophrah, during the time that he was judge in Israel. Again, his non-military public duties as judge, although they are not described, were presumably not performed in such a manner as to separate him necessarily from his domestic life. It would seem that neither Deborah nor Gideon needed to move to a capital city or preside over a centralized government elsewhere.

Most of the stories in Judges 3–16 concern events that affected only a small territory and relatively few people within Israel. Although even some of the core stories are phrased as if they concerned the entire league of twelve tribes, most likely "all Israel" was not the scope of the original narratives. Examination of those stories that do enumerate participants shows them to be concerned almost entirely with small-scale battles. This is not to suggest that they involved only one tribe or an even smaller group; clearly, some cooperation between tribes is indicated. But we are left with the impression that the participation of the entire league of twelve tribes was either extremely rare or downright lacking. The point is that the power *structure* was not centralized, even where concerted effort was possible. We do not even find evidence of a centralized priesthood in these core stories, or, in fact, any mention of a central shrine, of the ark, or of centralized religious festivals. The picture painted here is of a society that was not directed by a central authority in any of its efforts, save Yahweh's authority, acknowledged by covenant, to make emergency demands on the people in times of crisis.

There is also some slight evidence of the formation of social and economic classes. The literature tells us that the ideal in the period of the judges was non-hereditary, charismatic leadership. Yahweh was the only king in Israel, and the earthly leaders, the judges, were "raised up" by Yahweh for the purpose of delivering Israel from some specific crisis (see Judg. 2:11–19). But in Judges 9:1–6, a nascent hereditary ruling class seems to be in evidence. We are told that Abimelech, one of Gideon's sons, proposes to the rulers of Shechem that it is better that he rule over them than that all seventy of Gideon's sons rule over them (for Gideon's seventy sons, see Judges 8:30). The implication is that the choice facing the Israelites in Shechem was not *whether* some individual or group in Gideon's family would continue to rule them but rather *which element* in the family would serve them best. We should note here that this story concerns the city of Shechem, where the *ba῾ălê šŏkem,* the "rulers" of Shechem, made Abimelech king. But Shechem is probably a special case, in that it was a sizable city, and a city with a background of Canaanite kingship. Jephthah, in chapter 11, had been denied any inheritance and was outcast because his mother was a prostitute and not a legal wife, but he was offered a "chiefship" by his former enemies in return for his defeating the Ammonites, perhaps another example of a concentration of power. We have further evidence of economic or social inequality in the notices of the "minor judges," with often an emphasis on their family wealth: Jair's thirty sons who rode on thirty asses, if this is indeed a family notice and not a political one, in Judges 10:3–5;[35] Ibzan's large family in 12:8–10 and the presumably expensive marriage arrangements made for them all; Abdon's seventy asses for his sons and grandsons in 12:13–15. Even though many of these elements are somewhat folkloric and may not reflect any particular historical event, it is still worth noting that the stories speak of a period when certain wealth and social distinctions were made. Such hierarchy did not seem out of place to the storytellers.

Admittedly, these are only shadows of the kind of detail we would like to have. The fact that the judges were thought to be appointed by Yahweh for their tasks gives us no information about the *societal* bases for authority, and no details of the decision making that must also have taken place. The only exceptions are the Shechemite kingship of Abimelech (described above) and the emergency recruitment of Jephthah by the elders of Gilead and subsequent ceremony "before Yahweh" at Mizpah (Judg. 11:1–11). Abimelech was certainly not the norm among deliverers, and so his story does not really help us in determining how the authentic judges might have been chosen. But Jephthah's story perhaps gives us a glimpse of the human side of the choosing of a judge: We see the fear and desperation of the elders of Gilead and we see that they turned to the only person they thought could help them. Yahweh's stamp of approval was delivered only some time later.

One feature is relatively easy to analyze for this time. We can say without doubt that there are periods of serious social dysfunction reported. In fact, nearly all of our characters are involved in stories that have to do with emergencies in the lives of the people. Judges 5:6 describes the period vividly: Caravans ceased and travelers kept to the byways. One of the functions of the judge was to be savior of the people, and the saving was needed precisely because the situation was critical. Judges 6:1–6, for example, describes a time in which the Midianites even destroyed the food and cattle and flocks of the Israelites, so that they had no means of sustaining themselves, apart from what they could hide. The Israelites were said to hide in caves in the mountains, certainly a sign that the normal social and economic system had broken down under the weight of external pressures. Each of the stories proceeds to describe in similar fashion a situation of severe oppression and lack of control, usually because of a neighboring power.

Finally, we have some evidence of the kinship system. Polygyny was practiced, as we might expect: Gideon's seventy sons were borne by his "many wives," and Abimelech's mother was Gideon's concubine. It would seem that inheritance and status were patrilineal, but they could be restricted to legally recognized arrangements. Note Jephthah's situation in Judges 11:1–2, mentioned above: Gilead's other sons make Jephthah's inheritance an issue, and so it was presumably not absolutely ruled out; yet these other sons and the recognized wife had the power to deny him inheritance, because his mother was a woman "other than" Gilead's legal wife, a prostitute, in fact.

In summary, then, Israel in the time of the judges was a rural, agrarian society, with some urbanization, as seems probable from the situation in Shechem in Judges 9, and from archaeological finds.[36] During a period distinguished by its lack of tranquillity and its social upheavals, there was no central administration and generally only ad hoc leadership in local affairs. This is a far cry from a centralized, hierarchical, and dynastic monarchy. There is, nevertheless, some evidence that social and economic classes existed. Although the evidence is slim and is mostly a matter of one group accumulating more wealth than another, it is possible that hereditary ruling groups are implied in some stories, especially those concerning urban Shechem. The marriage customs were what we would expect: patrilineal and sometimes polygynous. Public life and private life were apparently not widely separated; there is, at least, no evidence that they were, and some slight evidence that they were not.

With this brief overview of the society in Israel during the period of the judges in mind, we now turn to a description of women's roles and status within that society. We have seen already that women could fill leadership roles in this era of decentralized power and ad hoc leaders. Although women are seldom seen as the ones who make war in any society, and the same is true for biblical Israel, we do have in these stories two women who were intimately involved in a war. Deborah in Judges 4 was a prophet and a judge. Her function as judge in the battle with the Canaanites was to declare the battle a holy war, in other words, to legitimize the battle. As we have seen, Barak would not go to war without Yahweh's representative with him (4:8). Deborah is also said to deliver to Barak Yahweh's oracle that described the actual battle plan (4:6–7).

In the later prose version in chapter 4, Deborah called Barak to summon the troops to battle, but in the earlier Song of Deborah, in chapter 5,[37] verse 12 commands Deborah: "Awake, awake, Deborah; awake, utter a song"—not the song in Judges 5, since the self-reference makes no sense in the middle of the poem, but, as some commentators have seen,[38] a song to muster the troops, to call them out for battle. *Awake, awake* is typical language in the Hebrew Bible for a call to arms; Isaiah 51:9 comes immediately to mind: "Awake, awake, put on strength, arm of Yahweh." In Judges 5:12, the poet is calling on Deborah to get the battle going, and so her song here must be the vehicle for bringing out the troops.[39]

So while Deborah is indeed the only deliverer who has a military man working with her, the older version in the song, while mentioning Barak, gives an even greater military role to Deborah than the more familiar prose version. And while we do not see Deborah carrying weapons and fighting, we do not see Barak fighting either. It is part of the genre of "holy war" battles that they are won, not by their human participants, but rather by Yahweh acting on Israel's behalf. In this case, the battle is said to be won by Yahweh's routing of Sisera's troops (Judg. 4:15), or by the stars and the torrent Qishon (5:20–21).

There seems to be a reluctance on the part of some commentators to see Deborah as a true judge, alongside the other deliverers in the book. This reluctance probably lies behind the acceptance by some modern commentators of the old theory that Lappidoth (Deborah's husband according to Judg. 4:4) and Barak were the same person, and that Deborah, therefore, derived her status from her marital relationship with Barak, who is seen as the *real* judge in this episode.[40] Granted it is Barak who is mentioned in the New Testament book of Hebrews (11:32, along with other Israelite heroes), and probably Barak who is meant in 1 Samuel 12:11 in the list of deliverers, rather than the unknown Bedan. We might conclude from this substitution that some later Israelite historians, like many of their modern counterparts, had trouble accepting the notion of a female judge. But the text itself (Judg. 4–5) is clear that Deborah was a judge and there is really no reason to doubt the text here. In fact, our analysis of the society in Israel at this time, as well as analogies from other cultures, suggests that such a situation is entirely appropriate and believable.

Finally, in connection with Deborah, a word should be said about the title "mother" used of her in Judges 5:7: "Until you arose, Deborah, until you arose, a mother in Israel." This most domestic of terms is here transformed by its use in such a public context, and is simply, I think, comparable to "father" as a leadership title within the prophetic tradition, as in 1 Samuel 10:12 and 2 Kings 2:12.[41] Deborah's identification as a mother may also be seen within the poem as a balance to the final lines, which deal with Sisera's *mother* and her reaction to the battle.

At the end of the battle with the Israelites, the Canaanite general, Sisera, is said to flee from his defeat to the tent of Jael. There was a peace treaty between Sisera's king, Jabin, and the family of Jael's husband, and so Sisera sought refuge in this friendly territory. Jael first offered hospitality to the soldier, but both Judges 4 and 5 (in slightly different versions) relate that in the end she killed him with a tent peg. Although Jael's killing of Sisera need not be seen as the act of a soldier, it can certainly be said that she coolly and deliberately dispatched the leader of the enemy army. She was also, as I pointed out above, remembered in the same breath with Shamgar, who was, according to Judges 3:31, a military hero. We are presented with only one story of his prowess, and a rather incredible one at that: that he killed six hundred Philistines with an ox goad.[42] There would seem to be no reason to categorize Jael's act as unique and Shamgar's as military, except a gender bias. Benjamin Mazar long ago pointed to the Kenite Jael's possible priestly role and suggested that Sisera sought out her tent not only because her people and his had a peace treaty but also because her tent was in fact pitched at a sanctuary and Sisera reasonably expected refuge there.[43]

The analysis of Israel's society presented here leads to similar insights into the leadership of Gideon and of Jephthah. Evidence of societal upheavals and the lack of centralized hierarchical authority can be used to explain the rise to power of these two men, neither of whom could claim a favorable social position within Israel. And in fact, both question the choice of such lowly or outcast characters to deliver their people. But it is precisely in troubled times and decentralized systems that power may be wielded by people who in more settled times and structured systems would most likely not be defined as fit to rule.

Alongside descriptions of their heroic acts, women are pictured in more traditional roles. Deborah and Jael, for instance, are identified as the wives of their respective husbands. At the beginning of Samson's story in Judges 13:1–7, a divine messenger appears, bringing a message to Samson's mother. His message is a pronouncement of her impending pregnancy, but it also includes instructions on how the child is to be raised. These instructions were not given to Manoah, the child's father, who in fact only heard the message because he seemed to be doubtful of his wife's story. Clearly, the mother was given the instructions because she would be in large part responsible for the child's upbringing. Again, even if these stories are fanciful, we still can glean the attitude of the storytellers from the details, and also learn their understanding of their own society.

It is difficult to ascertain whether women in this period had systems of rank and value that were separate from those of the overall society. Our only hint occurs in the story of Jephthah's daughter. Jephthah, the outcast son of a prostitute, is called back by the elders of Gilead to lead his people in war against the Ammonites (Judg. 11–12). After the spirit of Yahweh came upon Jephthah (confirming him as judge), and just before he engaged the Ammonites in battle, Jephthah made a vow to Yahweh: If Yahweh would allow Jephthah to win the battle, then Jephthah would offer to Yahweh, as a burnt offering, whoever first came out of the doors of his house to meet him when he returned home victorious. Jephthah wins, of course, and is greeted when he returns by his daughter, his only child. The daughter affirms that a vow to Yahweh must be carried out, but she asks for two months to go away to the mountains to mourn her virginity before she dies. The very end of the story is intriguing: Jephthah's daughter goes away to mourn her virginity, not alone, but accompanied by her female companions, and these companions served as the model, in popular thought, for a women's ritual mourning each year. Whatever the actual origin of this women's ritual,[44] the concern for a young

29

woman's plight, shown in this story as a concern shared by other young women, suggests a closely bound society of females with female concerns and their own means of dealing with such concerns. These women share with the daughter not only her preparations for her impending death but presumably also the dilemma posed by the opposition of her strong faith in Yahweh and her desire to live and have a family.

Jephthah's daughter had come to meet him as he returned from battle "with timbrels and with dances," and we know from other evidence in the Hebrew Bible that women were traditionally the ones who met the returning warriors with songs (see, for example, 1 Samuel 18:7, and the several war songs attributed to Miriam, Deborah, and Hannah). The story of Jephthah's daughter raises the issue of the religious status of women in Israel during this period. There is clearly at least one women's ritual, described above, whether it was actually the later proscribed Tammuz ritual (see note 44) or whether it was acceptable Israelite ritual. Furthermore, I would argue that in an Israelite context, the action of a man who vows a human sacrifice would not be seen neutrally, but would rather be judged negatively by the audience, and that Jephthah, rather than being simply unfortunate, was seen as thoughtless at best and faithless at worst.[45] The story can be seen, then, at least implicitly, as critical of Jephthah, while his daughter is shown in an entirely positive light—in Israelite terms, if not our own. She certainly considers herself part of the covenant community, and, therefore, must see that a vow to Yahweh is upheld, whatever the consequences.

These stories provide very little information on women's sexuality. We can see in the Samson stories that an unmarried woman's father has power over her sexuality. It was the father of Samson's wife who "gave" her to Samson's "best man" after Samson walked out on her in anger. It was the same father who "offered" her younger sister as a substitute (Judg. 15:1–2). Presumably after a marriage, a woman's sexuality was controlled by her husband; because he was denied this right to control, Samson reacted badly to his former father-in-law's actions. (Admittedly, this story, if it exhibits any authentic memory of the times, mixes the attitudes of Israelites and Philistines toward this issue, and is probably not a good test case.) There is little information about women outside this system of control. As I mentioned earlier, Jephthah was not allowed to inherit, but the reason given for this is not that his mother was a prostitute, but rather that she was a woman "other than" Gilead's wife; apparently Jephthah's mother was in no position to demand inheritance rights for her children, over against the children of the legal wife. The two women with whom Samson was involved other than his wife—the prostitute in Gaza and Delilah—although Philistines and not Israelites, were also not reprimanded in the text for their way of life. Presumably prostitution was an accepted way for a woman to make a living in this period, although a woman outside the usual system of sexual control could be punished by the denial of rights to her offspring.

Polygyny is a factor in Abimelech's story and it is possible that he acted separately from all his brothers because he had a different status within the family. His mother was not Gideon's wife, but a concubine. It is interesting that Abimelech's power base was his mother's family in Shechem, although it seems he was living in Ophrah with his father's family (he is said to "go to" Shechem in Judg. 9:1). Jephthah's case is similar. Since his mother was a prostitute, the situation is not polygyny, strictly speaking. Still, he was resident in his father's house (11:7) when he was disinherited; the hierarchy of sons depended on the hierarchy of mothers.

It is clear from what we have seen that Israelite women in this era, having several sources of power, did not need to rely strictly on men for their power. We have discussed Deborah's, and possibly Jael's, position within a decentralized authority structure as being equal to that of the men in the same office. Sisera's mother also is portrayed as a woman of exalted position, but in Canaanite society rather than Israelite. Although such a woman might have derived her power from her son's position, she might also represent one of the elite women who are trained to rule when men are absent. Jephthah's daughter, although she was powerless before an oath to Yahweh, as was her father, still had the power and the support of her society to carry out the vow and her preparations for it in the manner that suited her.

In other cases, women achieve their ends by working through a man. Sexual politics was involved in Samson's dealings both with his wife and with Delilah. Each one played on her expected feminine role in order to get information from Samson, which she then used to her own advantage—the wife to save her life and her family, Delilah to earn money from the Philistine lords who had approached her. We have already seen the possible hierarchy within Gideon's polygynous household.

A less transparent, but perhaps real, sort of power is the wisdom and faith of several women. Deborah is presented as certain that the battle against the Canaanites is a proper one and that Yahweh is in favor of it, while Barak needs reassurance; it is Deborah's line of reasoning that is followed in this case. Similarly, as was mentioned above, Jephthah's daughter was clearsighted about the necessary course of affairs following her father's vow, while Jephthah could merely whimper; in this case the daughter was at least able to influence the manner of her death. Finally, Samson's mother is portrayed as the intelligent half of his parents, while Manoah lacked faith in his wife's word and memory, was slow to figure out the identity of their divine visitor, and in the end was afraid for his life. His wife had to explain to him that Yahweh would hardly have bothered to announce the birth of a son and the grand career of that son only to kill them immediately afterward, something that could have been done at any time. Samson, it might be added, took after his father rather than his mother.

The status of women in any society may be measured against that of men, and it is apparent in our stories that the major female characters often fare better in the narrative than do the men they are involved with: Deborah alongside Barak; Jael versus Sisera; perhaps Jephthah's daughter as opposed to Jephthah; Samson's mother and father; and it is no new insight to say that women got the better of Samson, time and time again. One is tempted to suggest that some of these stories in fact derive from women's literature, literature composed by and/or preserved in women's circles. I make that suggestion not simply because they are stories that are favorable to women, as if men would not preserve such stories. Rather, a more important observation about these narratives in the context of women's literature is that women's lives and issues are often central: The women's ritual in the story of Jephthah's daughter is one example, and the poem in Judges 5 is another. Judges 5 is really a very female piece of literature. It describes the battle with the Canaanites precisely from the perspectives of the women in the story: the women involved in the fighting and killing, and the women waiting to hear the results of the battle. Even the women who are assumed to be part of the victor's spoils are mentioned. We do traditionally refer to the song as the Song of Deborah and we know that women are credited with singing the battle songs in ancient Israel. Still it is worth reaffirming, because this poem is not simply a song about a famous woman or one that might have been sung by women, but is, in fact, a poem whose entire focus is the lives of women.

In sum, women's status and roles as seen in Judges 3:12–16:31 are more varied than they might have been at other times in biblical Israel: Men were not always the sources of power. This is not to say that women were dominant over men, even in this period; still, the characterization of the era as one of decentralized and ad hoc power would lead us to expect wider possibilities for women in public and powerful positions, and this is precisely what we have found.

It is always true that the results of one's research depend to a certain extent upon one's focus. A description of the status of women in ancient Israel as gleaned from the stories in the Hebrew Bible signals a new focus for biblical scholarship, and the results we have obtained are, therefore, quite different from those found in typical research in that field. Because we have asked new questions, the answers and insights we have generated have been new also, and significant, both to those who wish to know about life in ancient Israel and to those who are interested in the kinds of lives women have lived in different places and times. Furthermore, the importance of the portrayal of women's lives in biblical Israel is not limited to those who actively practice a biblical religion. Interpretations of biblical passages have had and still have an enormous effect on much of the world; consequently, we all benefit from the methods developed within and for the new scholarship on women. Descriptions of Israelite society and of the roles Israelite women played through time have evolved from a combination of interests in both the history of women's lives and the history of Israel's religion, a coalescence rare in biblical studies and women's studies alike, and these descriptions have developed without many of the assumptions of previous generations. Because of the impressive and ongoing work of a new group of scholars whose major interests are the description and analysis of women's roles and status in varied societies, we can now be more precise in our scholarship—as historians of women, in our analysis of women's lives, and as Bible scholars, in our longstanding quest to understand ancient Israelite society.

Notes

1. There are several good discussions of this development. See for example the following articles in Berenice A. Carroll, ed., *Liberating Women's History* (Urbana: University of Illinois Press, 1976): Gerda Lerner, "New Approaches to the Study of Women in American History" (reprinted from the *Journal of Social History* 4 [1969]), and "Placing Women in History: A 1975 Perspective"; Berenice A. Carroll, pp. ix–xii in the Introduction; Hilda A. Smith, "Feminism and the Methodology of Women's History." See also Joan Kelly-Gadol, "The Social Relation of the Sexes: Methodological Implications of Women in History," *Signs* 1 (1976): 809–823; Carl N. Degler, *Is There a History of Women?* (Oxford: Clarendon Press, 1975), and "Women and the Family," in Michael Kammen, ed., *The Past before Us: Contemporary Historical Writing in the United States* (Ithaca: Cornell University Press, 1980), pp. 308–326; and Carroll Smith-Rosenberg, "The New Woman and the New History," *Feminist Studies* 3 (1975): 185–198.

Various articles offer sample questions that should be asked in a women's history. See Smith-Rosenberg, "The New Woman and the New History"; and three articles in the Carroll anthology: Ann D. Gordon, Mari Jo Buhle, and Nancy Schrom Dye, "The Problem of Women's History"; Sheila Ryan Johansson, " 'Herstory' as History: A New Field or Another Fad?"; Lerner, "Placing Women in History."

2. They were presumed to have been left out because of the male bias of societies in general and of historians, the vast majority of whom have been male, in particular.

Several of the writers mentioned in note 1 make the distinction between the new women's history and compensatory women's histories: Kelly-Gadol, p. 810; Johansson, pp. 400–405; Carroll, pp. x–xi; Smith-Rosenberg, pp. 186–187; Gordon, Buhle, and Dye, pp. 75–92 passim.

3. And see further Smith-Rosenberg, "The New Woman and the New History," pp. 188–189, who comments that the development of women's history as a "subspecialty" within social history implicitly suggests that even this new historical writing does not really take women into account. For a critique of writings about women in America, see Linda Gordon, Persis Hunt, Elizabeth Pleck, Rochelle Goldberg Ruthchild, and Marcia Scott, "Historical Phallacies: Sexism in American Historical Writing," in Carroll, ed., *Liberating Women's History*, pp. 55–74.

4. See the discussion of historians' views of women and religion in America in Kathryn Kish Sklar, "The Last Fifteen Years," in Hilah F. Thomas and Rosemary Skinner Keller, eds., *Women in New Worlds:*

Historical Perspectives on the Wesleyan Tradition (Nashville: Abingdon, 1981), pp. 48–65.

5. " 'Herstory' as History," pp. 405–406.

6. I realize I am combining methodologies here; some historians introduce new periods, others use the familiar periods. See the explanations in Lerner, "Placing Women in History," pp. 362–363, where she suggests new schemes of periodization; Kelly-Gadol, "The Social Relation of the Sexes," pp. 810–812.

7. This is the prevailing opinion among anthropologists. See Eleanor Burke Leacock's Introduction to Frederick Engels, *The Origin of the Family, Private Property, and the State* (New York: International Publishers, 1972), pp. 34–35, and Kathleen Gough's review of Kate Millett's *Sexual Politics* in *Monthly Review,* February 1971, pp. 52–53.

8. "The Social Relation of the Sexes," p. 816.

9. See Smith, "Feminism," p. 382; Johansson, " 'Herstory' as History," pp. 416–417. JoAnn McNamara and Suzanne F. Wemple chronicle women's loss of power in the church as it gained a stable base and hierarchical structure. See "Sanctity and Power: The Dual Pursuit of Medieval Women," in Renate Bridenthal and Claudia Koonz, eds., *Becoming Visible: Women in European History* (Boston: Houghton Mifflin, 1977), pp. 90–118.

10. See the following three articles from Michelle Zimbalist Rosaldo and Louise Lamphere, eds., *Woman, Culture, and Society* (Stanford: Stanford University Press, 1974): Rosaldo, "Woman, Culture, and Society: A Theoretical Overview"; Sherry B. Ortner, "Is Female to Male as Nature Is to Culture?"; Lamphere, "Strategies, Cooperation, and Conflict among Women in Domestic Groups." See also Rayna R. Reiter, "Men and Women in the South of France: Public and Private Domains," in Rayna R. Reiter, ed., *Toward an Anthropology of Women* (New York: Monthly Review Press, 1975), pp. 252–282.

11. Nancy Chodorow, "Family Structure and Feminine Personality," in Rosaldo and Lamphere, eds., *Woman, Culture, and Society,* pp. 43–45; Rosaldo, "Woman, Culture, and Society," pp. 17–18, 23–25.

12. Karen Sacks relates this observation to class exploitation in "Engels Revisited: Women, the Organization of Production, and Private Property," in Rosaldo and Lamphere, eds., *Woman, Culture, and Society,* p. 220.

13. "The Use and Abuse of Anthropology: Reflections on Feminism and Cross-cultural Understanding," *Signs* 5 (1980): 389–417.

14. Ibid., p. 399.

15. This phenomenon is discussed, for example, in Engels, *The Origin*

of the Family, pp. 137–179, 221; Sacks, "Engels Revisited," pp. 208–213, 220–222; Ann J. Lane, "Woman in Society: A Critique of Frederick Engels," in Carroll, ed., *Liberating Women's History,* pp. 16–17, 22–24; Margaret Benston, "The Political Economy of Women's Liberation," *Monthly Review,* September 1969, pp. 13–27.

16. Ethnicity and race also feed into a class analysis of a given society. The following discussion is based on Johansson's summary in " 'Herstory' as History," pp. 412–416.

17. Smith, "Feminism," p. 382; Degler, *Is There a History of Women?,* pp. 12–13. McNamara and Wemple, "Sanctity and Power," use this concept throughout their discussion of women in the Middle Ages.

18. Smith, "Feminism," pp. 374, 382.

19. Kinship relationships in Genesis have been explored by Robert A. Oden, Jr., "Jacob as Father, Husband, and Nephew: Kinship Studies and the Patriarchal Narratives," *Journal of Biblical Literature* 102 (1983): 189–205; Mara E. Donaldson, "Kinship Theory in the Patriarchal Narratives: The Case of the Barren Wife," *Journal of the American Academy of Religion* 49 (1981): 77–87.

20. This is the central question in Lamphere, "Strategies, Cooperation, and Conflict."

21. This is Rosaldo's suggestion in "Woman, Culture, and Society," pp. 38–39.

22. See Johansson, " 'Herstory' as History," p. 404; for the Hebrew Bible in particular, see Phyllis Bird's excellent article "Images of Women in the Old Testament," in Rosemary Radford Ruether, ed., *Religion and Sexism* (New York: Simon and Schuster, 1974), esp. pp. 48–57.

23. Lamphere, "Strategies, Cooperation, and Conflict," p. 9. Rosaldo points out that "it is necessary to remember that while authority legitimates the use of power, it does not exhaust it, and actual methods of giving rewards, controlling information, exerting pressure, and shaping events may be available to women as well as to men" ("Woman, Culture, and Society," p. 21). Both writers cite relevant literature in their discussions.

24. Rosaldo, "Woman, Culture, and Society," pp. 37–38.

25. Lamphere, "Strategies, Cooperation, and Conflict," pp. 104–106; Susan Harding, "Women and Words in a Spanish Village," in Reiter, ed., *Toward an Anthropology,* pp. 293–294.

26. Lamphere, "Strategies, Cooperation, and Conflict," pp. 107–108.

27. Lamphere speaks of a woman's ability to "recruit aid" for her

undertakings. Can she do this on her own, and can she do it with success equal to that of men in her society? (ibid., p. 100).

28. Johansson, " 'Herstory' as History," pp. 419–421.

29. See Leacock, Introduction, pp. 33–36; Rosaldo, "Woman, Culture, and Society," p. 37; Lane, "Woman in Society," p. 14.

30. Johansson, " 'Herstory' as History," p. 421; Lamphere, "Strategies, Cooperation, and Conflict," p. 108.

31. Johansson, " 'Herstory' as History," pp. 425–426.

32. This is Johansson's suggestion (ibid., pp. 426–427). She uses Elizabeth I of England as an example and affirms that "she was not just a lucky accident"; rather, her ability to rule resulted from her extensive training, which she received because she lived in a period when many women were educated.

33. I am leaving out the Conquest account and the Deuteronomistic introduction, and am ending with the Samson stories because they reflect a societal background similar to the rest of the material covered in this paper. Judges 16 is generally conceded to be taken from a separate source (see, e.g., Robert Boling, *Judges* [Anchor Bible; Garden City, N.Y.: Doubleday, 1975], p. 36), but Delilah fits well into the scheme outlined here. Chapters 17–21 are considered separately from chapters 1–16 by every commentator I have read. The sources of these chapters are still a matter of dispute.

34. See, for example, Boling, *Judges,* p. 23. These dates are not uncontested. Most scholars will agree that some core information may actually go back to Israel in the time before the monarchy, but the literary problem of extracting the core from the extensive Deuteronomistic editing is immense. With all due caution, I have used only information that seems to me to be relatively free of editorial reworking; in particular, since many of the social data I will be presenting are incidental to the theological program of the editors, I feel somewhat more secure in judging these to be passed-over details, and therefore more likely to be authentic.

35. Boling, *Judges,* p. 187, argues that "son of" in this list refers to political affiliation rather than kinship.

36. See G. Ernest Wright, *Shechem: The Biography of a Biblical City* (New York: McGraw-Hill, 1965), p. 123.

37. The poem is judged older than the prose version on grammatical and orthographic grounds.

38. For example, George Foot Moore, *Judges* (International Critical Commentary; New York: Charles Scribner's Sons, 1895), pp. 149–150.

39. In this case, we might prefer to read with an ancient Greek variant, rather than the Masoretic (Hebrew) text. The variant reads, "Awake, awake, Deborah; arouse the myriads of the army." Patrick D. Miller makes a similar argument in *The Divine Warrior in Early Israel* (Cambridge, Mass.: Harvard University Press, 1975), pp. 92–94.

40. See, for example, Boling, *Judges,* p. 95, or Moore, *Judges,* p. 113.

41. Note also the use of "son(s) of" for followers in 1 Kings 20:35; 2 Kings 2; Amos 7:14; and elsewhere. Boling, *Judges,* p. 257, sees the term "father" in Judges 17:10 and 18:19, as well as Deborah's description here as "mother," as indicating the person in charge of oracular questioning of the deity, and he points to Judges 18:4–6 as an example of this function.

42. There are, furthermore, problems with this story and its relationship to similar ones elsewhere in the Hebrew Bible. See Moore, *Judges,* p. 106.

43. Benjamin Mazar, "The Sanctuary of Arad and the Family of Hobab the Kenite," *Journal of Near Eastern Studies* 24 (1965): 297–303. See further, Frank Moore Cross, *Canaanite Myth and Hebrew Epic* (Cambridge, Mass.: Harvard University Press, 1973), p. 201.

44. C. F. Burney suggested a connection with other virgin sacrifice stories, or with weeping rituals for Tammuz or another dying and rising god (*The Book of Judges* [New York: KTAV, 1970], pp. 332–334). See also Theodor H. Gaster, *Myth, Legend, and Custom in the Old Testament,* vol. 2 (New York: Harper and Row, 1975), pp. 430–432, 534–535.

45. See Phyllis Trible's discussion of this story in *Texts of Terror: Literary-Feminist Readings of Biblical Narratives* (Philadelphia: Fortress, 1984), pp. 93–116. Boling calls Jephthah's "failure to trust" in his judgeship his "tragic flaw" (*Judges,* pp. 207–208). I would like to thank William Propp for pointing out that since the story is an etiological one, it is necessary for the daughter to die in order to explain the ritual noted in Judges 11:39–40. Although her death is often compared negatively with the rescue of Isaac in Genesis 22 and of Jonathan in 1 Samuel 14, it should not be; the three stories serve entirely different purposes.

Three

Female Sexuality in the Hindu World*
Frédérique Apffel Marglin

Westerners' understanding of female sexuality in the Hindu world
has been strongly colored by cultural meanings from Western traditions. All too often, familiar meanings have been projected onto
less familiar Hindu cultural facts. The Hindu world is complex; its
religion has no dogma and no universally recognized priestly hierarchy. The Hindu tradition honors local practices and traditions,
and it has no mechanism to make any given local institution conform to a general pattern. If a uniform Hindu religion can be identified, it resides in widely shared basic principles rather than in a
single canon. The word *Hinduism* encompasses a broad array of
traditions, sects, and religious-philosophical schools.

The image of the world-renouncing ascetic of Hinduism has been
emphasized out of all proportion to its true relevance to a majority
of the Hindu population. Writers such as Albert Schweitzer as well
as scholars such as Max Weber have contributed to the popular
Western perception of India as the land of the *sadhu* and other
more or less emaciated spiritual seekers. The tradition of the
world-renouncing ascetic—typified by Śankara's Advaita Vedanta
—is important, but Western and Western-inspired Indian scholarship has given it a prominence that does not correspond to its
place among the practices of a great part of the population. It is
perhaps not a coincidence that this strand in the Hindu tradition
is more similar to the religious traditions of the Western world,
particularly in matters concerning female sexuality, than other

* I wish to express my deepest gratitude to Lawrence A. Babb for having read with great care a first draft of this paper. His detailed, insightful, and meticulous suggestions have helped to make this paper a much
better work. Any shortcomings are entirely my responsibility.

strands such as the tantric tradition. Only fairly recently have scholars, both Western and Indian, been able to tackle the more radical forms of tantrism (in which cultic sexual activity figures prominently) without feeling obliged to justify a scholarly interest in practices that not very long ago were called obscene.

It is difficult to say whether Western bias concerning the meanings attached to female sexuality derives from simple projection or from an inappropriate application of the values of the ascetic to other strands within Hinduism that are very different from it. My contention is that in eastern India at least, the cultural meanings attached to female sexuality by the average person differ radically from those that exist in the Western tradition or in the tradition of Hindu asceticism.

What follows is a critical look at the widely shared scholarly view that the malevolence of Hindu goddesses who are represented without a male consort results from the danger residing in female sexuality that is not under the control of a male consort. Hindu goddesses who are represented with a male consort have benevolent natures, and many scholars argue that this is the direct result of male taming and control. My previous study of the rituals of the female dancers and singers of the temple of Jagannātha in Purī, Orissa, has led me to view female sexuality in a different light.[1] Alongside the negative cultural valuation of sexuality and menstruation embodied in the fact that sexual intercourse renders one impure, and that a menstruating woman is impure and treated like an untouchable, there is a positive valuation. This positive valuation is expressed by the term *auspicious:* Both sexual intercourse and menstruation are impure but auspicious. A whole axis of value, quite different from the axis of value represented by purity and impurity, emerges with the realization that auspiciousness and purity are not the same at all.[2] These different meanings have not been well understood, probably because the impurity of sex and menstrual blood is so similar to their impurity in the Judeo-Christian tradition; the similarity results in a hasty overidentification. To this, one can add the Western difficulty in accepting apparently contradictory moral values for the same phenomenon.

"Social Reality" and "Symbolic Reality"

Most of the dramatis personae in this essay are goddesses and gods, and the reader may wonder how their doings relate to those of simple mortals living in the context of what is sometimes called social reality. In other words, what is the relationship between religious images of female sexuality and the sexuality of women in India? Some clarifications are in order before we can proceed. First of all, I am concerned here, not with "sexual behavior," but with the cultural meanings that a particular society attaches to female sexuality. Cultural meanings are encoded in rituals and myths as well as in other cultural expressions. Ritual and myth do not belong to a different order of reality from other practices, such as kinship arrangements or the maintenance of the caste system. All human practices, be they the telling of stories about deities or the observance of caste rules, have an element of conventionality. But some practices are more formal, more conventional than others. And rather than differentiating between "social reality" and "symbolic reality," one should speak of a continuum from least formal to most formal practices, the former corresponding to everyday life and the latter to those special times and places that all cultures set aside and describe as ceremonies, festivals, rituals, or the like. One could well apply to ritual a contrast drawn by Paul Ricoeur between speech that takes place between two or more people and a text. Speech is a dialogue, whereas a text, being autonomous and objectified, does not involve any immediate give-and-take. One could say that everyday practice is a transaction between actors embedded in contingency, whereas ritual practice is relatively fixed, and therefore not tied to a "situation of transaction which flows from one agent to another, exactly as spoken language is caught in the process of interlocution." [3] The very fixity of ritual, its formal nature, distances it from contingency, and thus ritual and myth can create their own imaginary world in the same way that a text creates its own world. This imaginative world of myth and ritual, inhabited by goddesses, gods, demons, ghosts, ancestors, and other beings, should not be thought of as a reflection of the everyday world, but as part and parcel of it. I would argue, following Ricoeur's thought, that in the same way that writing fixes the evanescent spoken words by capturing what can be identified and reidentified in what has been said, ritual captures what can be identified and reidentified in what has been done, in social practice. Ritual is to the everyday flow of interaction what literature is to the flow of speech in a dialogue. In other words, ritual is the poetry of everyday practice. [4]

41

Female Sexuality in the Hindu World

The prevalent Western understanding concerning the nature of the malevolence of single goddesses has been formulated most clearly and succinctly by the anthropologist Lawrence Babb.[5] I use the term *Hindu single goddess* as a generic, to refer to a variety of goddesses who are most frequently represented iconographically without a male consort.

Babb has argued that even though in the Sanskrit tradition the goddess is spoken of as being married to a god, in the lived experience of temple ritual and iconography the goddess is often represented as having no consort. When asked, visitors to those temples often recognize that ultimately the particular goddess, who has her own name and seems to be distinct from the goddess associated with Śiva, is identical to the Great Goddess. In her local context, the goddess becomes multiple. She has a local name and is represented alone. Often a male god is also present but in an inferior position, playing not the role of husband but the role of doorkeeper, or of "keeper of the fields" (*kṣetrapāla*). For example in the temple of Mahāmāyā in Raipur, Madhyapradesh, studied by Babb, the most important goddess temple of that city, the two divinities associated with the goddess are Lal Bhairav and Kal Bhairav (Red Bhairav and Black Bhairav). These are two sinister figures placed on either side of the door leading into the inner sanctum of the goddess. The priest of the temple explains that Bhairav is the terrible form (*krodh rup*) of Śiva. In such a context, Śiva is subordinate to the goddess. He is no longer represented as her husband but as a servant who protects the goddess. When the goddess is thus represented alone or with a male in an inferior position, she is the recipient of blood sacrifice, which is never the case when she is represented in her role of consort to a male god who is in a position of superiority. According to Babb, the couples Śiva and his wife Parvatī, Vishnu and his wife Lakshmī, and the royal incarnations of Vishnu and Lakshmī in the *Rāmāyaṇa,* namely, Rāma and Sītā, stand for exemplary social values. When the goddess is alone or in a position of ascendancy, with or without her male acolytes, she acquires the sinister attributes of the goddess herself. Under such a form, the goddess is not conceived as an exemplar of social values but as the personification of a dangerous force that threatens even the gods and must be contained. Babb recognizes that such a goddess can be persuaded to help her devotees, but an important theme of her cult is the appeasement of her thirst for blood. The goddess in such a local context stands for a dangerous force in the Hindu pantheon. When the goddess is shown in her role of consort to her lord, this dangerous and sinister force is transformed into its opposite; the goddess becomes the tender wife, the source of wealth and progeny. When the goddess is placed in the context of a restraining social relationship, that is, in a relationship of marriage, she transforms herself into a benign force. According to Babb, "An appetite for conflict and destruction is thus transformed into the most fundamental of social virtues, that of wifely submission." [6] Babb concludes, "In general, masculine divinity seems to act as a restraining factor while feminine divinity is associated with a potentially destructive force that must be restrained." [7] Such restraint is accomplished in the conjugal relationship. The power inherent in the goddess, emanating from her femininity, is a dangerous power that must be tamed, dominated, and thus controlled by the male.

We have thus a picture of femininity as inherently dangerous, prone to conflict and destructiveness; this dangerous female power is transformed into a beneficent force in the conjugal relationship by virtue of the restraining force of the male. I will be taking up several points in this interpretation, beginning with the aspect of wifely submission as representing the most fundamental of social virtues; that is, with the hierarchical aspect of male-female relationship.

Gender Hierarchy

Indian society requires almost total submission on the part of the wife. The injunction to treat one's husband as a god, encoded in the sacred law literature, is far from a dead letter in contemporary Hindu social life. The following verse from Manu, one of the authors of the sacred law codes (ca. fourth to fifth century A.D.) pithily states the rule: "By a girl, by a young woman, or even by an aged one, nothing must be done independently, even in her own house. In childhood a female must be subject to her father, in youth to her husband, when her lord is dead to her sons; a woman must never be independent." [8]

The wife must blindly and unquestioningly obey her husband,

who is her superior. Here we encounter the same set of meanings as those found in the hierarchy of caste. Even though the norm in Hindu India is for spouses to belong to the same caste or subcaste, women as a group are classified for many purposes as all being of the same low status. Women born in the highest castes do not undergo the initiation ceremony that transforms a male child from a low status *śūdra* into a high status, twice-born man. Except in the case of pollution observances in the event of a death or a birth in the kin group, women observe the rules of purity and impurity in the same manner as persons belonging to the lowest social category (above the line of untouchability). The hierarchy of caste rests upon the observance of rules of purity and pollution;[9] thus the inferiority of women vis-à-vis men is indeed a matter of purity and pollution.

The terms *purity* and *pollution* refer to two classes of phenomena.[10] On the one hand, these terms refer to notions of intactness or integrity, especially of the body; violations of the boundaries of the body, such as menstruation, elimination, wounds, and mutilations, create impurity. Death and birth as well belong to this class of phenomena, since they threaten or violate the integrity of the body. On the other hand, the terms *purity* and *impurity* also refer to the hierarchy of caste: Lower castes are considered less pure than higher ones. The privilege that the superior castes enjoy at the expense of the inferior castes emerges clearly in the various rules that regulate the relationship between castes and are phrased in the language of purity and impurity. There is an unmistakable aspect of power in those concepts, the kind of power evidenced in the subordination of one person or group of persons to another. It is entirely possible that women, being the source of two powerful states of impurity, namely, menstruation and birth, from which men are exempt, are classified as lower, and therefore less pure than men. This set of cultural meanings has led most scholars to see the status of Hindu women as similar to but worse than that of Western women.

Auspiciousness and Inauspiciousness

Purity and impurity and the values they represent, namely, integrity, order, and hierarchy, do not exhaust the Indian cultural landscape. The terms *auspiciousness* and *inauspiciousness* speak of different values and a different sort of power. Up to now, these concepts have been considered to be more or less synonymous with those of purity and impurity, but they are not alike. The terms *auspiciousness* and *inauspiciousness* speak of a nonhierarchical power. To introduce these values, let me retell a myth about Lakshmī, the wife of Jagannātha, the central deity in the temple of Purī.

Lakshmī seeks permission from her husband to go outside the temple and visit households in the town on the occasion of her festival in the month of Mārgaśira (Nov.–Dec.). He grants her the privilege and she visits many households but finds that her worship is improperly carried out. She wanders toward the settlement of the untouchables and enters the house of an untouchable woman who is carrying out her worship exquisitely. Lakshmī is extremely pleased and shares the untouchable's food offering. By so doing, according to caste rules, she becomes polluted and an untouchable herself until she undergoes the proper purificatory rites. Upon her return to the temple, she finds her husband and his elder brother (Balabhadra, who along with their sister Subhadrā is also enshrined in the main temple) blocking the entrance gate. They have learned of her whereabouts and Balabhadra, knowing her to be polluted, prevails upon his younger brother—not without difficulty—to repudiate his wife. The language of the elder brother expresses vividly the hierarchically inferior position of the wife; after having told his younger brother that without bathing, Lakshmī would enter the temple and pollute them, Balabhadra tells him to drive her away. Jagannātha pleads with his elder brother, pointing out that Lakshmī is not easily replaceable. He begs his brother to forgive Lakshmī's fault and to give her another chance. To this Balabhadra replies, "A wife is really only the shoe that covers the foot. If one has a brother then one can get ten million more wives!" Notwithstanding such unambiguously hierarchical—and patriarchal—language, Lakshmī addresses her husband, "Move out of the way, I'm coming in!" Not exactly the words of wifely submission. After brilliantly arguing with her husband, and thereby infuriating him, she is prevented from entering the temple and is sent away. Before leaving, she curses her husband: "Receive my curse, Oh Bhabagrahi [another name for Jagannātha]. If the sun and the moon really move, ah Jagannātha, you won't get any food. You will be poor for twelve years. You won't be able to get food, water, or clothes. When I, a Candāluṇī [an untouchable woman] give you

45

food, then you will eat!" The two brothers do indeed wander for
twelve years as destitute beggars unrecognized by anyone, and are
finally driven to beg food from the house of a Candālunī who
turns out to be Lakshmī.

This story is told to explain the origin of the custom peculiar to
the temple of Jagannātha in Purī of sharing the food offering
among all castes. The brahmin and the untouchable can take food
from the same pot without the higher one becoming polluted. This
was the concession Lakshmī extracted from the two brothers for
agreeing to return with them to the temple. Lakshmī, the goddess
of auspiciousness, prosperity, and well-being, acquiesces in the
logic of hierarchy and purity-impurity and does not enter into the
temple; instead she holds another sort of power. This different
power revolves essentially around food and water, that is, around
life maintenance. In this sphere she is supreme. The story seems
to make a point about Lakshmī's disdain for caste status. Lakshmī
does not purify herself before she tries to reenter the temple, nor
does she do so afterward. She willfully retains the status of an untouchable woman. In the full version of the story the point is underscored, for after being thrown out by her husband, she has a
palace built for herself on the outskirts of town, beyond the pale
of the clean castes, just as the settlement of the untouchables is
situated on the outskirts of town.

Lakshmī's power is awesome, ultimately greater than that of her
husband and brother-in-law, since they are reduced to begging food
from her untouchable hands, an action sure to bring a loss of status
in caste society. The story underlines the point that female power is
great, that it revolves around life maintenance, and that it is an
antihierarchical power. It is not a power-over-others but the power
of life. Woman's power of life maintenance through the control of
cooking and food distribution in the household is culturally perceived as a variant of woman's power to give life and to nourish
the unborn child as well as the infant. Such a power is culturally
highly valued and clearly recognized; it is called *śakti,* the female
power of life. It is to these values that the terms *auspiciousness* and
inauspiciousness apply. The same author who so radically condemned women to submission seems to recognize their power.

Women must be honoured and adorned by their fathers, brothers,
husbands, and brothers-in-law, who desire (their own) welfare.

Where women are honoured, there the gods are pleased; where they are not honoured, no sacred rite yields rewards. Where the female relations live in grief, the family soon wholly perishes; but that family where they are not unhappy ever prospers. The house in which female relations, not being duly honoured, pronounce a curse, perish completely, as if destroyed by magic.[11]

Such a view is certainly consonant with the story of Lakshmī's curse.

The Danger of Male Celibacy

The evidence I have presented so far does not address the question of the potentially destructive force of feminine divinity, which must be restrained by a masculine divinity. Babb's argument implies that there is a dangerous force that is inherently female. Only the male can restrain, control, and neutralize this dangerous female force. I suggest, however, that danger resides, not in the female per se, but in celibacy, whether practiced by a female or a male. Furthermore the danger emanating from the celibate state exists only in the context of this world of birth-death-rebirth (samsāra), and not in the world of the one who pursues liberation from that cycle. From the point of view of the goals of renunciation, celibacy, far from being dangerous, is essential for the one embarking on such a journey. In the world-renouncing traditions, women are excluded from the search for liberation. Hence, in those traditions, the female celibate state can only be dangerous, never positive and necessary, as it is for the male renouncer.

Babb notes the following myth, a local variant of a great traditional myth.

> In ancient times there was a Maharaja named Dakshaprajapati, who ruled in Himachal Pradesh. A daughter was born to him, to whom the name Parvati was given. The astrologers said that her fate in life would be a good one, but that she would have to perform severe *tapasya* (renunciation or austerity) in order to obtain a husband.
>
> After some years had passed, the Maharishi Narad (a famous sage) arrived at the Maharaja's palace and informed his host that Parvati would become the wife of Mahadev (Shiva). This, he said, would come about as the result of her renunciation. When she was old enough for marriage, Parvati went to the jungle and there began her *tapasya*. Seeing the severity of her renunciation, Indra became

47

worried, thinking that she might become more powerful than the gods. So he sent Kamdev (the god of sexual desire) to divert her. This was unsuccessful. Indra sent the Saptarishis to tell her that because of her *tapasya* she might choose a husband from among Vishnu, Brahma, and Shiva. Shiva himself then sent the Saptarishis to Maharaja Dakshaprajapati to inform him of the impending wedding, and in the end the wedding was celebrated with great magnificence.[12]

What is striking in this story is its parallel to the many tales of the austerities of male ascetics who by the heat of their penances threaten the throne of Indra, king of the gods.[13] This story about the austerities of Parvatī is quite similar to the stories of the *tapasya* of male ascetics. One of the festivals held in the temple of Jagannātha, the Sandal Wood Festival (Candan Jātrā), illustrates the parallel.

The main themes of Candan Jātrā are water and eroticism. The female temple dancers (*devadāsī*) call the festival a water play (*jala krida*), an expression with strong erotic connotations. Candan Jātrā lasts forty-two days and ends on the eve of the beginning of the Chariot Festival (*ratha jātrā*), which corresponds with the arrival of the monsoon in late June or early July. The first day of Candan Jātrā corresponds with the beginning of the construction of the chariots to be used during the Chariot Festival. Thus the beginning as well as the end of Candan Jātrā is linked to the next festival ushering in the monsoon.

The season preceding the Chariot Festival, during which the Sandal Wood Festival takes place, is the hottest, driest time of the year. During the Sandal Wood Festival, the activity of the *devadāsīs* in the temple is greatly increased and takes on a special character. During the rest of the year, the *devadāsīs* perform their ritual for Jagannātha, who is their husband. During Candan Jātrā, they perform for Jagannātha's elder brother, Balabhadra, twice a day. Besides those two daily occasions, the *devadāsīs* sing or dance three times in the temple and two times on a boat placed for this occasion in one of the largest artificial lakes of the city. In the boat, a *devadāsī* sings and dances in front of the representative images of Jagannātha and his two wives, Lakshmī and the earth goddess, Bhūdevī. During the ritual the boat is rowed around the tank once in the morning and once in the evening, during the first twenty-one days of the festival.

Thus during Candan Jātrā the *devadāsīs* perform seven times a day; they perform only twice a day in the temple during the rest of the year. Although they perform twice daily for Balabhadra during Candan Jātrā, they do not perform on the second boat, on which his representative image is placed, but only on the boat that carries Jagannātha's representative image and those of his two wives. On Balabhadra's boat, a young man dressed as a woman performs.

In the ritual performed by a *devadāsī* for Balabhadra, the theme of the seduction of an ascetic is acted out. The ritual sequence, which takes place twice a day for the whole forty-two days of the festival, illuminates the meaning of male celibacy and of female sexuality. It is called a secret performance (*gupta seba*), and takes place on the threshold of the inner sanctum, with all doors leading to it being closed so that no one can witness the ritual. Only three brahmin temple priests are present, seated on the platform on which the three main images of this temple are standing, namely, Jagannātha, his elder brother, Balabhadra, and their sister, Subhadrā. The priests fan the deities while the *devadāsī* sings a song for Balabhadra. All the lamps are extinguished, which produces total darkness, since the inner sanctum of a Hindu temple has no windows. The deities are considered to be naked at this time; in fact they wear a single thin loin cloth. While singing, the *devadāsī* takes off the upper part of her garment; and thus she sings her song while partly denuded. The song speaks of the poet's longing to see the Chariot Festival and the white clouds of the monsoon.

Male nudity and female nudity seem to carry different meanings. The folk explanation for Balabhadra's nudity is that it is simply an attempt to escape the scorching heat of the sun. But Balabhadra in this context is associated with Śiva the ascetic, thus leading one to a more strictly religious interpretation. Nudity here conveys asceticism; in such a perspective, nudity, far from being a search for relief from the heat, is in fact the very opposite. Typically, the ascetic goes about nude, a state that concretely expresses his detachment from worldly concerns as well as his intent to mortify the flesh by not protecting it from the elements. Female nudity communicates something different. Alf Hiltebeitel has focused on the heroine Draupadī, the wife of the five Pāṇḍava brothers in the *Mahābhārata*. In a famous scene, the eldest of the five Pāṇḍava brothers plays dice with his arch rival and cousin, the Kaurava prince. The Pāṇḍava loses everything he owns, including his kingdom and, driven by the passion and logic of the game, wagers his four brothers, then himself, and finally their common wife, Draupadī, and loses all. The game takes place in the men's audience hall. The women are out of sight in the women's quarters. The Kaurava prince orders the highborn princess, Draupadī, to be fetched and brought into the hall to be appropriated. After some reluctance on the part of those he ordered, Draupadī is finally dragged by her flowing hair into the men's hall. Thereupon, one of the Kaurava prince's men (a man named Karṇa) orders her to be disrobed. This is the ultimate humiliation and a symbolic rape. While this is going on, Draupadī appeals to her five husbands, who stand by motionless, immobilized by their honor and the duty to keep their word. By divine intervention Draupadī's garment becomes endless and the more it is pulled, the more it renews itself. Draupadī cannot be disrobed. According to Hiltebeitel's persuasive interpretation, Draupadī's garment symbolizes the earth's vegetation, Draupadī herself representing the earth and her powers of regeneration. The man who orders Draupadī's disrobement, Karṇa, is the son of the sun. During the hot season, the Indian earth is scorched and denuded, her garment reduced to a minimum. The *devadāsī*'s partial nudity during the secret ritual may thus be a metaphorical allusion to the state of the earth during the season of the festival, which is the hottest time of the year.

There is another set of meanings contained in the secret ritual of the *devadāsī*. The *devadāsī* is also a courtesan and therefore cannot be dissociated from sexuality; the unveiling of her breasts may also be interpreted as a seductive gesture. This interpretation is reinforced by the rest of the *devadāsī*'s attire. For this ritual she wears a modified costume. A *devadāsī,* as befitting her status of one who is always auspicious, that is, always a married woman, wears the signs of marriage: the round red dot on the forehead and the red line in the parting of the hair; many bangles on both wrists; ringing anklets and toe rings; lac on her feet. For this ritual the *devadāsī* wears a vertical red line on the forehead, pushes her bangles up on her forearms so they will not jingle, and wears no jingling anklets, no perfume, and no lac on her feet. All this signifies that she comes to Balabhadra clandestinely, with no telltale jingles, feet marks, or sweet smell. She is decorated but in a modified fashion emphasizing secrecy, a secrecy ensured by the closed doors and the darkness. She has come for an illicit meeting in which she attempts to seduce Balabhadra. The *devadāsīs* are the wives of Jagannātha, not of Balabhadra, and during the rest of the year they perform for their husband. During the secret ritual we have the well-known mythical theme of the seduction of an ascetic by a courtesan. Balabhadra is identified at this time with Śiva the ascetic, not Śiva the husband of Parvatī, since she is not represented with him.

The prototypical story of the seduction of an ascetic is found in the *Mahābhārata*'s episode of the seduction of the ascetic Riṣya-śringa.[14] The seduction of an ascetic by a courtesan opposes the heat of the ascetic gained through rigorous penances to the rains of the king of the gods, Indra.[15] Ascetic heat "challenges the throne of Indra" by the power it gains; the challenge often takes the narrative form of a drought plaguing the kingdom. The most effective weapon of the earthly king or the heavenly king (Indra) against the drying heat of the ascetic is the courtesan. By seducing the ascetic, the courtesan destroys his heat (and power), and the deed releases Indra's rains. It is now understandable why the *devadāsī* during the secret ritual sings of the poet's longing to see the next festival, the Chariot Festival, a festival of renewal that ushers in the rains. The seduction of the ascetic Balabhadra will put an end to the heat and the scorching of the earth. Male celibacy threatens the well-being of the realm, whereas sexual union through a woman's seduction brings about the beneficent and prosperity-bearing rains.

During Candan Jātrā, Balabhadra is secretly courted by a courtesan, but publicly he is apparently courted by a male transvestite. What messages relevant to our subject can be discovered in this episode? During the twice-daily display of Balabhadra in a boat, a young man dressed as a female temple dancer sings and dances. His style of dress, dancing, and singing is almost identical to that of the *devadāsī*. This means that the dance is unmistakably sensual if not openly erotic. Since the dance of the transvestite on Balabhadra's boat takes place at the same time as the dance of the *devadāsī* on Jagannātha's representative's boat, the parallel in time, space, and style cannot be ignored. Are we to interpret this ritual sequence as the homosexual seduction of Balabhadra by a transvestite? Many signs seem to point toward such an interpretation.

On the boat Balabhadra is accompanied by the images of five Śivas from five Śiva temples in the city. These five Śivas are called the five Pāndavas. It is clear then that at that moment Balabhadra is identified with Śiva and the five Śivas in turn are identified with the five brothers, heroes of the *Mahābhārata.* Since there are no women and no wives of the deities on Balabhadra's boat, the identification is with Śiva the ascetic, not Śiva the loving husband of Parvatī. Further, the transvestite dancer on the boat with the five Pāndavas brings to mind in a Hindu audience the episode in the epic when Arjuna (one of the five brothers) becomes for the duration of one year a transvestite teacher of dance and music. Hiltebeitel has shown that Arjuna's disguise or transformation is a necessary symbolic precondition and prelude to the regeneration of the Pāndava line, all but extinguished in the great battle that culminates the epic. All the sons of Draupadī are killed. Arjuna's son by another wife marries the princess to whom Arjuna taught dance and music. Their male offspring is ultimately the sole survivor and continuator of the Pāndava lineage. Thus in the epic Arjuna's transvestism is linked with lineal regeneration.

To these epic references must be added ethnographic references concerning male transvestites in general, who are called *hijras* and legitimize their way of life by reference to Arjuna's period as a transvestite.[16] Interestingly, the *hijras* are traditionally requested to dance and sing particularly on the occasion of the birth of a male child. They are considered to be able to confer fertility on householders desirous of offspring. The great majority of these transvestites are homosexual prostitutes.[17] There are striking parallels between the tradition of the *hijras* and the sacred eunuch priests of the ancient West Asian goddesses,[18] such as the genital self-mutilation in the name of a goddess and the practice of homosexual prostitution. Even though the transvestite dancer on the boat is not a *hijra,* but a young boy or teen-ager who in all likelihood will later lead a heterosexual life, the larger cultural context of transvestism in Hindu India must be drawn upon in the interpretive task. The transvestite dances for the five Śivas and for Balabhadra at the same time that the *devadāsī* dances and sings for Jagannātha's representative and his two wives on the second boat. The dances and songs of the *devadāsīs* are erotic, and so are those of the transvestite. Furthermore Śiva is also well known in his form of the half-man, half-woman hermaphrodite (Śiva Arddhanārīśvara). Serena Nanda in her ethnographic reports on the *hijras* of North and South India tells us that the *hijras* claim that they can bring on the fertilizing rains. To support this claim they tell a story strikingly similar to that of the seduction of an ascetic by a courtesan. In the reported version there is no explicit reference to the seduction of a man by a *hijra,* but the rains are brought about by the personal visit of the king to two transvestites passing through his city.

Balabhadra the ascetic is seduced secretly by a woman and publicly by a male transvestite. Both activities signify the same thing, namely, the assurance of the timely arrival of the fertilizing rains. Erotic activity, be it heterosexual or homosexual, has an auspicious outcome, since it brings on the renewing rains. The *devadāsīs* and the *hijras* have in common that they sacrifice their procreative powers, the former by renouncing marriage and children (*devadāsīs* are not supposed to procreate and therefore they adopt daughters to succeed them), and the latter by sacrificing their genitals to the goddess. The fertility of the land is brought about not by the fertility of women but by erotic activity. Given the androgynous nature of Balabhadra/Śiva, both homosexual and heterosexual activity are required to ensure that his ascetic heat will be vanquished.

The auspicious nature of female sexuality, its power to ensure the fertility of the land, is imitated by certain males who offer their masculinity to a goddess and identify with her and with her powers of renewal. The ritual sequence just examined, with its associated myths and larger cultural context, seems to point unmistakably to the role of sexuality from the perspective of this-worldly concerns, that is, the concerns of the kingdom: Female sexuality embodies a highly valued power, the power to bring on the fertilizing rains. In the Indian subcontinent, prosperity and the avoidance of famine depend on the timely arrival of the monsoon rains. These concerns are those of the peasants, and of all those who depend on the land. In this perspective, asceticism is linked with drought and is therefore dangerous.

The Danger of Female Celibacy

The example of Parvatī's austerities, mentioned above, seems to suggest that female asceticism has the same dangerous effect as male asceticism. The austerities of Parvatī also endanger the throne of Indra. As Babb's retelling puts it, "Seeing the severity of her renunciation, Indra became worried, thinking that she might become more powerful than the gods." In her case Indra uses a weapon similar to that used against male ascetics, namely, Kamdev, the god of sexual desire. Such a weapon is the male counterpart of the heavenly courtesans (*apsaras*) or the earthly courtesan, and it has the same effect of putting an end to ascetic practices and producing a sexual union.[19]

When a male ascetic such as Balabhadra or Riṣyaśringa performs extreme *tapasya,* he produces a heat that threatens a kingdom. The kingdom stands for worldly concerns of regeneration and renewal, and is distinct from the otherworldly concerns of those who pursue a path that leads to liberation from the cycle of birth-death-rebirth. This means that the pursuit of liberation turns its back on concerns of regeneration and renewal.[20]

Female sexuality is thus inherently auspicious, the source of the regenerative powers of women, of the earth, and, by metaphorical extension, of the cosmos. Danger lies in celibacy, the foremost requirement in any ascetic practice. The danger of celibacy is impartially distributed between males and females. Goddesses represented alone or with a male in a subordinate position convey the celibate state of the goddess. Spatial arrangements are not the only signs of a goddess's celibacy. The single goddesses are often represented iconographically with loose flowing hair, which signals their celibate state. (Loose, disheveled, uncombed hair also signifies a state of impurity such as menstruation or a death in the kin group. During such periods, a woman is not to be approached sexually.)[21]

The danger of the single goddesses emanates from their celibate state and not from their female sexuality. From the perspective of this-worldly concerns of regeneration and renewal, sexual union signifies the achievement of the regeneration of a lineage or the renewal of the land and the realm. Celibacy, male or female, is a dangerous state, not absolutely, but from the point of view of regeneration whether cosmic or lineal, the former being the cosmological dimension of the latter. The sexuality of the *devadāsī* is linked with the renewal of the land, but is dissociated from reproduction and lineal regeneration. The *devadāsīs* are not chaste wives but unmarried courtesans who should not procreate. The sexuality of the married woman is linked with lineal regeneration, and such regenerative powers have cosmological resonances.

The celibacy of the male produces a heat linked to drought. Female celibacy may also produce heat, since during her menstruation a woman is said to be heated, and when the goddess earth menstruates, one of the days of her menses is called burning earth.

The foremost single goddess is Durgā, who was born from the combined energies of all the major male gods; these energies combined to form a great fire out of which appeared a fully grown, mature woman, the great goddess Durgā. She was created by the gods to vanquish their arch rival, whom they were unable to overcome. Durgā is called the maiden (*kumārī*), which is taken to mean not necessarily physiological virginity but an unmarried state. Durgā represents fiery energy and she alone conquers the great demon. Durgā's myth of origin highlights the fact that single goddesses are not always malevolent. Durgā's victory over the great buffalo demon is salvific and entirely beneficent.

Single goddesses may be both the cause of destruction and protection against calamities. This essentially ambivalent characteristic is most clearly evidenced in such goddesses as Sitaḷā, the goddess of smallpox. Her name means "the cool one," which is often taken to be a euphemism. I do not think the name is euphemistic but refers instead to the beneficent pole of her nature, which cures those stricken with the disease and thereby cools their fever. A person burning with the fever of smallpox is said to be possessed by this goddess, who is both the disease and its cure. I would interpret this characteristic in terms of the regenerative powers of women, particularly of women's sexuality.

Conclusion

Regeneration is a cyclical process, part of an endless spiral of birth, growth, maturation, decay, and death. From this perspective, death is not an end but the necessary transition to rebirth and regeneration. This is pithily captured by the following Sanskrit saying: "Again birth, again death, again sleep in the mother's womb." For Hindus, death is like a sleep in the mother's womb. The regenerative powers of women include and even necessitate decay and death. At the beginning of this essay I spoke of the power of life that females possess in the Hindu world; I might more accurately speak of the power of life and death. This power, called *śakti,* in its benevolent aspect covers all that is called auspicious and in its malevolent aspect all that is called inauspicious. But we are confronted by a single process, which in its unfolding may be positively or negatively valued or even both at times. Unlike the principle of the pure and the impure, the principle of the auspicious and the inauspicious does not represent a mutually exclusive dichotomy. The principle of the auspicious and the inauspicious does not conform to a dualistic conceptualization, and the opposition is not an exclusive binary one. Some events and persons can be at once auspicious and inauspicious. In the case of the single goddesses, their power of life and death, their *śakti,* can both destroy and renew. From all these observations we can conclude that it is not the inherently dangerous and malevolent nature of female sexuality that needs to be tamed and controlled by the male in order to transform it into benevolent wifely submission, since such an inherent nature does not exist. The character of single goddesses is ambivalent because their *śakti,* their potency, can go in two directions. In a conjugal or any sexual relationship female *śakti* is stabilized as auspicious.

Even though the nature of the ambivalence and the potential for danger in male celibacy may be different from that in female celibacy, it is clear that male celibacy can and often does destroy auspiciousness. This is brought out clearly in the relationship between drought, and therefore famine, and male celibacy. Thus, there is as much evidence for stating that within the values of this world, of the kingdom, male asceticism can be dangerous. The issues reside not in a dangerous female sexuality but in the ambivalent potency of female and male celibacy. Sexual union "tames" and softens the male as much as it does the female in the Hindu world.

There is a symmetry between the dangerous powers emanating from male and female celibacy. Sexual union signifies renewal and prosperity, whereas celibacy may signify a danger to regeneration and renewal. The association between the goddess's single status and her dangerous power derives from her celibacy; dangerous power is not inherent in her as a female. Further, the benign nature of the goddess as consort of a male god is the result, not of the male taming and controlling her inherently dangerous nature, but rather of the benevolent and auspicious nature of the union between male and female. Parvatī's hard-won conjugal union with Śiva could be interpreted as a taming and transforming of the great god. From being a fearful ascetic he becomes a loving family man.

Babb's emphasis on the inherent danger of females and on the necessity of male control may be colored by a Western belief in the danger of uncontrolled female sexuality; a more appropriate, more biblical term for danger would be *evil,* with its phonological link to Eve, the name of the original temptress.

Notes

1. F. A. Marglin, *Wives of the God-King: The Rituals of the Devadasis of Puri* (Oxford: Oxford University Press, 1985).

2. Ibid.

3. Paul Ricoeur, *Hermeneutics and the Human Sciences* (Paris: Cambridge University Press and Editions de la Maison des Sciences de l'Homme, 1981), p. 203.

4. Most of the myths and rituals discussed here have been observed and recorded in Purī, Orissa, on the eastern seacoast of India. I have also examined myths found in various texts such as the two great epics, the *Mahābhārata* and the *Rāmāyaṇa,* or in one of the many texts containing the deeds of the gods, which are called "old stories" (*purāṇas*). My approach thus does not follow a strictly empirical methodology, since it mixes data actually observed and recorded with textual data. The rationale for such an approach is that textual sources can throw light on field data; to deprive oneself of such sources is to be needlessly narrowly empirical. Although not all residents and visitors to a town such as Purī are literate, the textual tradition is kept alive through oral retellings and other forms of representation such as folk theater and dance. My data come primarily from temple practice. Temple worship as it is carried out in Purī, whether in the great compound of the temple of Jagannātha or in any of the innumerable smaller shrines of this sacred pilgrimage center, can only superficially be associated with any one sectarian tradition. Even though the temple of Jagannātha, built in the twelfth century A.D., is generally considered to be a Vaishnavite (dedicated to Vishnu, one of the three great gods of the Hindu pantheon) shrine, it contains many elements of other sectarian traditions such as the Shaivite (of the great god Śiva) and Śāktā (of the great goddess, sometimes called the great Śakti) traditions. Besides these three main sectarian traditions, the rituals and myths in Purī exhibit local features that cannot be attributed to any particular sectarian tradition, and form part of what can be called popular Hinduism. I have based my remarks on people's practices; sometimes, but not always, the persons whom I observed and from whom I recorded stories identified themselves as belonging to a particular sectarian tradition. Most of the time, my informants said they belonged to no sectarian tradition at all, and this seems to be the case

for the majority of the people. These persons do what they do because it is customary.

5. Lawrence A. Babb, "Marriage and Malevolence: The Uses of Sexual Opposition in a Hindu Pantheon," in *Ethnology*, vol. ix, no. 2, 1970; and Lawrence A. Babb, *The Divine Hierarchy: Popular Hinduism in Central India* (New York: Columbia University Press, 1970).

6. Babb, *The Divine Hierarchy*, pp. 235–236.

7. Ibid., p. 229.

8. Manu, *The Laws of Manu*, vol. v, trans. Georg Bühler (New York: Dover, 1969), pp. 147–148.

9. Louis Dumont, *Homo Hierarchicus: The Caste System and Its Implications* (Chicago: University of Chicago Press, 1970).

10. F. A. Marglin, "Power, Purity, and Pollution: Aspects of the Caste System Reconsidered," in *Contributions to Indian Sociology* n.s. vol. 11, no. 2, 1977; and Babb, *Marriage and Malevolence*.

11. Manu, vol. III, pp. 55–58.

12. Babb, *The Divine Hierarchy*, pp. 149–150.

13. For translations of several such stories, see Wendy O'Flaherty, *Asceticism and Eroticism in the Mythology of Śiva* (Delhi: Oxford University Press, 1975), pp. 42–51.

14. For a retelling and a discussion of the Riṣyaśringa myth, see O'Flaherty, *Asceticism and Eroticism*, pp. 42–51.

15. For a lengthier and more in-depth treatment of this theme, see F. A. Marglin, *Wives of the God-King: The Rituals of the Devadasis of Puri* (Oxford: Oxford University Press, 1985), chap. 3.

16. Serena Nanda, *"The Hijras of India: Cultural and Individual Dimensions of an Institutionalized Third Gender Role,"* manuscript, 1984.

17. Ibid.

18. Walter Kornfeld, "Prostitution Sacrée," in *Supplément au Dictionnaire de la Bible* (Paris: 1972).

19. Hiltebeitel discusses at length the meaning of Draupadī's vow not to bind her hair and to remain in a symbolic condition of menstrual defilement for the whole thirteen years of the exile. This means that Draupadī remains celibate during that time. Draupadī's celibacy also has dangerous consequences; it forces the Kauravas and the Pāṇḍavas to wage a bloody and destructive war in which Draupadī's five sons are killed. See Alf Hiltebeitel, "Draupadī's Hair," *Purusārtha* 5 (1981). Thus Parvatī's *tapasya* to get a husband is not the only example of female celibacy. A search in the literature would, I suspect, turn up other examples of female austerity.

20. This schema does not hold for two major traditions, namely, the devotional *bhakti* movements and the tantric traditions. In those traditions, transcendence or liberation may be attained without having to turn one's back on worldly concerns but rather through them.

21. For a thorough investigation of the symbolism of women's hair, see Hiltebeitel, "Draupadī's Hair."

Bibliography

Babb, Lawrence A. "Marriage and Malevolence: The Uses of Sexual Opposition in a Hindu Pantheon" in *Ethnology*, Vol. IX, no. 2, 1970.

————. *The Divine Hierarchy: Popular Hinduism in Central India,* Columbia University Press, Chicago, 1975.

Dumont, Louis. *Homo Hierarchicus: The Caste System and Its Implications,* University of Chicago Press, Chicago, 1970.

Hiltebeitel, Alf. "Śiva, the Goddess, and the Disguises of the Pāṇḍavas and Draupadī," in *History of Religions*, Vol. 20, nos. 1 & 2, 1980.

————. "Draupadī's Garment," in *Indo-Iranian Journal*, Vol. 22, 1980.

————. "Draupadī's Hair," in *Puruṣārtha*, Vol. 5, 1981.

Kornfeld, Walter. "Prostitution Sacrée," in the *Supplément au Dictionnaire de la Bible,* Paris, 1972.

Manu. *The Laws of Manu,* translated by Georg Bühler, Dover Publications, New York, 1969.

Marglin, Frédérique A. "Power, Purity, and Pollution: Aspects of the Caste System Reconsidered," in *Contributions to Indian Sociology* n.s., Vol. 11, no. 2, 1977.

————. *Wives of the God-King: The Rituals of the Devadasis of Puri,* Oxford University Press, Delhi, New York, Oxford, 1985.

Nanda, Serena. *The Hijras of India: Cultural and Individual Dimensions of an Institutionalized Third Gender Role,* Manuscript, 1984.

O'Flaherty, Wendy Doniger. *Asceticism and Eroticism in the Mythology of Śiva,* Oxford University Press, Delhi, 1975.

Ricoeur, Paul. *Hermeneutics and the Human Sciences,* Cambridge University Press and Editions de la Maison des Sciences de l'Homme, Paris, 1981.

Four

Paul's Views on the Nature of Women and Female Homoeroticism*

Bernadette J. Brooten

Paul's condemnation of sexual love relations between women in Romans 1:26 is central to his understanding of female sexuality, nature, and the relationship between women and men. Because of the role of Christianity in the Western world, the New Testament's ethical advice, its images of women and of men, and its attitudes toward sexuality have helped to shape Western concepts of the family and of the proper place of women in society, as well as legislation on marriage and sexuality.

Paul's Letter to the Romans, written in the formative stage of Christianity, came, in the course of time, to be normative for Christian theology. It is one of the most widely read and preached-upon books of the New Testament. In the present church debate on ordination and sexual orientation, Paul's teaching on sexual love relations between women and between men (Rom. 1:26–27) plays an important role. In contemporary public policy debates, fundamentalist groups opposing the right of lesbians and gay men to be protected from discrimination in employment, housing, or custody of their children often quote the Letter to the Romans as an authority.

Sexuality has to do with power. An important insight of the

* This article was written within the context of the "Frau und Christentum" project of the Institut für ökumenische Forschung, University of Tübingen, West Germany. I would like to thank the Stiftung Volkswagenwerk, which is funding this project, as well as the following members of the project team for providing critical comments, typing the manuscript, and doing bibliographical work: Inge Baumann, Christina Bucher, Jutta Flatters, and Linda Maloney. I am currently preparing a book-length study on the topic of the present essay in which I plan to include more extensive documentation and critical discussion.

61

women's movement has been that, as women, we cannot determine the direction of our lives as long as others control our bodies. Feminists have discovered that sexuality is not simply a matter of romantic love, nor is it a changeless, purely biological phenomenon; rather, sexuality is determined by societal structures. By looking at ethical teachings on female sexuality, as well as by studying the ways in which women experience sexuality, we can learn about hierarchy, about superordination and subordination in a given society. Thus, to understand female sexuality is not simply to understand just one other area of women's lives. It is to understand an area of female existence in which power is acutely expressed.

It is essential to distinguish between what men have taught about women's sexuality and how women have experienced sexuality. What Paul taught is not to be identified with what early Christian women thought or how they lived. Paul's thinking has contributed, nevertheless, in a significant way to the Christian construction of female sexuality, and is therefore intertwined with Christian women's lives. The purpose of this study is to understand Paul within his cultural context. This can help us to examine critically our own thinking about female sexuality and nature, and our appropriation of Paul's thought within our own cultural context.

A central message of Paul's Letter to the Romans is that all who believe in Christ are justified. In Romans 1:18 to 3:20, Paul sets the background for this message by describing how all human beings are in need of justification, how without Christ they live under the power of sin and stand condemned. Everyone has had the opportunity to know God through God's created works, and therefore human beings are without excuse for having turned from God to idols. The result is serious, according to Romans 1:24–27 (RSV).

24 Therefore God gave them up in the lusts of their hearts to impurity, to the dishonoring of their bodies among themselves, **25** because they exchanged the truth about God for a lie and worshiped and served the creature rather than the Creator, who is blessed forever! Amen. **26** For this reason God gave them up to dishonorable passions. Their women exchanged natural relations for unnatural, **27** and the men likewise gave up natural relations with women and were consumed with passion for one another, men committing shameless acts with men and receiving in their own persons the due penalty for their error.

Thus, Paul sees sexual relations between women and between men to be a result of idolatry; they signify estrangement between human beings and God.

The focus of this essay is Romans 1:26, in which Paul speaks of the unnatural relations of their women. While the condemnation of male homosexual acts in verse 27 is related to that in verse 26, the issue is not parallel and cannot be subsumed under sexual love relations between women. It is my thesis that Paul's condemnation of female homoeroticism is closely connected with his view that there should be gender differentiation in appearance because of the man's being the head of woman (see 1 Cor. 11:2–16). Paul could well share with other contemporary authors who commented on female homoeroticism and proper female sexual roles the view that sexual relations between women implied that women were trying to be like men, that is, to transcend the passive, subordinate role accorded to them by nature. Indeed, I interpret Paul's words "exchanged natural relations for unnatural" to mean that the women exchanged the passive, subordinate sexual role for an active, autonomous one. If I am correct, it should be clear that Paul's condemnation of sexual love relations between women is of fundamental significance for his understanding of female sexuality.

Female Homoeroticism in the Greco-Roman World

Paul's theological thinking about women was culturally conditioned by his environment. To understand his views, we must determine where Romans 1:26 fits into the ancient spectrum of views on female homoeroticism. Understanding the historical context is necessary so we do not interpret Paul anachronistically, but rather locate his thinking within the contemporary discussion about female sexuality of his own time.

Jewish Authors

The Hebrew Bible does not prohibit sexual relations between women, although it does forbid male homosexual intercourse: "If a man lies with a male as with a woman, both of them have committed an abomination; they shall be put to death, their blood is upon them" (RSV, Lev. 20:13, cf. Lev. 18:22). Postbiblical Jewish literature does take up the issue of sexual intercourse between women. *The Sentences of Pseudo-Phocylides,* a Greek poem probably written by a Jewish author of the Diaspora, contains a section on proper sexual behavior, marriage, and family life.[1] Following upon a prohibition of male homosexual behavior is a similar prohibition to women: "And let not women imitate the sexual role [literally, "marriage bed"] of men" (line 192). The author describes male homosexuality as a transgression of nature (line 190) that is not found in the animal world (line 191). The reader is warned not to let a son have long, braided or knotted hair, as long hair is for voluptuous women (lines 210–212). Further, beautiful boys are to be protected from homosexual advances and virgins kept locked up until their wedding day (lines 213–216). The sexual ethics presented in the poem are thus based on strict gender differentiation in dress and sexual role. Girls are to be kept fit for marriage and, once married, are not to stray outside the boundaries of marriage. A woman having sexual relations with another woman is viewed as imitating a man.[2]

Sifra, a rabbinical commentary on Leviticus composed of sayings from the tannaitic period (before ca. 220 C.E.), also discussed the issue:

> Or: "You shall not do as they do in the land of Egypt . . . and you shall not do as they do in the land of Canaan" (Lev. 18:3). One could [interpret it as meaning] that they may not build buildings or plant plants like them. Therefore scripture teaches, "You shall not walk in their statutes" (Lev. 18:3). . . . And what did they do? A man married a man and a woman a woman, and a man married a woman and her daughter, and a woman was married to two men.[3]

Thus we see that, in light of the lack of a biblical verse prohibiting sexual relations between women, another verse in Leviticus is taken as referring to such relations. This is not a specific negative commandment. Rather, the Egyptians and the Canaanites are described as practicing male homosexual and lesbian marriage, and the Israelites are forbidden to follow statutes that allow such things.

In the Jerusalem Talmud, the compilation and editing of which was completed around the fifth century C.E., there is reference to women having intercourse with each other, literally to "swinging back and forth" with each other.[4] The text records a difference of opinion between two rabbinical schools of the first century on whether such intercourse made women unfit for the priesthood, that is, unfit to marry into the priesthood and to eat the priestly offerings. The background is that a priest may not marry a woman who has committed harlotry (Lev. 21:7), and the high priest must marry a virgin (Lev. 21:13). The question is whether sexual relations between women counts as intercourse, thereby making marriage to a priest forbidden. According to the text, the School of Shammai says that it does count, and the School of Hillel does not count sexual relations between women as making a woman unfit for marriage into the priesthood. Later Jewish sources also occasionally discuss the issue.[5]

In sum, the earliest Jewish sources (known to me) on sexual relations between women are from the Roman period. The emergent awareness of the issue may indicate increased openness on the part of women and possibly a greater frequency of sexual expression within female friendships, for anxiety about a phenomenon usually shows that it in fact exists. Paul's inclusion of women fits in well with the Jewish concern developing at precisely his time.

Non-Jewish Authors

The earliest clear reference to female homoeroticism in Greek literature[6] seems to be that in Plato's *Symposium*.[7] Aristophanes, in discoursing on the origins of humanity, speaks of *hetairistriai,* women who are attracted to women, as having their origin in primeval beings consisting of two women joined together. This parallels the original creatures who were two men joined together and those who consisted of one woman and one man. Aristophanes imagines that each human being seeks a partner of the gender to which she or he was originally attached. In Plato's last work, the *Laws,*[8] he speaks of sexual relations between men and between women as "contrary to nature" (*para physin*), and adds that "the first who dared to do this acted through lack of self-control with respect to pleasure." [9] Thus, the passage in the *Symposium* presupposes that same-sex love is as natural and normal as heterosexual love, while that in the *Laws* does not. The reason for the discrepancy is unclear.

In the third century B.C.E., Asclepiades composed an epigram on two Samian women, Bitto and Nannion, who did not want to live in accordance with the laws of Aphrodite; instead, deserting sexual activities of which she would approve, they turned to other, "not beautiful" ones. Asclepiades calls upon Aphrodite to hate these women, who are fleeing intercourse within her realm. An ancient commentator added as an explanatory note that he was accusing them of being *tribades,* which is the most common Greek term for women who engage in same-sex love.[10]

In the Latin literature of the early Empire, there are a number of references to a woman's expressing her love for another woman sexually, and all of them are derogatory. Seneca the Elder (ca. 55 B.C.E. to 40 C.E.) composed one of his fictitious legal controversies around the case of a man who caught two *tribades* in bed, his wife and another woman, and killed them both. One declaimer describes the husband's first reaction: "But I looked first at the man, to see whether he was natural or sewed-on." Another declaimer notes that one would not tolerate the killing of a male adulterer under these circumstances, but adds that if he "had found a pseudo-adulterer. . . ." The reader is left with the shock of the monstrosity, having been led to see that the husband's act was justified.[11]

Ovid's (43 B.C.E. to 18 C.E.) *Metamorphoses* contains the tale of two girls, Iphis and Ianthe, who loved each other and were engaged to marry.[12] Because of her husband's wish to have a boy, Iphis's mother had raised her as a boy and concealed it from her husband. Iphis now bemoans her predicament, saying that the love she possesses is "unheard of," and even "monstrous." If the gods wished to destroy her, she bewails, they should have given her a "natural woe," one "according to custom." Among animals, females do not love females, she says, and, in her despair, she wishes she were no longer female. Iphis knows that she should accept herself as a woman and seek what is in accordance with divine law and love as a woman ought to love. And yet she loves Ianthe, though knowing that "nature does not will it, nature more powerful than all." [13] It is against the background of the tragedy of freakish circumstances—against divine will, against nature, against custom, unheard of—that the reader is relieved when Isis intervenes and changes Iphis into a boy, making the marriage possible.[14]

The poet Phaedrus (died mid 1st c. C.E.) composed a fable in which he describes the origin of *tribades* and passive homosexual men (*molles mares*) as an error on the part of Prometheus. For Prometheus, on returning intoxicated and sleepy from a dinner party, mistakenly placed female sexual organs on male bodies and male members on women. "Therefore lust now enjoys perverted pleasure." [15]

66

Martial (ca. 40 to 103/104 c.e.) dedicated two epigrams to Philaenis, "tribad of the very tribads."[16] He depicts Philaenis as sexually aggressive toward both boys and girls, the latter of whom she, "quite fierce with the erection of a husband," batters eleven in a day. She spends much time on athletics: handball, heavy jumping weights, wrestling. She engages in the pleasure of being whipped by a greasy teacher.[17] Before dining she vomits seven portions of unmixed wine. After consuming sixteen meat dishes, she returns to the wine. "When, after all of these things, her mind turns back to sex, she does not engage in fellatio, which she thinks is not manly enough." Instead she "devours girls' middles." Martial can only scorn the logic of this last act, for how could she consider cunnilingus manly? He also says of Philaenis "you rightly call the woman with whom you copulate a girlfriend."

In a third epigram,[18] Martial addresses one Bassa, a woman whom he had first thought to be as chaste as the famed Lucretia, for he had never seen Bassa coupling with men and had heard no scandals about her. On the contrary, she was always surrounded by women. But now he realizes that she was a *fututor* (m., "fucker").[19] Her "monstrous lust imitates a man." That without a man there should be adultery is worthy of the Theban riddle.

In interpreting Martial one must be cautious. The vulgar and violent language and imagery we encounter here are not peculiar to these three epigrams, but are typical of Martial's style. Of particular note is his precise imagery. A *tribas* is a woman who is trying to be like a man. Philaenis is unlimited in her sexual prowess, trying to win as many boys and girls as she can by her aggressive pursuits. The reference to what seems to be sadomasochistic pleasure at the hand of the trainer is designed to evoke special horror in the reader. Could it be that the voluntary submission to violence symbolizes Philaenis's control even over violence toward herself? It appears here that a man's violence toward a woman is a cultural outrage only when she allows such violence. By virtue of such autonomy, Philaenis has ceased to be a woman, as culturally defined, and has become a man. To Martial, it can then appear only ridiculous that she show interest in female genitalia. For how could anyone of sound mind consider cunnilingus (because it can be pleasurable to women?) virile? Thus, for all her carryings-on, Philaenis is not a real man after all. Martial generates a creative tension in the poems by exaggerating women's attempts to be virile and then exposing these attempts as ridiculous. But they are not simply laughable. Such behavior is dangerous, and therefore deserves the term *monstrous*.

Judith P. Hallett, in a very insightful paper entitled "Autonomy as Anomaly: Roman, and postclassical Greek, reactions to female homoerotic expression," [20] suggests that Martial consciously portrays Philaenis as physically masculine, as physically capable of penile penetration (for example, of the boys).[21] She further notes that in the epigrams on Philaenis and elsewhere, Roman authors depict female homoeroticism as Greek and therefore distanced from their own reality. This occurs through such devices as the use of Greek[22] or Greek loanwords, of which there are a number in Martial's epigrams on Philaenis. The word *tribas* itself is a Greek loanword and must have evoked a nuance of foreignness. Hallett's hypothesis is this:

> To some extent, therefore, this male preoccupation with physical masculinity, and particularly penis possession, as a necessary component of female sexual autonomy and homoeroticism, and this characterization of female sexual autonomy as distanced and non-Roman, seem to reflect an effort to describe such female behavior in symbolic language, as an imaginary super-deviation from the limits of prescribed female sexuality explicable to Roman males only in male terms.[23]

Hallett argues that whereas Roman men passed beyond the passive sexual stage during which they could be penetrated by another male when they reached their early twenties, Roman women were to remain in the passive role throughout their adult lives. The easiest way to understand women's rejection of the passive sexual role was to imagine that they, like the men, had passed on to the next stage, which implied penetrating behavior.

Juvenal's (ca. 67 C.E. to ?) *Sixth Satire* contains a reference to women who set down their litters at the ancient altar of Chastity in Rome: "and in turn they ride horseback, and what is more they throb with the moon as a witness." [24] Elsewhere Juvenal has a woman, Laronia, contrast women with homosexual men, saying that among women "such an abominable specimen of conduct" will not be found.[25]

Authors writing in Greek in the Roman period were also nearly always quite negative in their depictions of female homoeroticism.

The philosopher and biographer Plutarch (ca. 45 to ca. 120 C.E.) is an important exception. He describes boy-love in the Sparta of the legendary founder of the Spartan constitution, Lycurgus, in rather favorable terms as promoting the education of the youth. By way of side comment, Plutarch adds, "though this love was so approved among them that also the noble and good women loved the virgins; there was no jealous love in it." [26] There is no mention that such love might be perverse or abominable. Nevertheless, we should not assume that Plutarch's admiration of ancient Spartan customs meant that he would have accepted love relations between women, or female sexual autonomy, in his own day. [27]

The references to female homoeroticism in Greek authors of the second century C.E. and beyond represent a continuation of the motifs outlined thus far. The novelist Iamblichus (after 100 to ?) characterizes the love of Berenice, the daughter of the king of Egypt, for Mesopotamia, with whom she slept, as "wild and lawless amours." [28] In his *Dialogues of the Courtesans,* the second-century author Lucian devotes the fifth dialogue to an experience that Leaena has had with her fellow courtesans Megilla and Demonassa. Megilla, a wealthy woman from Lesbos, has succeeded in seducing Leaena, in spite of Leaena's shame at the strange activity. It turns out that Megilla sees her true self as Megillus and Demonassa as her wife. She wears a wig to conceal her short hair and says that although she does not have a male organ, she does have some sort of substitute. Leaena refuses to describe the exact nature of the sexual encounter, since it is too "shameful." [29] Also cast in the dialogue form is the *Amores* by Pseudo-Lucian (probably early 4th cent.) in which one of the discussants speaks of "tribadic licentiousness," and describes female homoeroticism as women behaving like men. [30]

In his treatise on dream interpretation, the second-century author Artemidorus mentions dreams in which one woman sexually possesses another. [31] The second-century treatises *On Chronic Diseases* and *On Acute Diseases* by Soranus are only available to us in the Latin translation by the African medical writer Caelius Aurelianus (5th cent.). Here we read of the disease of the *tribades,* so called because of their interest in both kinds of love, although they prefer women, whom they pursue with a jealousy that is almost masculine. [32]

A number of ancient astrologers mention sexual relations between women, which they see as a disorder caused by the stars and the planets. Ptolemy (2d cent.) writes of *tribades* who are "lustful of sexual intercourse contrary to nature," who "perform the deeds of men," and who sometimes even designate their partners as "lawful wives." Elsewhere he speaks of *tribades* as "castrated (men)." [33] Vettius Valens (mid 2d cent.) speaks of *tribades* who are "licentious, servile, perpetrators of filth." [34] Manetho (probably 4th cent.) refers to *tribades* as ones who "perform deeds after the manner of men." [35]

In sum, most of the writers discussed do not seem to find a place for female homoeroticism within the realm of the lawful and natural, although the Aristophanes of Plato's *Symposium* and Plutarch in describing the Sparta of Lycurgus do represent another view. Among the other authors there is a strong tendency to depict *tribades* as like men, or trying to be like men (Seneca the Elder, Martial, Phaedrus, Lucian, Pseudo-Lucian, Caelius Aurelianus in his translation of Soranus, Ptolemy, Manetho, Firmicus Maternus, and possibly Artemidorus). The real issue may be that of women overstepping the bounds of the female, passive role assigned to them in Greco-Roman culture. The underlying issue would then be female sexual autonomy. If this is indeed the real issue, it would explain why Martial, for example, associates assertive sexual behavior toward males with the *tribas* Philaenis.[36] Lucian and Ptolemy speak of the women calling their partners wives.[37] The authors in question describe female homoeroticism as against the laws of Aphrodite and not beautiful (Asclepiades), monstrous (Ovid, Martial), unnatural (Plato, Ovid, Ptolemy, by implication Seneca the Elder), shameful (Lucian), and lawless (Iamblichus). According to Caelius Aurelianus's translation of Soranus, homoeroticism was a disease of the mind, to be treated by controlling the mind; in Phaedrus's view it was the result of a divine error; and in the astrologers' view, it was caused by the stars and the planets.

Other Sources

Two Greek vase paintings that document erotic attraction between women should be mentioned here, even though they are from an earlier period. A plate dating to circa 620 B.C.E. from the Greek island Thera depicts two women, of approximately equal height, in a typical courting position; that is, one is placing her hand below the chin of the other.[38] An Attic red-figure vase (ca. 500 B.C.E.) shows one woman caressing the clitoris of another.[39] We cannot exclude the possibility that the second vase was used for male titillation; the vase was a *kylix,* a drinking vessel for wine. But this could hardly be the case with the first, since both women are fully clothed; in the second they are nude. Neither vase depicts the women as in any way masculine or pseudomasculine, and they differ from the Greek vases showing male couples, nearly all of which consist of a bearded adult and a beardless youth.[40]

Also relevant is the image of the poet Sappho in the Roman period. The earliest Sappho biography (P.Oxy. 1800, fr. 1, 2d to 3d cent.) notes, "She has been accused by some of immorality and of being a lover of women." Horace, in commenting on her verse technique, calls her "masculine Sappho," but this may not be a reference to her sexuality.[41] Both Plutarch[42] and Maximus of Tyre[43] compared her with Socrates, who was known for his preference for men. Ovid writes that she loved girls and takes up the legend that she fell in love with a man, Phaon, who did not love her in return, a story that is possibly a reaction to the image of Sappho as one who loved women.[44] On the Christian side, the second-century writer Tatian describes Sappho as a *hetaira* and as a "love-crazy harlot of a woman, who sang her own licentiousness." [45] The context is a list of disparaging remarks concerning fourteen Greek women writers, the works of nearly all of whom are lost to us. According to the *Suda,* a medieval lexicon that contains many earlier traditions, Sappho was accused by some of "shameful love" for women.[46] Thus, beginning in the Roman period there is an increasing preoccupation with Sappho's love for women, usually combined with disapproval of that love. This fits in well with the broader development noted thus far for the Roman period: an increased attention to and vehement rejection of sexual relations between women.

Paul's Condemnation of Female Homoeroticism

In Romans 1:18–32, Paul describes a series of tragic *exchanges.*[47] Human beings, though they had the opportunity to recognize God through God's created works, exchanged the truth about God for a lie and worshiped images resembling those same created works. As a result of this fundamental disorder and confusion in human be-

71

ings' relation to God and to God's creation, other exchanges occurred: God handed them over to impurity, to the dishonoring of their bodies (verse 24); God handed them over to dishonorable passions (verse 26); God handed them over to an unapproved intellect and unfitting conduct (verse 28). The disorder and confusion that are idolatry are repeated in the disorder and confusion of same-sex love (verses 26–27)[48] and of other forms of unfitting behavior (verses 29–32).

We have seen that the motif of the *tribas* becoming, being, or trying to be like a man recurs throughout the discussion of *tribades* in the literature of the Greco-Roman world. *Tribades* are women who cross the boundary of their femaleness as it is culturally defined. They are an anomaly, for they fit neither the proper category of female nor that of male. The structure and terminology of Romans 1:18–32 and of 1 Corinthians 11:2–16 show that Paul was deeply concerned that what he saw to be the order of creation be maintained with respect to sex roles and gender polarity. Like other ancient authors who discuss *tribades,* Paul saw female homoeroticism as an improper crossing of boundaries, a blurring of the categories of male and female.

Impurity in Romans 1:24

The insights of anthropology can help us understand the complex concept of impurity. Mary Douglas argues that one must study purity laws in a systematic way.[49] With respect to ancient Israel, she writes:

> The purity laws of the Bible . . . set up the great inclusive categories in which the whole universe is hierarchised and structured. Access to their meaning comes by mapping the same basic set of rules from one context on to another.[50]

There is a symmetry among the classifications for animals, peoples, sacrificial victims, priests, and women. According to Douglas,

> the underlying principle of cleanness in animals [in Leviticus 11 and Deuteronomy 14] is that they shall conform fully to their class. Those species are unclean which are imperfect members of their class, or whose class itself confounds the general scheme of the world.[51]

These considerations are of help in interpreting the concept of impurity in Romans 1:24.

The exchange of natural relations for those contrary to nature in verses 26–27 is a concretization of the "impurity, to the dishonoring of their bodies," described in verse 24.[52] Thus, same-sex love constitutes impurity and a dishonoring of one's body. The categories of classification, namely, "male" and "female," are now no longer clear. Sexual intercourse with a member of the opposite sex implies clarity of sex roles; with a member of one's own, confusion. The biological male could become like a female, as culturally defined, and the biological female—could she become like a male? A class is created that "confounds the general scheme of the world." This crossing of gender-role boundaries is one clear point of contingency between female and male same-sex love. Paul's contemporary, the Jewish philosopher Philo of Alexandria, writes of male homosexuality:

> In former days the very mention of it was a great disgrace, but now it is a matter of boasting not only to the active but to the passive partners, who habituate themselves to endure the disease of effemination, let both body and soul run to waste, and leave no ember of their male sex-nature to smoulder. Mark how conspicuously they braid and adorn the hair of their heads, and how they scrub and paint their faces with cosmetics and pigments and the like, and smother themselves with fragrant unguents. For of all such embellishments, used by all who deck themselves out to wear a comely appearance, fragrance is the most seductive. In fact the transformation of the male nature to the female is practised by them as an art and does not raise a blush. These persons are rightly judged worthy of death by those who obey the law, which ordains that the man-woman who debases the sterling coin of nature should perish unavenged, suffered not to live for a day or even an hour, as a disgrace to himself, his house, his native land, and the whole human race. And the lover of such may be assured that he is subject to the same penalty. He pursues an unnatural pleasure and does his best to render cities desolate and uninhabited by destroying the means of procreation. Furthermore he sees no harm in becoming a tutor and instructor in the grievous vices of unmanliness and effeminacy. . . .[53]

Philo's presupposition that sexual intercourse implies an active and a passive partner (normally a man and a woman), his view that passive male homosexuals become like women, in fact are afflicted with the disease of effeminacy, and his abhorrence of

73

cross-dressing are not untypical of ancient condemnations of male homosexuality.[54] Both Paul and Philo disapprove of male homosexuality; both use the term *para physin,* "unnatural" or "contrary to nature";[55] both reject men wearing hair styles also worn by women (see 1 Cor. 11:2–16); and both imagine physical recompense for male homosexual behavior. Further, as Diaspora Jews, both lived with the conflict between the open male homosexuality around them and the Levitical prohibition thereof.

Underlying Philo's words is disgust, and even horror, at the ambiguous, anomalous being created by male homosexuality. This fits in well with the understanding of the impure as that which does not conform fully to its class.

For Paul, the opposite of impurity is righteousness (Rom. 6:19) or holiness (1 Thess. 4:7; 1 Cor. 7:14). According to Mary Douglas, "Holiness requires that individuals shall conform to the class to which they belong. And holiness requires that different classes of things shall not be confused." [56] In 1 Thessalonians 4:3–8 it is holiness that separates Christians from "the gentiles who do not know God." Holiness implies abstention from forbidden sexual intercourse, that each man should "take a wife [literally, "vessel"] for himself in holiness and honor" (RSV, 1 Thess. 4:4;).[57] Here holiness defines Christians as separate from the outside world, and is manifest by maintaining the proper boundaries within the realm of sexuality.

In Romans 1:24–27, dishonor and shame are closely related to impurity. Bruce Malina, in applying anthropological categories to New Testament studies, writes:

> From a symbolic point of view, honor stands for a person's rightful place in society, his social standing. This honor place is marked off by boundaries consisting of power, sexual status, and position on the social ladder. From a structuralist functionalist point of view, honor is the value of a person in his or her own eyes plus the value of that person in the eyes of his or her social group.[58]

The "dishonoring their bodies among themselves" (verse 24) and the "dishonorable passions" (verse 26) would then mean that those engaged in same-sex love no longer occupy their rightful place in society. Malina contends that honor is not the same for women and men.[59] In the passage at hand, the men have relinquished the honor due their sex. "Their women"—note the subordinating, relativizing word *their*—have not maintained the shame due their sex,[60] and have departed from their proper sexual role. Thus, having crossed the boundaries delineating their respective social positions, their positions in the order of creation, they live in impurity and dishonor. In contrast, a Christian man who respects these boundaries will take for himself a wife in "holiness and honor" (1 Thess. 4:4–8).

It is not an accident that same-sex love is underscored in Romans 1:24–27 as a repetition of the pattern of exchange found in idolatry. Idolaters, that is, followers of all the Greco-Roman religions except Judaism, exist totally outside the realm of holiness. It is therefore clear that a complete confusion of categories, or impurity, should exist among them. The confusion of maleness and femaleness stands for fundamental "symbolic confusion." [61] That Paul saw sexual purity to be more basic than, for example, the cleanness and uncleanness of foods is evident in his statement that the terms *clean* and *unclean* do not apply to foods (Rom. 14:20–21; cf. 1 Cor. 8, 10; Gal. 2:11–14) while he continued to apply the classification system of impurity and holiness to sexuality (cf. 1 Cor. 5:1–13, 7:14; 1 Thess. 4:3–8).

Romans 1:26 and 1 Corinthians 11:2–16

In 1 Corinthians 11:2–16 Paul is addressing himself to a concrete conflict in a community founded by himself, one that he knows well, whereas Romans 1:26–27 is meant for a community not founded by him and is in the context of a discourse on universal human sinfulness. In spite of the differing contexts, 1 Corinthians 11:2–16 helps us to see why Paul describes same-sex love as "impurity" and as the "dishonoring of their bodies among themselves." He sees a blurring of the distinction between the sexes as contrary to nature and against the hierarchy: God, Christ, man, woman. 1 Corinthians 11:2–16 (RSV) reads:[62]

> **2** I commend you because you remember me in everything and maintain the traditions even as I have delivered them to you. **3** But I want you to understand that the head of every man is Christ, the head of a woman is her husband, and the head of Christ is God. **4** Any man who prays or prophesies with his head covered dishonors his head, **5** but any woman who prays or prophesies with her head unveiled dishonors her head—it is the same as if her head were

shaven. **6** For if a woman will not veil herself, then she should cut off her hair; but if it is disgraceful for a woman to be shorn or shaven, let her wear a veil. **7** For a man ought not to cover his head, since he is the image and glory of God; but woman is the glory of man. **8** (For man was not made from woman, but woman from man. **9** Neither was man created for woman, but woman for man.) **10** That is why a woman ought to have a veil on her head, because of the angels. **11** (Nevertheless, in the Lord woman is not independent of man nor man of woman; **12** for as woman was made from man, so man is now born of woman. And all things are from God.) **13** Judge for yourselves; is it proper for a woman to pray to God with her head uncovered? **14** Does not nature itself teach you that for a man to wear long hair is degrading to him, **15** but if a woman has long hair, it is her pride? For her hair is given to her for a covering. **16** If any one is disposed to be contentious, we recognize no other practice, nor do the churches of God.

In this passage Paul requires strict gender differentiation with respect to hair style and headdress. Women and men should not look the same. For Paul, this is a theological issue. The reasons for gender polarization in dress are that the man is the head of the woman, just as the head of the man is Christ and the head of Christ is God; that woman is the glory of man, while the man is the image and glory of God; and that woman was created from man and for him. There is a difference between woman and man, a difference that implies woman is to be oriented to her head, to man, in whom she has her origin. (Paul's concessive remarks in verses 11 and 12 do not alter this basic structure.) The boundaries between femaleness and maleness are not to be blurred by women cutting their hair short or men wearing it long. Nor is long hair on women sufficient to mark the difference; women require a veil as a visible sign of their place in the order of creation.

As in Romans 1:26–27, Paul appeals to nature: Nature teaches that for a man to wear long hair is a "dishonor" (*atimia* [RSV] "degrading") to him (while for a woman it is "shameful," *aischron,* to wear short hair, and an unveiled woman "dishonors," *kataischynei,* her head). Thus, nature is the basis for strict gender differentiation in dress. For a man to defy nature means a loss of honor; that is, he no longer occupies his rightful place in society.

This discussion of headdress and hair style is quite reminiscent of the ancient discussions of same-sex love. For the man, the fear is that by looking like a woman a man loses his masculinity and can sink to the level of a woman. Short hair on a woman is one of the signs of her becoming like, or trying to become like, a man. One thinks of the Megilla/Megillus of Lucian,[63] who pulls off her wig to reveal short hair and announces herself to be Demonassa's husband. A woman cannot sink to the level of a man. She can only make ridiculous, yet nevertheless threatening, attempts to rise to that level.

Several exegetes have recognized that same-sex love could be an issue in 1 Corinthians 11:2–16. Early church discussions on same-sex love often included reference to the passage.[64] In the nineteenth century, Johannes Weiss wrote that the woman who shaved her head was trying to look like a man for lascivious reasons, that the "lesbian vice" of perverse women was at stake here.[65] The most recent scholar to see such a connection is Jerome Murphy-O'Connor, who detects in the Corinthian behavior a response to Galatians 3:28:

> If there was no longer any male or female, the Corinthians felt free to blur the distinction between the sexes. . . . The consistent infantilism of the Corinthians rubbed him on the raw, and the hair-dos raised the disquieting question of homosexuality within the community.[66]

Paul and Female Nonsubordination

Paul is not simply opposed to nonsubordination of the female. By recommending celibacy to women (1 Cor. 7:8–9, 25–35, 39–40) he actually promotes women as anomalies, as not directly subordinate to a husband. Further, by quoting the baptismal formula, "There is neither Jew nor Greek, there is neither slave nor free, there is neither male nor female; for you are all one in Christ Jesus" (RSV, Gal. 3:28), he is opening the way for a blurring of gender roles that could alter social structures. That the slogan was powerful is evident, for he quotes a different version of the formula, one without the "male and female" portion, in 1 Corinthians 12:13, probably because he recognizes that the Corinthians had indeed understood the implications of the phrase "not male and female." Paul acknowledges the work of women in the gospel (Rom. 16:1–16; Phil. 4:2–3), as well as women's right to prophesy in the liturgical assembly (1 Cor. 11:5). If the admonition to women to be silent in the churches and subordinate is by Paul (1 Cor. 14:33b–36) and not a later interpolator, it would be a further example of the already documented tension in his thinking. Thus, any ambiguity about gender roles in the Christian community resulted at least partly from Paul himself. But when pressed, as in the case of gender differentiation in appearance in Corinth, he calls for strict differentiation and bases it on a hierarchical ordering of the sexes, at the same time omitting the "not male and female" phrase that apparently endangered established gender roles. Perhaps it was precisely Paul's promotion of celibacy, itself a potential threat to patriarchal marriage, that caused him to be so adamant about gender polarization, implying female subordination, in dress and in sexual intercourse. Against the belief of the end being near and Christ being the head of both man and woman, Paul could allow a woman to devote herself solely to Christ, thereby circumventing a male head in the form of a spouse. What he could not accept was women experiencing their power through the erotic in a way that challenged the hierarchical ladder: God, Christ, man, woman.[67]

Conclusions and Implications

This brief survey of sources has demonstrated that little tolerance for sexual love relationships between women can be found among male Greco-Roman writers. This is different from the recorded attitudes toward male homosexuality, which are quite mixed. The sources reviewed should teach us that it is methodologically questionable to subsume love relations between women under male homosexuality, as the following examples show. John Boswell, from whom I have learned much in spite of our differing interpretations, summarizes his findings on Roman society:

> . . . intolerance on this issue was rare to the point of insignificance in its great urban centers. Gay people were in a strict sense a minority, but neither they nor their contemporaries regarded their inclinations as harmful, bizarre, immoral or threatening, and they were fully integrated into Roman life at every level.[68]

Robin Scroggs, upon completion of a survey of ancient sources on male homosexuality, writes:

Thus what the New Testament was against was the image of homosexuality as pederasty and primarily here its more sordid and dehumanizing dimensions [such as lack of mutuality]. One would regret it if somebody in the New Testament had not opposed such dehumanization.[69]

Scroggs specifically notes that he is speaking here only of male homosexuality. His discussion of women occurs in a four-and-one-half-page appendix entitled "Female Homosexuality in the Greco-Roman World." [70]

Boswell and Scroggs, drawing upon the same sources, come to radically different conclusions. Boswell claims that his thesis applies to women; Scroggs does not. What is clear is that the conclusions of neither apply to women. The Roman authors surveyed *did* regard sexual relations between women as harmful, bizarre, immoral, and threatening. And one would be hard pressed to say that the authors discussed disapproved of women giving sexual expression to their affection for one another because it was dehumanizing by being, for example, nonmutual. On the contrary, hierarchy seemed normal to the authors discussed; what was abnormal was women not submitting to it. There is no good reason for Scroggs not to have asked why the sources on women do not support his thesis on men.

It should be noted that what I have been discussing is not lesbian history, that is, the history of women who found their primary identification in other women and who may or may not have expressed that sexually.[71] Rather, I have been treating sources that attest to male attitudes toward, and male fantasies about, lesbians, and the men writing are heavily genitally oriented. These male attitudes are important for women's history insofar as they shaped the culture in which women lived. The extent of that determination remains to be established. The conclusions for women's history can only be tentative and general. The increasing preoccupation with sexual relations between women in the Roman period could indicate that lesbians were living more openly and were perceived as a greater threat. Two ways of dealing with the lesbian threat are utter silence and vehement rejection, whereby a sudden shift in method is not unusual. The sources surveyed seem to represent such a shift from silence to open rejection, although marginalization and containment through the technique of silence continued throughout the period discussed.

One must be clear about the significance of these sources for Paul, and not assume that Paul personally knew or read any of the sources discussed. Indeed, some were written after the Letter to the Romans. The sources are relevant because their broad variety documents attitudes that were most likely known to him and his readers. In light of widespread disapproval of female homoeroticism, Paul's condemnation is not surprising, nor is his use of the expression *para physin,* "unnatural" or "contrary to nature." The motif of a woman becoming or trying to become like a man was most probably known to him, as well as men's association of female homoerotic activity with sexual aggressiveness and licentiousness, which may be a way of describing—in caricature—female sexual autonomy. Further, it may not be an accident that Paul takes up this question in his Letter to the Romans. In the decades surrounding that letter, several authors who had been trained or lived in Rome (Seneca the Elder, Ovid, Martial, Phaedrus) expressed themselves on the matter, as did Juvenal (Rome) and Soranus (Rome and Alexandria, according to the fifth-century translation) in the early second century. This geographical clustering results partly from the high level of literary productivity in Rome in this period, but may also indicate a special concern with this issue in the city of Rome.

According to the sources, Paul and his culture understood maleness and femaleness hierarchically. The structures of Paul's culture were based on a hierarchical definition of maleness and femaleness, a definition that found an acute expression in the rejection of physically intimate love relations between women and in the accompanying requirement of gender polarity in physical appearance. It is this definition that is behind Paul's condemnation of female homoeroticism. Therefore this issue cannot be dismissed as a marginal question affecting only a small number of women. Anyone concerned about the human costs of a definition of women and men based on enforced polarity and hierarchy must take on the issue of the Christian rejection of lesbian existence, as well as that of male homosexuality, for which Paul is a primary source.

The churches and theology have the task of thinking through the implications of the fact that Romans 1:26 cannot be extricated from its immediate context or from Pauline thinking about women and men. In Paul's eyes a woman who physically expressed love for another woman was repeating the pattern of idolatry, that is, of estrangement from God. It is inconsistent to call for equality between the sexes and yet to require that women either orient themselves toward men or remain celibate. Consistency would also require that if one declares Romans 1:26 (and 27) not to be normative for theology, one cannot adopt the rest of Pauline theology and theological anthropology. Therefore, a careful analysis and fundamental rethinking of Paul's theology is required. Since Paul's thought has deeply affected Western society, this is a task for everyone, not just for Christians.

Notes

1. Lines 175–227. P. W. Van der Horst, trans., *The Sentences of Pseudo-Phocylides,* Studia in Veteris Testamenti Pseudepigrapha 4 (Leiden: Brill, 1978), pp. 225–257. Van der Horst dates the work to between ca. 30 B.C.E. and 40 C.E., and suggests Alexandria as the place of origin (Van der Horst, *Sentences,* pp. 81–83).

2. Were line 192 not in its present context, it could also refer to a woman imitating a man sexually in another way, such as by taking the sexually active role in heterosexual intercourse. Disapproval of lesbians and disapproval of nonpassive heterosexual women are not unrelated to each other, as will be seen below.

   Another Greek-language Jewish source deserving mention is Psalms of Solomon 2:14–15, which speaks of the daughters of Jerusalem having defiled themselves with a "confusion of mingling." This could refer to incest or to intercourse with animals or with other women.

3. A. H. Weiss, ed., *Sifra* (Vienna: Schlossberg, 1862), on Lev. 18:3 (Aharei Mot, Parasha 9). Translation my own.

4. *Y. Gittin* 49c. 70–71.

5. Babylonian Talmud: *Shabbat* 65a–b; *Yebamot* 76a (see the medieval commentator Rashi on both passages); Maimonides, *Mishneh Torah,* '*Issurei Bi'ah* (Forbidden Intercourse) 21:8; '*Even Ha'Ezer* 20.2.

6. The fragment of Parmenides quoted in Caelius Aurelianus, *Chronic Diseases* 9.134–135 (5th cent. C.E.), does seem to refer to both women and men, and could thus be considered a yet earlier mention. See the edition and translation by I. E. Drabkin (Chicago: University of Chicago Press, 1950), pp. 902–903.

7. 191E.

8. 636B–C.

9. John Boswell points out the possible ambiguity of the phrase *para physin*, but does not address himself to the expressions "daring or shameless act" or "lack of self-control." See his *Christianity, Social Tolerance, and Homosexuality: Gay People in Western Europe from the Beginning of the Christian Era to the Fourteenth Century* (Chicago: University of Chicago Press, 1980), pp. 13–14, n. 22.

10. Hugo Stadtmueller, ed., *Anthologia Graeca* 5.206 (Leipzig: Teubner, 1894), vol. 1, pp. 168–169; see schol.[B].

11. *Controversiae* 1.2.23.

12. *Metamorphoses* 9.666–797.

13. *Metamorphoses* 9.726–763.

14. The story of Caenis/Caeneus, a woman with no interest in sexual intercourse with men who was changed into a man, should also be mentioned here. Ovid is one of the main sources for the tale: *Metamorphoses* 12.171–535.

15. Phaedrus, *Liber Fabularum* 4.16. Phaedrus probably composed the fables of book 4 when he was an old man. See Peter L. Schmidt, *Der Kleine Pauly*, s.v. "Phaedrus." Note that actual physical organs are involved. Does the author consider them necessary for the female to play the active role in sexual intercourse?

16. *Epigrammata* 7.67, 70. A woman named Philaenis was known in the Greek-speaking world as the author of a book on sexual positions, although some considered the attribution of the work to her to be malicious. See Pauly-Wissowa, *Real-Encyclopädie der classischen Altertumswissenschaft* 19, 2 (1938), p. 2122. Martial may have had this association in mind.

17. Cf. Juvenal, *Saturae* 6.423.

18. Martial, *Epigrammata* 1.90.

19. The verb *futuo* used in line 2 of 7.70, which I have translated as "copulate," is from the same root. Both refer to men's copulating with women.

20. Unpublished paper presented at the Fifth Berkshire Conference on the History of Women, Vassar College, New York, June 1981.

21. Peter Howell also sees Martial as envisaging physical penetration in 1.90 (Bassa) and 7.67 (Philaenis). He notes that some women are said to have a clitoris large enough to "be able to copulate, or even sodomise," but sees it as more likely that the use of an artificial phallus is meant. See Howell, *A Commentary on Book One of the Epigrams of Martial* (London: Athlone Press, 1980), p. 298. Phaedrus's depiction of *tribades* possessing actual male organs would also support Hal-

lett's interpretation, especially since Martial knew and used the work of Phaedrus. See Schmidt, *Der Kleine Pauly,* s.v. "Phaedrus."

22. See Seneca, *Controversiae* 1.2.23.

23. Hallett, "Autonomy," p. 15.

24. Juvenal, *Saturae* 6.306–313. E. Courtney gives references to metaphors for horse riding applied to sexual activity (*A Commentary on the Satires of Juvenal* [London: Athlone Press, 1980], p. 298). Ludwig Friedländer describes the issue here as "tribadic fornication" (*D. Iunii Iuvenalis Saturarum Libri V. Mit erklärenden Anmerkungen,* 2 vols. [Leipzig: S. Hirzel, 1895], vol. 1, p. 319).

25. Juvenal, *Saturae* 2.43–48. Laronia does not necessarily represent Juvenal's view, and it seems nearly certain that he is referring to sexual activity among the women mentioned at 6.306–313.

26. Plutarch, *Vitae, Lycurgus* 18.9.

27. For Plutarch's views on female marital duties, see especially his treatise *Conjugal Precepts* (*Moralia* 138A–146A). On this work see Kathleen O'Brien Wicker, "First-Century Marriage Ethics: A Comparative Study of the Household Codes and Plutarch's Conjugal Precepts," in James W. Flanagan and Anita Weisbrod Robinson, eds., *No Famine in the Land: Studies in Honor of John L. McKenzie* (Claremont, Calif.: Institute for Antiquity and Christianity, 1975), pp. 141–153. It is female subordination, rather than female autonomy, that Plutarch advises in this treatise.

28. This fragment of Iamblichus, *Babyloniaca,* was preserved in the *Bibliotheca* of the tenth-century patriarch Photius. See René Henry, ed. and trans., *Photius: Bibliothèque,* 8 vols. (Paris: "Les Belles Lettres," 1959–77), vol. 2, pp. 44–46. See also the critical edition of the fragments of Iamblichus by Elmar Habrich (Leipzig: Teubner, 1960), pp. 58–65, and the discussion in Boswell, *Christianity, Social Tolerance, and Homosexuality,* p. 84, Boswell's translation of *ekthesmos* as "inordinate" rather than "lawless" or "contre nature" (Henry) is not supported by the evidence; see the references for *ekthesmos* in the standard Greek lexica: Liddell-Scott-Jones, Lampe, and Preisigke.

29. See also Alciphron (2d cent.), *Letters of Courtesans* 14, which contains an account of an all-female party with erotic overtones.

30. *Amores* 28.

31. *Oneirocritica* 1.80.

32. *Tardarum passionum* 4.9.132–133.

33. *Tetrabiblos* 3.14; 4.5.

34. *Anthologiarum Libri* 2.36.

35. *Apotelesmatica* 4.24. See also the fourth-century Latin writer Firmicus Maternus, who, in his systematic work on astrology, repeats the motif of women becoming like men (*Matheseos Libri VIII* 7.25.1).

36. See also Caelius Aurelianus, *Tardarum passionum* 4.9.132 ("women who are called *tribades* because they perform both kinds of love").

37. A third second-century author who speaks of women is the Christian Clement of Alexandria: "Men passively play the role of women, and women behave like men in that women, contrary to nature, are given in marriage and marry" (*Paedagogus* 3.3.21).

38. K(enneth) J. Dover, *Greek Homosexuality* (Cambridge, Mass.: Harvard University Press, 1978), CE34, discussion on p. 173; G. M. A. Richter, *Korai: Archaic Greek Maidens* (London: Phaidon, 1968), pl. VIII-C.

39. Dover, *Greek Homosexuality*, R207, discussion on p. 173; John Boardman, Eugenio La Rocca, and Antonia Mulas, *Eros in Griechenland* (Munich: List, 1976), pp. 111–112; J. D. Beazley, *Paralipomena: Additions to* Attic Black-Figure Vase-Painters *and* Attic Red-Figure Vase-Painters *2d ed.* (Oxford: Clarendon, 1971), p. 333.

40. Whether the use of dildos is relevant here is not certain. See Dover, *Greek Homosexuality*, pp. 102–103, 132–133; Sarah B. Pomeroy, *Goddesses, Whores, Wives, and Slaves: Women in Classical Antiquity* (New York: Schocken, 1975), pl. 12; Robin Scroggs, *The New Testament and Homosexuality: Contextual Background for Contemporary Debate* (Philadelphia: Fortress, 1983), pp. 141, 143.

41. *Epistulae* 1.19.28. See also Horace's reference to Folia of Ariminum, to whom he attributes "masculine libido," in *Epodon* 5.41–46.

42. *Moralia* 406A.

43. 18.7.

44. *Tristia* 2.365–366; *Heroides* [XV]; cf. also Ovid, *Metamorphoses* 9.666–797.

45. *Oratio ad Graecos* 33.

46. Ada Adler, ed., *Suidae Lexicon,* 1 vol. in 5 parts (Leipzig: Teubner, 1928–38; repr. Stuttgart: Teubner, 1967–71), vol. 1.4, pp. 322–323.

47. On Romans 1:18–32 as a whole, see the commentaries on Romans by C. E. B. Cranfield, Ulrich Wilckens, Heinrich Schlier, Ernst Käsemann, Otto Michel, C. K. Barrett, Hans Lietzmann, M. J. Lagrange, and William Sanday and Arthur Headlam, which contain references to further literature. For a survey of views on the structure of the pericope, which is an especially disputed point, see Wiard Popkes, "Zum Aufbau und Charakter von Römer 1.18–32," *New Testament Studies* 28 (1982): 490–501. On Romans 1:26–27 see also Boswell, *Christian-*

ity, Social Tolerance, and Homosexuality, pp. 107–117; Peter Coleman, *Christian Attitudes to Homosexuality* (London: SPCK, 1980), pp. 88–93; Else Kähler, "Exegese zweier neutestamentlicher Stellen (*Römer 1, 18–32; 1. Korinther 6,9–11*)," in Theodor Bovet, ed., *Probleme der Homophilie in medizinischer, theologischer und juristischer Sicht* (Bern: Paul Haupt; Tübingen: Katzmann, 1965), pp. 12–43.

48. My primary reason for interpreting verse 26 as referring to same-sex love, and not to another form of sexual behavior that Paul would call unnatural, is the word *likewise* of verse 27, which clearly refers to male homosexuality. If it were to refer to women taking the active role in heterosexual intercourse, the interpretation that follows would still hold. There does not seem to me to be sufficient basis for taking it to refer to anal or oral intercourse.

49. See esp. *Implicit Meanings: Essays in Anthropology* (London: Routledge and Kegan Paul, 1975); *Natural Symbols: Explorations in Cosmology* (New York: Random House, 1970); *Purity and Danger: An analysis of concepts of pollution and taboo* (London: Routledge and Kegan Paul, 1966). See also Sheldon R. Isenberg and Dennis E. Owen, "Bodies, Natural and Contrived: The Work of Mary Douglas," *Religious Studies Review* 3 (1977): 1–17; Jacob Neusner, *The Idea of Purity in Ancient Judaism: The Haskell Lectures, 1972–1973*. With a Critique and a Commentary by Mary Douglas, Studies in Judaism in Late Antiquity 1 (Leiden: Brill, 1973).

50. In Neusner, *The Idea of Purity*, p. 139.

51. *Purity and Danger*, p. 55.

52. For this interpretation see Ulrich Wilckens, *Der Brief an die Römer*, EKK 6,1–3 (Zurich: Benziger; Neukirchen-Vluyn: Neukirchener, 1978–82), vol. 1, p. 109, and others.

53. *De specialibus legibus* 3.37–39, trans. F. H. Colson, *Philo*, Loeb Classical Library (Cambridge, Mass.: Harvard, 1937), vol. 7, pp. 499, 501; cf. Wilckens, *Der Brief*, vol. 1, p. 325; *De Abrahamo* 133–139; *De vita contemplativa* 59–63.

54. For sources on male homosexuality in antiquity, see esp. Robin Scroggs, *The New Testament and Homosexuality;* Boswell, *Christianity, Social Tolerance, and Homosexuality*, pp. 61–87; Dover, *Greek Homosexuality*. On male cross-dressing, see esp. H. Herter, "Effeminatus," *Reallexikon für Antike und Christentum* 4 (1959): 620–650.

55. See Helmut Koester, "*Physis*," in Gerhard Kittel and Gerhard Friedrich, eds., *Theological Dictionary of the New Testament*, vol. 9 (1974), pp. 251–277, esp. pp. 262, 264–265, 267–269, 271–275.

56. *Purity and Danger*, p. 53.

57. See Wayne A. Meeks, *The First Urban Christians: The Social World of the Apostle Paul* (New Haven: Yale University Press, 1983), pp. 100–101, 228.

58. *The New Testament World: Insights from Cultural Anthropology* (Atlanta: John Knox, 1981), p. 47.

59. Ibid., pp. 42–48.

60. In commenting on Romans 1:26, John Chrysostom writes that it is "more disgraceful that the women should seek this type of intercourse, since they ought to have a greater sense of shame than men" (*PG* 60.417).

61. Ruth Tiffany Barnhouse's book bears the apt title *Homosexuality: A Symbolic Confusion* (New York: Seabury, 1979).

62. It is not possible to discuss here the complex exegetical issues of 1 Corinthians 11:2–16 (such as the meaning of *kephalē* or the reasons for believing that the passage has something to do with veiling). For a different interpretation, see Elisabeth Schüssler Fiorenza, *In Memory of Her: A Feminist Theological Reconstruction of Christian Origins* (New York: Crossroads, 1983), pp. 46, 226–230, 239–240; see also the literature cited there.

63. Note that Lucian is a second-century author and therefore later than Paul. See also Lucian, *Fugitivi* 27.

64. For several of these references, see Bernadette J. Brooten, "Patristic Interpretations of Romans 1:26," in Elizabeth A. Livingstone, ed., *Proceedings of the Ninth International Conference on Patristic Studies* (forthcoming).

65. *Der erste Korintherbrief*, 9th ed. (1910; repr. Göttingen: Vandenhoeck and Ruprecht, 1977), p. 272.

66. "Sex and Logic in 1 Corinthians 11:2–16," *Catholic Biblical Quarterly* 42 (1980): 490. See also Richard Kroeger and Catherine Clark Kroeger, "St. Paul's Treatment of Misogyny, Gynephobia, and Sex Segregation in First Corinthians 11:2–6 [*sic*]," in Paul J. Achtemeier, ed., *Society of Biblical Literature 1979 Seminar Papers*, vol. 2 (Missoula: Scholars Press, 1979), pp. 213–221; John P. Meier, "On the Veiling of Hermeneutics (1 Cor. 11:2–16)," *Catholic Biblical Quarterly* 40 (1978): 219, n. 15; Robin Scroggs, "Paul and the Eschatological Woman," *Journal of the American Academy of Religion* 40 (1972): 297; C. K. Barrett, *The First Epistle to the Corinthians*, Black's New Testament Commentary (London: Black, 1968), p. 257.

67. See Audre Lorde, *Uses of the Erotic: The Erotic as Power* (New York: Out and Out Books, 1978).

68. *Christianity, Social Tolerance, and Homosexuality*, p. 87. It is

important to underscore the great value of Boswell's book; he includes sources that do not support his thesis, which is one of the marks of good scholarship.

69. *The New Testament and Homosexuality*, p. 126.

70. Ibid., pp. 140–144.

71. On the definition of the term *lesbian,* see Adrienne Rich, "Compulsory Heterosexuality and Lesbian Existence," *Signs* 5 (1980): 631–660; see also the responses by Martha E. Thompson in *Signs* 6 (1981): 790–794, and by Ann Ferguson, Jacquelyn N. Zita, and Kathryn Pyne Addelson in *Signs* 7 (1981): 159–199.

On women's history in antiquity as distinct from male attitudes toward women, see Bernadette J. Brooten, "Early Christian Women and Their Cultural Context: Issues of Method in Historical Reconstruction," in Adela Yarbro Collins, ed., *Feminist Perspectives on Biblical Scholarship* (Chico, Calif.: Scholars Press, 1985).

Five

Black Women's Literature and the Task of Feminist Theology

Delores S. Williams

With the birth of the various liberation theologies in the 1960s and 1970s, the imaginative literature of oppressed peoples began to be recognized as an important source for theology. Black liberation theologians used the works of black poets and dramatists to inform their understanding of the black experience.[1] White feminist scholars in religious studies used women's imaginative literature to illuminate the character of women's experience.[2] Recently black feminist scholars entered the fields of theology and ethics. Some of them maintain that the works of black women writers provide valuable resources for constructing the theoretical frameworks needed to assess the theological and ethical significance of black women's social and religious experience.[3]

Like these other interpretations by black and feminist scholars, this essay affirms the value of imaginative literature as a source for theology and for shedding light on the nature of women's experience. In the works of some Afro-American women writers, I have found three models that help to elucidate the nature of black women's experience. I have found these models embodied with particular clarity in three texts. In Margaret Walker's *Jubilee* I will focus on what I have called the communal life-support model in order to interpret the personal and religious transformation of its protagonist, Vyry. Lucy, in Zora Neale Hurston's *Jonah's Gourd Vine,* personifies the tragic victim model. In Alice Walker's *The Color Purple* the central character, Celie, is transformed by her experience of what I shall call the catalyst and moral-agent model. In the second part of the essay, I will explore the implications of these models and the stories in which they are embedded for the larger task of black and feminist theology.

Jubilee: Vyry's Story

In the communal life-support model, the actions and life tasks of the major female characters sustain unity and community within social groups in both black and white society. In Margaret Walker's *Jubilee* the slave woman Vyry nurtures the slave master's family and her own black family.[4] Similarly, Vyry's mother, Sis Hetta, by sleeping with Master Dutton (his wife refuses to do so), enables the Dutton family to remain intact.[5] The consciousness and actions of both women are conditioned by the demands of the slavocracy and the slave community, and their personal needs are inextricably bound to community needs and goals.

These women undergo both positive and negative transformations. Hetta and Vyry experience the negative personal transformation that slavery inflicted upon black women, as Walker's description of the change in Hetta's body—and spirit—makes painfully clear. Hetta had once "looked like some African queen from the Congo. She had a long thin neck and she held her head high." [6] But as the result of bearing children for the slavocracy, she was "no longer . . . slender and lovely."

> Her breasts were long and flabby; her belly always bloated, whether she was big in family way or not, and her legs and thighs were now covered with large broken blood vessels that made it painful when she stood long or walked far. . . . She was a sullen-looking woman . . . who rarely smiled.[7]

Walker's whole plot is, in fact, structured around the central themes of bondage and freedom. Vyry's character unfolds in episodes dramatizing value conflicts between characters caught in various kinds of bondage. At one point, for example, Vyry courageously confronts Master Dutton about her right to marry the free-issue Negro Randall Ware. She asks Dutton, "Does you think it's a sin for me to want to be free?" Informed by traditional ethical principles condoning slavery, Dutton tells her that slavery is right because "here in Georgia it's very hard to manumit a slave, you know what I mean—set you free. I don't have the right to break the law." [8] Dutton tries to convince Vyry that she will survive better as a slave than as a free woman. He tells her:

> Look around you at the poor white people who are free. You don't want to be like them, now do you? . . . Can't feed their pot-bellied

younguns; always dying of dysentery and pellagra. . . . Do you think you would be better off if you were like them? And being black and free! Why, my God, that's just like being a hunted animal running all the time! [9]

But Master Dutton cannot shake his slave daughter's moral conviction that slavery is wrong. Knowing that Vyry does not believe him, "he was withered before her scorn. He had no additional weapon to fight such scorn and he was forced to drop his eyes and hang his head." [10] This moral confrontation between opposing ethical principles shows Vyry's courage in the face of possible danger: Master Dutton can punish her severely for suggesting that slavery is wrong and she ought to be freed.

Vyry's other characteristics—her devotion to her social role and tasks, her endurance and ingenuity, her shrewd survival intelligence and deep spirituality—emerge through value conflicts involving both the slave quarters and the Big House. Her commitment to her role as mother is obvious when she objects to Randall Ware's plan for her escape. Although Ware apparently values Vyry's freedom more than the freedom of their small children, Vyry cannot imagine freedom without her children. When she tries to escape, she is captured because she refuses to leave her children in slavery.

Vyry endures the cruel treatment she receives from the slave master's wife. She realizes that this cruelty stems from a major value conflict between Master Dutton and Big Missy Selena Dutton, a conflict centering on Master Dutton's relationship with Vyry's mother, Hetta. According to Dutton, "it was better for a young man of quality to learn life by breaking in a young nigger wench than it was for him to spoil a pure white virgin girl." [11] He cannot understand why Selena is shocked when she finds out about his relationship with Hetta, for to him "miscegenation was no sin. . . . It was an accepted fact of his world. What he could not understand . . . was . . . how her loving parents had kept the facts of life from her." [12] Nevertheless, Big Missy Selena is jealous of Hetta, even though she does not want to sleep with Dutton herself. She argues with her husband about his black children and out of unhappiness treats Vyry brutally.

Within the communal life-support model of *Jubilee,* women's need for a survival intelligence is emphasized. Vyry's endurance is assured by the shrewd intelligence she develops under the tutelage of Mammy Sukey and Aunt Sally. Plantation politics, for instance, involves learning how to be visible and accessible while simultaneously keeping out of Big Missy's way. The art of physical survival is learned as well: Vyry picks up the correct knowledge of the effects of roots and herbs.[13] Most important, Vyry develops a deep spirituality that psychologically sustains her in the time of trouble.

Spiritual education begins for Vyry when she is very young. And value conflicts are obvious from the beginning. Aunt Sally, Vyry's mentor, explains the menstrual cycle to her in relation to its negative possibilities. But Vyry associates the menstrual cycle with the positive aspects of Christian ritual. Referring to the first menstruation, Aunt Sally tells Vyry:

> It's what makes you a woman. Makes you different from a no-good man ... make you ... have younguns and be a sho-nuff mammy all your own. ... [But] men ain't nothing but trouble, just a breath and britches and trouble ... don't let a no-good man touch you, else he'll big you up sho-nuff.[14]

Thus, for Aunt Sally, the coming of womanhood signals danger for women. Nevertheless, Vyry anxiously awaits her womanhood because, for her, its coming signals something good. She is happy because "womanhood meant [her] baptizing. ... Come spring ... and the creeks ... would rise and all the swollen streams flow down to the river, Brother Zeke would baptize her." [15] For Vyry, the coming of womanhood connects her with an important spiritual event, a spiritual cleansing. And later, when she becomes a mother, her deep spirituality surfaces as she gathered "her children in her arms and prayed because praying was all she knew to do." [16]

Under the conditions of bondage, all aspects of her survival intelligence work together to help Vyry both endure and make the transformations needed for her family to survive the slave system.[17] Although she emerged from her confrontation with Master Dutton feeling hopeless,[18] Vyry experiences many positive transformations after emancipation. Once despondent about the meaninglessness of slave existence, she becomes hopeful. Once passive, she becomes assertive in her relationship with her husband, Innis Brown. She decides when and where they will build their second home. She establishes a relationship with the town's white people, who join forces to help Vyry and Innis build their house.

Vyry is transformed spiritually. During slavery she only prayed for the safety of black children and for black freedom. After emancipation she sees herself and her family connected to all people through their common condition of sinfulness. Therefore, she prays with a concern for all humankind. She acknowledges, "Lord, we ain't nothing but sinful human flesh. . . . We is evil peoples in a wicked world, but I'm asking you to let your forgiving love cover our sin, Lord." [19]

Out of her experience of transformation from slave to free woman, Vyry emerges a resilient person participating in making a new history for black people. Whereas she once depended upon the slavocracy for food, shelter, and clothing, Vyry the free woman relies upon her own resources to help sustain her family economically. She sells eggs and vegetables to the townspeople. She increases her income by becoming the town's midwife. She tries to establish a new, hospitable relationship between Southern white and black people. When the Ku Klux Klan burns her home and destroys her family's possessions, Vyry joins her husband in rebuilding their lives and fortune in another location.

Hence communal life support ultimately yields an image of a transformed black woman who, as Innis Brown observes, "has stood so much outrage." Vyry shows

> a wisdom and a touching humility. . . . It was more than her practical intelligence, or her moral fortitude; more than the fundamental decency and innate dignity . . . she was touched with a spiritual fire and permeated with a spiritual wholeness. . . . Peasant and slave, unlettered and untutored, she was nevertheless the best true example of the motherhood of her race, an ever present assurance that nothing could destroy a people whose sons had come from her loins.[20]

Everything transformative that happens to this black woman occurs within the context of her commitment to support community, group, and family goals and aspirations. More often than not, she is a strong mother who is "crazy about her children" [21] and uses her intelligence, strength, and courage to sustain the black family structure. Black males in the family depend upon, admire, and respect these attributes. But this woman is not devoted exclusively to the personal ambitions of men. Rather, her energies are exerted on behalf of her entire family. Idealized though it may be, the image of the transformed woman presented according to the communal life-support model is a successful, energetic, spiritually whole person.

Jonah's Gourd Vine: **Lucy's Story**

Unlike the woman who is transformed in the communal life-support model, the black woman as tragic victim is isolated, dedicated to the goals and aspirations of one person, a male. While communal life support ultimately enables a woman to become transformed into a whole person, the woman as tragic victim is slowly destroyed by her self-denying love for a man. Where the communal life-support model shows that certain aspects of black community goals and aspirations can enhance the positive transformations of black women, the tragic victim model shows that another side of black community values can contribute to the negative transformation and death of a woman.

Both Margaret Walker in *Jubilee* and Zora Hurston in *Jonah's Gourd Vine* use the language and lore of black folk culture to communicate their message and to comment on the action. But Walker and Hurston use different folk forms to tell the stories of the primary female characters. At the beginning of most chapters, Margaret Walker uses folk poems or the lyrics of spirituals and work songs to comment on the action. Zora Hurston (in *Jonah's Gourd Vine*) uses rituals from black folk religion and characters from black folklore to portray symbolically the relation between the primary female character and other characters. Walker's and Hurston's common use of the folk idiom communicates a central message—that black women's lives are bound to an Afro-American subculture that may work both for and against black women's liberation struggles.[22]

Though Hurston claims *Jonah's Gourd Vine* is about "a Negro preacher who is neither funny nor an imitation Puritan ram-rod in pants," [23] the novel is also about a female victim who is tragic in a classic sense. Lucy, a noble character, does not deserve the outrage she suffers. She is ultimately transformed from a vital, aggressive, and talented person into a defeated wife dying of tuberculosis. Lucy recognizes her tragic mistake. On her deathbed she tells her youngest daughter, Isis, "Don't you love nobody bet-

ter'n you do yo' self. Do, you'll be dying befo' yo' time is out." [24]
Lucy has loved her husband, the Reverend John Pearson, better
than herself, and Pearson has loved womanizing best of all.

To portray her tragic victim, Hurston uses biblical figures, black
folk images, ritual, and the depiction of conflicting religious systems; through these forms we see Lucy's victimization and ultimate
transformation. First, Hurston illustrates problems in Lucy's personal and social situation by portraying a minor female character
who has experienced a positive transformation. Amy, the mother
of Preacher John Pearson, who has undergone a social transformation from slave to free woman, is a perfect foil for Lucy.

Whereas Lucy is delicate and physically weak, Amy is physically
strong, her strength almost equaling that of a man. She works in
the fields along with her husband, Ned. In physical fights with Ned,
Amy is a worthy opponent. Hurston graphically describes one such
fight.

> Ned . . . brought the whip down across Amy's back. . . . She wheeled
> to fight. The raw hide again. This time across her head. She charged
> in with a stick of wood. . . . This had happened many times before.
> Amy's strength was almost as great as Ned's. . . . Forced to the wall
> by her tigress onslaught, Ned saw that victory for him was possible
> only by choking Amy.[25]

Whereas Lucy is economically dependent upon John, Amy earns
her own living. Slavery has equipped Amy with the same skills as
the male field hand Ned. Her consciousness has been conditioned
by a fundamental principle of the slavocracy—that every able black
person must be a worker. Lucy grows up after emancipation in a
relatively comfortable nuclear family where girls are prepared to
become housewives.

As the novel progresses, Hurston reveals that Lucy's relationship with her husband, John, has slowly undermined her physical
and emotional health. Into Lucy's final scene, Hurston introduces
a folklore figure: the spider. As she lies dying, Lucy notices a big
spider weaving its web on the ceiling. Isis, Lucy's youngest daughter,
asks if the spider should be killed. Lucy says no. She attempts to
divert her attention from death by watching the movements of the
spider. Yet, hard as she tries, she cannot detect it in the act of
spinning its web. At the very end, she even stays awake at night.

Despite Lucy's all-night vigil she never saw the spider when he moved, but at first light she noted that he was at least a foot from the ceiling but as motionless as a painted spider in a picture.[26]

Hurston's use of the spider points to the folklore hero Anaise, the spider, the trickster who never gets caught. The spider spinning its web is symbolic of John and his twenty-two-year-old relationship with Lucy. Lucy can never see the web that John weaves around her life. Even when community gossip about John's sordid relationships reaches Lucy, she does not act. Rather, she helps John maintain the posture of an honorable family man before his questioning congregation. Thus John, like the trickster spider, lives beyond accountability.

Although some literary critics deplore what they see as an exaggerated use of folk language and folklore in *Jonah's Gourd Vine*,[27] Hurston's introduction of the spider into Lucy's death scene works effectively to emphasize Lucy's tragic plight. This relation of character and symbol reinforces the idea of a negative transformation for which Preacher John (the trickster) is responsible. Hurston makes sure the reader understands that Lucy has experienced a personal transformation from an aggressive, talented, and vital young person to a suffering servant-wife giving her life for the aspirations and goals of a philandering husband. In the end, the reader agrees with the book's narrator: "The vital Lucy was gone." [28]

Even though Hurston does not bring them together in a scene in the book, Lucy and the gourd vine also seem to bear a symbolic relation. If one assumes that Hurston endows Preacher John Pearson with some of the attributes of the biblical figure Jonah,[29] one can draw parallels between the function of the gourd vine for Jonah and the function of Lucy for Preacher John Pearson.

The biblical plant "came up over Jonah, that it might be shade over his head, to save him from his discomfort. So Jonah was exceedingly glad because of the plant" (Jon. 4:6–7). Like the plant, Lucy is the shield for John's irregular actions, and she saves him from the discomfort of having to answer to the church for his profligate conduct. Like the plant, which is attacked by a worm and dies, Lucy is attacked by a fatal tuberculosis virus. God says to Jonah, "You pity the plant for which you did not labor, nor did you make it grow" (Jon. 4:10). Certainly John has taken Lucy's service for granted, with little concern for her emotional and physical well-being or growth.

Finally, Hurston's use of ritual and conflicting religious systems illustrates how various forces in the community contribute to Lucy's destruction and death. Her relationship with John is affected by the voodoo rituals practiced by Aunt Dangie Dewoe and paid for by Hattie Tyson, John's lover and second wife. Working against Lucy and on behalf of Hattie, Aunt Dangie Dewoe performs an elaborate ritual. She

> crept to her altar in the back room and began to dress candles with war water . . . lit the inverted candles on the altar, saying as she did so, "Now fight! Fight and fuss til you part" . . . she rubbed her hands and forehead with war powder, put the catbone in her mouth, and laid herself down in the red coffin facing the altar and went into the spirit.[30]

Shortly afterward, Lucy takes to her bed and dies. But before her death, Lucy confronts John sternly and directly about his neglect of his family and his relationship with Hattie Tyson. For the first time, John becomes enraged and strikes her. Lucy, a Christian all her life, has consistently prayed to God about her relationship with John. But Christianity affords Lucy no rituals as elaborate or, Hurston implies, as effective as those Aunt Dangie Dewoe practices.

As tragic victim, Hurston's major female character is destroyed by her subservience to male goals and by her self-denying love relationships. An admirable character in many ways, she does not take the action necessary for her own liberation. Rather, she experiences the ultimate transformation: death. Hurston's tragic victim suggests an important lesson to the reader: Woman's greatest gift to herself is self-love. From this love proceeds all positive action and neighborly care.

The Color Purple: **Celie's Story**

The third possibility for transformation is a process by which black women help other black women take the moral action necessary for gaining control of their lives. Black women help other black women become moral agents redefining right and wrong from the perspective of female experience. This process involves a catalyst: a liberated, self-confident black woman who accelerates the movement of another woman away from the psychological, sexual, and emotional abuse that has plagued her. The female catalyst does not change with the process; rather, the other woman undergoes personal, social, and religious transformations that help her to become a whole, self-confident person. As she progresses from bondage to full moral agency, she reconstructs her notions about morality, God, sexuality, and the meaning of human relationships. The female catalyst guides her through the changes necessary for her liberation.

While the communal life-support model portrays an image of a transformed woman whose wholeness is related to community needs and goals, the model of the catalyst and moral agent portrays a woman whose wholeness is based on the successful social and spiritual healing of a black female self-concept. Communal life support as it is depicted in *Jubilee* presupposes the importance of women's lives for the historical extension and well-being of social collectives. The catalyst and moral-agent model presupposes the significance of women's personal growth, development, and well-being for the transformation of social collectives. Both suggest that women's stories and transformations are central in determining the nature and quality of relationships in the black community.

More clearly than any other work, Alice Walker's *The Color Purple* demonstrates the catalyst and moral-agent model. The black female singer Shug Avery is the catalyst who motivates Celie to move from the bondage of domestic violence to the freedom of self-asserting confidence.

Before she meets Shug, Celie has been sexually, psychologically, and emotionally abused by the males prominent in her life. Her stepfather rapes her first when she is fourteen years old. Because she knows very little about her body, she is surprised when she gives birth to two children by him. She marries Mr. Albert, who beats her constantly. Her husband and stepfather psychologically condition her to believe herself stupid. They separate her from the people she loves. Her stepfather gives away the children he has fathered by her. Her husband banishes her sister, Nettie, from their house and, for years, hides the letters Nettie writes to Celie. Celie begins to believe that her sister is dead. Oppression and violation render Celie emotionally numb.

When Shug Avery and Celie become friends, Celie's emotional resurrection begins. The first emotions Celie feels are self-hate and awe. She confesses to herself, "I hate the way I look. I hate the way I dress. Nothing but church going clothes in my chifferobe." [31] During a singing appearance, Shug publicly affirms Celie's worth by telling the audience the story of the new song she has written. The story is about Celie, and Shug has named the song "Miss Celie's Song." Filled with delight and awe, Celie admits that this is the "first time anybody made something and name it after me." [32]

After this incident, Shug guides Celie through educational experiences that awaken her emotions and change her life completely. Shug begins Celie's education by introducing Celie to her own body. Even though she has been sexually involved for years, Celie is not acquainted with her body's erotic zones. Shug points these out to Celie and gives her a mirror with which to inspect them. With this discovery, Celie begins to understand her own sexuality. She is not sexually attracted to men. She has loved and admired Shug ever since first seeing Shug's picture when Mr. Albert dropped it years ago, and she now realizes her attraction to Shug is also sexual.

The public affirmation of her identity by Shug and her new knowledge about her body and sexuality teach Celie that it is important for women to claim their own identity. When Squeak, Harpo's girlfriend, tells Celie that her real name is Mary Agnes, Celie advises her: "Make Harpo call you by your real name. . . . Then maybe he see you even when he trouble." [33] Celie also learns another important lesson. Females must affirm each other as they struggle to free themselves from male domination and abuse. Again, Shug is the catalyst for this learning experience instigated when Celie tells how she has been sexually abused by men. There is an emotional catharsis; Celie cries and cries as she confesses, "Nobody ever love me." [34] Shug expresses her love for Celie, and they consummate their love in sexual union. Having experienced this fulfilling love, Celie is able later to say at Sophia's mother's funeral, "I love folk." [35]

Finally, Celie openly expresses anger when she discovers that her husband has for years hidden from her letters from her sister, Nettie, and has allowed her to believe Nettie was dead. Restrained by Shug, Celie does not kill Mr. Albert, which her anger leads her to try. Rather, she openly declares her independence from him. Confronting him for the first time, Celie calls him a "lowdown dog" and says she is leaving him "to enter into creation." [36] Again, Shug provides Celie the security she needs to carry out this threat. Shug takes Celie back to her own home in Memphis, and makes it clear why she is inviting Celie. Shug says to Celie, "You not my maid. I didn't bring you to Memphis to be that. I brought you here to love you and help you get on your feet." [37] Shug helps Celie develop her sewing talent into a thriving business.

When Celie returns to Georgia, where her husband and his children reside, she is a completely transformed woman with a new morality, a new sense of herself, and a new financial independence. She is now a whole person. Celie has achieved this by reconstructing her notions about sexuality, morality, God, and the meaning of human relationships. Celie now believes a woman's sense of right and wrong should have more authority over her actions than what people think or say about her. When she realizes her image of God is an old white man who prohibits her from noticing her connection to nature, she concludes, "It is like Shug say, you have to git man off your eyeball before you can see anything a'tall." [38] Once she affirms this, she can confront the men who have abused her. She can step into creation and become a moral agent taking full responsibility for her life.

Most important, the new Celie has a more profound understanding of human relationships. She believes that each person in a relationship should be free to live beyond the social conditioning associated with masculine and feminine roles. Hence, she encourages Mr. Albert to begin sewing, since he wanted to sew when he was a child but did not because people called this woman's work.

Celie also reconstructs her notion of how love ought to operate in human relationships. Once she had thought love meant each person in the relationship had exclusive claims on the other's expressions of love. Celie changes her mind when Shug leaves her to go off with a young man. After many tears and much depression, Celie realizes that love is also free in mutual relationships. She concludes, "Shug got a right to live too. . . . Just cause I love her don't take away none of her rights. . . . Who am I to tell her who to love? My job just to love her good and true myself." [39] When Shug tells Celie she is coming home, Celie says, "If she come, I be happy. If she don't, I be content. . . . I figure this the lesson I was supposed to learn." [40]

With Shug as the catalyst, Celie has learned to be content with herself transformed from an abject, abused, self-hating "girl" to a self-confident woman taking responsibility for her own life. Such a change has yielded a moral agent whose entry into women's history inaugurates a new understanding of morality in her community. Mr. Albert, once Celie's rigid oppressor, begins to believe that every person has the right to explore and define his or her sexuality. He has learned his own heart story and begins, like Celie, to understand that the purpose of his life is to question, to affirm the mystery of human origins. And the more he affirms "wonder . . . the more I love." [41] This understanding of love, in contrast to his old notion of love as an emotion connecting a man and a woman, establishes a positive link between him and all others in the community.

Thus, in the catalyst and moral-agent model demonstrated by Alice Walker in *The Color Purple,* one woman's personal growth causes transformations in the social collective called the family. When the novel begins, Celie is caught up in the oppression generated by relationships in the nuclear family. Celie's marriage to Mr. Albert establishes another nuclear family where the primary male oppresses everybody. But when the novel ends, the family structure has become an extended one where people are grafted on like new skin on burned flesh. So Celie refers to her children as "our children," meaning she, Nettie, Samuel, Shug, Mr. Albert, Sophia, and Harpo will provide care and nurture for the children and each other. Sophia and Harpo care for Squeak's and Harpo's child when Squeak leaves to seek a career in music. Squeak and Harpo nurture Sophia's and Harpo's children when Sophia is jailed. Odessa, Sophia's sister, is also involved in the extended family. In the end, everybody is connected to everybody else through love, care, and nurture. It is no wonder Celie addresses her last letter to the universe, to "Dear God. Dear stars, dear trees, dear sky, dear people. Dear everything. Dear God." [42]

The Theological Task

These three different literary models—those of communal life support, tragic victim, and catalyst and moral agent—reveal different processes by which women's personal, social, and religious transformations are effected. Vyry's movement (*Jubilee*) from the so-

cial position of slave to assertive free woman, spiritually and emotionally whole, involves a process of humiliation, suffering, struggle, and commitment. Lucy's transformation (*Jonah's Gourd Vine*)
from a vital, aggressive young woman to a suffering servant-wife
is effected by humiliating experiences that erode her physical and
emotional stamina. Celie (*The Color Purple*) becomes a whole person as the result of a series of positive educational experiences
monitored by her primary supporter, Shug Avery.

Yet there are common assumptions beneath these very different
models for women's transformation. The first assumption is that
a racial history (along with a gender history) determines the character of Afro-American women's experience. The second assumption is that black female liberation and black family liberation are
inseparable. The third is that Afro-American and white attitudes
toward the black woman's sexuality affect her struggle to survive
and to change. Critical reflection upon all of these assumptions can
inform the task of feminist theology.

The three literary models reflect two dimensions of Afro-American racial history. One is the oppression of black people by white
people (females and males). Each novel depicts incidents showing this shared oppression. In *Jubilee* Big Missy Selena Dutton
and her overseer, Grimes, brutalize male and female slaves alike.
In *Jonah's Gourd Vine,* the white judge is as disrespectful to John
Pearson as he is to Hattie Tyson. In *The Color Purple* Celie's
natural father is lynched by white men, and Sophia is beaten almost to death by the white mayor.

The second dimension of this racial history is a cultural heritage
rooted in the Afro-American folk tradition. The use of black folk
language, lore, and religion by Zora Hurston, Margaret Walker,
and Alice Walker brings the themes of this tradition to the surface.
In addition to Afro-American folk tales, themes of survival, bondage, liberation, cunning, and spiritual awakening are also present
in the novels. This cultural heritage shapes the experience of both
black males and females, as reflected in the novels. Celie often
remarks that she knows how to survive. Brother Ezekiel uses his
cunning to outwit slave owners and to help other slaves escape.
Vyry and other slaves use their knowledge of roots and herbs to
help the slave community survive when white doctors hesitate to
attend them. Lucy's warning to her daughter about giving too
much to love relationships is meant to help her daughter survive.

John Pearson's spiritual awakening leads him to the pulpit to become a preacher. Many of the black characters in these three books experience some aspect of bondage. Some become liberated (for example, Celie, Vyry, Innis Brown, and Randall Ware). All struggle to survive the harsh realities of black life in an oppressive white world.

Racial history in all its dimensions is a prism through which one can see important features of Afro-American women's experience derived from racial oppression and cultural traditions shared with all black people. This understanding that women's experience derives some of its character from a racial history men and women share (perhaps equally) illuminates white women's reality as well. According to the nature of the relationships depicted in the novels, part of white women's experience includes their participation with white men in the oppression of black women and other black people.[43] A cultural heritage rooted in a tradition of racism is part of this racial history. Margaret Walker's *Jubilee* and Alice Walker's *The Color Purple* find in this tradition the themes of violence, injustice, exploitation, and death.

Just as it illuminates Afro-American and white women's experience, racial history informs the task of feminist theology in several ways. Since feminist theologians claim women's experience as an important source for Christian theology, the notion of racial history encourages theologians to expand their definitions of women's experience so that women are realistically portrayed both as oppressors and as victims. This expanded portrayal of women's experience is necessary if North American feminist theology is not to be limited to the social and religious reality of white middle-class women, and if tensions are to be eased between black and white women in the church and in society.

Once women acknowledge the fact of racial history, the task of feminist theology will be to use sources that reflect this history. Many of these sources come from the communities of oppressed people of color. This means, then, that insights from these sources will inform the proposals of feminist theologians in a significant and visible way. The socioreligious experience and concerns of Afro-American women can become more prominent in feminist theology than they have been in the past.

Perhaps the most important task imposed by the notion of racial history upon feminist theology is to urge feminist theologians to construct critical principles for biblical interpretation that clarify God's message of liberation to those women who, like the biblical woman Hagar, are oppressed by the collaborative efforts of other women (such as Sarah) with men (such as Abraham). The question is this: Does the liberating word that feminist theology addresses to women who view the world from the underside of history (white women) have the same liberating effect for those women who view the world from the *underside of the underside* of history (black women)? Regardless of the answer one gives to this question, feminist theologians—black and white—will be aided in their work if they consider how racial history shapes the experience of Afro-American and white North American women.

Female and Family Liberation

Margaret Walker, Zora Hurston, and Alice Walker apparently assume that black women's liberation (and transformation) must be accompanied by the liberation of the black family. Vyry, Innis Brown, and Vyry's children are liberated together, along with other black slaves. Celie's final liberation and transformation is juxtaposed with Celie's husband's liberation and transformation. At the end of *The Color Purple,* Celie and her entire extended family enjoy a peaceful, happy state of liberation. In *Jonah's Gourd Vine,* Lucy is not liberated. Neither is her husband, John Pearson, liberated from the bondage of carnal lust, which leads to his premature death. After Lucy dies, their children leave John's house. There is no evidence in the book that anyone has achieved liberation.

This notion that black women's liberation is inseparable from black family liberation suggests additional analytical tasks for feminist theology. More class analysis is needed in the work of feminist theology if the kind of oppression suggested by this notion is to be understood. Sociologist Charles V. Willie has emphasized the differences in values, income, aspirations, and relation to the larger society that exist between middle-class, working-class, and lower-class black families.[44] With black women as well as with the black family, these class differences could mean that the character of oppression varies from class to class. But regardless of class differentiation, the black family is, as Andrew Billingsley observes, "a social system inextricably bound up with and heavily influenced by the major institutions of the larger society." [45] Barbara Sizemore identifies American institutional values as white European superiority, male superiority, and the superiority of people with money.[46] If one acknowledges the effects of these values on the black woman and the black family, then race, gender, and class must *all* enter into feminist analysis of black women's oppression. Whether Marxist categories are the most appropriate for analyzing this woman-family oppression is an open question. But the fact remains: One cannot understand the full scope of black women's oppression and the terms for their liberation unless one understands the oppression of black families in North America. Beyond the analysis of this oppression, feminist theologians should address an important theological question: What is God's liberating word to black women and to black families struggling with oppression? Promising and perplexing possibilities emerge when one uses the New Testament to deal with this question. As central themes in the New Testament, healing (of the body) and transformation (of the spirit, and from death to life) seem to be promising words to oppressed black women and their families.[47] Jesus heals family members without regard to gender— for example, Simon Peter's mother-in-law (Matt. 8:14–15; Luke 4:38–39); the resurrection of the ruler's daughter (Matt. 9:18–26; Luke 8:40–56) and of the widow's only son (Luke 7:12–16); and the transformation of the spiritual state of males and females (casting out demons).

The emphasis on community building in the New Testament also offers a liberating word. The Book of Acts tells of the "company of those who believed . . . and no one said that any of the things . . . he possessed was his own . . . they had everything in common. . . . There was not a needy person among them" (Acts 4:32–34). When Ananias and his wife, Sapphira (both members of the company), tried to hoard some of their money, both fell dead when the Apostle Peter and the community members confronted them with their deed (Acts 5:1–11). These passages suggest that all family members can be whole spiritually and physically, and that the best economic arrangements for oppressed families are socialist arrangements.

Perplexing questions also emerge when one views other New Testament passages in light of the black woman's and the black family's struggle to achieve the unity necessary for liberation. What model of unity does one see when Jesus tells a man to relinquish responsibility to his family and go instead to spread the gospel (Matt. 8:21–22; Luke 9:59–60)? Does the author of Matthew 10:34–44 suggest that one member of a family can resist other members of the family who impede service to God? That would appear to be his intent: "For I have come to set a man against his father, a daughter against her mother, and a daughter-in-law against her mother-in-law; and a man's foes will be those of his own household" (Matt. 10:35–36). What message is communicated about the role of the father in the family as Joseph recedes and soon disappears from the stories of Jesus' life and ministry?

The explication of these problems would take another essay and much exegesis. This study merely intends to indicate some problems and possibilities and to reiterate that many black women —like Zora Hurston, Margaret Walker, and Alice Walker—see the black woman's oppression inseparably connected to the oppression of the black family (including males and females). Liberation for the black woman must include liberation for the black family. To make this understanding of joint oppression and liberation accessible to theology, the theologian must *simultaneously* use race, gender, and class analysis to forge inclusive categories for theology informed by the black woman's and the black family's experience.

Sexuality and Feminist Theology

Finally, the three literary models described in this study are grounded in the assumption that white North American and Afro-American attitudes toward black women's sexuality affect black women's struggle to survive, to change, and to be liberated. In her portrayal of Hetta, Margaret Walker emphasizes that in the American slavocracy, white people regarded the black woman's body as property to be used to gratify white male lust, to wet-nurse white children, and to be an ever present fountain of life for families of the ruling class. Hetta, a young woman, dies from this activity. Alice Walker's portrayal of Squeak, or Mary Agnes (who is raped by the white sheriff), reminds the reader that even after slavery white males still regarded the black woman's body as "readily" available for all kinds of exploitation. Lucy and John's marital problems reveal that some black males (John) have appropriated the slave master's patriarchal attitude toward female sexuality: that is, the wife's body for procreation and the other woman's body for pleasure. John's attitude ultimately leads to Lucy's death.

By contrast, other views in the black community about women's sexuality can help women in their struggle for transformation and liberation. Shug's view that women should be independent and control their own bodies supports Celie's liberation struggle. Mr. Albert's liberation is evident in his conclusion that all people should express their sexuality in any way they desire. Therefore, Celie has the right to choose lesbianism for herself. Celie's family expresses no disapproval of Shug's and Celie's lesbian relationship.

Some feminists have shown that patriarchal conceptions of the hierarchical relation between culture and nature have led to the devaluation of the female body.[48] Black feminist Bell Hooks explains that black womanhood and black female sexuality have been consistently devalued in North America since the days of the slavocracy.[49] It is useful to explore questions about female sexuality from the perspective of oppressed women confronting white male conceptualizations that lead to the subjugation, exploitation, and abuse of women's bodies.

Feminist theologians can gain important insights by attempting to appreciate black perspectives. Within the black community, certain negative ideas about the black woman's sexuality are related to aesthetic values black people appropriated through the conditioning fostered by colonialism. Black women's sexuality and attractiveness are often associated with skin color and quality of hair. If a woman is light skinned and has "good" hair (it blows in the wind), she may be thought to be more desirable. Her reproductive capacity is valued not for itself but because she can produce lighter-skinned children who will be treated better by the white ruling class than darker-skinned people are treated. As one black woman claims, "Color is something most of us are quite irrational about. It's hopelessly confused with sexuality and God knows what else." And as another black woman says, "One reason the whole thing is so hard to deal with is that nobody really talks about it." [50] The task of feminist theology is to talk about it as part of the attempt to analyze the complexities of women's oppression. Perhaps the disciplines of aesthetics, ethics, and folk religion studies can provide some analytical tools to accomplish this task. This work is needed if black feminists are to deal with some of the tensions separating black women from one another and from white women and thereby inhibiting liberation efforts.

Conclusion

Almost twenty years ago, theologian John Macquarrie reminded us that the theological task "needs to be done over and over again, as new problems, new situations and new knowledge come along." [51] This is no less true for feminist theology—as long as we understand that new problems, new situations, and new knowledge *do not invalidate* the theological work of those brave ones who pioneered the new. Every woman engaged in theological and religious studies is indebted to feminist scholars who struggled so that women's concerns could gain a central place in theological discourse.

Building on the work of these scholars, I have attempted to show that an assessment of black women's experience, as it appears in literary works by black women, brings new insights and questions to the task of feminist theology. By coming to understand black women's experience, perhaps feminist theologians can begin to design a methodology that will allow the tensions between women to be resolved in creative theological statements reflecting real inclusiveness. The literature used in this study illustrates the symbiotic relation between the imagination and the theological task. Women's imagination and women's reason must not be separated. The imagination must have equal status with reason in theological construction, so that the voices of many diverse women can speak of the God they know. When all is said and done, perhaps feminist theologians will discover that *in their work together* they have passed along courage, faith, intelligence, and wisdom to succeeding generations of women seeking equality in the church and in the world.

Notes

1. See James Cone, *A Theology of Liberation* (New York: Lippincott, 1970).

2. See Carol P. Christ, *Diving Deep and Surfacing* (Boston: Beacon Press, 1980).

3. Dr. Kate G. Cannon, Assistant Professor of Ethics at Episcopal Divinity School in Cambridge, Massachusetts, is doing pioneering work

in Zora Neale Hurston's writings as a source of information about black women as moral agents.

4. Margaret Walker, *Jubilee* (New York: Bantam Books, 1966), pp. 72–74.

5. Ibid., pp. 3–31.

6. Ibid., p. 7.

7. Ibid., p. 12.

8. Ibid., p. 121.

9. Ibid.

10. Ibid.

11. Ibid., pp. 7–8.

12. Ibid., p. 9.

13. Vyry escapes punishment from the overseer because she knows the names of roots and herbs (ibid., pp. 83–84).

14. Ibid., p. 45.

15. Ibid.

16. Ibid., p. 135.

17. See the passages on Vyry's attempted escape (ibid., pp. 137–145); see also Vyry's instruction to another slave woman about how to survive on the plantation (p. 109).

18. Ibid., p. 125.

19. Ibid., p. 381.

20. Ibid., p. 407.

21. Ibid., p. 408.

22. Black folklore contains many models of independent women who are equal to men. The blues songs project models of dependent women bound to unhappy love affairs. These are positive (the folklore models) and negative models (the blues) for women's liberation struggles.

23. Zora Neale Hurston, *Jonah's Gourd Vine* (Philadelphia: Lippincott, 1971), p. 5.

24. Ibid., p. 207.

25. Ibid., p. 22.

26. Ibid., pp. 209–210.

27. See Darwin Turner, *In a Minor Chord: Three Afro-American Writers and Their Search for Identity* (Carbondale: Southern Illinois University Press, 1971).

28. Ibid., p. 214.

29. See Lillie P. Howard, *Zora Neale Hurston* (Boston: Twayne Publishers, 1980).

30. Ibid., p. 201.

31. Alice Walker, *The Color Purple* (New York: Harcourt Brace Jovanovich, 1982), p. 64.

32. Ibid., p. 65.

33. Ibid., p. 75.

34. Ibid., p. 97.

35. Ibid., p. 188.

36. Ibid., p. 170.

37. Ibid., p. 179.

38. Ibid., p. 168.

39. Ibid., p. 228.

40. Ibid., p. 240.

41. Ibid., p. 239.

42. Ibid., p. 242.

43. In *Jubilee,* Big Missy Dutton and the overseer, Grimes, jointly brutalized the slaves (pp. 142–149). In *The Color Purple,* the mayor and his wife exploited Sophia (pp. 87–92).

44. Charles V. Willie, "The Black Family and Social Class," *American Journal of Orthopsychiatry* 44 (1974): 50–60.

45. Andrew Billingsley, *Black Families in White America* (Englewood Cliffs, N.J.: Prentice-Hall, 1968), p. 3.

46. Barbara Sizemore, "Sexism and the Black Male," *Black Scholar* 4 (March–April 1973): 2–11.

47. These are promising words because of the present problems confronting the family. At a conference on the black family, sponsored by the Nashville Urban League at Fisk University in the spring of 1984, several problems were explored. These were the deteriorating health of family members, the relatively high mortality rate among black infants, the absence of fathers in the home often because of imprisonment, war, or early death, and the relations between males and females. Many workshop reports spoke of the changes needed in the black family and in America's way of dealing with the black family.

48. See Rosemary Radford Ruether, *Sexism and God-Talk* (Boston: Beacon Press, 1983), pp. 72–92. Also see Sherry B. Ortner, "Is Female to Male as Nature Is to Culture?", in Michelle Zimbalist Rosaldo and Louise Lamphere, eds., *Woman, Culture, and Society* (Stanford: Stanford University Press, 1974), pp. 67–87.

49. Bell Hooks, *Ain't I a Woman* (Boston: South End Press, 1981), see pp. 15–86.

50. In John L. Gwaltney, *Drylongso* (New York: Random House, 1980). See the narratives by Celia Delaney and Angela McArthur, pp. 83–86 and 76–82, respectively.

51. John Macquarrie, *Principles of Christian Theology* (New York: Charles Scribner's Sons, 1966), p. vii.

Six

Primordial Purity and Everyday Life: Exalted Female Symbols and the Women of Tibet

Anne C. Klein

How many women have observed cultural icons of the female—
Vogue models, the Venus de Milo, or the Virgin Mary—with the
surprised or painful realization, "This is not me"? And how many
have acknowledged in the next moment the enormous influence
such symbols have in shaping their goals and self-perceptions?
Insights like these constitute a personal recognition that female
symbols and the lives of women are separate yet deeply connected
realities. The importance of distinguishing the two has been a
major insight of women's studies and the women's movement, with
implications of these insights being investigated by theologians, historians, sociologists, psychologists, and others. The interplay between spheres of symbolic and social reality has a special interest
for students of religion, since religion frequently provides a culture with its most influential symbolic structures.[1] Yet the precise
pattern of influence is difficult to trace.

   The interaction between female religious imagery in Tibet and
the social roles—lay and clerical—of Tibetan women presents a
complex and compelling case in point. Such female imagery is a
vital component of the Buddhism that, at least until the Chinese
takeover in the late 1950s, permeated all levels of Tibetan society.
Female images of the divine, that is female enlightened Buddhas,
abound; profound and positive female imagery is a major element
of Tibetan Buddhist art and practice. Furthermore, Buddhist philosophy appears to support an egalitarian vision and to affirm a
cluster of values one would expect to work positively for women.
The question is this: Are these positive indications mirrored by
women's place in society?

   If ever there was a country where religious perspectives might be expected to mold social realities, it would be Tibet. This was a culture steeped in religion, with traditions that had existed virtually unchanged since the fourteenth century and many aspects dating from the twelfth century or earlier. A fifth of the male population entered monastic life.[2] Virtually every home, however poor, had a Buddhist shrine where offerings and prayers were made daily, and the enormous intellectual, literary, and artistic energies of the population were focused almost exclusively on the religious sphere.

Aside from the evidence of exalted imagery, what would lead one to believe that women might achieve greater equality because of Buddhism? A guiding principle of Great Vehicle or Mahayana Buddhism (the form in which that religion has mainly been known in Tibet, China, Japan, Korea, Vietnam, and Nepal) is its conviction that all minds are eminently purifiable, and thus women and men are equally able to achieve enlightenment or Buddhahood. Moreover, philosophical treatises, especially in Tibet, deal at length with the fallacies of various kinds of assumed dualisms, including dualisms that many feminist theologians consider a major and cross-cultural factor relegating women to secondary status. The Buddhist rebuttal of dualism, developed at length on the theoretical level, is said to be integrated experientially through meditative rituals. Many rituals focus on female enlightened Buddhas such as the Great Bliss Queen.

Tibetan Buddhist symbolism glorifies female embodiments of wisdom (*ḍākinī, mkha' gro ma*) and enlightened heroines. Whose needs do such symbols address? Does positive female religious imagery have positive effects on the social realities of women? We know that glorification of the Virgin Mary in the West has not generally done so. Would different types of female images operate any differently? Does the mere presence of female deities, or the apparently equal status of male and female deities, affect the social situation of ordinary women? When, as in Tibet, the female form is considered an exalted metaphor of religious meaning, are women's bodies more respected or affirmed? More broadly, what can we learn about the relationship between religious symbols and social conventions?

First, we must understand what we can about women in Tibet, and then analyze specific symbolic elements of their culture in order to assess the relationship between the two. Moreover, in a country whose clergy was numerically and politically significant, it is necessary to take separate account of laywomen and female religious, whether celibate or married. Several possibilities traditionally existed for women—to marry, become a nun, remain as a homebound religious, or live as a wandering tantrika or practitioner of esoteric Buddhism. Men had roughly equivalent options, but with more access to associated forms of power.

In considering the influence of religious, social, and iconographical elements and profound religious doctrines, the philosophical and experiential aspects of Buddhism, on social structures and individual lives, we come to the most difficult and fundamental question of all. To what extent can we assess the mutual influence of symbols and social realities? Further, is the imprint left by religious elements on the social or political order proportionate to their significance in the religious sphere? Some feminist theologians have found evidence that major elements of Christian theology which are negative for women represent neither the most profound Christian vision nor the last word on biblical interpretation. For example, Rosemary Ruether writes:

> Feminist theology is not asserting unprecedented ideas; rather, it is rediscovering the prophetic context and content of Biblical faith itself.... On one level, this means that feminist theology ... strips off the ideological mystifications that have developed in the traditions of Biblical interpretation and that have concealed the liberating content.[3]

Moreover, the misogyny of Christianity and other traditions can be seen as a distortion that derives from or promulgates a presumption of male primacy.

> All the categories of classical theology in its major traditions—Orthodox, Catholic and Protestant—have been distorted by androcentrism. This not only makes the male normative in a way that reduces women to invisibility, but it also distorts all the dialectical relationships of good/evil, nature/grace, body/soul, God/nature, by modeling them on a polarization of male and female.[4]

To make maleness normative is to accede it a centrality that in Christianity is better reserved for principles such as love or vitalizing faith. The goal is a methodology that can account for dynamics developed outside a given religion yet able to sanction principles or practices that contradict the values of the religion. Whereas originators of a religious tradition may question, open, or transcend traditional social roles, their successors tend to return to more conservative positions. Jacob Needleman describes what he takes to be a powerful instance of this tendency in the West:

> With Constantine, Christianity as a world religion takes form and decisively branches away from what might be called Christianity as an inner path. From that point on, there are two main histories of Christianity, a distinction, to my mind, far more fundamental than the various other aspects of Christian culture through the ages.... Even the history of monasticism in its relation to the Church does not necessarily coincide with these two histories I am speaking of, however much it may seem to during certain periods of time. This rather elusive idea of two histories is how I have come to regard the origins and development of Christianity.[5]

The term *inner* in my analysis refers to aspects of a tradition directed toward personal or spiritual transformation; *outer* refers to aspects primarily enmeshed with or influenced by sociopolitical variables. The inner and outer aspects naturally impinge on each other, but the Buddhist tradition retains a meaningful distinction between them. Mahayana and non-Mahayana Buddhists, who offer different definitions of the ultimate religious goal, agree that all persons are capable of achieving an *identical type of spiritual transformation* called liberation or enlightenment. At the same time, especially in tantra, it is openly recognized that the path to enlightenment, including the symbols and visions associated with this, can vary considerably. This openness is important in establishing the viability of and necessity for female as well as male representations of Buddhist divinity, in contrast to the male-dominated Christian symbols. In terms of Christianity we can, with Ruether and Needleman, try to distinguish the inner from the outer, and thereby to determine whether the former is any less androcentric than the latter. By applying these categories cross-culturally, we may eventually find patterns by which to identify and even predict historical or metaphysical junctures at which religion is apt to foster or impede an egalitarian society and the development of egalitarian individuals.

The issues and questions indicated above will be addressed through observing and analyzing three spheres in Tibetan culture: the social, symbolic, and individual. The variety of roles available to individuals in combination with the multileveled social strata—farmer, nomad, noble—create a complex schema. The difficulty of doing justice to this complexity is compounded by the relative paucity of reliable ethnographic material on pre-Chinese Tibet and by the virtual nonexistence of material depicting the lives of ordinary women, especially those outside the religious life. We will therefore focus on three topics. First, I will briefly describe the life of Ayu Khandro, a contemporary woman who moved dramatically between the social and religious spheres. Second, I will summarize what is known about the social realities of women in family, state, and church; this material is largely concerned with the outer religion. Third, I will note major elements of female symbolism common to both inner and outer aspects of Tibetan Buddhism.

Ayu Khandro's life is a paradigm for the juxtaposition of two major areas of life for Tibetan women—the outer social realm and the inner arena of religion with its exalted female imagery. The fantastic elements of her biography cannot receive special attention here but are included in order to complete the picture of how a certain Tibetan religious practitioner came to be regarded in her own time.

The Life of Ayu Khandro

The woman who was to live to the age of 115 and spend the last fifty years of her life in meditation was born in eastern Tibet in 1839.[6] As the youngest child, she tended her family's goats and sheep until, at age seven, she went to stay with her aunt, whose solitary life centered on religious practice. The girl took pleasure in what her aunt taught, and helped with the retreat by fetching water and cooking.

When Ayu was fourteen, she accompanied her aunt and parents to a series of religious teachings given by a lama with whom their family was long acquainted. Others also came, including a wealthy family known to Ayu's aunt. Ayu's parents, eager to make a connection with such a family, arranged for Ayu and a son of this family to marry. Ayu pleaded that the agreement be broken. The aunt took her part, explaining how happy the girl was and how much she wished to continue her training. The parents would not revoke the match, but did agree to wait until Ayu was nineteen.

In the intervening years Ayu continued to study with her aunt, attend initiations, and receive further instruction at certain monasteries. When, with her aunt, she undertook her first retreat, her meditation focused on Tara, an important female deity associated with the Great Bliss Queen. Subsequently, the aunt again protested to the family that Ayu wished to continue her practice and did not wish to marry, but the marriage took place.

In the autobiography Ayu dictated to a student in 1945, two years before her death, she reported that she was not an excellent wife and not good at family responsibilities. Given the wealth of her husband's family and that she had no children, her chief responsibilities were probably managing servants. After three years of married life she became ill with occasional paralysis, possibly caused by epilepsy. She became increasingly weaker until she was unable to walk. The family lama from whom she had previously received instruction came to visit. Her disease had likely come about, he said, because she had interrupted religious practice against her will. She must continue with this endeavor and not remain as a wife; otherwise she would die.

Ayu's husband agreed to the lama's advice. She was taken to stay with her aunt, near the lama's hermitage. Within the year she had recovered completely. Her husband and sisters provided food; her husband also contributed money, so she did not need to work and could concentrate on studying and meditation.

Some years later the family's lama died and at the funeral his students, including Ayu and her aunt, sat together in meditation. As Ayu emerged from her concentration she saw that her aunt, then sixty-two years old, had died, seated in full meditation posture, back straight and legs crossed. She remained in that position for three days after her breath had ceased; this was taken as evidence of her spiritual attainments.

Ayu was thirty. She spent the next fifteen years traveling throughout Tibet, sometimes accompanied by other women or men tantrikas. She studied with numerous teachers, visiting them in isolated retreat or in monasteries. She became especially adept in a practice known as cutting attachment (*chod*). This is a meditation strongly associated with one of the most famous female adepts in Tibet, Ma-ji Lap-dron (*Ma-gcig-lab-sgron*), who is considered an incarnation of the Great Bliss Queen Yeshey Tsogyal.[7] In this practice, one visualizes that one's consciousness leaves one's body and enters the form of a fierce goddess. She then transforms one's now lifeless human body, imagined to have become as large as a mountain, into a nourishing nectar that is then offered to hosts of deities, humans, hungry ghosts, and other beings, high and low.[8] Ayu and her companions spent years walking up and down the rugged terrain, sounding drums and bells to accompany their chants of the liturgy of cutting attachment.

When she was forty-four, Ayu was invited to stay at her former husband's house, where she continued her practice and gave instructions to him and other family members. Subsequently she undertook a retreat while her husband arranged for a permanent meditation hut to be built on a site selected by her through a vision some years before. In this vision she had seen a small hill with an egg-shaped cave whose thick darkness gave way to multicolored light that allowed her to see through its walls when she entered. She had then attempted to make her way to the place she had seen, known as Dzong-sa in eastern Tibet. But the area had been flooded by a river and she was forced to wait on a nearby hill. After three days and nights of continuous meditation, she had another dream or waking vision in which there seemed to be a long white bridge arching over the flood. She thought, "Good, now I can cross," at which point it was no longer a dream, for she had reached her destination without knowing how she came there. People in the area said she had flown across the ravine. She denied this, saying her crossing had happened as she described.

Ayu completed several retreats here until, at the age of fifty-four, she determined she would remain there in retreat for the rest of her life. This she did, but between daily meditation sessions she would occasionally give instruction to students at their request. She was known especially for her adeptness in the Great Sphere Heart Essence, one of the main liturgical traditions in the most ancient order of Tibetan Buddhism. She developed a meditation practice, which she selectively taught others, centered on Sinhamukha (the Lion-faced One), an esoteric deity known as the secret female form of Padmasambhava.

Ayu had numerous students, both male and female; one of these, sent by his own monastic preceptor especially to learn the Sinhamukha and other practices from her, requested her life story and wrote down what she said. He later heard the reports of her death. Though 115 years old, she was without any signs of ill health. She told those around her that in three weeks she would die and they should prepare for the funeral. "This is a time of change, everything will be disturbed, I'd rather depart," she said. For twenty days she ceased her meditation sessions and received visitors, giving much advice and teaching. Toward the twenty-fifth day, at an hour when normally she would be completing a meditation session, she was found to have passed away in meditative posture. Many of her disciples reported that she remained upright for two weeks, during which time her body became very small. A sudden hot spell brought trees and flowers into bloom unseasonably.

By the time she died she was known as a living Vajrayogini. Vajrayogini (the Adamantine Female Yogi) is a deity identified with the Great Bliss Queen Yeshey Tsogyal. The existence of this and other enlightened female figures undoubtedly made it possible, if not easy, for Ayu to be regarded as a realized woman. She had not been born to this position, but had gained it through her own efforts. Ayu Khandro was obviously not a typical woman, but she typifies aspects of the kind of life open to many women and, moreover, a life to which many Tibetan Buddhist practitioners, male and female, deeply aspired. Let us observe how the opportunities she encountered relate to the broader social picture.

Women in Tibet

The Tibetans have an adage, "Every doctor has his prescriptions, every lama his own religion." We might well add, "and every valley its own social structure." Given the extraordinarily rough terrain and lack of roads or motorized vehicles in Tibet, it could hardly be otherwise. Almost every valley might be days or weeks by horse or foot from the next settled area, and consequently each valley has its own customs. This diversity makes it impossible to generalize accurately about Tibet as a whole. Our focus will be on the women and symbolism of eastern Tibet—the Kham and Amdo regions where Ayu Khandro lived and which were the stronghold of the Nyingma or ancient order of Tibetan Buddhism. Some contrasts will be drawn between this area and Lhasa, the largest urban center in the country, site of the three largest monasteries in Tibet, the seat of the early Tibetan kings, and the capital of the central Tibetan government since the seventeenth century. Thus, sociologically, Lhasa was in a class by itself in Tibet.[9] We will examine women's status in the context of work roles and education for lay and clergy, religious vocations, and family structures and marriage customs prior to the Chinese takeover in 1959.

Work and Education

Among most classes the parity of women with men was greatest in the area of work. For example, eastern Tibetan nomads, groups of families traveling with their yak-hair tents and grazing animals, shared a hard and simple life. Their staples were a rich tea made with salt and butter, *tsampa* (parched barley), yogurt, cheese, and meat when available. Clothing, made from wool and animal skins, was sewn by men (among the larger population, both men and women spun yarn).[10] Men and women dressed alike, their garments equally suited for active work. Women were primarily in charge of the "white" or milk products, the essential cheese, milk, and yogurt. This responsibility was so vital and so closely associated with women that its symbolism was woven into the nomad's wedding ceremony.

Tibetans as a race are famous for trade, and women of virtually all classes appear to have been active in this sphere. Among the horse herders of eastern Tibet, men were typically unwilling to conclude a sale, however favorable, in the absence of their wives.[11] Foreigners, both Western and Chinese, encountering this phenomenon were amazed. One traveler put it this way:

> By what means have these women gained such a complete ascendency over the men, how have they made their mastery so complete and so acceptable to a race of lawless barbarians who but unwillingly submit even to the authority of their chiefs, is a problem worthy of consideration.[12]

In Lhasa, too, women were the family shopkeepers and some had their own businesses.[13] There is no evidence that female infanticide, known to have occurred in India, was ever practiced in Tibet. At the same time, despite a certain equality in work, a preference for male offspring existed at least in some locales. For example, in Lhasa parents followed the custom of slipping a ring onto the male infant's penis as soon as it was born, lest some mischievous demons change it into a girl.[14]

Egalitarianism also existed in mores governing public modesty. Unlike neighboring India, where women in many areas developed

119

internal diseases because of the impropriety of relieving themselves in public and the lack of private places to do so, men and women were equally free in this regard in Lhasa and elsewhere; the *chuba,* or long dress worn by women, made this possible without any physical exposure. Thus there was nothing to prevent women as well as men from heading toward the city to conduct trade, circumambulate the temples, meet acquaintances, and so forth. Women were free to strip to the waist at public bathing spots, since breasts were not regarded as shameful or sexual; this particular taboo was reserved for legs, which both men and women were required to keep covered.

In more recent times, girls were almost as likely as boys to receive lay education, but the traditional monastic universities—major institutions of the religious and political spheres—have always been closed to them. Indeed, wherever hierarchical structures were emphasized, as they were in Tibet's monastic order and theocratic political system centered in Lhasa, women were excluded from power.[15] In terms of our categories of "inner" and "outer" this is significant. The internalized state cultivated by practitioners of the Great Bliss Queen and other rituals specifically counters deeply ingrained notions of hierarchy or opposition.[16] Nevertheless, externally, Tibetan society, especially where political or economic power accrued, was intricately hierarchical. This fact is reflected in the colloquial Tibetan language, particularly as spoken in Lhasa, which contains an elaborately graded honorific vocabulary for most important words; one's choice of words clearly indicates whether one is speaking with equals, or with persons above or below oneself in social standing.

Religious Vocations

Women who wished to devote themselves to religion could choose between becoming a celibate nun or being a tantrika. Most typically, but not necessarily, nuns lived together in nunneries, which, unlike some monasteries, were never politically powerful. They tended to be small and did not offer the educational opportunities provided by the larger monasteries, the largest of which were really university complexes. Women tantrikas, usually of the Nyingma or Gagyu orders, might or might not marry and were likely to spend the greater part of their lives on pilgrimages, receiving instruction from isolated or monastic tantric teachers, or in retreat. Ayu Khandro was in this respect a typical tantrika. Women in all classes could choose to become nuns.

Nomad women sometimes came to a kind of religious vocation in another way. In general there were more available women than men among these groups; many men were killed in quarrels and many others became monks. The unmarried women were known as *ka-ma,* "hearth ladies," because in their youth they slept by the family hearth and did the dairy work (just as the young bride did).[17] Not as highly regarded as Buddhist nuns or tantrikas, the *ka-ma* nonetheless received a certain respect as religious practitioners. They dressed like Buddhist nuns, although they may or may not have shaved their heads as nuns did. In their later years they would join the monks' circle of tents and concentrate on religious practice, supported, as were the monks, by their families.[18] There was apparently no male equivalent to this role.

Another type of religious vocation, documented mainly in the Lhasa area, was that of oracle for deities known as protectors of the religion (*chos kyong, dharma-pāla*). Female oracles of this type married; on their death their daughters took over the role.[19]

Women in convents, an outer religious institution, were socially subsidiary to men in monasteries. Indeed, since the formation of a Buddhist order of nuns in India during the fifth century B.C. women have been institutionally subordinated to male clergy.[20] Inner religious values of equality were encapsulated by the larger androcentric social situation, despite the considerable egalitarianism within the family.

Family Structures

Monogamous marriages were the rule in Tibet, but polyandry and (secondarily) polygamy were not uncommon. The issue was not so much personal preference as inheritance logistics. A farmer with three sons and insufficient land to leave each son enough property to sustain a new family might arrange for a single woman to be their common bride. This custom was especially common among herders in the northern plains and western Tibet.[21] Polyandry was most widespread in the Tsang area, outside Lhasa, where soil was poor and estates large, requiring many people to look after them. Polygamy was less common, by some accounts the option only of rich men who could afford two or three wives.[22] Nevertheless, parents with several daughters and insufficient inheritance for each might arrange for a single man to be their common husband. In the case of divorce child custody customs varied. In some places, boys stayed with the father, girls with the mother; in other areas the mother most commonly took the children. In the case of illegitimate children, at least among nomads, the father was required to make a one-time payment to the mother if neither desired to marry.[23]

In the absence of extensive ethnographic materials on family roles in daily life,[24] a close look at wedding customs among the nomads and nobility will serve to illustrate certain facets of male-female divisions of responsibility and power.

Weddings were arranged by parents and other relatives of the prospective bride. Among the nomadic peoples, a father or uncle of the groom visited the girl's home and requested both parents to give their daughter in marriage. A girl was not likely to be consulted in the matter, just as Ayu Khandro was not. The prospective groom would more likely already have had a say. Typically, the girl's parents do not agree immediately. However, their giving flimsy reasons for refusing was a subtle invitation to the petitioners to pursue the matter further. The girl's parents often required the request to be made three times, thereby establishing the esteem in which their daughter was held and, possibly, eliciting the best financial offer from the groom's family. Once the girl's parents gave their consent by accepting gifts, often with a show of reluctance, the match was made. Among the Lhasa nobility, and probably elsewhere, a special gift known literally as the "breast [milk] fee" (*nu ring*) was given to the girl's mother, thereby acknowledging her role as the girl's nurturer.[25] These gifts were meant to reflect the groom's family's wealth: according to their capacity, the groom's family gave items such as silk cloth, silver, horses, and multicolored cotton fabrics.[26]

Once these gifts were accepted, neither the prospective bride nor groom could be betrothed to another without legal censure.[27] The bride's family later gave gifts in equal measure to what they received. Thus although numerous accounts speak of Tibetan wives as being "bought," this seems not precisely the case, at least among nomads. At the same time, the "match" was certainly discussed in economic terms. Among nobles in Lhasa, gifts from the groom's family were piled on a platform onto which the bride dismounted from her horse; she rode up to this plaftorm but did not dismount unless servants in her party deemed the gifts sufficient.[28] Yet, in descriptions of nomadic wedding customs the Tibetan word for the groom's family is literally "takers of the bride," and the bride's family is referred to as "the givers of the bride." [29] In her role as bride, the woman herself is the chief commodity.

At most levels of society husband and wife apparently shared equally in day-to-day tasks or business matters. Either party could initiate a divorce. In these aspects of married life there was parity, making it all the more notable that the wedding traditions contained elements problematic for women. One occurs prior to the actual ceremony, and one during the ceremony itself.

The first is a custom known as "taking the bride's hat." As the bride approached the groom's vicinity, two horsemen came out to meet her. At that time, two of her own brothers—specified as *ming bo,* brothers born of the same parents—rustled her hat with their horsewhips. The horsemen then jostled to take her hat; the rules governing this act are based on strong if inexplicable superstitions. The hat had to be taken from the left or right; if it was taken from the girl's front or back, either the groom's or the bride's family, respectively, would be angry—sometimes so angry that an actual fight ensued.[30] This could not have been a soothing experience for the girl, and certainly conveyed a sense of being a passive hostage in this major event of her life.

The central feature of the nomadic wedding ritual was the Yogurt Vow.[31] Yogurt is in general considered an auspicious food. On this occasion it was also eaten to indicate the dairy work the bride would do and to ensure that she would make good yogurt.[32] Although this is said to be the most important of the marriage rituals, there was no ceremonial equivalent for the groom. This might signify that the husband's work roles are not as closely tied to gender as are female roles. Thus, whereas women may conduct trade and so forth as the men do, men do not make yogurt.

The bride's ritual accouterments emphasized her role as nurturer and sustainer, just as the special fee to her mother paid homage to this role. Yet, we have seen that this was by no means the only role she would play in family life: she would probably be active in trading, for example. To what extent were these family roles embodied in religious symbolism, and to what extent were they transcended?

Symbolism

> MA, Mother, essence of the enlightened mind
> MO, Woman, the self-arisen primordial wisdom
> Whatever I say, it is your name.[33]

Tibetan religious iconography is staggering in its diversity. Nevertheless, a representative portion can be drawn from the Great Sphere Heart Essence (*kLong chen snying tik*) lineage of the Nyingma order of Tibetan Buddhism. Nyingma is the oldest of the four main Tibetan orders and the Heart Essence is among the best known of its many groups of practices. The Great Bliss Queen Yeshey Tsogyal, an important deity known in various forms and under different names throughout east Asia, is featured in rituals of the Heart Essence liturgies. She and other female enlightened figures illustrate elements of female symbolism that are central to current Nyingma practice. The bulk of the material discussed here is from eighteenth-century Nyingma discussions of the symbolism associated with the Great Bliss Queen, drawn from works by abbots of the Do-drup-chen monastery in the Do Valley, between the Kham and Amdo regions of eastern Tibet.

The female element, variously described, is all-important to the practice and understanding of Tibetan Buddhist symbolism. It occurs in three closely related aspects: female deities; explicit female body imagery wherein portions of the deity's body symbolize specific philosophical concepts; and the female characterization of the ground or essential nature of everything that exists, including the deity's and one's own mind and body.

Because phenomena are actually manifestations or the play (*līla, rol ba*) of this essential nature, all that exists is an embodiment and a display of its vitality. Thus, "Whatever I say, it is your name." In this way the three lines quoted above indicate the relationship between female deities or female body imagery and the feminine ground of these. All visualized symbols, whatever other significance they hold, are thus also understood as embodiments of the empty essence or primordial purity that is considered their true nature. Engagement with these symbols is aimed primarily at gaining access to this reality, which the practitioner learns to recognize as the actual substance of all symbols. This reality is classified as feminine. Specific import of the individual symbols is explained in great detail in liturgical texts; but no matter how skilled the practitioner may be in visualization or symbolic interpretation, the ritual or meditation is not fulfilled unless these appearances are experienced as united with their primordial basis. The deity's body, ornaments, instruments, and so forth must all be seen as the "stuff" of emptiness.

This "stuff" or "great sphere" is considered accessible, through routes that vary according to culture and circumstance, in identical form to all persons. Thus, great importance is given to the flexibility of symbolic structures: the divine here must not be limited, as it often is in Western traditions, to specific forms of expression— for example, the male or the virginal. This means that in the Tibetan Mahayana tradition one can speak of an "essence"—comprising compassionate wisdom or primordial purity—toward which the tradition as a whole is directed. This is an essence that thoroughly defies the properties of exclusivity and reductionism that are hallmarks of this concept in Western religious and philosophical discourse.

In brief, Tibetan iconography exhibits two modes of female symbolism: the female roles or metaphors occurring in liturgy, which to some extent reflect cultural sex roles, and the transcendent female symbols of the great sphere (*kLong chen*) which is emptiness. This distinction will govern our analysis.

That there are numerous levels on which to understand the Great Bliss Queen Yeshey Tsogyal is indicated in a typical description of her:

> From the mouth of a lotus was born
> The swift goddess, heroic liberator,
> Who went forth in human form
> Amid the snowy mountains of Tibet.
>
> Externally [she is] Sarasvati [Yeshey] Tsogyal
> Internally, the actual venerable Lady Tara
> Secretly she is Vajravarahi.[34]

Here the terms *external* and *internal* refer primarily to the mythical elements of the Great Bliss Queen symbol system, whereas "the secret" most directly concerns the more practical aspect—the level on which a religious practitioner makes "actual contact" not only with the symbol or its meaning but also with the primordial purity that is literally considered to be its true content. These two major strata of Buddhist symbology here are roughly equivalent to Needleman's categories of external and internal religion.[35] I suggest that these two levels—external and internal, mythic and experiential, symbol and symbolized—have different implications for women and different degrees of significance in the social realm.

Mythic Dimensions

Yeshey Tsogyal, historically identified as a queen of the eighth-century Tibetan king Tri-srong-day-tsen, is considered a fully enlightened being, a Buddha, who appeared as an ordinary Tibetan girl so that people of her country might easily form a relationship with her, visualize her, and attain enlightenment through conjoining this visualization with teachings of the Nyingma Great Perfection tradition (*rDzogs chen*), which were preserved by her.

> The name [Yeshey Tsogyal] and the form of the "Daughter of the [Tibetan] Kar-chen family" was displayed by [Yeshey Tsogyal] largely for the sake of those who, for the time being, do not see [her more exalted manifestation as] Vajravarahi [in which she appears in the] form of a fully perfected deity. Among the practices of the Guru [Padmasambhava] especially intended for Tibetans there are many whose chief deity is [The Great Bliss Queen] Yeshey Tsogyal.[36]

In describing her role as preserver of the teaching, the liturgical commentary makes an explicit connection with women's roles, noting that in the world it is the man who seeks wealth and the woman who keeps it safely, both activities being required if wealth is to increase.[37] This tendency to conserve is analogous to Yeshey Tsogyal's role in the preservation of Nyingma traditions. According to the commentator,

> ... in the world, a woman maintains the fund of resources; in the same way ... the sustainers (*dhāraṇī*) ... who hold and accumulate the doctrine manifest ... in the form of female deities and so forth.[38]

Yeshey Tsogyal is the supreme preserver of the "resources" that constitute the Nyingma teachings. In the literature on her—biographies, liturgy, and extensive commentaries on the liturgy—her role as preserver or bestower is exalted to the point that Padmasambhava's role as preceptor appears secondary. On the other hand, in the liturgy associated specifically with Padmasambhava, Yeshey Tsogyal is hardly mentioned, although she is present as his consort. Thus, even though she is designated as a teacher in her own right, it is Padmasambhava, known as the Precious Guru (Guru Rinbochay), who is mainly venerated as originator of the teachings being practiced. She is the nurturer and distributor of these, which she dispenses through the ages, "like timely messages" for those intent on emulating her state of realization.[39]

> ... due to her merciful compassion for the disciples of this area [Tibet, she] prayed the Great Lotus Master [Padmasambhava] to turn limitless wheels of the doctrine [that is, to teach extensively the meaning of] secret mantra and she collected his spoken word. So that the continuum of these volumes would not vanish, she requested the concealing of innumerable treasures which could not be damaged by humans, non-humans, demons, or the elements.[40]

Yeshey Tsogyal is thus in part depicted as a kind of sublime housekeeper. Yet she is also associated with vibrant activity and venerated for such heroic behavior as successfully pursuing her religious quest through great adversity. Even more than the liturgy, her biography reveals her as an embodiment of zestful energy, courage, and perseverance. Her biography, in fact a religious epic, was compiled in the eighteenth century and, like the liturgical texts, contains elements that are much older.

In the course of her training Yeshey Tsogyal faced and overcame numerous difficulties. To give one example, she described an incident early in her practice:

> I sat where I was, totally detached, thought-free. "She must be a *yeti*" they cried and proceeded to shoot their arrows at me, beat me with their clubs, stab at me with their spears and slash at me with their knives. But no matter in what way they attacked me or with what weapons, they caused absolutely no harm to my body. They gave me the name Invulnerable Tibetan, and not knowing what to do they dispersed to their homes.[41]

Yeshey Tsogyal did not passively endure degradation and worse; the context of this passage emphasizes that she was beyond danger or discomfort precisely because of her actively cultivated realization. That such ability can come to anyone who practices is a deeply held Buddhist conviction. Praise of Tsogyal as a fully accomplished yogini, emphasizing her extraordinary influence and charisma, is meant as an incentive to others. According to Tsogyal herself, some time after the event described above:

> [the king] invited me to Samye [the first Buddhist monastery established in Tibet] . . . the translators, courtiers, ministers, and queens led by the king, Mutri Tsenpo, all paid me honour and served me with humility . . . fifteen hundred new monks were ordained at one time, and [the king] appointed the Indian sage Kamalaśīla as the new Abbot. I gave instruction to the newly ordained monks, and they went to Chimphu to begin in their meditation, which bore nothing but positive results.[42]

Like Ayu Khandro, Yeshey Tsogyal was a charismatic teacher in her own right. This characterization is notable, for although Tsogyal is venerated as a preserver of the Great Perfection tradition and in this role mirrors Tibetan women's responsibility for the milk and yogurt, she is not limited to this role. To see her only as a preserver would be too narrow, even on the mythic level. Mythic characterization of her expands this through descriptions of her activities, miraculous and otherwise. These fall mainly into two categories: her arduous ascetic practices (remaining on a glacier for three years with scarcely food or clothing, for example) and bringing the means of enlightenment to others. These are classic elements to be found in any Buddhist story of liberation. The close relationship with a guru, which is particularized in Tsogyal's biography as her consortship with Padmasambhava, fits the classic pattern. She also seeks her own male consorts, one of whom she ransoms with money given her for the miraculous act of raising a rich Nepali family's child from the dead. Most central is her status as an enlightened Buddha whose spiritual attainment is equal to Padmasambhava's. Although she appeared to develop this realization through depending on him she had actually been enlightened prior to her birth in Tibet.

Thus, on the mythic level Tsogyal seems to incorporate a certain regalization of woman as preserver that transcends and reinforces women's traditional roles. She is also characterized by modes of religious development that are common to stories of male and female enlightenment.

Body Symbols and the Primordial Ground

Yeshey Tsogyal is not just a mythical figure; she is a visualized symbol. Meditators cultivate an ability to imagine her in every detail and with brilliant color. Each part of her body is a focus for complex doctrines of Buddhist ontology, epistemology, and teleology. Yet her form, like the form of any deity in advanced tantric practice, is not the only focus for the practitioner, notwithstanding the training it takes to "see" and understand this figure. The primordial reality, the empty nature or basis, embodied as Yeshey Tsogyal is of deeper significance, both doctrinally and experientially.

I wish to contrast this style of religious practice in ritual with the model of ritual as delusion presented by Mary Daly as the Big Lie of the Eucharist.[43] Daly maintains that training participants to accept bread and wine as the body and blood of Christ, a change Catholic theology deems the greatest change there is, "prepares the way for further deception." [44] Her perspective is shaped by a conviction that such transubstantiation cannot in any sense occur. But her view is also shaped by two other assumptions: there can be no possible value in imagining such a change and there is no other valid way of construing the meaning of this ritual.

I am not arguing with Daly's valuable insight that the Eucharist or any other ritual enactment may become an injunction to delusion. Rather I want to suggest that the extent to which participation in the ritual has negative valuation (which, given our cultural framing of female identity as passive and "outside" reality, is particularly dangerous for women) is a function of the degree to which one ignores its possibilities in praxis. For example, one might engage in the Eucharist, understanding it as a viable means of transforming, not the bread and wine, but one's own inner life *in a way that one has already consciously determined* it should be transformed. The rite might be experienced as a contact with divine love or joy, imbibed so deeply that it resonates within as a possibility for oneself. To the extent that participants can distinguish their actual capacities from their ideals, this would no longer be passive participation in a lie. Such vibrant appropriation of any rite is difficult. It unites probing self-knowledge with a heightened engagement in ritual, a combination that is the antithesis of self-deceptive rote reiteration. A tradition's or an individual's failure to emphasize genuine contact with religious meaning, not just with the symbols of that meaning, invites alienation from and degeneration of a religious tradition, and facilitates an emphasis on surface symbols to the virtual exclusion of inner meaning. To recognize this is to perceive an important dynamic connecting the narrowing of a tradition's repertoire of symbols with its negative imaging of women. Such narrowing greatly impedes genuine contact— something that is difficult in any circumstance. In Needleman's words,

> The actual contact of forces is much, much more rare and difficult than one imagines. Surely, the great symbols of this contact, if they are mistaken for the inner event itself, can actually take one farther away from the truth. How much of the degeneration of Christianity—and of all religions—is due to this. In ritual, is not the aim the actual contact of forces within the individual? [45]

The androcentrification of religion is a major example of the altered role of symbol structures. Androcentrification depends in large measure on failing to focus on the "inner event," thereby becoming mesmerized by the surface of symbols. In Christianity, this is exemplified by the rigid imaging of divinity as male. This image has become so dominant as to overshadow what is arguably the all-encompassing nature of the divinity that it incompletely represents.

The role played by social, economic, and political forces in the degeneration of religious tradition is widely recognized. The deterioration of religious practice because of religious stultification must also be acknowledged. In these ways a religion can come to artificially exclude persons and areas of experience that correspond to the symbols excluded from the religious sphere. This is deadening. Any symbol or ritual is passive-fying in Daly's powerful vocabulary when it fails to open up experience—possibly to change it, but never to deny it—and proceeds irrespective of it.

Yeshey Tsogyal, appearing as the vibrantly red, unclothed Great Bliss Queen, is meant to symbolize a reality in which both men and women, divine and human, are equally grounded. It is not a question of experiencing this "reality" simply because it is said to be there, but because such experience is seen to have a healing and vivifying effect on those who successfully cultivate it.

As already indicated, Yeshey Tsogyal symbolizes this reality in two ways. Certain parts of her body are symbols by which the meditator calls to mind what has been learned or intuited regarding this metaphysical ground. The female organ itself (*bhāga*) signifies the "expanse of reality that is without limits or center." [46] This expanse, generally synonymous with emptiness in the Nyingma presentation, does not have a purely negative connotation. As the ground of all things it is their source and in this sense a womb.

> This womb of the mother-consort [Yeshey Tsogyal] is reality; it is the source of all Buddhas, the basis of all coming and going; the place of arising of all existents. [47]

The Judeo-Christian God created the world out of nothing. This nothingness stands outside the framework of existence. In the doctrine of *ex nihilo* the source, which is nothingness, must be left behind for existence to be manifest. [48] There is an important correlation between this position and Western psychological perspectives. In Western psychology, any inclination to reassociate with the maternal womb is viewed as regressive, impeding individuation and growth. By contrast, in the liturgy discussed above, the womb expanse is the matrix of production and of the things produced; it is not something left behind in the process of creation. In this context the wish to renew association with the womb or source is seen not as regressive but as developmental. It points to the birth of an understanding that fully recognizes the enduring source of existence, which is embodied as a female organ.

In most iconographical representations, the naked Great Bliss Queen's *bhāga,* entrance to the womb, is clearly visible. It is also represented by other symbols, most notably that of two equilateral triangles superimposed, like a star of David. Tibetan texts refer to this symbol as the source of phenomena and explicitly compare it to the "place of generation" of the consort Yeshey Tsogyal. [49]

Emptiness is the "place of generation" of all things, not because it is abstracted potential, but because it is the quality of things that makes it possible for them to be produced, function, and cease. Only in this sense can it be considered a ground of being; it is not on an ontological, physical, or metaphysical plane separate from the things that exist and are qualified by it. Thus, in enacting the liturgy and accompanying visualization of the Great Bliss Queen, *everything* visualized is understood to be a compassionate bodying forth of emptiness. Indeed, in preparation for practice of the ritual, the student studied and meditated to understand the emptiness that inheres in one's own person—especially one's mind. Ideally, it is from within an understanding of this dimension, in which far and near, subject and object, or creation and emptiness are seen to converge, that the visualization of the Great Bliss Queen emerges. She is a compassionate manifestation of the vibrant, empty, spacelike sphere of reality. In practices where a male deity is featured, he is seen as an embodiment of the emptiness principle in just the same way. Thus, although emptiness itself, as well as the consciousness that unites with it, is considered feminine, it appears equally as male, female, or inanimate thing. Everything that exists is "one taste" in being free from all types of reification as this or that. This allows the incorporation of an infinite variety of symbols and corresponding experience into religious activity.

In this view, male and female retain their individual character and functions but cannot properly be defined by these alone. No one pretends that it is easy to acquire a perspective harmonious with the doctrines of emptiness or primordial purity; from the perspective of the tradition itself, it is not paradoxical to find sexism or other prejudices in Buddhist societies. Practitioners are often reminded of how difficult it is to know things as empty. Thus, the presence of an egalitarian principle cannot automatically translate into an egalitarian society. The lack of widespread social egalitarianism suggests the extent to which the major principle of Buddhism can be lost and raises questions about socioeconomic, psychological, and other factors adversely affecting women. To the extent that an egalitarian or nondualistic perspective lies at the heart of Buddhist theory and practice, it is difficult for Buddhism to be used in support of a sexist or otherwise oppressive society.

It is difficult, and perhaps at this point impossible, to separate failure of religious vision from other psychosocial factors that combine to marginalize women. It is nonetheless a distinction that can sharpen analysis and methodology. This has been an attempt to trace certain dynamics operating between the religious and social spheres in terms of the relationship between female symbolism and women in society. Many further questions can be raised regarding the social effects, if any, of intense cultivation of certain meditative states of mind. For example, Buddhists claim it is possible to overcome, on the perceptual and cognitive level, all sense of subject and object as cut off from one another. Many religions describe different degrees or types of nondualistic experience. Are persons trained in such views less likely to perceive women as a secondary "other"? Are the techniques or meditations giving rise to such experience equally accessible to women and men? Assuming that transformation to some type of nondualistic perspective can be actualized, does the presence of individuals so accomplished significantly affect or become affected by social structures? Does this experience enhance or deplete the lives of women, the poor, or other marginalized groups? These issues must be dealt with cross-culturally. This discussion has been an effort to focus attention on one aspect of these larger questions, the relation of symbols to social realities.

Conclusion

Through focusing on specific customs, we have noted that although Tibetan women had considerable parity with men in the work sphere, both birth and wedding customs contained negative associations for women. Most significantly, women were almost universally excluded from places of power. Such exclusion is discordant with principles of egalitarianism at the heart of Buddhism; nevertheless, the female symbolism that expresses this principle is found side by side with symbolism that does not overtly challenge the nurturing role popularly associated with wives and mothers.

Such female symbolism is a vital component of Tibetan Buddhist practice and iconography. With some elements it reinforces cultural stereotypes, with others it transcends them—thus further confounding the issue of whether stereotypical female roles derive primarily from religious tradition or elsewhere. Further, how does social reality affect expression of the religious life? For instance, to what extent did Ayu Khandro's charisma harken back to symbolized female wisdom figures, and to what extent to the living example of her aunt? To what extent did she benefit from the egalitarianism of Buddhism, and to what extent from her own determination and the cooperation of her husband?

The ephemeral nature of these issues points to the difficulty of characterizing the effect of symbolic structures on society. Although Tibetan women apparently had more autonomy and status than their Asian sisters in China, Japan, or India, in general their lot

133

did not mirror the exalted status of the symbolized female. Why not?

The reasons why inner religious egalitarianism fails to translate into social egalitarianism are complex. The amalgamation of social, political, or economic power is one obstacle. Women were most systematically excluded from the monastic centers of power such as those that characterized the Gelukba order; in outlying areas, nuns or female tantrikas of the Nyingma order might study and sometimes live within the monastic confines. Female figures such as the Great Bliss Queen were more prevalent in Nyingma areas, and the opportunity for women practitioners was also greater there. Positive female imagery and the importance of female deities contributed to the relative ease with which women were accepted into the religious life. As in the case of Ayu Khandro, the family might object, but women were welcome in all Buddhist orders as nuns, and in orders not heavily monastic, it was possible for women to achieve considerable status as practitioners or teachers. Yet, as already noted, at the junctures of religious and political power, women were excluded.

From the Indo-Tibetan Buddhist perspective, a metaphysical juncture also becomes apparent. To become stuck in narrow symbolic expressions, or to fail to use symbols inclusively, is in part a product of the same type of error that the principle of emptiness or primordial purity is intended to contradict. Such error involves an inappropriate reification, not only of a symbol such as Yeshey Tsogyal (or a male Judeo-Christian God for that matter), but of the idea of truth itself. To the extent that "truth" is considered embodied otherwise than as a lived reality, or to the extent that "truth" is considered capable of being valued over and against living persons, there is room to push such persons aside in the name of that "truth." In a Buddhist context this can happen when the essential nature of things, emptiness or primordial purity, is treated as if it had a life of its own, apart from those persons and things whose nature it is. That sets the scene for women to be characterized in less exalted ways.

The ambiguity of women's situation is reflected in female symbolism. On the mythic level, woman's social role as nurturer and preserver is mirrored yet transcended in Yeshey Tsogyal's identity as preserver of the teaching and an awe-inspiring wisdom figure. Wedding customs also emphasized the nurturing role for women even though in family life her activities extended to other areas. The more intricate symbolism of the primordial ground or womb is the most unambiguously positive symbol for women and the most difficult symbol to translate into social reality. This is largely because the experience and subsequent incorporation of this principle requires a change in attitudes and perceptions to which one is deeply and unconsciously habituated.

It is primarily at the point of personal and communal integration that the flow from an egalitarian principle to a social reality is thwarted. There is no escape from this difficulty. For those who see religion as potentially able to transform individuals and societies, this is the place to take note of how religion affects what Needleman calls "the inner state of the subject." [50] This is religion's most vital domain. When a spiritual tradition's external institutions, symbols, or social structures are alienated from this domain, a religion's capacity to underwrite injustice increases. If Tibet is any indication, as I believe that it is, failure at any level—public or private—to emphasize personal appropriation of the inner religion as the starting point for social, symbolic, and other permutations of religious perspective is a major factor impeding full translation of, for example, positive female symbolism into full social equity for women. This appropriation would not be easy, nor its effects predictable. It is not at all obvious how one would extrapolate the significance of, say, primordial purity in social terms. Nevertheless, the first step is to define what must be remedied. In naming patriarchy and tracing its shape in a religious heritage, feminist scholars have uncovered the most prevalent instance of religion's failure to translate its core principles into social equity. From this derives an imperative to maintain that religious core as a presence distinct from the symbols embodying it and to alleviate failure of translation by articulating this core more clearly, as well as by reincorporating or newly creating the heart of religious experience.

Notes

1. See Clifford Geertz, *The Interpretation of Cultures* (New York: Basic Books, 1973), pp. 90–94.

2. R. A. Stein, *Tibetan Civilization* (Stanford: Stanford University Press, 1972), pp. 139–140. Originally published as *La Civilisation Tibetaine* (Paris: Dunod Editeur, 1962).

3. Rosemary Radford Ruether, *Sexism and God-Talk* (Boston: Beacon Press, 1983), p. 31.

4. Ibid., p. 37.

5. Jacob Needleman, *Lost Christianity* (New York: Bantam Books, 1982), pp. 16–17.

6. From an unpublished Tibetan manuscript dictated by Ayu Khandro, written by and in possession of Namkhai Norbu, professor at the Instituto Universitario Orientale, Naples. For a complete translation of Ayu's autobiography see Tsultrim Allione, *Women of Wisdom* (London: Routledge and Kegan Paul, 1984), pp. 236–257.

7. For a biography of Ma-ji Lap-dron, see Allione, *Women of Wisdom*, pp. 142–187.

8. For a description and the liturgy of this practice, see Khetsun Sangpo Rinbochay (Ithaca, N.Y.: Snow Lion Press, 1982; London: Rider, 1982), pp. 161–166.

9. For much of the discussion that follows I rely on ethnographic records made prior to the 1959 Chinese takeover of Tibet and on women's autobiographies. Half of the population is nomadic. For a discussion of the origins of the nomads, see Stein, *Tibetan Civilization*, pp. 109–112. See also the detailed study based on travels among them in 1951 in Namkhai Norbu, *Byong 'brog gi lam yig* (A Journey into the Culture of Tibetan Nomads) (Arcidosso, Italy: Shang-Shung Edizioni, 1983).

10. Charles A. Sherring, *Western Tibet and the Indian Borderland* (1916; repr. Delhi: Cosmo Publications, 1974), p. 329.

11. William Woodville Rockhill, *The Land of the Lamas* (1891; repr. New Delhi: Asian Publication Services, 1975), p. 229.

12. Ibid., p. 230.

13. Tseten Dolkar, *Girl from Tibet* (Chicago: Loyola University Press, 1971), pp. 13, 18.

14. Ibid., p. 8.

15. There were exceptions to this. The Nu-wang tribe in eastern Tibet, which was a political enterprise of sufficient luster to establish an embassy noted in Chinese Sui dynasty accounts of A.D. 586, was ruled by women until A.D. 742, when a male was elected. Subsequently this district was absorbed by Lhasa. The female sovereign's house had several hundred female attendants; the men had nothing to do with

government, their activities being limited to battles and cultivating the land. See Sherring, *Western Tibet*, p. 338.

16. See A. Klein, "Non-Dualism and the Great Bliss Queen," *Journal of Feminist Studies in Religion* 1 (1984).

17. Norbu, *Byang 'brog gi lam yig*, pp. 188–189, gives this term as *ga ma*. According to Tulku Thondrup, a Nyingma Lama from a nomadic family of the Golok area in Tibet, the term *go-ga-ma*, synonymous with the above, has wide usage.

18. Ibid.

19. Sir Charles Bell, *The People of Tibet* (Oxford: Clarendon Press, 1928), p. 169.

20. I. B. Horner, *Women Under Primitive Buddhism* (London: Routledge and Kegan Paul, 1930), reprinted in Delhi, Motilal Banarsidass, 1975. Horner suggests that this institutional bias was a concession to prevailing Indian mores in the context of which even forming an order of female clergy was a radical step. See also Nancy Falk, "The Case of the Vanishing Nuns," in *Unspoken Worlds: Women's Religious Lives in Non-Western Cultures,* edited by Nancy Falk and Rita Gross (San Francisco: Harper and Row, 1982).

21. Bell, *The People of Tibet*, pp. 193–194. For an autobiographical account of marriage arrangements in one of Tibet's most powerful noble families, see Rinchen Dolma Taring, *Daughter of Tibet* (London: Camelot Press, 1970), esp. pp. 66–104.

22. Bell, *The People of Tibet*, p. 192.

23. Norbu, *Byang 'brog gi lam yig*, p. 225.

24. For a good general discussion of Tibetan families, see Stein, *Tibetan Civilization*, pp. 94–109. For a focus on marriage customs among Tibetans on the Nepal border, see Barbara Aziz, *Tibetan Frontier Families* (Durham, N.C.: Carolina Academic Press, 1978), pp. 134–185.

25. Alan Winnington, *Tibet: Record of a Journey* (London: Lawrence and Wishart, 1957), p. 101; Bell, *The People of Tibet*, p. 179.

26. Norbu, *Byang 'brog gi lam yig*, pp. 190–191.

27. Ibid., p. 190.

28. Winnington, *Tibet*, p. 101.

29. *bag ma len mkhan* and *bag ma gtong mkhan*, respectively.

30. Norbu, *Byang 'brog gi lam yig*, p. 198.

31. Ibid., p. 202.

32. Tulku Thondrup in private conversation.

33. Nga-wang-den-dzin-dor-jay (Nga-dbang-bden-'dzin-rdo-rje), *kLong*

chen snying gi thig le'i mkha' 'gro bde chen rgyal mo'i grub gshung gi 'grel pa rgyud don snang ba (Commentary on the Practice for Emulating the Skyborne Lady, the Great Bliss Queen, from the "Great Sphere Heart Essence" Tradition of Long-chen-rab-jam) (New Delhi: Sonam Topgay Kazi, 1972), p. 15.6.

I thank venerable Tulku Thondrup for extensive discussions clarifying and supplying context for this *Commentary* and for the *Notes* cited below.

34. kLong-chen-rab-'byam, *kLong-chen-nying-tik* (n.p., n.d.), reprinted in *Aum* 356: 1–4; quoted by Jig-may-den-bay-nyi-ma ('Jigs-med-bstan-ba'i-nyi-ma) in *Rig 'dzin yum ka bde chen rgyal mo'i sgrub gzhung gi zin bris bde chen lam gzang gsal ba'i gron ma (Notes on the Basic Text for Emulating the Mother Knowledge Bearer, the Great Bliss Queen: A Lamp Clarifying the Good Path of Great Bliss)* (Gantok: Collected Works of Do-drup-chen, 1975), p. 470.1.

35. Needleman, *Lost Christianity,* p. 32.

36. Jig-may-den-bay-nyi-ma, *Rig 'dzin yum ka,* pp. 473.4ff.

37. Consider the following (ibid., p. 472.6):

A householder's wife said, "My good Lord, if you search [for wealth]

And I save [it], this house will be wealthy and prosper before long.

38. Ibid., p. 473.2.

39. Ibid., p. 474.4.

40. Ibid., p. 471.1.

41. Keith Dowman, trans., *Sky Dancer: The Secret Life and Songs of the Lady Yeshe Tsogyel* (London: Routledge and Kegan Paul, 1984), p. 84.

42. Ibid., p. 137.

43. Mary Daly, *Pure Lust: Elemental Feminist Philosophy* (Boston: Beacon Press, 1984), pp. 50–53.

44. Ibid., p. 51.

45. Needleman, *Lost Christianity,* p. 32.

46. Nga-wang-den-dzin-dor-jay, *kLong chen snying thig,* p. 43.1.

47. Ibid., p. 43.5.

48. For the major examination of this distinction to date, see Keiji Nishitani, *Religion and Nothingness* (Berkeley: University of California Press, 1982), esp. pp. 95–129.

49. Nga-wang-den-dzin-dor-jay, *kLong chen snying thig,* p. 44.2.

50. Needleman, *Lost Christianity,* p. 55.

Seven

"Your Servant, My Mother": The Figure of Saint Monica in the Ideology of Christian Motherhood

Clarissa W. Atkinson

Monica, the mother of Saint Augustine, has served for centuries as a model of Christian motherhood and a saint for Christian mothers. Her image, first drawn by her son in his autobiography, emerged and reemerged in later ages, always with modifications suited to a symbol for a new time. She represented ideal maternity, but the ideal took different forms in successive chapters of the history of parenthood and of Christianity. The shifting image of Monica sheds light on the development of an ideology that was promoted, for the most part, by celibate men, but has had a substantial impact upon Christian women.[1] However remote they are from the realities of people's lives, ideologies help to shape the expectations and assumptions within which women give birth and raise children. "Motherhood" is an idea and a social institution as well as a personal reality, and women who mother children (whether or not they give birth to them) necessarily participate in motherhood as defined and understood in their own societies.[2]

Our notions of good and bad motherhood are derived in part from models that live in the imaginations of individuals and societies. Like the "wicked stepmother," the "good mother" is a figure of fantasy, based on historical and religious and legendary models. In the Christian tradition, Mary is the preeminent Good Mother, but although ordinary women might emulate her virginity and her maternity (perhaps both, at different times in their lives), she was unique—not only because she was simultaneously virgin and mother, but also because her child was God. Good motherhood is almost as difficult to define as it is to achieve, and it is helpful to pull out strands, specific figures and images, from the rope that ties us to the ideologies of a particular religious or cultural tradition.

139

Within the history of Christianity, one such strand is the story of Monica—lived and recorded in the fourth century, constantly changing its shape and its emphases, and still powerful after sixteen centuries. The story has been used repeatedly, sometimes explicitly, to show mothers how to be good, as goodness was variously defined by the clerical men who held up her image and exhorted women to follow.

Monica in the *Confessions*

A successful autobiographer must be an artist in the reconstruction of memory. The circumstances, events, thoughts, and feelings that made up the writer's past are filtered through the lens of present needs, attitudes, and expectations. From the perspective of the present, certain episodes or relationships assert themselves as primary or crucial, while others disappear, "forgotten" as irrelevant to the shaping of a life into a story, a sermon, a poem, or a self-portrait. No autobiographer was more conscious than Saint Augustine of the protean nature of memory, or more respectful of the power of the will to make meaning. In his *Confessions* he set out to integrate the emotional and intellectual aspects of his conversion, to "make sense" of his feelings. He wrote of his childhood and youth from the vantage point of middle age, intending to discover and draw forth from his early experience whatever was of value in his maturity.[3]

Modern scholars have pointed out that to write the *Confessions* was to undertake a form of therapy.[4] If this is so, it is not surprising that a major aspect of the therapeutic work was to remember, reorganize, and come to terms with his relationship with his mother. Augustine was explicit about the priority he assigned to that task.

> There are many things which I do not set down in this book, since I am pressed for time. My God, I pray you to accept my confessions and also the gratitude I bear you for all the many things which I pass over in silence. But I will omit not a word that my mind can bring to birth concerning your servant, my mother.[5]

Because his relationship with Monica was central to his *Confessions,* Augustine included a wealth of detail, both words and feelings along with the biographical "facts." We have much more information about Monica than about other fourth-century women, but our knowledge is limited by the special, intimate perspective of a son who perceived his mother as focused entirely on himself and his salvation. He was a close, attentive witness with no claim at all to "objectivity."

Monica was the wife of a difficult, demanding man. She had two other children, a household, and a place in the Christian community, but from his birth in C.E. 354 to her death in 387, Augustine was her mission and her destiny. Her own assumptions about the meaning of her life, as these were perceived and interpreted by her son, were expressed in the comment she made a few days before her final illness.

> My son, for my part I find no further pleasure in this life. What I am still to do or why I am here in this world, I do not know, for I have no more to hope for on this earth. There was one reason, and one alone, why I wished to remain a little longer in this life, and that was to see you a Catholic Christian before I died. God has granted my wish and more besides, for I now see you as his servant, spurning such happiness as the world can give. What is left for me to do in this world? [6]

From this distance we cannot know whether these words reflect more accurately Monica's single-mindedness or her son's self-absorption; it may be both. The feelings of mother and son may have become so identified that their distance was erased, as in the early dream in which Monica, despairing, was told to look carefully, to "see that where she was, there also was I. And when she looked, she saw me standing beside her on the same rule." [7]

Augustine described his mother's upbringing in "one of those good Christian families which form the body of your Church," [8] and her marriage to Patricius, the unfaithful, hot-tempered man whose respect she won by her patience.[9] The major theme of her life, the pursuit of her son's soul, is a familiar story: when he tried to leave North Africa without her knowledge, she was "wild with grief . . . for as mothers do, and far more than most, she loved to have me with her." [10] She followed him to Italy and died there in the blissful certainty of his changed life. At the end, she renounced even the wish to be buried beside her husband, confident at last that God would "know where to find me when he comes to raise me to life at the end of the world." [11]

Augustine faithfully recounted and praised his mother's virtues. She was patient and strong, a peacemaker, obedient to ecclesiastical authority but persistent in the righteous cause of her son's salvation. She never admitted defeat, nor was she concerned about her own comfort and security when these interfered with her mission. Such virtues, of course, can be variously interpreted, for powerful, relentless, single-minded women are not always seen in a favorable light. Augustine, who at the age of twenty-eight had to leave for Italy under cover of night to avoid his mother, remained her child until (at thirty-two) he became her brother in Christ. This long childhood, or state of dependence and resistance, was extremely difficult, perhaps especially for a man who conceived of childhood as neither happy nor blessed. The "innocence" of childhood did not exist for him: "It was, then, simply because they are small that you used children to symbolize humility." [12] Mother and son existed in a state of extreme tension until after his conversion, when their relationship was transformed into one of siblings who were equally children of God. [13]

No matter how difficult Augustine found his mother when he scorned her "womanish advice" [14] at sixteen or left for Italy at twenty-eight, he never doubted her role in his salvation. Servant of God and agent of grace, Monica mediated his conversion by her prayers and tears. "In the flesh she brought me to birth in this world; in her heart she brought me to birth in your eternal light." [15] Monica did the work of the church as Augustine later conceived of that work, "compelling her lost sons to return," serving as "the instrument by which those who are found in the highways and hedges . . . are compelled to come in." [16] Like Monica, the church sought out and corrected the recalcitrant, nourished the feeble, and educated the immature. Long after their complex relationship was resolved by his conversion and Monica's death, the ecclesiology and theology of Saint Augustine were haunted by that powerful, pursuing maternal figure. As Peter Brown has said, "When he speaks of the 'hand' of God 'stretching forth' to 'snatch' him, he is thinking, more often than not, of Monica." [17] Not only the church but also God, whose grace could be neither dismissed nor denied, acted as a mother toward her sons, who were the elect.

Augustine's predestined salvation was accomplished through "my mother, your faithful servant, [who] wept to you for me, shedding more tears for my spiritual death than other mothers shed for the bodily death of a son." [18] Her tears resembled the water of baptism and the wine of the Eucharist, sacramental fluids whose purposes were accomplished *ex opere operato* ("on grounds of the performance of the rite").[19] Neither Monica's patience nor even her faith could have achieved such a work; in Augustine's theology, we do not earn our salvation or that of another through our merits, but by God's grace, which may be poured out in the sacraments. The power of Monica's tears was recognized by "the church" in the person of the bishop to whom she turned for comfort and advice when Augustine was involved with the Manichaeans. "Leave me," the bishop said, "and go in peace. It cannot be that the son of these tears should be lost." [20]

Certain letters and sermons and other writings of Augustine reveal aspects of Monica's personality and presence that do not appear in the *Confessions,* and for that reason tended to be lost to the "Monica" of later centuries. At Cassiciacum, where Augustine and some companions retired after his conversion to read and study and talk, she was not simply an honored guest (or a housekeeper) but a participant in the conversations of her son and his friends. Augustine said that Monica reached "the very height of philosophy" during a discussion of the good life. The company, "forgetful completely of her sex, believed some great man was seated with us." [21] In another dialogue, Monica herself commented that women were not usually included in philosophical discussions or mentioned in books of philosophy. Augustine replied that the character and talents of the participants were more important than their status.[22] More was involved than inclusiveness, which did not much concern Augustine or his colleagues. They were concerned about faith, and in the *Dialogues* of Cassiciacum, Monica is not simply herself, but the representative of uneducated Christians whose faith might be more valuable than the learning of philosophers. Furthermore, she was not just any woman, but a vehicle of illumination, blessed with the gift of mystical vision in dreams and the special ability to "distinguish between [God's] revelations and her own natural dreams." [23] In the *Confessions,* too, she was perceived as one bringing light; after all, it was Monica (not a bishop or philosopher) with whom Augustine reached out at Ostia to touch wisdom itself.[24]

The Figure of Monica in the Middle Ages

Augustine buried his mother at Ostia, honoring her last request for his prayers; he passed on the request to future readers of the *Confessions*. The enormous, continued popularity of that work ensured that the "historical Monica" (that is, Augustine's Monica) would not be lost, although she has been variously interpreted by successive generations. In the early medieval centuries, there was no public Monica, nor any formal veneration of her memory. Certainly she was known to those who knew the *Confessions,* but for the first millennium after her death, her influence was exerted most significantly through her impact upon her son. Augustine's understanding of God, the church, and human nature was painfully constructed out of the experience, conflict, and deep reflection of a genius whose psyche had been shaped in crucial ways by her unforgettable mother.

A few traces of attention to Monica's memory survive from the early centuries. An epitaph was carved into her tombstone early in the fifth century; a fragment of the original marble was discovered in 1945.[25] The verses were copied by pilgrims, and some copies survive, the earliest from the eighth century. But a few travelers do not constitute a cult, and there was no substantial recognition of Monica until the twelfth century. In 1162, a regular canon of Arrouaise traveled to Italy and took some of Monica's bones home to northern France. Augustinian canons and others who followed Augustine's rule[26] began to celebrate her feast on May 4, the eve of the conversion of her son. After her name and feast were admitted to the calendar, Monica's reputation spread with the Augustinians all over Europe. In the twelfth century the canons were busy promoting saints connected with their tradition, and Monica was a natural candidate for their attention.

Beginning in the thirteenth century, Monica began to assume some prominence in the devotional life of Christian people. The *Confessions* always remained the major source of information about her, but there were other sources, including popular *Lives* of Augustine and especially the chapter devoted to him in the *Golden Legend*. That collection of holy tales, collected and written down by Jacobus de Voragine in the thirteenth century, had a major impact on preaching and storytelling. It announced what was generally believed about the saints, and it also fed and formed the common understanding of their virtues, attributes, and activities. In the *Legend,* Monica appeared as the "mother who wept for Augustine and sought to lead him back to the truth of faith," and the chapter included the story of the bishop who assured her of the salvation of the "child of so many tears."[27]

By the later Middle Ages, the phrase and the notion of the "son of tears" had entered the consciousness of certain Christian parents. The phrase began to occur apart from any direct reference to Monica or Augustine, indicating the power and appeal of the story and the transformation of biography into mythology. Two of the eight children of the fourteenth-century saint Birgitta of Sweden were described by their mother as sons of tears. Their stories, related in her influential *Revelations,* helped in turn to establish and affirm a particular ideology of parental power and responsibility.

At the deathbed of her young son Bengt, Birgitta wept inconsolably, not so much for the loss of her child as over her conviction that his parents' sins were responsible for his illness. When the devil taunted Birgitta, Christ came to her defense. He announced that the disease had natural causes, that the boy would receive a heavenly crown, and that

> he shall now be called Benedict, son of tears and prayers, and I will make an end of his suffering. Five days later, a sweet song was heard, as if a bird sang between the boy's bed and the wall, and the boy's soul departed, and the Spirit said: "See what the tears have done: now the son of tears has crossed over to his rest."[28]

Bengt had never been strong, and in the months before his final illness Birgitta had been away from him, pursuing her vocation as pilgrim and seer. His death came at a time when she was tormented by conflict between her family and her vocation, afflicted with bad dreams about her children, and consoled by visions affirming her revelations and her way of life.[29] In a storm of grief and guilt at the death of her child, it must have been comforting indeed to hear the very words that were addressed to Saint Monica, paragon of Christian mothers.

The life of Birgitta's son Karl, who died shortly before his mother, was very different from that of his young brother. Karl was a perpetual source of anxiety, the only one of Birgitta's children to betray his upbringing or to shame his parents. But even

Karl was redeemed by the devotion to the Virgin that he had learned from his mother, and Mary came to assist his soul into the next world.[30] Despite that assistance, Birgitta continued to fret over the status of Karl's soul until she experienced an extraordinary vision. Her son stood in front of Christ as Judge: Mary, with an angel, stood on one side, the Devil on the other. The Devil complained that he had been robbed of a sinner's soul, and Mary replied that she had spared Karl because he loved and served her. The Devil argued that Karl, at an age when he could recognize sin for what it was, deliberately chose worldly pleasure over heavenly rewards. Then the angel spoke up and said that Karl's mother, realizing that her son was vulnerable to temptation, helped him "with workes of mercy and longe prayers." [31] She made him fear God so that he confessed and was absolved as often as he sinned. The Devil protested that he still had a whole sack of sins for which Karl had not had time to make restitution before his untimely death. When he looked, however, the sack was gone, and the angel announced that Birgitta's tears, pleasing to God, had broken the sack and destroyed the list of sins. Even venial sins were erased by his mother's "prayers and labour. For sche loued his soule with alle hir herte." [32] In the final dramatic scene, the Devil—crying and roaring—realized that he had lost even the memory of the sins and the name of the sinner. Then "the angel answered: his name is callid in heuen 'the son of teeres.' " [33]

Birgitta never mentioned Monica or Augustine in connection with the deaths of her sons. In the case of Bengt, her tears brought Christ to end the child's suffering, but Bengt's story is so unlike Augustine's that it is probably more significant that the comfortable words, "son of tears," echoed in her imagination. Karl's story is more revealing, for Birgitta obviously believed that she had obtained for him at least a "disposition to contrition," [34] and that her tears pleased God. She exerted her maternal power not only in the Christian upbringing of a child, but also for his salvation. Even though she had not been able to teach and persuade Karl to be good, she had prayed and wept for him effectively. Karl was no Augustine, but Birgitta might be a Monica—a saintly, powerful woman whose child was redeemed through her tears. The ideology of motherhood, at least for women with aspirations to sanctity for themselves, associated power and suffering, goodness and sorrow. Birgitta was one of several late medieval saints who were wives and mothers.[35] Such women, who experienced sharp conflict and anxiety over sexuality and family ties, could find reassurance and guidance in the story of Monica, whose maternal power was a force in heaven as well as on earth. Birgitta's *Revelations* were translated, copied, and widely read in fifteenth-century Europe, circulating the ideology of motherhood inherent in the notion of the "son of tears."

Among those who knew and admired Birgitta and her *Revelations* was Margery Kempe, a fifteenth-century English woman with a son who cost her many prayers and tears and whose sins produced a "face . . . full of weals and blubbers as if he were a leper." [36] In the *Confessions* Augustine had described his spiritual condition in physical terms; in Carthage his "soul fell sick. It broke out in ulcers." Later he saw himself "deformed and squalid . . . tainted with ulcers and sores." [37] Augustine spoke metaphorically; Margery Kempe, literally, but she certainly knew the story of his conversion, and she always referred to "St. Austin" in the context of reformed sinners.[38]

Margery firmly believed that her prayers and tears saved her son. At first she tried persuasion, and "many times she counselled him to leave the world and follow Christ, insomuch that he fled her company and would not gladly meet with her." [39] When he defied her, Margery asked God to teach him a lesson, and the young man suffered greatly. Soon he came back to his mother to ask her to beg God's forgiveness, "for he supposed, by her prayers, Our Lord sent him that punishment and therefore he trusted by her prayers to be delivered there-of." [40] She did as he asked and he was cured, physically and spiritually. At his early death his mother noted gratefully that "in good life and right belief, he passed to the mercy of Our Lord." [41] Both mother and son were convinced that her prayers caused his troubles and also his return to divine favor; God could not, or would not, deny the petitions of a holy mother. By the end of the Middle Ages, "good" Christian mothers possessed extraordinary powers and responsibilities for the spiritual state of their children.

Renaissance Woman

In fifteenth-century Italy the symbolic figure of Saint Monica developed in new directions while her cult, which was promoted by various influential persons and groups, became increasingly popular. Interest in Monica was greatly stimulated by the transfer of her relics from Ostia to Rome on April 9, 1430. Unlike the informal removal of some of her bones in the twelfth century, this transfer, or "translation," was an official act of the Roman Church. The influence of the Order of Augustinian Hermits was an obvious factor in the awakening of interest in their founder's mother,[42] but interest was not limited to the friars. The translation provoked a variety of responses, expressed in sermons and paintings and pilgrimage. The Augustinians promoted interest in Monica, but they could not have created such a widespread and enthusiastic reception unless she touched people's lives or satisfied needs that were not met in other ways.

The Augustinian humanist Andrea Biglia wrote a famous sermon on the occasion of Monica's translation—famous primarily because it was attributed (until quite recently) to Pope Martin V, who was given a great deal of credit for the renewal of devotion to Monica.[43] The attribution lent papal prestige to the sermon, which has been called the bull of canonization of Saint Monica.[44] In the fifteenth century, new candidates for sainthood had to undergo the official processes of the church. Monica was not a new saint, but her cult was new, and the supposed sermon of Martin V lent it a kind of official status.

The real author of the sermon was born in Milan in 1395 and joined the Augustinian Hermits in 1412. His scholarly career was short but productive; he taught rhetoric, poetics, and moral philosophy in Florence, Bologna, and Siena, and wrote extensively on literary and religious subjects. Biglia began his sermon on the translation of Monica with an account of her virtues as these were described in the *Confessions*. He praised the soul and body of the saint—her womb, her breasts, her arms—reminding hearers that Monica's entire body should be honored for bearing and caring for such a son. He described the discovery of her relics at Ostia and the procession that carried them to Rome, comparing the delight of the crowd on that occasion with the joy of the Roman crowd in antiquity when the Great Mother was brought from Phrygia.[45] The analogy displays more clearly the learned humanist than the devout friar, but it also expresses an underlying sense that Monica was not simply Augustine's mother but "Mother" Herself. The translation was glorified by miracles; a mother brought her sick child, and the crowds grew enormous when the child recovered from a desperate illness. When a second party returned to Ostia for the sarcophagus in which Augustine himself had placed his mother's body, there were more miracles, many of which involved the restoration of sight to blind persons. Biglia suggested that God wished by this method to honor the mother of the great doctor whose teaching illuminated the church, and also the tears she shed over her son.

Miraculous healing was expected of saints, as were acts of extraordinary charity toward the poor and sick. In another sermon attributed to Biglia, Monica was portrayed washing feet and binding up wounds. Biglia called her "the handmaiden of the poor"; in a contemporary Augustinian sermon, she was compared to the Magdalene.[46] The friars wanted their saints to possess the essential saintly virtues and abilities, and in fifteenth-century Augustinian writings, Monica acquired powers and attributes that had not been recorded in her son's autobiography.

Biglia was only one of several humanists who were attracted to the figure of Monica, and not all of them were Augustinians. Her "translation order" (an official document) was prepared by Maffeo Vegio, Datary of the Curia, who was in charge of the pope's correspondence. Vegio was born near Milan in 1406, wrote and taught poetry at Pavia, then joined the brilliant throng of scholars and artists who lived in Florence while the Curia was there during the Council of Florence (1439–43). When the papal court returned to Rome, he became a canon of Saint Peter's and a special favorite of Pope Nicholas V. In later years his interests turned more and more toward religious subjects, and he wrote saints' lives, religious poetry, and studies of Roman Christian antiquities. Vegio was responsible for the construction of Saint Monica's Chapel in the Church of San Agostino in Rome, where her remains were finally entombed. He paid for a new marble sarcophagus, composed her epitaph, and wrote several treatises in honor of mother and son. He was buried in Saint Monica's Chapel.

Vegio was one of several fifteenth-century humanists who were deeply interested in infancy, childhood, and education. These men were fascinated by human development—their own as well as that of others—and it was natural for them to look back to Augustine; with a few twelfth-century exceptions, medieval thinkers had not paid much attention (at least in writing) to their own psyches and their moral and mental formation. In his treatise *De educatione liberorum,* Vegio repeatedly recommended to parents the example of Monica. Chapter 20, in book 1, is entitled "So that parents may imitate the example of blessed Monica, mother of the blessed Augustine, in these matters." [47] He began at the beginning; like most contemporary writers on morals and family life he believed that women should nurse their own children. If this was impossible because of illness, then the wet nurse must be chosen very carefully. Vegio assumed that he had acquired shyness and timidity from his own nurse "as if he had taken in her heart and soul with the milk." [48] He may also have remembered Augustine, who at Monica's breast "suckled dutifully on his name, the name of your Son." [49] It was a common assumption that infants imbibed mental, physical, and moral traits along with the milk of mother or nurse.

Intellectual training had to be based on sound physical care, for education began at birth and shaped the whole person.[50] Classical literature, the staple of humanist education, was wasted on pupils whose characters and morals were not properly formed, and the classics had to be presented in a Christian context. Augustine, along with Ambrose and Jerome, was an excellent model of a classically trained Christian, and Monica was the ideal teacher for a young child. Because human beings were composed of body, mind, and spirit, schooling had to include Christian as well as classical texts and to prepare young people for life not only in this world but also in the next. Vegio's treatise was one of many Renaissance writings on education and family (for example, Alberti's *Della Famiglia*) that were well received and frequently reprinted.

In the 1450s Vegio wrote a new life of Monica drawn from the letters and sermons of Augustine as well as the *Confessions.* In that and earlier works he assembled a picture of Monica as the ideal elementary teacher who forms and sustains and nourishes the young child, so that it becomes capable of higher education, both spiritual and intellectual.[51] Rejecting medieval monastic and scholastic training, Renaissance humanists sought new teachers and new curricula. For the first time in many centuries, parents were recognized as first and best teachers, "natural" educators endowed by God with the authority and the responsibility to shape Christian souls along with minds and bodies. The humanists' confidence about the compatibility of classical and Christian learning, and their attention to human development, made the *Confessions* a major source for their educational theories. Even apart from the special interests of the Augustinians, Monica was a useful exemplar of Renaissance values.

Not only friars and scholars were interested in Monica. Even if the ecstatic crowds greeting her relics were exaggerated by Biglia, substantial numbers of pilgrims did visit her tomb. Many of these must have been women with children, for Eugenius IV established a "confraternity" of Christian mothers in Monica's name. Artists as well as afflicted mothers were caught by the general enthusiasm, and episodes from the *Confessions* became common subjects of painting and sculpture. That tendency was encouraged when Augustinian priors were required to have likenesses of Monica placed in their churches so that "devotion to the mother of our Father might be increased." [52] Aesthetic and literary and religious impulses tended to support one another during the Renaissance, when artists as well as philosophers and preachers found ways to praise divine and human beauty.

In the 1460s, Benozzo Gozzoli produced a series of paintings based on the life of Augustine for the Church of San Agostino at San Gimignano. The figures in these lively, colorful scenes resemble Renaissance courtiers, with fifteenth-century clothing and hair styles. As a young mother leaving her son for his first day at school, Monica is dressed entirely in white; her purity and refinement set her apart from the hearty confusion of the scene. In the painting of her death, she sits upright on the bed, dominating the group of watchers. Augustine stands by, gazing upward at the Christ Child, who approaches within a circle of light linked visually to the halos of mother and son. At the foot of her bed two naked children romp with a dog, unlikely participants at Monica's death, but common figures in Renaissance paintings.[53] Her wedding was portrayed by several artists, including Antonio Vivarini, whose painting (in the Gallerie dell'Accademia in Venice) sets Monica and Patricius in the middle of a group of larger and older-looking figures; the bride and groom look like children among the adults. The older, widowed Monica was usually painted wearing a wimple and carrying a book. In the painting by Girolama di Benvenuto (Fogg Museum, Cambridge), she appears with Augustine, the Madonna and Child, Nicholas of Tolentino, and John the Evangelist. Here Monica is an imposing figure who stands above her son, looking down at him and only at him, ignoring the Mother and the Child.

Artists, like humanist preachers, frequently presented Monica as teacher as well as mother, and they paid special attention to the childhood and youth of Augustine. Apparently they shared the widespread contemporary interest in families, especially in child raising and the relationships of parents and children, or, more accurately, of parents and sons.[54] Augustine's family was a popular subject, second only (among religious family groups) to the Holy Family itself, which was increasingly a focus of devotion and artistic attention. In the fifteenth century Saint Anne's cult flourished; people turned, as to a doting grandmother, to the mother of the mother of Christ.[55] The cult of Saint Joseph, promoted by such prominent churchmen as Bernardino of Siena and Jean Gerson, provided a model for married men, fathers of families.[56] By the last centuries of the Middle Ages, celibacy was no longer the exclusive path to holiness. There was a growing number of married saints, modeling new forms of spirituality for lay people, both male and female, and providing encouragement and training for those who hoped to raise good Christian children. Neither Saint Joseph nor Monica was a "new" saint, but they were represented by writers and artists in ways that called forth new kinds of devotion. Monica the teacher was important to those whose responsibilities included the care and upbringing of children. Women who lived with difficult or abusive husbands and recalcitrant children identified with Monica and were consoled by her cult, and their devotion was encouraged by their spiritual advisers. The cult of Monica as a substantial phenomenon began in Renaissance Italy, but it was not confined there. With the advance of Christianity throughout the world in early modern times, the figure of Monica, with its attendant ideology, spread through Europe and far beyond.

Motherhood Reformed

The renewal of interest in family issues and enthusiasm for family life that began in the later Middle Ages took new turnings during the reformations of the sixteenth century. The renunciation of "works" as a means of salvation led Martin Luther and his followers to decry monastic vows and clerical celibacy. Protestant pastors became exemplars of reformed family life as well as reformed theology. Husbands and wives, mothers and fathers, were taught to perceive their family roles and relationships as sacred callings. But Protestants, who denounced the veneration of saints as works righteousness, had little use for Saint Monica. For a time, Protestants preempted much of the energy and lively interest in family relationships that had been reflected in the attention paid to the "new" saints of the fifteenth century. The Roman church was slow to respond, tending (after the Council of Trent) to insist on parochial privileges, obligations, and rights over those of the family, whether nuclear household or wider kin group. In what John Bossy has called a "panic about Protestantism," [57] the hierarchy turned its back on "family" as it was being presented in Protestant books and sermons—that is, as a primary source of energy and consolation for individuals, as the kindergarten of Christian education, and as the major arena in which persons of all ages and conditions lived out their faith.

After the Council of Trent (1545–63), the Roman Catholic church retrenched on matters of gender and sexuality as well as domesticity. The council reaffirmed the necessity of celibacy for clergy and of cloister for all women religious, marking a step backward in the relationship of the male hierarchy of the church and the women whose lives were devoted to God, especially those who wished to serve God through service to their neighbors. The enormous practical and spiritual energy generated by the Catholic Reform inspired individuals and groups of women as well as men to discover and develop new modes of religious life, including, for women, teaching and nursing outside the convent. Thanks to the conservatism and sexual fears of the Fathers of Trent, and to the impact of the council on generations of bishops, much of that energy was dissipated in the struggle over cloister.[58]

Monica reemerged as a powerful and significant figure in the early seventeenth century under the sponsorship of Francis de Sales, founder of the Order of the Visitation and a leader in the French Catholic reform. De Sales, born in Savoy in 1567, became in 1602 the bishop of Geneva (in exile, since Geneva had been a stronghold of Protestantism since 1535). He preached and wrote extensively on the spiritual life, and his *Introduction to the Devout Life* was a central text in the renewal of lay Catholic spirituality. Saint Francis was a successful director of souls and specialized in the direction of women. Their requests for advice and consolation, and his replies, formed the basis of his *Introduction,* which offered a mode of mystical spirituality supposedly accessible to "everyone," meaning soldiers and housewives as well as monks and nuns. Of course it was not for "everyone"; like his letters of spiritual counsel, it addressed the needs of wealthy, wellborn people with the leisure to develop their spirituality in this manner. Nonetheless, his disciples were very different from contemporary groups such as the Jesuits; most of them were women, and many of them lived "in the world," with ties and obligations besides those of religion.

Saint Francis regarded himself as a missionary to the Huguenots, and he was well acquainted with the religion of Calvinist Geneva. He must have recognized the attraction of the notion of worldly vocation, the sanctification of ordinary life preached by Protestants. Like them, he believed that a holy, God-centered life could be lived at court or in the countinghouse as well as the convent, and that family roles were as valuable as the roles of professional religious (although he appreciated, as Protestants did not, the work of monks and nuns). He understood that domestic spirituality required special forms of expression, and he tried to develop a suitable system for married women. Convinced of the goodness of marriage and domesticity, Francis referred directly and positively to conjugal love. He believed that married people should be "moderate" in their sexual relationship, but he affirmed the basic goodness of physical intimacy against a powerful tradition that ignored or belittled human sexuality. Protestant reformers had lost no opportunity to parody and exaggerate as well as to differ with Roman Catholic teachings on marriage and sexuality, emphasizing the misogynist attitudes and "useless" lives of priests and nuns. Francis was notable among those reformers who helped the Catholic church to recapture a portion of the middle ground, continuing to praise and insist upon celibacy for those who could give their attention completely to God, but celebrating the special contributions of those who lived in families.

Monica was a perennial favorite in Francis's catalogue of married saints. Along with "the blessed Virgin, together with St. Joseph, St. Louis . . . and a hundred thousand others," [59] she was helpful to those who lacked the opportunities for single-minded devotion offered by the cloister. Her image and example played a significant part in his direction of his most famous disciple, Jane

154

Frances de Chantal. When Mme. de Chantal met Francis de Sales in 1604, she was a young widow with four children. She had made a vow of chastity after her husband's death in 1601, and had even thought of going to the Holy Land to live as a kind of permanent pilgrim. She may have known of Saint Birgitta's widowhood, children, and pilgrimage to Jerusalem, although she did not mention the Swedish saint. She certainly knew about Saint Elizabeth of Hungary (d. 1231), who was one of the first and most influential of the holy wives and mothers of the later Middle Ages. Mme. de Chantal consciously attempted to imitate Elizabeth, who had stubbornly avoided remarriage and devoted the bulk of her time, energy, and fortune to prayer and to the poor and sick. Mme. de Chantal's first director even resembled, in his excesses, the infamous Conrad of Marburg, who abused Elizabeth.

Some time before she met Francis, Mme. de Chantal experienced a vision of a man in clerical dress whose presence brought her great joy; she heard a voice saying, "This is the man beloved of God and among men into whose hands you are to commit your conscience." [60] Their intense relationship endured until Francis died in 1622. It is documented by an extensive correspondence— unfortunately one-sided, since Chantal burned most of her own letters when they were returned to her after Francis's death.

In letters to female penitents with children, Francis repeatedly reminded them that Monica's Christian motherhood began before her son was born, when she dedicated the unborn child to God. He associated Monica with the mothers of Thomas Aquinas and Bernard of Clairvaux, each of whom offered a precious child to God. Francis suggested that Mme. de Chantal try to appreciate the "religious" character of her life at home: her enclosure was the world, and her abbess, the Virgin. Her novice-mistress was Saint Monica, who could best supervise the spiritual formation of a true widow and mother.[61] When Chantal was worried by temptations and despair he wrote, "Together with your Mistress live long in tears without getting anything in return; in the end God will raise you up and fill you with rejoicing and will make you see the desire of your heart." [62] Francis took a hand in the raising of Chantal's children and a special interest in her only son, Celse-Bénigne. For a time, both adults may have believed that the boy would some day reward their attention as Monica's son rewarded hers. Francis wrote in 1604:

For the next point, it is indeed true that I cherish your son Celse-Bénigne and your other children with very special love. As God has put into your heart the desire to see them wholly dedicated to his service you must bring them up with this end always in view. . . . Have a copy of the *Confessions* of St. Augustine and read it carefully from the eighth book onwards: then you will get to know St. Monica when she was a widow and looking after her son, Augustine, and you will find much to console you in your own task. As for Celse-Bénigne, generous motives must be implanted in him . . . while notions of worldly glory must be cried down; but this should be done little by little. As he grows up we shall, with God's help, think of what particular course to take.[63]

Like Birgitta's Karl, Celse-Bénigne was no Augustine. He was a troublesome boy who grew into a violent man, and in adolescence he created one of the memorable scenes in the annals of Christian motherhood. In 1610, after years of waiting and planning, Mme. de Chantal left home to become the first member and superior of the new Order of the Visitation, an institute planned and developed by Francis with her assistance and cooperation.[64] At that time Celse-Bénigne was fourteen years old—nearly adult by the standards of that time, and already being educated away from home under the supervision of his grandfather. The eldest of his three sisters (then aged twelve) was married to Francis de Sales's younger brother, his youngest sister had recently died, and the middle girl would accompany her mother to Annecy, in Savoy, where the first house of the order was located. Mme. de Chantal had suffered through considerable trials as she prepared to leave home, but less from her children (whom she expected to continue to watch over) than from her old father and father-in-law, who were loath to give up her companionship and services. When the time came to say goodbye, and a sizable crowd had gathered, Celse-Bénigne wept and begged her not to leave him. As she moved toward the door he threw himself over the threshold and cried out, "I am too weak to hold you back, but at least it shall be said that you trampled on your own child." [65] The scene clings to the memory of Mme. de Chantal, who has been praised for her determination, denounced as an unnatural mother, and "excused" by those who believe that the boy's relatives put him up to it. Clearly, the model of Monica and Augustine was not a perfect fit. Augustine left his mother: she did not leave him. Mme. de Chantal did leave her son, although she continued to worry about his debts, his duels, and his salvation until his early death. She was much more concerned about him than about his sisters. When her eldest daughter died in childbirth, she wrote to her nephew:

It has truly . . . been a great grief to me to be deprived of the presence of this dear, amiable daughter, but . . . [I] embrace the divine will which has sent me this sorrow. There is much to console me in her happy and holy death, while I am almost in despair at the thought of the state of soul of your cousin (Celse-Bénigne). . . . Oh! the incomparable anguish of this affliction! No other grief, my dearest nephew, can come near to it.[66]

She was much comforted when her son died, not in a duel, but in a "good and Christian death" in battle.[67] He was neither a saint nor a genius, and his mother, no matter how much she worried, could not keep him always at the center of her attention. Her own spiritual life, her relationship with Francis de Sales, and (after 1610) her work in the Order of the Visitation increasingly claimed precedence over family concerns. De Sales and Chantal had planned their foundation so that women with family obligations could fulfill their responsibilities, and she herself continued to manage some of her children's affairs. But the model of Monica as novice-mistress, appropriate while Mme. de Chantal lived at home, was quickly outworn when she was no longer a novice or "in the world." Monica's child (at least according to his own account) kept his preeminence in his mother's life until his conversion, at which time her work was done. Mme. de Chantal had her own work, quite separate from her son's salvation.

Nevertheless, Monica remained significant to Mme. de Chantal in ways that probably were not suggested by her director. When she was dying, far from her beloved home at Annecy, she had read to her Augustine's account of the death of Monica and was comforted by the saint's indifference about her burial place, believing that Monica's resignation was "meant for her." [68] She listened also to the story of the vision at Ostia, the ecstatic mystical experience of mother and son. While she was dying, Saint Vincent de Paul was in Paris, praying for her soul. He experienced a vision of "a small globe of fire which rose from the earth to join a larger, more luminous globe, the two together then soaring up higher to mingle and lose themselves within an orb infinitely great and shining." [69]

Vincent understood the vision to refer to the mystical union of Mme. de Chantal and Francis de Sales, consummated in heaven when Chantal died. His sense of their relationship must have come largely from what Chantal told him—and for her, the vision of Ostia may have symbolized and expressed her own experience of mystical partnership with Francis de Sales. Celse-Bénigne never grew beyond the bad boy, but Francis—the saintly bishop who was a genius—could be identified with the adult Augustine.

It is extremely unlikely that Mme. de Chantal would consciously reject anything given or suggested to her by her director. Saints are multivalent symbols, used at different times by different persons for totally different ends. Francis used Monica the novice-mistress and the mother of the son of tears to teach patience, to preach a vocation to widows and mothers, and to strengthen the identification of motherhood and suffering. It is possible that Chantal, at least by the end of her life, may have replaced the Monica of Francis with a Monica of her own—the mystical companion of a beloved and extraordinary man.

Modern Times

Francis de Sales and Mme. de Chantal established the name and image of Monica in the Catholic piety of early modern Europe, especially in France. Teachers and clergymen who counseled and preached to women pointed to Monica's virtues, her rewards, and her sufferings. And as time went on, more and more of their hearers *were* women. By the middle of the nineteenth century, it was overwhelmingly women—not men—who came to confession and who filled the pews of parish churches on Sunday mornings. With mixed emotions, embattled leaders of the Roman Catholic church began to recognize their dependence on the faith and work of "ordinary" women.

In the struggle with "modernism" that occupied the hierarchy of the Catholic church in the nineteenth century, clerical leaders looked around for allies and discovered women: nuns, laywomen, female saints, and the Virgin Mary. Barbara Corrado Pope has discussed the phenomena of the Marian Age: both the official pronouncements of the church, from the definition of the Immaculate Conception in 1854 to the Assumption of the Virgin in 1950, and its acceptance, endorsement, and sponsorship of certain Marian apparitions and the associated mass movement of pilgrims to the new shrines.[70] Pope points out that the hierarchy made good use of some common nineteenth-century assumptions about men and women, their attributes, and their proper spheres. Not only in Catholic France, but in England, Germany, and the United States, middle-class shapers of culture expected women to be pious, self-sacrificing sufferers whose (limited) energies were expended on behalf of home, family, and church.[71] They were expected to use their influence to keep their sons—and, if possible, their husbands and brothers—out of the snares of vice, secularism, heresy, and unbelief.

Leaders of the French Catholic church assumed that symbolic as well as real women possessed specific "feminine" powers and attributes. Their most important model of womanhood was Mary, whose Son could never refuse her requests. But there were other powerful female saints, and Monica in particular was well suited to the needs of the church in the Marian Age. When the Dutch painter Ary Scheffer (d. 1858) painted the vision at Ostia in a romantic scene of ecstatic union, he struck a chord that sounded repeatedly during the nineteenth century. The painting sparked the enthusiasm of a series of biographers and devotional writers, including Émile Bougaud, whose *Life of Saint Monica,* written in 1865, perfectly exemplifies the "Monica" of that time. The first edition sold out in a few weeks. In the preface to the second, the author expressed his gratification at the many letters he had received from mothers of families, testifying to the inspiration and consolation supplied by his book.

Bougaud wrote the book, he said, to make mothers aware of the divine forces within them, to call them to their crucial work by exhibiting the purest, most perfect love in human history: a love that increased through tears and trials to triumph at last in the perfect communion symbolized by the vision at Ostia. To one mother he wrote, "Your son will be what you make him—good, pure, noble, fearless, fearing God—if you yourself have these virtues." [72] The mother worried that she would not be able to foresee and outwit the dangers to a young man in modern society, but neither she nor Bougaud questioned her responsibility to "save" her son. Bougaud simply reassured her of her duty and her power, strengthening her confidence and determination.

The message of the *Life of Saint Monica* was not restricted to mothers, although they were its primary target. Fathers, especially single fathers like the "incomparable" Frémyot, father of Mme. de Chantal,[73] were included in the challenge and the promise. Behind every saint or hero stood a great parent, usually a mother, whose achievements were crucial to their nation and their church. The preface to the second edition ends with this:

> Alas! neither bishops nor priests can re-make modern France unless Christian mothers will come to their aid. God has entrusted to mothers the cradle of man—the cradle, that is to say, of almost everything.[74]

Unless souls were followed, guarded, and guided by their parents from infancy through adolescence, and beyond, the modern world might sweep them away. Mothers, rightly indoctrinated in "traditional" values, were encouraged to use their influence even in the political sphere, as long as they used it on the right side and as long as the soul of a child was at stake. Bougaud repeated a story of an Irish patriot tempted by fears for his family to vote against his conscience. His aged mother appeared just in time, seized his arm, and cried, "Remember your soul and your freedom!" [75]

Bougaud believed that even Augustine, who loved his mother intensely, could not write about her as she deserved. He used Augustine's narrative, but filled it out with traditional stories and with the opinions and commentary of learned doctors and saints. The idea for the book came from Francis de Sales, who had recognized the value of Monica as a model for married women, and especially for the mothers of young Augustines. Bougaud described Mme. de Chantal weeping at the altar over her son, who had recently been involved in a duel and was in danger of the guillotine. Through her tears she heard Saint Francis saying, "Read the eighth book of the *Confessions*," and when she obeyed, she rediscovered Augustine saved by his mother's tears. She was immediately consoled by the belief that her own tears would save Celse-Bénigne— a presentiment that (in Bougaud's opinion) turned out to be correct.[76] Recalling that Francis's advice had helped mothers very much at a time when the Protestant Reformation caused them to fear for the souls of their children, Bougaud thought the same advice was even more necessary in his own time. With morals more corrupt than ever, with the homes and even the cradles of infants threatened by the horrors of "modernism," Bougaud advised:

Read the story of St. Monica; learn from that wife and mother to pray, to weep as she did, to hope always and never to be discouraged; and do not forget that if young men run today toward such great dangers, it is only because there are not enough tears in the eyes of their wives and mothers.[77]

A woman who was not sorrowful was not doing her work for the Faith, or for France.

In a comment on the growth and development of the cult of Monica, Bougaud remarked that she had to wait nearly a thousand years for the attention she deserved. God intended Monica for women with sons like Augustine, and during the Age of Faith, children had not wandered so far from their childhood religion. Monica was not easily visible during the Middle Ages because her image shone brightly only to eyes filled with tears. On the eve of Luther's Reformation, her tomb was opened and her image placed on the altars of Christendom. But she was not seen in her glory until Bougaud's own time, for no age had ever needed her so badly. For the first time since pagan antiquity, he said, boys of sixteen turned away from their early training and grew old without asking what they owed to their creator, or whether they had souls; they existed without hope or faith or the "gentler joys." Beside most of these wretched men were women—wives, mothers, sisters, or daughters—who saw the truth and were heartbroken.[78] For those women he wrote the *Life of Saint Monica.*

Bougaud was much encouraged by the increasing attention to Monica that he observed around him, and to which he contributed so much. In 1850 a little group of sorrowful mothers met in a chapel in Paris to pray and weep for their children. The idea caught fire; it became a formal Association of Christian Mothers under the patronage of Saint Monica, and spread through Europe and far beyond. In 1856, the association became an archconfraternity. The archbishop of Paris, meeting with representatives of the group to announce its elevation in status, took the opportunity to preach.

Ladies, if you wish to be true Christian mothers, keep your eyes on Saint Monica. . . . Follow the example of that holy mother, who by her prayers led her son into the ways of piety, and with God's help made him a great saint . . . perhaps you too have wept over your son. . . . Invoke Saint Monica; imitate her. It is impossible that the mother of Augustine would not remember in Heaven her cares on

161

earth, or that she would not take pity on your heart and win for you the conversion of a much-loved son or his persistence in virtue.[79]

Bougaud ended his book on a note of personal gratitude. Just as every true mother had to be in some respects a priest, so every priest required a mother's heart in order to help young Augustines find their way back to the Faith. At a time when church and family were hard pressed to keep the next generation within the fold, Monica taught him how to do the work of a priest.[80]

Bougaud's *Life of Saint Monica* inspired imitations in several languages. In 1910, the Catholic Truth Society of London published a *St. Monica* by Lady Herbert, a translation and abridgment of Bougaud. The introduction continued to offer the book to "the anxious, fearful mothers of these days";[81] apparently "these days" were no less threatening in 1910 than in 1865. But by 1928, when F. A. Forbes produced a new *Life of St. Monica,* there were new threats, and the introductory paragraph struck a different note.

> This book is above all things the story of a mother. But it is also the story of a noble woman—a woman who was truly great, for the reason that she never sought to be so. Because she understood the sphere in which a woman's work in the world must usually lie, and led her life truly along the lines that God had lain down for her; because she suffered bravely, forgot herself for others, and remained faithful to her noble ideals, she ruled as a queen among those with whom her life was cast. Her influence was great and far-reaching, but she herself was the last to suspect it, the last to desire it, and that was perhaps the secret of its greatness. The type is rare at the present day, but thank God! there are Monicas still in the world. If there were more, the world would be a better place.[82]

Like many another female figure before and since, Monica had been drafted into the battle against women who departed from the ideal—in this instance, the "new woman" of the 1920s. In H. F. Blunt's *Great Wives and Mothers* (1927), Monica was presented primarily as "the great patroness of grieving mothers" and the exemplar of "true motherhood," but the author did not fail to note that she "regarded her husband as her lord and master." [83] A publisher's imprint on the title page associates this work with others in a special class of pious literature with a purpose, stating that "clean literature and clean womanhood are the keystones of civilization." [84] Lives of Monica continue to appear, of course, and to change with changing times. In Luke Farley's *Saints for the Modern Woman* (1961), the chapter on Monica is entitled "Prototype of Prayer in Domestic Difficulties," and the author asserts that tact is a woman's best defense against being beaten by her husband.[85]

For her son, to whom we owe everything we know about Monica, she was Mother, and even Motherhood itself, as is every mother until her child grows up. Augustine's perceptions of Monica, and his relationship with her, were woven into his understanding of human beings and of God. His portrait of her survived, and because he was the most influential Christian theologian between Paul and Luther, her memory endures, shaping Christian notions of what motherhood should be. Augustine was not only her original biographer and creator of the historical Monica, but the first of a long line of clerical men who promoted her cause.

Although individual Christians knew about Monica during the Middle Ages, and the story of the son of tears became part of a maternal mythology, public celebration of her cult did not begin until the fifteenth century, when Italian Augustinians, artists, and humanists made her the subject of sermons, paintings, and treatises. She was always represented primarily as Mother, but also as the best of all teachers, whose work was essential to predispose the child to receive both higher education and divine illumination. Humanists believed that people could be taught to be good, and Monica, who pushed and dragged her son to sainthood, was a powerful symbol of the value of education.

In the early seventeenth century, the Roman Catholic church gathered its spiritual forces for the long struggle against Protestantism—a struggle that went beyond political and even theological ends to be acted out in households, families, and schools. Protestant reformers insisted that family and household were sacred, and that wives and mothers, as well as virgins, had a holy calling. Catholics had no intention of abandoning the ideal and practice of committed celibacy for their religious elite, but they had begun to appreciate the value to the Faith of "ordinary" women, who were essential to the church and to their families. Saint Francis de Sales used the model of Monica to keep Mme. de Chantal happy at home while her children were young, to reassure her about her son, and to serve as a "novice-mistress" in the formation of her spirituality. The record of Mme. de Chantal's incorporation of the model is much less clear, but I believe that *her* Monica, the mystical companion of Augustine, supported her vocation out of the world, away from home and family.

French Catholic clergy, hard pressed by "modernism" in the nineteenth century, turned for help to real and symbolic women. Women came to church, and women spoke in the confessional of their struggles with atheistic or indifferent husbands and sons. By supporting and promoting the new Marian Age, and by publicizing the virtues of female saints, the church enlisted feminine influence in heaven and on earth. Bougaud presented Monica as the personification of powerful, persistent motherhood. Her tears were salvific; her mission, the preservation of Augustine for the church. Her devotees were encouraged to be mothers of new sons of tears, and their mission was the preservation of the church from enemies within and without.

Historical personages fulfill the needs and expectations of different ages, changing as the times change. Men as well as women are made into symbols and legends; for such a figure as Francis of Assisi—or Abraham Lincoln—there is truth in the phrase "Now he belongs to the ages!" I believe, further, that the phenomenon is especially marked when the symbol is female, perhaps because women (even living women) are so often the objects of male fantasy. In past centuries, when very few women recorded their thoughts or feelings or observations, history was made almost entirely by men, who projected their wishes onto female figures and used such figures to teach and correct real women.[86] The process of saint making, occurring over centuries, offers an excellent opportunity to watch the birth, growth, decay, and transformation of ideologies. In the case of female saints, we observe the development of men's notions about "good women"; in the particular case of Monica, about "good mothers."

The image of Monica, varying through time, reappeared in many forms as new spokesmen defined her virtues and advertised her cause. Augustine's Monica still lives, but each age makes its own symbols, and each symbol speaks with many voices. According to one student of the *Confessions,* Monica spoke to her son with the voice of God, becoming "almost transparently the maternal presence of God Himself." [87] Through the figure of Monica, Christian women have been persuaded to incorporate and represent that "maternal presence of God"—a heavy requirement, but a persistent element in the ideology of Christian motherhood.

Notes

1. The impact of Christian ideologies is not restricted to Christians. European explorers, missionaries, and colonists carried not only their faith but also the attendant ideologies of their cultures to many parts of the world during the early modern period, and it is still true that persons who do not identify themselves as "religious" are profoundly affected by messages and symbols that originated in religious systems but have become figures and patterns in the secular culture.

2. The history of motherhood is now being studied as one aspect of the growing field of family history. Much of the interesting work is concerned with the eighteenth and nineteenth centuries: for example, Elisabeth Badinter, *Mother Love* (New York: Macmillan, 1981). The notion of motherhood as an institution was clearly stated by Adrienne Rich in *Of Woman Born* (New York: Norton, 1976); see also Dorothy Dinnersteen, *The Mermaid and the Minotaur* (New York: Harper & Row, 1976). In *The Reproduction of Mothering* (Berkeley: University of California Press, 1978), Nancy Chodorow approaches the subject from the perspective of psychoanalysis; in *The Politics of Reproduction* (Boston: Routledge and Kegan Paul, 1981), Mary O'Brien works from the perspective of political science.

3. In *Augustine of Hippo* (Berkeley: University of California Press, 1969), Peter Brown wrote: "The *Confessions* is very much the work of a man who had come to regard his past as a training for his present career" (p. 162).

4. Among the several scholars who have discussed the *Confessions* as a form of therapy are Brown, *Augustine*, chap. 16, and Margaret R. Miles, "Infancy, Parenting, and Nourishment in Augustine's *Confessions*," *Journal of the American Academy of Religion* 50 (1982): 349–364.

5. R. S. Pine-Coffin, ed. and trans., *St. Augustine: Confessions* (London: Penguin Books, 1961), bk. 9, chap. 8.

6. Ibid., chap. 10.

7. Ibid., bk. 3, chap. 11.

8. Ibid., bk. 9, chap. 8.

9. Augustine praised his mother for her successful circumvention of

Patricius's violence; when other women appeared with bruised faces, Monica reminded them that they were bound "to serve their husbands, and from that time onward they should remember their condition and not defy their masters" (ibid., bk. 9, chap. 9). Apparently, both Monica and Augustine believed the women were responsible for the beatings.

10. Ibid., bk. 5, chap. 8.

11. Ibid., bk. 9, chap. 11.

12. Ibid., bk. 1, chap. 19. Miles discusses Augustine's horror of infancy in "Infancy, Parenting," p. 353. She also points out (pp. 362–363 that when he wrote the *Confessions,* Augustine had not worked out the full doctrine of original sin which he developed later in conflict with the Pelagians. I believe that the notion of the newborn child as a kind of "carrier" of original sin is adumbrated here.

13. Augustine asked God to inspire readers of his book to remember "those who were not only my parents in this light that fails, but were also my brother and sister, subject to you, our Father, in our Catholic mother the Church, and will be my fellow citizens in the eternal Jerusalem" (ibid., bk. 9, chap. 13). This development in his relationship to his parents is discussed by Miles, "Infancy, Parenting," pp. 359–360, and by Robert J. O'Connell, *St. Augustine's Confessions* (Cambridge: Belknap Press, 1969), pp. 106–119.

14. *Conf.,* bk. 1, chap. 3.

15. Ibid., bk. 9, chap. 8.

16. In the "Treatise Concerning the Correction of the Donatists," Augustine used the parable of the Great Supper to justify the coercion of heretics and schismatics by the church. See P. Schaff, ed., *Select Library of the Nicene and Post-Nicene Fathers,* vol. 4 (Buffalo: The Christian Literature Company, 1887), p. 62.

17. Brown, *Augustine,* p. 175.

18. *Conf.,* bk. 3, chap. 11.

19. H. A. Oberman, *The Harvest of Medieval Theology* (Grand Rapids: Wm. B. Eerdmans Publishing Company, 1967), p. 467.

20. *Conf.,* bk. 3, chap. 12.

21. Ruth Allison Brown, ed. and trans., *S. Aureli Augustini De beata vita* (Washington, D.C.: The Catholic University of America, 1944), p. 77.

22. P. Knoell, ed., *S. Aureli Augustini De Ordine Libri Duo* (Vindobonae, Hoelder-Pichler-Tempsky, 1922), pp. 142–143. Augustine claimed that his mother loved wisdom even more than she loved him, and that her great love of wisdom made her eligible to discuss philoso-

phy (*De Ordine* I.10.32). Peter Brown says that Augustine perceived Monica at Cassiciacum as an "oracle of primitive Catholic piety" (Brown, *Augustine,* p. 118).

23. *Conf.,* bk. 6, chap. 13.

24. The vision at Ostia (an experience of mystical ascent and union with the divine) is described in *Conf.,* bk. 9, chap. 10. O'Connell believes that Augustine's attitude toward Monica reveals that "the ancient world's view of woman is undergoing metamorphosis" (*Augustine's Confessions,* p. 114), that "in a theory of man as essentially soul, such contingent relationships as those of parents and children are doomed to slide about" (p. 110), and that at Ostia, they were "no longer 'mother' or 'son' but merely soul with companion soul" (p. 117), reaching an ideal state in which woman's inferiority was left behind. If in order to leave behind inferiority, one must also abandon bodies, relationships, and gender, the significance of the "metamorphosis" is strictly limited.

25. See A. Casamassa, "Ritrovamento di parte dell'elogio di S. Monica," *Scritti Patristici* (Rome, Facultas Theologica Pontificii Athenaei Lateranensis, 1955), vol. 1, pp. 215–218.

26. "Regular canons" were cathedral clergy living under quasi-monastic rule. In the late eleventh century, canons in southern France and Italy began to form communities with a formal structure of work, prayer, and celibacy, although they did not take monastic vows. Their lives and work were approved by the reformed popes, successors of Gregory VII, and their customs spread through Europe during the twelfth century. Many of these communities adopted the Rule of St. Augustine, which was based on a letter written by Augustine to a group of women in Hippo who had asked his advice about living a religious life together. The rule was general and flexible enough to be used by many different groups in the twelfth and thirteenth centuries, when the foundation of new orders with new rules was discouraged by the papacy.

27. Granger Ryan and Helmut Ripperger, eds., *The Golden Legend of Jacobus de Voragine* (New York: Arno Press, 1969), p. 487.

28. Isak Collijn, ed., *Birgerus Gregorii Legenda S. Birgitte* (Uppsala: Almquist and Wiksells, 1946), p. 21.

29. See Johannes Joergensen, *Saint Bridget of Sweden* (New York: Longmans Green, 1954), vol. 1, pp. 219–223. The Virgin reassured Birgitta as follows: "Mary, daughter of Joachim, who is the Mother of God, will be a mother to the children of Ulf and Birgita." Lennart Hollman, ed., *Den heliga Birgitta's Revelaciones Extravagantes* (Uppsala: Almquist and Wiksells, 1956), cap. 63, p. 185.

30. W. P. Cumming, ed., *The Revelations of Saint Birgitta* (London: Oxford University Press, 1929), pp. 117–118.

31. Ibid., p. 120.

32. Ibid., p. 122.

33. Ibid., p. 123.

34. In a fifteenth-century English manuscript of the *Revelations,* there is a marginal gloss: "Marke how pe modres prayers purchesyth disposicion to contricion of hyr sone," indicating that this point was understood and reinforced by a contemporary commentator on Birgitta's text (Cumming, *Revelations,* p. 120).

35. See my article " 'Precious Balsam in a Fragile Glass': The Ideology of Virginity in the Later Middle Ages," *Journal of Family History* 8 (1983): 131–143.

36. W. Butler-Bowdon, ed., *The Book of Margery Kempe* (New York: Devin-Adair, 1944), p. 202.

37. *Conf.,* bk. 3, chap. 1; bk. 8, chap. 7.

38. Butler-Bowdon, *Margery Kempe,* p. 230: "St. Austin" is listed with "Mary Magdalene, Mary of Egypt, and St. Paul."

39. Ibid., p. 201.

40. Ibid., p. 202.

41. Ibid., p. 205.

42. The Order of Hermits of St. Augustine (OSA) was a mendicant order based on a thirteenth-century union of eremitic communities, most of which were in northern Italy. Certain Tuscan communities requested that the pope unite them in one order under one rule; this was done in 1244, and in 1256, at the first general chapter of the order, the Italians were joined by communities from Germany, Spain, France, and England. Augustinian Hermits were friars who led mixed lives of action and contemplation, and they emphasized education for their members. By at least 1419 the order had begun to insist that its various houses celebrate the Feast of St. Monica. See Antonio do Rosario, OP, and Carlos Alonso, OSA, "Actas Inéditas de Diez Capítulos Generales: 1419–1460," *Analecta Augustiniana* 42 (1979): 39, 45.

43. For a thorough discussion of the authorship of the sermon, see Antonio Casamassa, "L'Autore di un pretoso Discorso di Martino V," *Miscellanea Pio Paschini* (Rome, Facultas Theologica Pontificii Athenaei Lateranensis, 1949), vol. 2, pp. 109–125. See also Rudolph Arbesmann, OSA, "Andrea Biglia, Augustinian Friar and Humanist," *Analecta Augustiniana* 28 (1965): 187, n. 117. In 1430, the chapter general of the order ordered perpetual masses for the soul of Martin V in recog-

nition of the translation of Monica; see Rosario and Alonso, "Actas Inéditas," p. 63.

44. Ludwig Pastor, *The History of the Popes,* vol. 1 (St. Louis: Herder, 1899), p. 231.

45. Arbesmann, "Andrea Biglia," p. 87, summarizes the sermon, including the comment on the Great Mother.

46. Valeria Leccesi, "Un Codice Quattrocentesco di Prediche di Autore Agostiniano Nella Biblioteca Francescana di Falconara Marittima," *Analecta Augustiniana* 44 (1981): 156.

47. Maria W. Fanning, ed., *Maphei Vegii Laudensis De Educatione Liberorum Et Eorum Claris Moribus, Libri Sex; A Critical Text of Books I–III,* Washington, D.C.: Catholic University of America Studies in Medieval and Renaissance Latin, vol. 1 (1933), p. 48.

48. Ibid., pp. 25–26. On wet-nursing in this time and place (and on Vegio), see also James Bruce Ross, "The Middle-Class Child in Urban Italy, Fourteenth to Early Sixteenth Century," in Lloyd de Mause, ed., *The History of Childhood* (New York: Harper & Row, 1974), pp. 184–196.

49. *Conf.,* bk. 3, chap. 4.

50. Vegio's educational theories are discussed by D. Bruno Vignati, "Maffeo Vegio, Umanista Cristiano," *Lodigiani Illustri* 9 (1959): 25–26.

51. Ibid., p. 25.

52. Rosario and Alonso, "Actas Inéditas," p. 61. The Augustinians commissioned painters and sculptors to create "images" of Monica; they also contributed to the beautification of her tomb in Rome (p. 59).

53. Ross, "Middle-Class Child," pp. 204–205, discusses the *putti* or "angel-children" of Renaissance painting and concludes that these "ideal" children tell us little about the lives of real children in that time and place. In Gozzoli's scene the children are not *putti* but real children, and their presence may say something about fifteenth-century attitudes toward birth and death, both of which generally happened at home, and not in an institution.

54. As Joan Kelly warned in her article "Did Women Have a Renaissance?" in Renate Bridenthal and Claudia Koonz, eds., *Becoming Visible: Women in European History* (Boston: Houghton Mifflin, 1977), it would be dangerous to assume that Renaissance educational theory applied to girls as well as boys. Most writers on education were men, and they were specially concerned with the raising of sons, despite the interest in women's education so often mentioned in traditional Renais-

sance historiography. On this subject, see articles by Margaret Leah King, including "Book-lined Cells: Women and Humanism in the Early Italian Renaissance," in P. Labalme, ed., *Beyond Their Sex: Learned Women of the European Past* (New York: New York University Press, 1980), pp. 66–90.

55. Martin Luther, among others, turned to Saint Anne when he was terrified by a thunderstorm; he promised her that if he survived, he would become a monk.

56. See the discussion by David Herlihy, "The Making of the Medieval Family: Symmetry, Structure, and Sentiment," *Journal of Family History* 8 (1983): 127–128.

57. John Bossy, "The Counter-Reformation and the People of Catholic Europe," *Past and Present* 47 (1970): 70.

58. See Bossy's "Editor's Postscript" to H. O. Evennett, *The Spirit of the Counter-Reformation* (Notre Dame: University of Notre Dame Press, 1968), p. 144.

59. John K. Ryan, trans. and ed., *St. Francis de Sales: Introduction to the Devout Life* (New York: Harper & Row, 1966), p. 59.

60. Quoted in Elisabeth Stopp, *Madame de Chantal* (London: Faber, 1962), p. 45.

61. Saint Francis believed that "if they [widows] are inclined to seek a man's love, they are not widows indeed" (*Introduction to the Devout Life,* p. 157). He objected to "true widows" wearing any ornaments, and chided Mme. de Chantal about the lace on her cap at one of their first meetings (Stopp, *Chantal,* p. 57).

62. Elisabeth Stopp, ed. and trans., *St. Francis de Sales: Selected Letters* (London: Harper & Row, 1960), p. 98.

63. Ibid., p. 68.

64. The Order of the Visitation was originally planned as a mixed (active and contemplative) order for women who were not suited to traditional convents because of physical infirmity or another reason. Saint Francis hoped to attract women like Mme. de Chantal, many of whom would be widows, who wished to lead a life of contemplative prayer while serving the poor and the sick of the neighborhood. Before very long, the hierarchy—in the person of the archbishop of Lyon—imposed perpetual cloister. The order was very popular; when Francis de Sales died in 1622, there were already thirteen houses.

65. Quoted in Stopp, *Chantal,* p. 110.

66. Sisters of the Visitation, trans., *Selected Letters of Saint Jane Frances Chantal* (New York: Kenedy, 1918), p. 60.

67. Ibid., p. 176.

68. Quoted by Stopp, *Chantal,* p. 249.

69. Ibid., p. 250.

70. See chapter 8, "Immaculate and Powerful: The Marian Revival in the Nineteenth Century," by Barbara Corrado Pope.

71. Much has been written on the subject of gender ideology in the nineteenth century, and on the notion of masculine and feminine "spheres" and attributes. See, for Germany, Marilyn Chapin Massey, *Feminine Soul* (Boston: Beacon Press, 1985). Middle-class English women were encouraged to model themselves on the "angel in the house," while American women participated in "the cult of true womanhood"; see the article of that name by Barbara Welter in *American Quarterly* 18 (1966): 151–162, 173–174. For a different approach to the uses of "women's sphere," see chapter 9, "In Christian Firmness and Christian Meekness: Feminism and Pacifism in Antebellum America," by Dorothy C. Bass.

72. Émile Bougaud, *Histoire de Sainte Monique* (Paris: C. Poussielgue, 1901), p. 26.

73. Ibid., p. 34.

74. Ibid., p. 22.

75. Ibid.

76. Ibid., p. 520.

77. Ibid., p. 56.

78. Ibid., p. 522.

79. Ibid., pp. 525–526.

80. Ibid., pp. 528–529.

81. Lady Herbert, *The Life of St. Monica* (London: Catholic Truth Society, 1910), p. iii.

82. F. A. Forbes, *The Life of St. Monica* (St. Louis: Herder, 1928), frontispiece.

83. H. F. Blunt, *Great Wives and Mothers* (New York: Devin-Adair, 1927), pp. 44, 68, 48.

84. Ibid., frontispiece.

85. "While wife-beating is certainly not recommended by anyone today, and although it is a cause for temporary separation in Church courts, Monica's advice ('Lay the blame rather on yourselves and your tongues. Guard your tongue when your husband is in a passion') could well be followed by some women of our day, who feel obliged to have the last word, infuriating to a dangerous pitch an already aroused temper on the part of their husbands" (Luke Farley, *Saints for the*

Modern Woman [Boston: St. Paul Editions, 1961], pp. 174–175).

86. The most extreme examples of legend and saint making have occurred in connection with women who were significant in both the religious and political spheres: Joan of Arc and Mary Queen of Scots. For the stories of their legends, see Marina Warner, *Joan of Arc: The Image of Female Heroism* (New York: Knopf, 1981), and J. E. Phillips, *Images of a Queen: Mary Stuart in Sixteenth-century Literature* (Berkeley: University of California Press, 1964).

87. O'Connell, *Augustine's Confessions,* p. 47.

Eight

Immaculate and Powerful: The Marian Revival in the Nineteenth Century

Barbara Corrado Pope

The nineteenth century witnessed a popular and official resurgence in the veneration of Mary throughout the Catholic world. Indeed, so great was this revival that leaders of the church call the years between 1850 and 1950 the Marian Age. The papacy demarcated this era by defining two controversial dogmas about the Mother of Christ: the Immaculate Conception, in 1854, and the Assumption of the Virgin, in 1950. The many reported apparitions of the Virgin throughout southern and western Europe, some of which gained widespread fame and church approval, were another sign of the rise in Marian fervor. Among these visions were those in Paris (1830), LaSalette (1846), Lourdes (1858), and Pontmain (1871), all in France; Fátima, Portugal (1917); and Beauraing (1932) and Banneaux (1933) in Belgium. With few exceptions, these apparitions aroused great hopes and fears, and their sites eventually attracted pilgrims from all walks of life.

The French visions set the pattern for later events. The image of the Immaculate Conception that Sister Catherine Labouré saw and recorded became the dominant image of the Virgin throughout Europe and the United States. And Lourdes remains the most popular of all Christian shrines and the most important site of miraculous healing in the world. In each of the last few years, over four million people have traveled to this little town in the Pyrenees. Lourdes still attracts twice as many pilgrims as Mecca, although, unike Mecca, it represents neither an obligation of religious practice nor a central focus of a world faith.[1]

How, then, can we understand the rise and endurance of modern Marian devotion? Some faithful Roman Catholics might answer that the renaissance in Marian devotion was part of a divine plan, that the Mother of God intervened in human history to counsel us about the need for redemption. Some Jungians might see in these events the reassertion of the female principle, either supernaturally or in the minds of those open to the message that religion and culture had become too masculine. Neither of these responses is fully satisfactory. Reports of visions and apparitions have been endemic to Catholicism. Some are approved, and attract great followings. Others are discouraged by the church, slighted and forgotten. I assume that at least part of the reason why these Marian apparitions took on such importance lies in their social, political, and cultural context, that is, in their purely human history.

An important part of that history is the onset of the modern French pilgrimage movement in 1873. The practice of journeying to a sacred place is common to Islam and Hinduism as well as to Christianity. In both ancient and medieval times, many Christians undertook long and arduous journeys to be cured of their spiritual or physical ills and to see and touch holy places and objects. But by the eighteenth century, most pilgrimages, at least in France, were local in character, and most of the practitioners were peasants following their village or "folk" traditions. Since the Catholic Reformation of the sixteenth century, there had been an increasing division between the official, orthodox church, bent on "purifying" the faith, and those who believed in extrasacramental miraculous powers.[2] Although pilgrimages were condemned as superstitious or pagan by some clergymen, many Catholics continued to journey to special holy places, where they could literally touch, or, in the case of fountains, immerse themselves in, the sacred powers, as their ancestors had done.

Frequently entire villages made annual treks to a nearby shrine, image, or fountain to offer sacrifices and pray for good crops, the health of their livestock, and cures for their own ills. Personal or national crises also induced people to participate in this form of sacrifice and prayer. Women, in particular, used pilgrimages for their own needs: to provide them with occasions for all-female sociability and to petition the Virgin or the local patron saint for aid with problems of sexuality and reproduction.[3] As Fatima Mernissi has shown in her work on contemporary Moslem saints' shrines in North Africa, these unorthodox traditions also offer women a sense of empowerment and autonomy.[4] It is not surprising that such activity could be seen as a danger to orthodox belief.

By 1873 the official attitude had changed, and the church had moved to tie these potentially subversive impulses to the sacramental system.[5] As we will see, the modern pilgrimage movement was an expression of political discontent as well as religious fervor, yet the sheer number of pilgrims involved reinforced the religious legitimacy of the new symbols. This new form of devotion was also an adaptation to an increasingly urban and industrial society. In the end it sapped the power of local French shrines and created a mass rather than "folk" religious culture, a culture tied to national and international rather than local systems. This religious culture relied upon modern mass production while it condemned modern political ideology.[6]

That Mary should be the focus of this new devotion is not surprising. The Virgin is the embodiment of what patriarchal Catholic theology had always defined as "good" feminine qualities: chastity, humility, and maternal forgiveness. At least since the late Middle Ages the faithful have seen her as the last resort, the intercessor between humanity and God who would help in times of direst need.[7] As nineteenth-century Catholics increasingly saw themselves in a state of siege against the modern world, they turned to those symbols that promised comfort. Further, Mary's supernatural role reflected what most French people knew in a more intimate way. In both the city and the country, women were the first teachers of moral lessons and religious stories. They were more often in charge of mediating dissension between paternal authority and their children.[8] Since religion and understanding were learned, so to speak, at mother's knee, it should not be surprising that the most readily seen and accepted visions took the form of a mediating mother.

The Apparitions

In 1830 the Virgin of the Miraculous Medal appeared several times to an uneducated country nun living at the Sisters of Charity in the Rue du Bac. During the first apparition the Virgin spoke at great length to the humble Catherine Labouré and warned that troubles would soon beset France. She prophesied that the cross would be treated with contempt and that blood would flow. This was the explicitly political content of the vision, which later interpreters took to predict the French revolutions of 1830, 1848, and 1871.

Labouré's later visions brought a more explicitly religious message and gave her a mission. The Virgin appeared within an oval; standing on a globe. Her feet trod on a snake, which represented Satan. She was dressed in white with a blue mantle (the colors of innocence and purity, and of royalist France). Her arms were extended downward and out. Her fingers were covered with rings of precious stones. From them radiated rays that symbolized the graces the Virgin would grant her devotees. Around the top of the oval ran the words "O Mary conceived without sin, pray for us who have recourse to thee." The vision asked that a medal be struck in this image.

Père Aladel, Labouré's confessor, showed a drawing of the image and explained its origins to the archbishop of Paris, Quélen, who authorized the pressing of the medals. Within ten years, millions of these images in gold, silver, and cheaper metals had been distributed throughout the world.[9] Accounts of miraculous cures and, especially, of spectacular conversions helped to spread the fame of this medal and fostered belief in its efficacy.

This image did not add any new elements to the symbolism of the Virgin, but its popularity did make some aspects more important than others and promoted a uniform, even universal notion of what she looked like. Both Bernadette of Lourdes and the visionaries of Pontmain described one of the stances of their apparitions as "like the Miraculous Medal, but without the rays." [10] Since these descriptions come from children living in relatively remote regions of France, these comments indicate how widely the image had spread. The coloration of blue and white (or simply white in some reproductions) reappeared at Lourdes, Fátima, Beauraing, and Banneaux. This is in contrast to earlier depictions of the Virgin, which were often multicolored and followed local cults.

Symbolically, Labouré's image of the Virgin projected a double message of hope and warning. The Virgin's outreaching arms seemed to beckon the sick, the alienated, and the lonely as well as sinners. The other prevalent attitude of succeeding visions would find Mary with her eyes lifted and hands clasped in prayer. This posture demonstrated her compassionate concern for humanity and her maternal willingness to intercede for the afflicted. It also expressed the increasingly popular hope that the divine Son could not refuse to grant any wish of his loving Mother.

Mary's crushing of the snake was the most direct iconographic link to the dogma of the Immaculate Conception. It signified Mary's own triumph over evil and especially her unique status as the only one of God's creatures never touched, even at the first instant of conception, by Original Sin. This dogma asserted that the vessel of Christ would never have been tainted by sin or temptation, that she was "pre-redeemed" in eternity before the coming of Christ in time.

According to church tradition, the most ancient proof of this special divine favor appeared in the third chapter of Genesis, when God told the ancient serpent, "I will put enmities between thee and the woman, between thy seed and her seed." The vision also recalled the woman and the dragon in the twelfth chapter of Revelation in the New Testament. Indeed earlier paintings of the Immaculate Conception had made the connection more explicit by depicting Mary as the woman of the Apocalypse, "clothed with the sun" and "with the moon at her feet." This accounts for some of the apocalyptic hopes and fears that were aroused with each new announcement of Marian apparitions.

Mary's triumph over sin was not merely a personal victory. She was also identified as Mother Church, and in this interpretation she represented the triumph of the spiritual family of Christ over sin and worldliness. The crushing of the snake could also signify the defeat of special kinds of sin. More and more, as we shall see, this came to mean the sins of the modern world, which ranged from the popularity of romantic novels to political and social revolution to an overweening human pride in the efficacy of science, materialism, and rationality. This message became more explicit in holy cards and in illustrated pamphlets, which added little phrases and texts to the original depiction.[11]

Thus while the outstretched arms of the Immaculate Conception promised mercy to the faithful, the iconography of this most widely distributed of Marian images also projected a militant and defiant message that through Mary the church would defeat its enemies.

Despite the apparent contemporary significance of its message and the tremendous popularity of reproductions of the image, Labouré's vision was not really a public affair. Labouré kept her identity a secret until she was near death, and the Rue du Bac did not become a popular shrine. Later apparitions were public events, propelled by messages for the faithful, abetted by publicity, and subject to the investigatory powers of church and state.

The first of these spectacular happenings occurred near LaSalette, a small town in the French Alps. On September 19, 1846, two shepherds, fourteen-year-old Mélanie Calvat and eleven-year-old Maximin Giraud, awoke from a nap to see a dazzling light in a ravine. Upon a closer look, they discerned a woman weeping. She beckoned them to her. Speaking in French, then in patois, this beautiful woman warned them that crop failures and famines would strike if the people did not stop blaspheming, learn to pray, and attend mass regularly. She told them that she had suffered greatly for their sins and could no longer hold up the arm of her Son, which would fall on them in punishment. Then she took each child aside and told each a secret. As she floated up toward heaven, she asked them to make her warnings known to all. This sad, majestic lady was dressed in white and gold and wore a crown. A golden crucifix hung from her neck, as did a hammer and pincers, torture instruments of Christ's Passion.

What ensued set the pattern for a social drama that would be reenacted several times during the next century. The actors (at LaSalette, Lourdes, Fátima, Pontmain, Beauraing, and Banneaux) were the child-peasant visionaries, a skeptical church, and an even more skeptical and hostile civil authority. In each case the children were subjected to threats and long hours of questioning aimed at finding contradictions in their testimony and (at LaSalette, Lourdes, and Fátima) at discovering their "secrets." In each case, the children stood firm. Word of the events spread through newspaper accounts and pamphlet literature. Before the church could investigate and define its opinion, pilgrims arrived. When the church did authorize the cults, it moved to define the meaning of the apparitions and control the celebrations. Special missionary orders came to serve at pilgrimage sites. Before all major gatherings, the sacrament of penance was strongly suggested and readily available. During the celebrations priests said mass, making the Eucharist, the ritual coming of Christ, the climactic event.

LaSalette was in many ways a test case, and at first the church was fully united neither about the veracity of the visions nor about how to proceed. Even after an investigation and official approval, LaSalette remained somewhat problematic, in part because of the intractability of its visionaries. Mélanie, who spent her adult life wandering from one religious order to another, was a particular source of embarrassment. She spoke often of the spiritual necessity of suffering and everywhere wore a scapular of her own design, which featured a bleeding sacred heart torn by sharp instruments and set between a pincers and hammer.[12] In 1870, after years of leaked information, she finally published her full "secret." This turned out to be a long diatribe on the sins of European nations and Catholic priests, replete with specific predictions about the coming of Lucifer and the reign of the Anti-Christ. Such behavior appealed only to the radical fringes of the Catholic right. For them the emphasis on sin and suffering reinforced the basic image of LaSalette: that of the weeping Virgin, complaining about the sins of the modern world.

Lourdes was much more fortunate in its visionary, the stolid Bernadette Soubirous, and in the multidimensionality of its message. Bernadette, the asthmatic fourteen-year-old daughter of a pitifully poor family, first saw her vision in February 1858 while gathering wood with her sister and a friend. When she told her companions of seeing a beautiful lady, word quickly spread. Soon Bernadette was being interviewed by local officials, a doctor, and rich, pious ladies of the town. One of the most photographed personages of the mid-nineteenth century, Bernadette exhibited to the world a stalwart, brooding, and (in her peasant dress) rather exotic presence. It matters little whether her quiet steady gaze was the result of confidence, docility, or befuddlement; her stubborn faithfulness, shrewd humor, and discretion inspired confidence in those who saw her and wished to believe her words. This was important because the protracted happening became a major news event.

Bernadette saw her vision seventeen times during the next five months, often in front of thousands of witnesses. Throughout she remained the perfect child of faith. When the vision told her to drink the water, Bernadette clawed the dry ground and ate mud; when asked to pray for sinners, she fell upon the ground in supplication. Bernadette also conformed with exactitude to the wishes of local churchmen, insisting only upon the truth of her visions as she had seen them. Bernadette's Virgin was beautiful, simple, and young. She wore a white robe and veil and a blue sash, and had two gold roses resting on her bare feet. She carried a rosary.

What the vision told Bernadette combined the old and the new, hope and atonement. As old as medieval apparitions was the request for the building of a church and a procession and the obedience of the visionary to numerous commands. Older still was the identification of a supernatural being with a miraculous fountain. In the Pyrenees villages, people associated healing water not only with old local Marian shrines but also with spirits of Celtic, pre-Christian origin. What was startlingly new was the apparition's identity. "I am," she replied to Bernadette's repeated question, "the Immaculate Conception."

The vision asked Bernadette to pray for sinners, told her she would suffer in this world and be happy in the next, and spoke the word *penitence* three times. The hope of Lourdes has always been focused on the magically discovered spring and the Virgin's command to drink it and wash in its waters. From the first, contact with the spring catalyzed miraculous cures and conversions. In its multidimensionality then, the Lourdes vision had much in common with Labouré's Virgin: it expressed both hope and warning, and stated a preference for a certain kind of symbolic representation, that of the Immaculate Conception.

Lourdes inspired many other visions. None gained church approval until Pontmain (1871), which occurred during the winter of the Franco-Prussian war. The claims of five peasant children that they had seen a smiling Virgin on a starry night in northwestern France had the charming quality of a fairy tale. The whole village gathered together at the news that a heavenly lady had appeared. But only a few boys and girls could actually see the oval containing the vision as it grew larger and drew nearer to earth. The lady wore a deep blue robe covered with gold stars. On her head sat a black veil and a gold crown. She held a crucifix. The children watched in amazement as a message was slowly written out beneath her feet, "But pray, my children. God will answer you soon. My Son is letting himself be touched by compassion." [13] When the town was not bombarded and all its soldiers returned unharmed, the vision and its message seemed to be verified. She became known as Our Lady of Hope, in contrast to the weeping woman of LaSalette or the more complex symbolization of Lourdes.

As one might expect, not everyone accepted the visions or the messages at face value. Skeptics scoffed; and the secular press denounced the apparitions as delusions or hoaxes or, worse, the manipulations of a wily clergy. Certainly not all Catholics accepted the truth of the visions, but many did. Against the disbelief of those who doubted the testimony of young, poor, illiterate peasants, they opposed the Christian paradox that the humble and ignorant could see the truth far better than the educated and worldly. This defense of the visions was in part an assault on the intellectual pretensions of the day, in part an expression of deeply felt piety, awe, and gratitude. It was an attitude that emanated from the very top of the hierarchy, the papacy itself.

The Role of the Papacy

Ever since the French Revolution of 1789, the Catholic church had found itself at odds with the intellectual ideas and political goals of important segments of Western European society. The secularization of the state and nationalism threatened the church's wealth and temporal power, just as the Enlightenment's reliance on empirical and scientific explanations challenged Catholic beliefs in tradition, revelation, and miracles. The revolutions of 1848, which swept across continental Europe, posed a direct threat to the papacy itself. Italian nationalists occupied Rome, assassinated a papal minister, and declared a republic. Pius IX (1846–78) was forced to flee. Although the pope soon returned to the Holy City, the issue of who would rule Rome under a united Italy poisoned the relationship between the papacy and Italian nationalists well into the twentieth century.

The experience of flight hardened Pius's resolve to combat what he saw as the sins and heresies of the modern world. The most famous salvo in this battle was the *Syllabus of Errors* (1864), in which Pius refused categorically to ally or reconcile himself with "progress, liberalism and modern civilization." He condemned the notion of human self-sufficiency in matters of knowledge and morality, labeling this attitude naturalism and "absolute rationalism."

The proclamation of the dogma of the Immaculate Conception also signaled his defiance. The declaration in 1854 of a "truth" that could not be proved by science, history, or critical analysis was a gauntlet flung at the proud pretensions of his enemies. In fact, the day after the definition, the pope explicitly emphasized its antimodernism. "The greatness of this privilege," he told a gathering of the faithful, will be a powerful means of confuting those who deny that human nature was corrupted by the first sin and who exaggerate the forces of reason in order to deny or lessen the benefit of Revelation. Finally, may the Blessed Virgin, who conquered and destroyed all heresies, uproot and destroy this dangerous error of Rationalism, which in our unhappy times not only afflicts and torments civil society, but more deeply afflicts the Church.[14]

The enthusiastic response that followed this declaration served to separate "real" Catholics from secularists, Protestants, and even lukewarm members of the faith. It also manifested a hope, the ultimate and inevitable triumph of the universal Church. In the final passage of the declaration of the dogma, Pius set forth the belief that Jesus could refuse his mother, the protectress of the Church, nothing. "What she asks, she obtains," he wrote. "Her pleas can never be unheard." [15] Thus like the Miraculous Medal icon, the dogma itself was both affirmative and defiant.

Observers outside the church viewed Pius's statements and actions as defensive and reactionary. But there can be little doubt that within Catholicism, the effect of his reign was to enhance the power of the papacy and successfully to exert its right to spiritual primacy. Although opposed to modern ideas, Pius did not eschew the benefits of modern communications. He relied upon the availability of trains to bring his bishops and people to Rome for frequent and widely reported audiences and celebrations. He was thoroughly aware of the beneficial role that the press could play in forming opinion, and he defended the aggressively rightist French editor Louis Veuillot against the complaints of the liberal bishops.[16] Despite or because of his intransigence, he attained wide popularity among the Catholic laity.

The culmination of his strategic efforts within the hierarchy was the declaration of papal infallibility in 1870. Some liberal bishops (mainly French bishops) opposed this move. But the power of the independent and liberal bishop was on the wane, for by the 1870s ultramontanism (the belief that one should look to Rome for leadership in all spiritual matters) had become the dominant political tendency in the church.

The culmination of Pius's efforts to win the allegiance of the laity was the successful promotion of a certain kind of piety. Pius and his immediate successors advocated new or renewed devotions that emphasized the affective rather than the rational or ethical

182

aspects of faith. That is, they chose to direct rather than to condemn or ignore emotional and potentially subversive religious impulses in order to maintain and increase Catholic influence. The adoration of the Eucharist, the Sacred Heart of Jesus, and Mary were emotional cults fully supported by the papacy; these cults form the major chapters in the history of Roman Catholic piety in the century before Vatican II.

Pius IX and his successor, Leo XIII (1878–1903), were personally devoted to the veneration of the Virgin. They approved coronations, whereby old statues of Mary received crowns in impressive ceremonies. They also confirmed the validity of new apparitions and miracles, and granted special indulgences for mass pilgrimages. They thoroughly believed, as the doctrine and popular icon of the Immaculate Conception indicated, that Mary could help the church in its time of dire need. Every October for ten years, Leo XIII, a pope generally reputed to have progressive political views, issued an encyclical exhorting the faithful to say the Rosary. In the first of these decrees (*Supremi Apostolatus,* 1883), he reminded Catholics that this prayer had saved the church from heresy and from the Turks in the sixteenth century. He hoped that contemporary devotion to Mary would similarly help Catholics to defeat secularism and materialism.

Catholic France, which considered itself to be the home of the Sacred Heart vision and the special realm of Mary, was both the inspiration and recipient of much of this papal activity. From the first, the apparitions in France reinforced Pius's belief in the rightness of his own views and seemed to verify Catholicism's claim to be the one true faith. Labouré's visions in 1830 and the consequent popularity of the Miraculous Medal helped to convince Pius that the time was ripe to declare the Immaculate Conception to be a true dogma of the church.[17] Four years after the declaration, the Lourdes visions were, literally, for this pope, a heaven-sent verification. From the point of view of temporal politics, too, it is not surprising that the popes regarded with special tenderness the appeal of French bishops for recognition of shrines and apparitions. In its quarrels with Italian nationalism, the church frequently looked to its "eldest daughter" for military aid. Rome also had an interest in shoring up traditional faith within the country that it considered to be the seedbed of modern revolutions. Thus the combined motives of faith and political sensitivity moved the papacy to confirm French Catholics' belief that they had been chosen by Mary.[18]

Catholic Piety in the Third Republic

This sense of being chosen provided French Catholics with a national unifying symbol when they most needed it. The last third of the century was an age of fervent nationalism. Yet during this period many French Catholics became extremely alienated from their own government, the Third Republic, founded in 1870. The conflict was exacerbated by the fact that many Catholics were ardent monarchists and many Republicans were avowed anticlericals. These positions, representing two very different world views, hardened into two irreconcilable political extremes during the tragedy of the Paris Commune at the very outset of the Republic.

The Commune was originally set up to resist the German siege of the capital during the Franco-Prussian War. After the siege, the Parisians came into conflict with the newly formed national government. The protosocialist Commune brought together all the radical left factions of the nineteenth century; the new government was very conservative and largely Catholic. The battle that ensued was the last great revolutionary uprising of the century, and the bloodiest. The Communards in their desperation set fire to many buildings in the capital and executed their most important hostage, the liberal archbishop of Paris, Darboy. The fighting between the conservative government troops and the Communards left more than twenty thousand Parisians dead; another thirty-eight thousand were arrested, and seventy-five hundred of these were deported to a penal colony. For the moment the forces of religion and order had triumphed. But their victory would not last through the decade.

For many conservative leaders, the appropriate response to defeat in war and to the bloodshed of the Commune was to make atonement for France's sins, which included the errors of the Republicans, anarchists, and socialists. The French church pledged itself to erect a monument for this purpose: the Basilica of the Sacre Coeur on Montmartre, overlooking Paris. In June 1873 fifty members of the conservative National Assembly made a penitential pilgrimage to Paray-le-Monial, the site of the original seventeenth-century vision of the Sacred Heart. To the Communards and their sympathizers, such a response to death and lost dreams was, at best, uncomprehending and, at worst, insulting, heartless, even laughable. It is little wonder that the Catholic monarchist right and Republican anticlericals heaped scorn on each other for the next half century.

Among the chief protagonists in this struggle were the Augustinian Fathers of the Assumption, whose role in religion and politics was so crucial that the historian René Rémond has labeled the years from 1871 to 1901 the era of Assumptionist Catholicism.[19] In 1883 the Assumptionists founded a daily, La Croix, which brought into play all the defensive tactics of nineteenth-century Catholicism. Its writers accepted with pride the accusations made against the church by rationalists. More, they exulted in their differences. But their paper not only defended, it attacked. La Croix equated revolutions and the Republic with Satan and his legions, mocked politicians with vitriolic sarcasm, and consistently blamed all problems (including crime, poverty, disease, and natural disasters) on the secular state.

The Assumptionists published the paper for Catholics. Two primary goals were to promote religious fervor and to give church members a sense of solidarity and community in the increasingly hostile environment of the anticlerical Republic. What made the order so influential was its willingness to apply modern technological and organizational means to these ends. They exploited with élan the possibilities inherent in mass literacy, transportation, communication, and production. Although they did not approve of universal suffrage, their paper, with its short dramatic headlines, sensationalistic reporting, and hyperbolic prose, successfully met the challenge of shaping opinion in a newly democratic, industrialized, modern society. To a large extent the Assumptionists managed to reach the disparate and isolated elements in Catholic society. Subscriptions to their paper cut across class lines and included an estimated twenty-five thousand members of the lower clergy, who could be counted on to spread the word.[20] Further, La Croix was only the most important publication produced and promoted by the Assumptionists and their press. Le Pèlerin, a weekly newsletter on pilgrimages founded in 1873, echoed La Croix's political and religious perspective. So did an estimated ninety-one regional newspapers.[21] In addition, La Croix and Le Pèlerin advertised and distributed mass-produced holy cards. The short, repeated dramatic phrases, satirical editorial cartoons, and holy images presented symbols or "opinion molecules" rather than rational, factual arguments.[22] Taken together they promoted a symbolic consciousness that invited subscribers to discover layers of mystical meanings behind objects and events. For example, the large cross on the masthead not only pictured the suffering of Jesus but also symbolized the suffering church in Rome and ghettoized Catholics in France.

The treatment of Bastille Day and Marianne, contrasted with that of the Assumption and the Virgin, is a more relevant example of how *La Croix* elaborated symbols for its readers. The newspaper's reportage of the "national orgy" on July 14 in Paris was always filled with sarcasm and predictions of doom. For days afterward, the paper would recount all the crimes or tragedies in the poor *quartiers,* claiming that these were caused either by drunkenness or barbaric celebration or the moral failures of Republican government. The paper was aroused to special fury in 1883 when a statue of Marianne was unveiled during the Bastille Day ceremony. Artists usually depicted this female symbol of the Republic as a brave warrior or a robust mother surrounded by children. *La Croix*'s front-page editorial derided her as "neither a queen nor a cook," compared her to the "impure Venus" created by "pagan demons," and finally called her a nothing. But they concluded, "she replaced something. She recalls Mary, queen of the Gauls" (July 16 and 17, 1883). This true queen had her feast on August 15. The real France, throne and altar France, had chosen the Assumption as its national holiday in the seventeenth century when Louis XIII dedicated his country to Our Lady. Front-page articles repeating this fact coincided with the onset of the yearly mass pilgrimages to Lourdes. Instead of disasters, the follow-up to this feast day featured miraculous cures and conversions.

The Assumptionists were eclectic in their use of symbols. They did not favor any subject of renewed devotion over others except insofar as some symbols had a national or historical significance that harmonized with their own sense of religious and political necessity. Thus they reported successful religious processions and fêtes, crownings at Marian shrines, and the legends of statues and saints. But their greatest and most consistent efforts were to instill a love for and familiarity with the cross, with Mary, and with the Sacred Heart of Jesus. Each May and June the paper ran stories to celebrate the months of Mary and the Sacred Heart. Pilgrimages and the church calendar were major news events for the Assumptionists and their readers because current events, like history, had a natural and supernatural realm and meaning.

The Assumptionists made their greatest contribution to establishing the realm of Mary in France by orchestrating a yearly cycle of pilgrimages. Leadership fell to them in 1872 when the order was asked to help with a large penitential pilgrimage to La-Salette. The next year the site was Lourdes, which drew a mere 492 people.[23] Ten years later, an estimated twenty thousand journeyed to Lourdes during August.

The initial reason for choosing Lourdes over LaSalette and Pontmain was logistical. The other two shrines were isolated geographically, whereas Lourdes (because of the fortuitous needs and influence of a local businessman) had its own train station by 1866. Certainly the Assumptionist style and temperament suited the LaSalette vision best. But if the Assumptionists could not regularly move masses of people to LaSalette, they could move its spirit, which emphasized the need for national repentance, elsewhere. They did this by providing spiritual leadership en route, by organizing events during the major August pilgrimage, and by publicizing their work.

Through their publicity and organization the Assumptionists allowed all of Catholic France to participate in the realm of Mary. At the furthest remove someone who simply read the newspaper could feel her or his faith affirmed by the firsthand account of the numbers of the faithful who went to Lourdes and the miracles that occurred. If one wanted to be more a part of the events, a subscriber could contribute money to the Lourdes campaign and help send a "poor sick one" on pilgrimage. A wealthier reader who could not get away might even take the entire responsibility for sending a *pauvre malade* and hope thereby to participate in the making of a miracle. After the return of the pilgrims, a Catholic who had stayed at home might attend the thanksgiving rites that local churches celebrated for the *miraculés* (or cured).

The sense of community that these concentric circles of participation generated came from the center itself: the pilgrimage. The anthropologists Edith and Victor Turner have described the pilgrimage as a liminoid or quasi-liminal experience. In undertaking this great journey, pilgrims place themselves outside their quotidian lives and customary social structures. Social divisions melt as all share the same hardships, the same rituals, the same status, and the same expectations and hopes. The participants feel a special closeness to the divine and a unity and oneness with others. This is a powerful sense of *communitas,* or unmediated communion, which the Turners call "a spring of pure possibility," the spring that makes miracles possible.[24]

To some extent, Lourdes pilgrimages were informed with the defiance inherent in the image of the Immaculate Conception and in conservative nationalism. One could choose to go alone to Lourdes as a believer or an observer. But most people came as part of a group. Parishes sometimes traveled together; so did entire regions. They carried the flags of the old provinces of France (rather than the emblems of the rationalized new *départements*), wore traditional costume, and sang special hymns that conformed to the history and cadences of their own *patrie.* These regional banners hung from the ceiling of the great basilica at Lourdes, manifesting "believing France's" disdain for merely legal boundaries and atomized democratic citizenship.

The National Pilgrimage for Men was the most avowedly political of these church-sponsored events. The *Missionaires du travail,* the religious order that served the Lourdes site, organized this rally because they believed that an exclusively male gathering would be a conclusive demonstration of the strength of traditional Catholic beliefs. Women and children, as both the anticlericals and the church knew, were easier to attract. The idea met with great success. The organizers stated that fifty thousand men made the first national pilgrimage in April 1899; eighty thousand attended two years later.[25] For those sojourners who felt mocked by their society, a pilgrimage to Lourdes showed them what their true homeland, a community of believers, would be like.

For Catholics, conditions in their temporal homeland, Third Republic France, became worse before they improved. As the century came to a close, the Assumptionists became increasingly involved in political campaigns. Their fatal misstep was to make *La Croix* a leading voice of anti-Semitic propaganda during the famous Dreyfus affair (1894–99), in which a Jewish army captain was unjustly accused of treason. *L'Affaire,* as the French called it, bitterly divided opinion throughout the nation. When Dreyfus was vindicated, the Republicans turned against their enemies. In 1900 the government temporarily expelled the Assumptionists from France. Five years later, it ordered the separation of church and state, which closed many more religious houses. But by that time the Assumptionists had left their mark. The mass pilgrimages to Lourdes had been permanently established.

The Meaning and Power of Lourdes

Despite the defiant tone found in much of the Assumptionists' work, it should be obvious that the Lourdes pilgrimage was not built upon political discontent and antimodernism alone. The Assumptionist monks, like their followers, were motivated by sincere religious belief and spiritual hope. They were fortunate that, almost by accident, Lourdes and not LaSalette became the pilgrimage site. Because the LaSalette vision mirrored the Assumptionist temperament so well, any mass pilgrimages based on it would have been permanently tied to aggressive antimodernism. Even the Pontmain apparition was more closely tied to a specific time, place, and mood than was Lourdes. Bernadette envisioned a truly polyvalent symbol that could evoke different emotional and intellectual responses. Her Immaculate Conception was simple and beautiful, yet she left a variety of messages that could lend themselves to many interpretations.

Because of the immediate political context, the Lourdes vision evoked new interpretations of old litanies. Mary, refuge of the sick and sinners, could also be Mary the refuge of Catholic France. In her Immaculate Conception, she vanquished not only Satan but also his Republican legions and materialistic ideas. Queen of heaven, she was also Queen of France, or at least the symbol of the "true France." Yet in her youth and simple clothes she could also be identified with the young, the poor, and the humble. Mary was truly a unifying symbol that could help French people overcome their class, regional, and local differences.

But even for the most politically motivated pilgrim, the Lourdes vision was something more. She was powerful, a miracle worker. The sources of these thaumaturgic powers were two: a belief in the special "privileges" accorded to Mary in Catholic ideology (her virginity, maternity, immaculate conception, and physical assumption) and the *communitas* the pilgrims en masse created at her shrine.

The most immediate attraction of Lourdes, of course, was the belief that Mary, Mother of God, had come there eighteen times. The belief in nineteenth-century apparitions is so strong that they were considered then, as now, "facts." [26] The "fact" of LaSalette or Lourdes is supported by the popular belief that Mary was physically assumed into heaven.[27] This tenet of faith makes the possibility of her reappearance more real. An actual physical presence is something to behold, to touch, and to feel. Pilgrims came and continue to come to Lourdes to feel Mary's presence.

The privilege of physical assumption is, in turn, connected to Mary's motherhood, virginity, and immaculate conception. There is a vast psychological and anthropological literature describing how both virginity and maternity confer powers on a person.[28] Virginity is a special condition of integrity or intactness. Within Catholicism, virginity is almost exclusively identified with sexual purity, a holy state that confers the power to transcend physical corruptibility. Mary's physical assumption is one sign of this empowerment; her ability to cure humanity's physical ills is another.

Motherhood, too, in myth and legend signifies the power over life and death. In a Catholic interpretation more directly informed by human experience, Mary as the mother of Jesus had the right to expect or ask him for favors. One of these favors was the preredemption of the Immaculate Conception, which Archbishop Dupanloup described as a privilege every son would give his mother if he could! [29] As the mother of humanity, Mary could mitigate the effect of divine judgment upon the children who came to her with their spiritual ills and abrogate the harsh laws of nature for those who sought a cure for their physical ailments.

It is this interpretation of Mary's maternity that has infuriated Protestant critics. Writing in 1855 (to protest the dogmatic definition of the Immaculate Conception), E. de Pressensé accused Catholics of a kind of neopaganism for their worship of a deity "made in their own [human] image" and for their adoration of "the gracious symbols of a feminized cult." [30] He wrote his pamphlet to recall Christians to their true symbol, the bloody cross. Giovanni Miegge made a strikingly similar analysis almost one hundred years later, just after the Assumption became an official dogma. Mary's compassion, he wrote,

> is outside the ethical, like the maternal instinct that without discrimination is always on the side of the son however depraved, and covers the guilt with indulgent complicity.

Calling the Mary cult merely "humanity's pity for itself," [31] Miegge accused Catholics of not understanding that Jesus was the true intermediary between harsh patriarchal divine laws and humanity.

Both Pressensé and Miegge were wrong, I think, in their assertions that Catholics did not understand Christ's compassion and suffering. *La Croix*'s crucifix and the widely distributed holy cards and statues of the red Sacred Heart of Jesus were highly honored and beloved symbols in Catholic France. Yet these two Protestant critics were correct in perceiving the unique attraction of the Marian cult at Lourdes. Even though the Sacred Heart was supposed to embody Christ's love for his people, in Third Republic France this symbol almost exclusively signified the need to atone for the modern sins that caused Jesus to bleed and suffer.[32] The "gracious femininity" of the Lourdes visions, then, did seem to promise a more indulgent forgiveness and compassion.

It was in this promise that the faithful placed their hope and trust as they approached the shrine. According to newspaper reports and Émile Zola's long realistic novel *Lourdes* (1894), most pilgrims came to Lourdes quite unencumbered by the niceties of dogmatic belief and definition. Again and again in *La Croix* and in Zola's book, sojourners referred to Mary quite simply as "the good Mother" or "the good" or "holy Virgin." By their rich description of the great Assumptionists' pilgrimages, these sources help us to understand how the believers themselves activated the miraculous powers of the symbol of the Immaculate Conception at Lourdes.

Each August, trains full of pilgrims traveled from Paris and other major cities, converging at Lourdes within days and hours of each other. Each train had a set of white hospital cars, where the "poor sick" were taken care of by the Sisters of the Assumption, volunteer doctors, *dames hospitalières,* and male *brancardiers* or stretcher-bearers. Using specially prepared manuals, priests and nuns took the pilgrims through a schedule of prayers and meditations. As the journey progressed, expectations mounted. Sometimes, as a July 1887 edition of *La Croix* put it, "the Virgin in her impatience to work miracles, healed sick pilgrims en route." [33]

At the site, a combination of ritual and social organization served to release the pilgrims from the mundane. For its actors, Lourdes, like all liminal experiences, was radically equalizing—so radical that it turned the world upside down. Here the sick and the poor, who were ordinarily shunted off to the margins of society, became the center of attention. The child with the misshapen limbs, the woman with the unsightly running sores, the coughing, grizzled tubercular man, were no longer despised, but served by the healthy and the rich. In *Lourdes,* Zola wrote of stretcher-bearers and volunteer nurses who came from every social class and practiced three days of real communalism every year; he told of aristocrats who took special pleasure in working long days and eating common meals that cost only three sous a day. For the sick, Lourdes represented at best the possibility of cure, and at the very least a means of overcoming isolation and alienation.[34] For the rich and healthy, it was the opportunity to fulfill a mission of perfect Christian charity. These role reversals helped to engender the religious experience that pilgrims sought, and gave them a taste of heaven, where all would equally join Mary in singing God's praises. In simple terms, the pilgrimage drew devotees closer to the divine.

So did the vigils, the outdoor and indoor masses, and the nightly candle-lit parade that spectacularly revealed the numbers of those who believed in the powers and mercy of Jesus and his mother. The sick looked forward most to the immersions at the bathhouses and the outdoor Benediction ceremonies, at which the Eucharist was paraded through the crowds. Almost all of the proclaimed miracles took place during these two events, when pilgrims could feel and see sacred objects. At the bathhouses the *brancardiers* and the sick all prayed to the Virgin as each patient was immersed in the waters of the fountain. During the outdoor Benedictions, the Son upstaged the Mother. The sick and the well spread out their arms in the characteristic Lourdes stance of supplication and prayer. Those who were able fell to their knees as the Eucharist passed. All asked for mercy and for miracles. Often during this rite, people would at last hear the long hoped-for cry, "I am cured." When this happened the pilgrims could feel, perhaps more dramatically than at any other time in their life, that they had been touched by divine power. With or without a total cure for their physical and spiritual ills, they gained something by experiencing Mary's realm at Lourdes.

The Heritage of Marian Apparitions

Lourdes has endured because of the fame of its miracles and its message of hope. The conservative nationalism that partly motivated its first great pilgrimages is no longer apparent. Lourdes is now an international shrine. Like much of the rest of the world, it is more commercialized, more bureaucratized, and more sanitized than in the past. But the Lourdes pilgrimage still provides believers with a sense of *communitas* and Mary's presence.[35]

But what is the legacy of Lourdes and the other apparitions for those who will never visit the shrine? Can we see in the Marian revival a resurgence of the "feminine principle" or a "feminization" of religion or culture?

The most famous treatment of the feminization of religion in the nineteenth century is Ann Douglas's *The Feminization of American Culture* (1977). In her discussion of American Protestantism one can distinguish three aspects or stages of feminization: a growing preponderance of women in congregations; the power that this preponderance gave women over religious life; and a "softening" of theology and religious symbolism that followed as a consequence. One does not necessarily have to accept the logic of her argument to make use of these distinctions. In the French Catholic experience, only the first and third aspects of feminization hold true.

Historians of France have long noted that religious practice fell more and more to women throughout the nineteenth century. This was true in the countryside as well as in the city, where a bourgeois ideology common to France, England, and America assumed that women were "naturally" more religious, whereas men were more "rational."

In contrast to Douglas's description of the American experience however, this trend did not lead to a female ideological ascendancy in the Catholic church. The male hierarchy, as we have seen, not only maintained but extended control of religious life by validating and popularizing certain affective religious practices and by tying them to the sacramental system.

The revival of the Marian cult can and has been interpreted as a "softening" of religious symbolism or a "resurgence of the feminine." [36] But it should be clear that this female symbolism has long been shaped and defined by men. By the time of the modern apparitions, over sixteen hundred years of Catholic theology had defined Mary as both Virgin and Mother. This depiction presented real women with a complex ideal of womanhood that they could not fulfill. For some women, it had the effect of denying female power, or the positive power of sexuality in human life. At the same time, the Virgin Mother provided a male, celibate clergy with a "safe" object of contemplation and adoration.

This does not mean that women did not respond to Mary. On the contrary, religious women enthusiastically took up her cause as it was defined by the newspapers, books, and holy images of their day. They admired Mary, the most powerful and ideal of mothers, because she knew the glories and tragedies of maternity without having had to experience its painful, impure, or bloody realities. Besides, a special identity between women and Mary was the product of a lifelong cultivation. Many girls had been told to model themselves after their Blessed Mother. Virtuous bourgeois convent students usually joined her sodality, the Children of Mary, and wore its special livery, the Miraculous Medal, for the rest of their lives.[37] As adults some still signed *Enfant de Marie* after their name. Mary's high position in the church was obviously a source of female pride. But as powerful as Mary was, her male-defined cult had serious limitations, particularly for women. These become clear when we consider what the nineteenth-century Virgin did *not* represent.

This Virgin had no connection with fertility and sexuality, the two most obvious attributes of any symbol of female divinity. This connection could only belong to an underground interpretation of the Good Mother's role. Although the connection was recognized and utilized in village rituals and local cults, it went unrecognized (officially at least) in the cults of the famous black Virgins, some of whom may have gotten their coloration from their connection with the earth and with pre-Christian goddesses.[38] From the perspective of these earlier images, the blue and white Virgin seems not only immaculate but also bloodless and disconnected from the earth and from the experiences of most women.

The Virgin, who did not have any control over fertility, also had little autonomy within "her" church. In official interpretations all evidences of her independence were slighted. But they were there. At Pontmain the vision's robes and headdress could be interpreted as priestly. At LaSalette the Lady (who never identified herself) made remarkable statements: *"I gave you six days' work. I have reserved the seventh for myself."* (Italics mine.) Certainly there was no suggestion that God was a woman! In fact, leaders of the church were not at all troubled by this lapse. They either ignored the first-person pronouns or dismissed them as a common means found often in the Hebrew Bible, whereby God spoke through his prophets.[39]

The Virgin of the apparitions is not the Mary of the Bible, who had doubts and hesitations during her life. Although she usually appeared alone, she was always cast as an intermediary, who had been given her privileges by a loving Son and prescient Father. Her *active* cooperation was not stressed. She was a vessel rather than the first disciple, who willingly acted out of faith.[40]

This is not surprising. In nineteenth-century Catholicism, discipleship and its historical successor, priesthood, belonged exclusively to males. A female model for sacramental and public leadership roles seemed inconceivable. Any official and public version of the apparitions would have to suit a celibate priesthood's sense of fitness. Mary the pure and passive vessel was an important part of the inherited interpretation.

Finally, if the apparitions had a prophetic mission, it only struck one social and political note. Although the visions appeared to the humble, they never carried a message of social transformation or suggested that the realm of Mary or the coming of Christ meant the overcoming of exploitation or oppression.[41] The political direction they augured was always backward rather than forward: in favor of kings and the old social order, and fearful of change.

This defensive antimodernism may be the most distinct legacy of the church-defined Marian cult of the nineteenth century. Major Marian apparitions still have a highly political and defensive function. The visions seen by the three children at Fátima (1917) echoed the warnings of the Lady of LaSalette. When Fátima's secret messages were revealed in the 1930s, their political spirit also recalled the earlier vision. This time, however, it was not famine or the Anti-Christ that threatened the church, but the spread of Russian Communism. Belief in these messages helped to inform Marian piety with an aggressive Cold War anti-Communism in the years preceding Vatican II. The Blue Army of Our Lady, formed in 1947 to fulfill the command of Fátima, at one time enrolled twenty million, who by their prayers hoped to vanquish the "red army of atheists." [42] The Rosary said against the Turks in the sixteenth century and against impiety in the nineteenth, was being recited in the 1950s over the radio for the conversion of Russia.

Now apparitions have turned against the changes within the

church itself. In places as culturally diverse as Garabandal in rural Spain and Bayside in New York City, Mary has appeared as the defender of the old pre-Vatican II faith.[43] Neither of these series of visions has been approved. But they draw large crowds and are only the most famous of similar happenings.

The Second Vatican Council (1962–65) signaled a break with the spirit of defensiveness and deemphasized certain kinds of piety. Even some of the mass-produced statues and holy cards brought into vogue during the nineteenth century have disappeared from the churches. Much of the attention of Catholic theologians is now focused on the search for resolutions to the problems of nuclear war, sexual politics, racism, economic exploitation, and the Third World. Pope John Paul II is deeply devoted to the Virgin and her apparitions. Unfortunately this piety may very well be related to his conservative attitudes on the issues of birth control, sexuality, and women's roles. Some liberation and feminist theologians have attempted to redefine Mary's role in the church.[44] But most of these progressive Catholics are at present more committed to redefining living women's roles than to rehabilitating a symbol weighed down by a heritage of defensive conservatism and male projection. This article suggests that the old saying, "As Mary goes, so goes the Church," [45] should be reversed. Rather we have learned: "As the Church goes, so goes Mary."

Notes

1. "Lourdes," *Wall Street Journal,* August 9, 1983, p. 8, states that Lourdes draws more than four million pilgrims, six times as many as Mecca. This comparison does not take into account the rising wealth of OPEC nations in the last decade. *Time* magazine's estimate that two million Moslems went to Mecca in 1982 seems more accurate (August 30, 1982, p. 32).

2. Thomas A. Kselman, *Miracles and Prophecies in Nineteenth-century France* (New Brunswick, N.J.: Rutgers University Press, 1983), p. 28.

3. Michael Marrus, "Cultures on the Move: Pilgrims and Pilgrimages in Nineteenth-century France," *Stanford French Review* 1 (1977): 206–212; Eugen Weber, *Peasants into Frenchmen: The Modernization*

of Rural France, 1870–1914 (Stanford: Stanford University Press, 1976), pp. 332–355.

4. Fatima Mernissi, "Women, Saints, and Sanctuaries," *Signs* 3 (1977): 101–112.

5. This is a major theme of Kselman's excellent book.

6. Marrus, "Cultures on the Move," pp. 205–206, 218.

7. Lawrence Cunningham, *Mother of God* (New York: Harper and Row, 1982), pp. 67–68.

8. Gerard Cholvy, "Le Catholicism populaire en France au xixe siècle," in Bernard Plongeron and Robert Pannet, eds., *Le Christianisme populaire. Les dossiers de l'histoire* (Paris: Centurion, 1976), pp. 201–202. The creation of a mother-teacher ideology among the bourgeoisie is a major theme of my dissertation, "Mothers and Daughters in Early Nineteenth-century Paris" (Ph.D. diss., Columbia University, 1981).

9. Père Aladel, *The Miraculous Medal,* trans. P. S. (Baltimore: John B. Piet, 1880), p. 71.

10. René Laurentin, *Lourdes. Histoire authentique,* vol. 3 (Paris: Lethielleux, 1962), p. 186, n. 25; René Laurentin and A. Durand, *Pontmain. Histoire authentique,* vol. 3 (Paris: Apostolat des Editions, 1970), p. 38.

11. A jubilee card on the tenth anniversary showed the sins of the world coming out in licks of flames under the serpent. Among the sins were errors, lies, impiety, and sacrilege. Another card, obviously for young girls, mentioned novels as a specific danger. I viewed these cards and much rare pamphlet literature at the Marian Library, University of Dayton, Dayton, Ohio. I am grateful to Brother William Fackovec for his kind assistance.

12. There is a picture of this scapular in G. LaFoy, "Le Secret de LaSalette," *Revue illustré,* October 5, 1908.

13. The actual words were: "Mais priez, mes enfants. Dieu vous exacera en peu du temps. Mon fils se laisse toucher."

14. Pius IX, "Timeliness of the Definition" (December 9, 1854), reprinted in *Papal Teachings: Our Lady,* sel. and arr. Benedictine Monks of Solesnes and trans. Daughters of St. Paul (Boston: St. Paul Editions, 1961), p. 83.

15. Pius IX, "Ineffabilis Deus" (December 8, 1954), in *Papal Teachings,* p. 82.

16. Pierre Pierrard, *Les Papes et la France* (Paris: Fayard, 1981), pp. 221–222; Paul Johnson, *A History of Christianity* (New York: Atheneum, 1976), p. 391.

17. Cunningham, *Mother of God,* p. 71; William McSweeney, *Roman Catholicism: The Search for Relevance* (Oxford: Basil Blackwell, 1980), p. 44.

18. McSweeney, *Roman Catholicism,* pp. 45–47.

19. René Rémond, *The Right Wing in France from 1815 to de Gaulle,* trans. J. Laux (Philadelphia: University of Pennsylvania Press, 1966), pp. 185–186.

20. Judson Mather, "*La Croix* and the Assumptionist Response to Secularization in France, 1870–1900" (Ph.D. diss., University of Michigan, 1971), p. 28.

21. Joseph Grenier, "To Reach the People: *La Croix,* 1883–1890" (Ph.D. diss., Fordham University, 1976), p. 140.

22. Mather, "*La Croix,*" p. 30.

23. Grenier, "To Reach the People," p. 413.

24. Edith Turner and Victor Turner, *Image and Pilgrimage in Christian Culture: Anthropological Perspectives* (New York: Columbia University Press, 1978), pp. 1–39, 243–255.

25. *L'Echo du pèlerinage national d'hommes à Lourdes* (avril 1899), p. 35, and Brother William Fackovec, *Lourdes Publications in French in the Clugnet Collection* (Dayton: University of Dayton, 1958), pp. 36–37.

26. For example, Louis Bassette's *Le Fait de la Salette, 1846–1854* (Paris: Cerf, 1965).

27. Turner and Turner, *Image and Pilgrimage,* pp. 154–155.

28. For example, on virginity see John A. Saliba, "The Virgin-Birth Debate in Anthropological Literature: A Critical Assessment," *Theological Studies* 36 (1975): 428–454; Joyce E. Salisbury, "Fruitful in Singleness," *Journal of Medieval History* 8 (1982): 97–106; Clarissa Atkinson, " 'Precious Balsam in a Fragile Glass': The Ideology of Virginity in the Later Middle Ages," *Journal of Family History* 8 (1983): 131–143. Kirsten Hastrup, "The Semantics of Biology: Virginity," in Shirley Ardener, ed., *Defining Females* (New York: John Wiley and Sons, 1978). On motherhood, see especially Erich Neumann, *The Great Mother: An Analysis of the Archetype,* trans. Ralph Manheim (New York: Pantheon, 1955), and the introduction and essays in James J. Preston, ed., *Mother Worship: Themes and Variations* (Chapel Hill: University of North Carolina Press, 1980).

29. Félix-Antoine-Philibert Dupanloup, "Mandement et Instruction Pastorale de Monseigneur l'Eveque d'Orléans sur l'Immaculée Conception de la Très-Sainte Vierge" (Orleans, 22 jan 1855), p. 50.

30. E. de Pressensé, *L'Immaculée Conception. Histoire d'un dogme*

catholique-romain ou comment l'hérésie devient un dogme (Paris: Ch. Meyrueis et cie., 1855), p. 16.

31. Giovanni Miegge, *The Virgin Mary: The Roman Catholic Marian Doctrine,* trans. Waldo Smith (Philadelphia: Westminster Press, 1955), pp. 153, 155.

32. Rémond, *The Right Wing,* pp. 185–186.

33. Grenier, "To Reach the People," p. 415.

34. Kselman, *Miracles,* pp. 62–79, and Henri Bernard, *Le Pelerinage: Une Response a l'aliénation des malades et infirmes* (Montreal: Oratoire Saint-Joseph du Mont-Royal, 1975).

35. For a recent description see Patrick Marnham, *Lourdes: A Modern Pilgrimage* (New York: Coward, McCann and Geoghegan, 1980).

36. This is a major thesis of Miegge's book. See especially chapter 7, "The Compassionate Mother," and "Conclusion: Mary in Dogma and Devotion." See also Carl Jung's comments on the declaration of the dogma of the Assumption in "Answer to Job," in *The Collected Works,* 2d ed., vol. 11 (Princeton: Princeton University Press, 1969), pp. 461–470.

37. Bonnie G. Smith, *Ladies of the Leisured Class: The Bourgeoises of Northern France in the Nineteenth Century* (Princeton: Princeton University Press, 1981), pp. 109–110; Aladel, *The Miraculous Medal,* pp. 272–273.

38. Leonard W. Moss and Stephen C. Cappannari, "In Quest of the Black Virgin: She Is Black Because She Is Black," in Preston, *Mother Worship,* pp. 53–72.

39. Bassette, *Le Fait de la Salette,* pp. 132–144 and Abbé Rousselot, *Manuel du pèlerin a Notre-Dame de la Salette* (Grenoble, 1848).

40. Victor Branick, "Mary: Model of the Charismatic as Seen in Acts 1–2, Luke 1–2, and John," in Branick, ed., *Mary, the Spirit of the Church* (Ramsey, N.J.: Paulist Press, 1980), pp. 28–43.

41. This is liberation theology's recent interpretation of the Gospel of Luke, which presents Mary as praising God for the divine favor he has shown her and for the new revolutionary order that her cooperation in redemption will help make possible. See, for example, Rosemary Radford Ruether, *Sexism and God-Talk* (Boston: Beacon Press, 1983), p. 153, and Robert M. Brown, *Theology in a New Key: Responding to Liberation Themes* (Philadelphia: Westminster Press, 1978), pp. 98–100.

42. "The Blue Army of Our Lady," *The Marian Era* (1965), VI, pp. 47ff.

43. See Joseph A. Pelletier, *Our Lady Comes to Garabandal* (Worcester, Mass.: Assumptionist Press, 1971), and "Faithful Reproductions: The Miraculous Photos of Bayside," *Boston Phoenix,* November 10, 1981.

44. See notes 40 and 41.

45. Turner and Turner, *Image and Pilgrimage,* p. 171.

Nine

"In Christian Firmness and Christian Meekness": Feminism and Pacifism in Antebellum America

Dorothy C. Bass

Women intent upon attaining their own emancipation have rarely been indifferent to the other great issues of their times. Indeed, feminists have often associated their own cause with other causes, partly out of a desire to make the world they aim more fully to inhabit a just and happy home for themselves and others. Among such associations, perhaps the best known has occurred between women's rights and black rights. Although the relationship between supporters of these movements has been tragically strained at many points, there was considerable overlap among supporters and philosophies during both the abolitionist movement of the nineteenth century and the civil rights movement of the twentieth.[1] More recently, activists and observers have shown substantial interest in the likelihood that the cause of women might be particularly tied to the cause of peacemaking. "War is not healthy for children and other living things," women peace activists have proclaimed in our time; in a world run by mothers, some add, the Pentagon would have to raise money through bake sales, and day care centers would receive federal funds. War and other forms of violence, such activists imply, are antithetical to the nurturing tasks that have defined the lives of most women. In what might be an oblique endorsement of these views, many more women than men surveyed by recent public opinion polls favor disarmament and other peaceful policies.[2]

While politicians seek to build the women's peace vote into a winning coalition, feminists ponder the implications of women's distinctive affinity with peace. Although most are pleased to forge an alliance between two good causes, recent feminist authors have also urged caution in embracing the images of women and men

201

implied by the expression *gender gap*.[3] When images of women as especially peaceable and nurturing are viewed in the light of women's historic subordination, critical questions emerge. Are women pacific or merely passive, active opponents of violence or accustomed victims within a system they dare not contravene? Should bellicosity be conceded to men as one of their gender traits, as if it belonged indelibly to their nature? Linking women and peace, it seems, can lead into an exceedingly complex tangle of stereotypes from which all, male and female, might emerge diminished.

These questions are not new. Paradoxically, the first generation of Americans to promote the image of women as distinctively peaceable was also the first to witness the emergence of an enduring movement on behalf of the emancipation of women. In the 1830s, a group of women and men committed both to thoroughgoing pacifism (which they called nonresistance) and to the equality of the sexes gave thoughtful attention to the ways in which images of women and men can contribute to the attainment of peace and justice. Their commitment began in opposition to the institution that in their time epitomized violence and hierarchy: the institution of slavery. Their commitment extended to include a challenge to the ways in which dominant views of "masculinity" and "femininity" may foster violence and hierarchy.

The intellectual and spiritual connection among the various unpopular causes espoused by this group of activists was a form of radical Christianity. The religious perspective of perfectionism, as interpreted by such leaders as Angelina and Sarah Grimké, William Lloyd Garrison, and Maria Weston Chapman, informed their quest for personal emancipation and social redemption, confirming their anger at prevailing injustices and raising their hopes of millennial fulfillment. Viewing their society from this perspective, they also saw widely accepted images of women and men in a new light. In their opposition to the violence of American economic and social life, these female and male reformers drew upon the dominant cultural image of women as the possessors of the pacific virtues, discovering there values worthy of cultivation in both men and women. But they also believed that "feminine" passivity had no place in the pacifism the gospel required. "Who will dare in Christian firmness and Christian meekness, to refuse to obey the *wicked laws* which require *woman to enslave, to degrade and to brutalize woman?*" the former slaveholder Angelina Grimké asked the Christian women of the South as she urged them to place obedience to God above obedience to man.[4]

This essay seeks to explain the origins, character, and implications of this episode in the history of American feminism. In an age when religion was the most common extrafamilial activity of American women, perfectionist feminism continued a tradition of female concern for public morality. Yet it also marked a turning point in the religious history of American women.

Images of Women in Antebellum Religious Reform

"In no country has such constant care been taken . . . to trace two clearly distinct lines of action for the two sexes," observed Alexis de Tocqueville after his tour of the United States in the mid-1830s.[5] The lives of women and men had always differed, of course, but Tocqueville was correct in thinking that the distinction was a matter of special concern for that generation of Americans. In the midst of the staggering economic, geographical, and demographic growth of the Jacksonian era, Americans were worried about the moral identity of their young, unruly, and as yet undefined republic, and to much of the Northern middle class the emerging cult of domesticity seemed to offer a route to cultural unity and moral certainty. The cultivation of private virtues in a domestic sphere under the aegis of women, proponents hoped, could preserve an orderly and Christian society by offsetting the unsteady and sometimes unsavory character of public life in a time of rapid social change.

The very fact that private life and public life—or, as nineteenth-century Americans put it, the domestic sphere and the public sphere—were conceptually separable is noteworthy. In the half-century since the Revolution, New England and its diaspora to the West had begun to change in ways that provided a basis for the separation and for the concepts by which it could be understood. The emphasis of economic life was shifting from household and agricultural production to commerce and industry, particularly in cities, and the overlap between home and work place that had prevailed in the seventeenth and eighteenth centuries diminished. As more men of the rising middle class worked away from home to earn cash for the commodities families had formerly produced

203

themselves, both the physical and the cultural distance between private life and public enterprise increased. Most women of this class continued to work in the home, of course; even those with outside employment usually returned within a few years to domestic pursuits, or combined the two. By the 1830s, the distinction between the social realities of men's and women's lives was apparent; the cultural result was a dualistic vision of gender and society.[6]

The cult of domesticity, which identified women with the private sphere and attributed to them the nurturing virtues appropriate to it, dominated American thought about womanhood by the 1830s. Although it could be interpreted in a wide variety of ways —in different hands it could isolate woman on a pedestal or lead to her better education for the tasks of motherhood—it generally included "the prevalent persuasion that there are virtues which are peculiarly masculine, and others which are peculiarly feminine," as the visiting English author Harriet Martineau put it in 1837.[7] Preached by Protestant clergymen and publicized in new, commercialized mass media aimed at the middle class, images of women as distinctively compassionate, self-denying, pure, and pious defined a chief moral and religious assumption of the age.

Among those who affirmed these images were religious leaders intent upon reforming the moral character of the young republic, who found many worthy assistants among the pious and benevolent women of the churches (where, after all, women far outnumbered men on membership rolls). In the Second Great Awakening (1795–1835), concern for religious renewal and social morality went hand in hand as evangelical churchmen sought, on the whole successfully, to win the American people's voluntary assent to piety and morality through revivalism, education, benevolence, and reform. In "female societies" gathered to support a variety of religious and humanitarian projects—missions, poor relief, education—women lent their aid without stepping beyond the boundaries of the domestic sphere; indeed, they could claim that their organized compassion was deeply consonant with their primary tasks and intrinsic nature. Evangelical women of New England and the middle states were most active in these efforts, but Unitarians in Massachusetts and Quakers in Pennsylvania were similarly engaged, typically meeting weekly to pray, study, and raise funds. Since their societies were usually auxiliary to all-male societies with the same purposes, benevolent women were viewed as helpmates in reform rather than as leaders; but even so, they often found their horizons stretched far beyond the walls of their homes by their engagement in the great moral and religious enterprises of their time.[8]

The greatest of these, at least in its threat to the social and economic structure of the United States of America, was the crusade for the immediate and unconditional abolition of slavery. Heralded by the Boston-based editor William Lloyd Garrison in 1831 and given national institutional expression at the founding of the American Anti-Slavery Society in 1833, abolitionism soon attracted the support of thousands of Northern women. These women shared with their brothers in the cause a prophetic rage against cruelty and an evangelical hope for the nation's speedy repentance from its worst sin; it is also likely that their own experience of subordination as women made them particularly responsive to the antislavery appeal.[9] In any case, the members of emerging female antislavery societies displayed, more vividly than had earlier activists, the radical potential of the ethical gender gap assumed by the cult of domesticity. "It is not in the nature of the female heart to look unmoved upon scenes of misery," they asserted as they pledged to turn all the force of outraged feeling against slavery.[10]

Innocently drawing on American culture's dominant images of women for the purpose of opposing America's most powerful political and economic institution, women abolitionists brought a distinctly "feminine" approach to their condemnation of slavery. "Whatever else it may be, slaveholding must be eminently a *domestic* evil," declared one group of abolitionist women. Defining the issue in this way served both to defend their activism in an unpopular cause their opponents thought was too political to concern women and to recruit the assistance of other women like themselves. "Upon all the relations that belong to [the family] circle, it wages war—and with deadly effect," the same group continued. "Can it be pretended that here is ground in which woman has no interest? Why, it is the ground on which she naturally moves. . . . HERE SHE LIVES." Identifying themselves with the domestic sphere, women abolitionists in the first half of the 1830s attempted to transform that sphere into a source of social regeneration. Perhaps the leading way in which they sought to exercise their private prerogatives for the public good was through their "influence," an indirect form of power ascribed to women by many thinkers in antebellum America. An expansive and imprecise social force, "influence" could encompass instructing one's children, remarking at tea that the sugar bowl contained free produce, and returning gentle advice about social issues for the love proffered by husbands and brothers. "Have ye no influence over those who are bound to you by the closest ties of relationship?" asked Elizabeth Margaret Chandler, the editor of the "Ladies Department" in *The Liberator* until her early death in 1834. Far from being sanctuaries from the cruel world, the homes of abolitionist women could exude an atmosphere of social involvement. "The pictures which adorn our parlors, and the songs and stories which animate our nurseries, may be made directly and powerfully subservient to the same object," wrote the Female Anti-Slavery Society of Chatham-Street Chapel of New York City. "Once set upon this end, we could readily devise a thousand ways to reach it." [11]

Whether singly in their own homes or in concert with one another—circulating petitions against slavery, raising funds to support male lecturers, or writing antislavery poems and pamphlets of their own—women abolitionists marshaled both the moral symbolism of private life and their own prodigious energies in a movement of crucial importance to their nation's life. Yet an understanding of reform so thoroughly grounded in the belief that the nature, rights, and duties of women were very different from those of men also suffered from at least two major contradictions. First, it disclosed a discomfort about the moral status of men that was shared by men and women abolitionists alike. And second, it restricted women even as it exalted Woman. Let us look at these more closely.

First, reformers' praise of the gentle traits of women was often accompanied by contrary assessments of male behavior in their commercial society. "Men are afraid, or perplexed with their social interests, or making calculations without or contrary to the book of God's word," wrote one abolitionist in 1835, "and therefore they are vacillating and uncertain." Women, on the other hand, had "no connection . . . with all those contradictory motives"; they were practically natural abolitionists. "Women of New England— mothers and daughters! if I fail to awake your sympathies, and secure your aid, I may well despair of gaining the hearts and support of men," cried Garrison in 1833.[12] Among reformers convinced of women's moral and religious superiority, such distrust of male morality was hard to dislodge. In Harriet Beecher Stowe's *Uncle Tom's Cabin,* for example, the depiction of the moral weakness and compromised lives of white men reveals a boundary beyond which it was difficult for domestic reform to pass; within the novel's scheme the efforts of salvific women can defeat the oppressive actions of individuals, but their ability to overcome the political and economic arrangements of society at large is left in doubt. Without a corresponding vision of the redemption of masculinity, the exaltation of femininity is insufficient to transform American life.

Second, even though the organization of compassionate women under the banner of domesticity opened for women substantial opportunities that had previously been closed, this arrangement continued to impose restrictions on their activities. Thus in 1836 Angelina Grimké, celebrating the fact that feminine benevolence had enabled *"woman* [to rise] to that influence and elevation in the world for which she was designed under the Gospel Dispensation," also took it for granted that woman should "frankly acknowledge [man] as 'the head' " and make her own contribution to reform a distinctly feminine one: "Her gentle influence is *felt* like falling dew—her soft & tender voice is heard in the heart, tho' never in the forum." [13] With the passage of time and the accumulation of experience, Grimké and a vocal minority of other abolitionist women would grow in both commitment to the cause and confidence in their own abilities; soon they would declare that the separate sphere to which they had been consigned was too small to contain them.

Under the pressure of these two contradictions, a revised view of gender and its ethical significance emerged as a central part of the program of one faction of abolitionists. Leading the intellectual and spiritual way toward this new vision was Maria Weston Chapman, a young officer of the Boston Female Anti-Slavery Society, who discovered in the religion of Christian perfection a set of images that transformed dominant understandings to offer full liberty to women even as it demanded full morality of men. Her statement of perfectionist feminism, later further developed by a community of men and women reformers, stands at a turning point in the history of American feminism.

The Emergence of Perfectionist Feminism

On October 21, 1835, a mob of some two thousand Bostonians assembled to disrupt the annual meeting of the Boston Female Anti-Slavery Society. Motivated by the antiabolitionist sentiment then at a zenith throughout the nation, these "gentlemen of property and standing"—mostly merchants—hoped to capture the well-known English abolitionist who was scheduled to address the meeting, but who in fact had already escaped. Thus thwarted, the mob had to make do with local game. First they bullied the women for an hour. Then they captured and dragged through the streets William Lloyd Garrison, who had agreed to address the women in the Englishman's absence.[14] In the face of this event, some of the women could not avoid noticing that the prerogatives of domestic and benevolent womanhood had proven to be paltry protection of their rights as reformers.

Among these was Maria Weston Chapman. Twenty-nine years old in 1835 and the mother of two small children, Chapman was remarkably well educated for a woman of the day, having served as the principal of the Boston High School for Young Ladies for the two years before her marriage in 1830 to a Boston merchant. In 1834, accompanied by a sizable assortment of Weston and Chapman sisters and cousins and aunts, the couple joined antislavery societies. On the day of the confrontation, Chapman stepped calmly forward as the besieged women's leader, speaking firmly to their assailants before directing the women to retreat to her own home.[15]

A few days later, Chapman sat down to write an account of the events of October 21. Her report was adopted by the Boston Female Anti-Slavery Society in November and soon published as *Right and Wrong in Boston*. Although it departed significantly from the earlier domestic understanding of female participation in reform, its implications seem to have gone unremarked both at the time and by later historians, perhaps because it was written by an author so angry that her prose is difficult to follow at some points. Nonetheless, Chapman here demonstrated the contradictions in prevailing views of gender and reform, advocating instead the merits of religious perfectionism as the basis for a feminist ethic of peace and justice.

First, she detailed the limitations of dominant images of women as a basis for reform activity. Although the respect accorded to the benevolent effusions of the feminine heart might protect the extra-familial activities of some women, Chapman wrote, it had hardly been ample protection for the members of the Boston Female Anti-Slavery Society. When the Fatherless and Widows' Society advertised a meeting, she noted dryly, "*those* ladies are designated as 'woman, stepping gracefully to the relief of infancy and suffering age'; and their treasury overflows with the donations of an approving public." When a meeting of women was held in support of an institution for the blind, "no one said *then,* 'women had better stay at home.' " Female antislavery societies, though acting "as other ladies' societies have *always* done," were being treated differently.[16] Moreover, the dominant images could too easily be turned against women; enforcing the most limited conceptions of woman's "sphere," after all, was among the mob's excuses for assembling. "Has it come to this, that the WOMEN of our country —not content with their proper sphere, the domestic fireside—must hold public meetings to encourage the efforts of a foreign emissary to destroy our peace?" thundered a typical critic in the Boston press. Chapman quoted him in her report as a reminder to her sisters that such alarms, whether based on a glib use of convenient stereotypes or real fear of the unmeasured potential of militant womanhood, found a ready audience in the America of 1835.[17]

No longer content to expand woman's sphere while assenting to its general characteristics, Chapman proposed in *Right and Wrong in Boston* an alternative understanding of gender based upon "the dearest human rights—rights equally dear to man and woman," [18] rights she grounded firmly in perfectionist conceptions of human nature and social morality. The first lengthy statement of perfectionist feminism, Chapman's argument asserted the equality of the sexes, but it also did much more. Directly challenging the segregation of public morality from private virtue, Chapman demonstrated that the ethics of gender were important not just to women but also to the well-being of society itself.

An exclusively domestic understanding of women, she wrote, was quite different from Christianity "as it fell from the lips of its founder." The reproof Jesus had administered to Martha was deleted in the corrupt religion of the present day; women now were "cumbered with much serving" and unable to attend to the words of the master, as Mary had done with his approval. Exclusively domestic duties made women "feeble and frivolous, and unable to discern the true duties of woman, wife and mother"; Chapman could call this nothing but sinful. Yet uppermost in her mind was not the division of physical labor but the division of moral labor, and here she was resolutely egalitarian. If something is "good for man, *to us* it follows also that it is good for woman." To those who "term it 'leaving our proper sphere, the domestic fire-side,' to feel and act like immortal souls," she responded, "We cannot, if we would, believe that this garment of womanhood wherewith our souls are invested, debars us from the privileges or absolves us from the duties of a spiritual existence." [19]

If womanhood was but a garment, from what *could* it debar its wearers? This forthright claim that nature had not revealed all its purposes in the details of physiology, coupled with the assertion that revelation was blind to gender, cut straight through accepted notions of divergent masculinity and femininity. Gender-distinct morality—appealing to phrases like "the retiring softness, so becoming in our sex"—was a gross compromise of the ethical demands of the gospel, Chapman contended. To understand God's commands as blind to gender would mean, for women, greater scope. For men and their institutions, however, adopting as their own the "gospel of PEACE" would have implications that were, if anything, even more radical. Casting her program in the language of millennial hope, Chapman identified pacifism as the key to a perfectionist revision of public and private life. "When men cease to treasure up wrath . . . by supporting naval and military establishments" and rely instead on the promise of God, "they will cease to rank the body higher than the soul, by placing strength of arm above strength of purpose," she wrote. Then the sex-biased morality of the present would be overcome; then "they will cease their labors to soften and enfeeble one half of the whole human race to the manifest injury of the whole." The result would be a new birth of Christian firmness and Christian meekness, for women and for men. "When they have advanced thus far in the Christian career they will have perceived that to ALL is the command given to be *gentle;* and that any other softness than this Christian virtue, is sin." [20]

Chapman's extension of the claims of female reformers expressed her personal rage at society's "enfeeblement" of women of her class, but this extension of claims was not only personal; it also explored the implications for gender relations of the intense religiosity of the abolitionist circle to which she belonged. The acknowledged leader of this group in most matters was William Lloyd Garrison—beloved by friends like Chapman though hated and feared as a dangerous radical by most of his contemporaries—and from him the Boston-based clique of radical abolitionists has taken its name.[21] Among other prominent Garrisonians were Lydia Maria Child, a popular author and reform journalist; Edmund Quincy, a gentleman of letters from one of Boston's most prominent families; and Lucretia Mott, a Hicksite Quaker of Philadelphia. Allied with these metropolitan liberals were a number of reformers whose backgrounds were more like that of Garrison, a lower-class Baptist from Newburyport: Henry C. Wright, a former hat maker and Congregational minister; Abby Kelley, a Quaker schoolmistress in Lynn; and her future husband, Stephen Foster, a New Hampshire farm boy and Union Theological Seminary dropout. In 1837–38, this group would for a time adopt into its midst Sarah and Angelina Grimké. The list could be expanded to include several dozen others, but these names suffice to situate the group and show that it defies simple sociological categorization.

The violence of 1835 also pressed Garrison to develop further his own statement of a perfectionist ethic. In the ensuing months and years, Garrison, Chapman, and other radical abolitionists developed a position that included some of the characteristic beliefs of the militant evangelicalism of their day, though transforming them as sectarians so often transform the dominant movements from which they come. Although the great majority of evangelicals would eschew the radical proposals of these perfectionists, the Second Great Awakening bequeathed to them a legacy of rich imagery linking social regeneration to the conversion of individual sinners on the one hand and the coming of the millennium on the other.

Perfectionism declared that complete emancipation from sin in all its forms is possible in this life.[22] Sanguine and simple, it stripped human beings and God of obscure or complicated motivations and posited direct accessibility between them. "Souls"—as human beings were usually called—could both know the will of God and do it. With all intermediaries between God and the soul abrogated, the "souls" who lived within perfectionism carried a heavy burden of individual accountability to God's will. Accompanying this was an intensely experienced liberation from the constraints of all authorities other than God—including, most decidedly, the church and the state. This was Christian anarchism.

It was also a form of Christian millennialism, though a more utopian form than that held by the majority of those who had been touched by the Second Great Awakening. Garrisonian perfectionism collapsed the distinction between the someday and the now, this life and the hereafter. Possessing the freedom to choose obedience to God over bondage to sin, human beings could reverse the tide of history and the purported fall of humanity. "Whatever the gospel is designed to destroy at any period of the world . . . ought now to be abandoned," declared a Garrisonian manifesto in 1838. Not content to achieve perfection after death, the Garrisonians claimed it in the here and now, as citizens of an already existing government of God. "We cannot acknowledge allegiance to any human government," this declaration continued; "we recognize but one KING and LAWGIVER, one JUDGE and RULER of mankind." [23]

The system of chattel slavery exemplified the perfectionists' vision of evil. To them, slavery was wrong precisely because it denied the accountability of the soul to God, blocking the channel between them with the usurped, violently wielded authority of the master. These abolitionists found that perfectionism suited and extended their reform in other ways as well. Perfectionism reinforced their impatience with gradualism, political compromise, and an imperfect social order. It required "universal reform"—the righting of many wrongs, not just the worst. It marshaled strong religious feelings to the doing of a task within the secular world.

Of the many corollaries of perfectionism none was more perfect than nonresistance. Taking literally the New Testament injunction to "resist not evil," these abolitionists urged slaves not to rebel by force of arms, governments not to wage war or hang criminals, and themselves not to fight back against their sometimes violent opponents. Violence was, after all, a form of coercion at direct odds with the freedom perfectionists granted each individual. If God governed the world, the religious argument ran, the faithful must trust in divine protection or, failing that, glory in a sanctified martyrdom. But the social argument carried a more radical tone: Nonresistance denied the power of the master or the husband or

212

the state to compel. As Maria Weston Chapman put it in 1835, "Scripture calls the Christian life a warfare, and in declaring that the weapons are not carnal, it fulfills one of its main purposes—to annul all distinctions but those of the soul." [24]

To "annul all distinctions but those of the soul" was to deny the authority of master over slave, husband over wife, and clergy or magistrate over people. Perfectionism's radically individualistic understanding of moral authority squarely challenged some of antebellum America's most cherished assumptions about men and women. Rejecting compromises with corruption, it demanded that the public sphere be as good as the private; reducing human beings to their souls, it questioned the primacy of physical gender as a determinant of behavior. Nonviolent, antipolitical, pietistic, it created a style of reform in which women theoretically could participate equally with men.

Women and Men in the Government of God

In the summer of 1837, the Boston Garrisonians arranged a lecture tour of New England for two former slaveholders who had become abolitionists, Angelina and Sarah Grimké. The Grimkés were expected by most abolitionists to speak only to groups of women, an acceptable task within the recognized bounds of female propriety. But even before they gave their first lecture, it was clear that something less acceptable was impending. Maria Weston Chapman, introducing the sisters in a circular to all the female antislavery societies, praised "the elevated and Christian point of view from which they behold the condition of woman: her duties and her consequent rights." "In all spiritual things," Chapman wrote, the duties of men and women were "identical," and as to "secondary pursuits, whether mercantile, mechanical, domestic, or professional," gender was equally irrelevant: "All are alike bound to the strenuous exercise of such faculties as God has given them." [25]

Well-educated women who had long chafed under the restrictions imposed by parents and religious leaders, the Grimkés were elated to become part of the perfectionist community in Boston. "At Friend Chapman's, where we spent a social evening, I had a long talk with the brethren on the rights of women and found a very general sentiment prevailing that it is time our fetters were broken," Angelina reported happily. "L. M. Child and Maria Chapman strongly supported this view." Sarah agreed with her sister's assessment, pronouncing herself "helped, strengthened, invigorated" by the Boston group. "There is some elasticity in this atmosphere," she concluded with satisfaction.[26]

The "elasticity" Sarah noticed in the Massachusetts atmosphere belonged, not to the population at large, but to the tiny perfectionist elite. As the sisters' fame preceded them from town to town, men as well as women came to listen, turning respectable all-female audiences into "promiscuous assemblies." Ministers led the cry of outrage against the Grimkés' infringements of womanly propriety, most notably in a well-known pastoral letter issued by the state's association of Congregational clergymen, and even many abolitionists joined in. But the Grimkés continued in their course, adding to their spoken and written arguments against slavery a new element: a defense of their right, as women, to act as full moral beings. Throughout the painful controversy, the two pioneer lecturers endured the "trials" to which they were subjected only with the aid of the personal and spiritual support they received from the little sect with which they cast their lot in 1837–38. Chapman, Garrison, and Henry C. Wright were particularly helpful, as were the ideas these three perfectionists had been discussing since 1835. "The more I contemplate this sublime doctrine of acknowledging no government but Gods, of loosing myself from all dominion of man both civil and ecclesiastical, the more I am persuaded it is the only doctrine that can bring us into that liberty wherewith Christ made us free," Sarah wrote in June 1837 as the storm broke around her. "At the present time this change in my feelings is a peculiar blessing, because I am engaged in a work that calls for much faith and I find from day to day the promise fulfilled." Angelina shared Sarah's conversion to "the blessed doctrine of Divine Government"—a doctrine providing both a lofty vantage point from which to criticize prevailing earthly dispensations and, more immediately, comfort to a radical acting in opposition to civil and ecclesiastical governments.[27]

Under the laws of God's government, the Grimkés and Chapman agreed, gender had, of itself, no moral content. "When human beings are regarded as *moral* beings," Angelina declared, "*sex,* instead of being enthroned upon the summit . . . sinks into insignificance and nothingness." Similarly, Abby Kelley, who would follow the Grimkés onto the lecture trail, challenged her critics to "show me the difference between a soul that may have taken up its abode . . . in a female tenement, and one that inhabits a male tenement." [28] On the basis of this anthropology, the Garrisonians collectively rejected the contemporary notion that the world was divided into separate female and male spheres, each with a distinctive morality, to describe the one sphere that was suitable to both women and men.

The crux of America's immorality, both Grimkés asserted in their 1837 writings on the rights of women, was "the anti-christian doctrine of masculine and feminine virtues." While encouraging in women passivity and unconcern for social injustice, this doctrine had "given to man a charter for the exercise of tyranny and selfishness, pride and arrogance, lust and brutal violence," Angelina charged. This catalogue of sins—the same ones to which abolitionists attributed slavery—resulted, she argued, from the false understanding of masculinity that was the reverse side of feminine retirement. To make war, to be stern, to acquire, to participate in a corrupt politics, "in common estimation belong to his character as a *man*." [29] If a just society were to be achieved, Americans had to remake the male role as well as the female one.

"To regard modesty and delicacy, and all the kindred virtues, as peculiarly appropriate to [women]," as Sarah Grimké put it, was one cornerstone of the Jacksonian era's dominant effort to balance virtue against expansion. A compensatory ethic based upon cultivating in the private sphere the wholesome and stabilizing qualities of selflessness, purity, and love, this effort obscured the absence of these virtues from the world of politics and economics. The *special* duty of woman was to embody in the private sphere "peace on earth, good will toward men," the domestic theoretician Catharine Beecher told Angelina Grimké as she urged her to relinquish public agitation. "Indeed!" the abolitionist responded, "did our Holy Redeemer preach the doctrine of *peace to our sex* only?" Grimké the daring lecturer agreed with Beecher the exponent of domesticity that women should not exert "coercive influences" or engage in "party conflict"; the crucial point between them was whether men should. If *everyone* followed "the precepts and examples of Christ," Grimké asserted, all would soon see that "after all, this appropriate sphere of woman is *just as appropriate* to man." [30]

215

What was this one "sphere" that could be inhabited, in equality, by both women and men? As Grimké suggested, it emphasized many supposedly "feminine" qualities; it "prize[d] the purity of *his* character as highly as . . . that of hers." Upon the death of Elizabeth Chandler, as "feminine" an abolitionist as ever there was, Maria Weston Chapman expressed her hope that "this character might become the general one . . . not of American *women* only, but of American *men*." Men who inhabited this new "sphere"— Garrison, Wright, Quincy, Foster, and others—chose to sway hearts as publicists instead of conquering them with ballots or swords. Their only weapons were the weapons they shared with women, and their position in society was, therefore, a somewhat "feminine" one. But this new "sphere" also had a "masculine" side. Since it included the lecture platform as surely as it did the home, women who inhabited it could stride between one and the other with an ease shocking to their contemporaries. "All who are valiantly in the warfare, cannot be out of their sphere," abolitionist editor Nathaniel Peabody Rogers of New Hampshire announced to a group of Garrisonian women, "and all who are not—cannot be in it." [31]

Nowhere were the full implications of this single moral standard for the lives of women and men as clear as in their nonresistance. To renounce violence even in self-defense, as nonresistance required, was not a passive repudiation of social engagement. It was, rather, an uncompromising critique of all forms of social action tinged with any degree of coercion, whether warfare or militia duty, capital punishment or spanking, slaveholding or voting. Its universal adoption, partisans believed, would end the corruptions of Jacksonian America and inaugurate the kingdom of God on earth.

A persistent theme in Garrisonian thought after 1835, nonresistance took on institutional form at a "peace convention" held in Boston in September 1838, when the New England Non-Resistance Society was founded and a Declaration of Sentiments written by Garrison and signed by seventeen women and eighteen men was issued. As citizens of God's government—with laws set by the example of Jesus—the signatories refused to participate in the coercive practices of human society, including "distinction of rank, or division of caste, or inequality of sex." To live under God's government was to renounce specific forms of power that many Americans took for granted: the power to defend by force oneself, one's nation, or even "the public peace"; the power to "bear arms, or to hold a military office"; and, "as every human government is upheld by physical strength," the power to hold any public office or elect others to do so.[32]

The many Americans who took such powers for granted were, of course, white adult males. Better weapons than these, the nonresistants declared, were ones associated in Jacksonian culture with the feminine. "The sinful dispositions of man can be subdued only by love," they affirmed, distilling in all innocence the plot of many a contemporary novel. Both efficacy in the task of "moral regeneration" and protection from the world's strife lay, they concluded, "in being gentle, harmless, long-suffering, and abundant in mercy."[33] Such were the virtues prized in that single sphere which they claimed would best suit both women and men and bring a perfect society with it.

Demanded by the logic of their religious position, the Garrisonians' understanding of the connection between feminism and pacifism represented a peculiar combination of persistent themes in the history of Christianity with the assumptions and urgencies of their own time. In the language of theology, their ethical program amounted to a declaration that human beings could escape in this life the grip of sin in both of its classic meanings: personal wrongdoing and cosmic alienation. Although the dominant interpretations of Christianity had held for centuries that human frailty was indelible—thus legitimating the temporal authorities' attempts to restrain it—dissenters had for as many centuries found hope of something better in the eschatological promises and moral stringencies of the Old and New Testaments. Taking seriously Jesus' command, "be ye perfect," the Garrisonians joined a long procession of Christian sectarians who had unequivocally renounced war and other forms of coercion, though their commitment to the renovation of public life prevented them from withdrawing into sectarian isolation.[34] Yet the perfectionists' transformation of particular images of women and men, undertaken in awareness of the ethical significance those images could carry, added a dimension to Christian pacifism that connected it, in a distinctive way, to the concerns and assumptions of their own time. In a culture that attributed virtue to women and resolution to men, the Garrisonian

217

image of a single sphere that was appropriate to both aimed to elicit from women the firmness and from men the meekness that would finally bring to fulfillment God's plan for peace and justice.

Since the variety of egalitarianism endorsed by these nonresistants depended as heavily upon the restriction of the male "sphere" as upon the expansion of the female one, the Garrisonians were free to attempt to put it into immediate effect among themselves. A reform movement in which neither sex voted or fought and both lectured and wrote was a movement in which women could participate equally with men. This principle transformed the arrangements in their organizations. Beginning in 1838, all state and national antislavery societies in which Garrisonians could command a majority hurried to grant the rights of full membership—vote, voice, and office—to women, and after an organizational schism in 1840 between Garrisonians and more moderate abolitionists, women played major roles in every aspect of Garrisonian reform. Although conflicting views of gender furnished only one source of the discord among abolitionist factions—disagreement over working within political and ecclesiastical structures was another—historians who have concluded that "the woman question" was only a peripheral issue in the division have been mistaken.[35] They have viewed the event solely from the perspective of men: after all, it can hardly be argued that the right of women to participate is a peripheral issue for women. They have also underrated the concern of this generation of Americans for the ethics of gender— ethics, the Garrisonians demonstrated, with significance not only for women but also for men, and for society as a whole.

During the next two decades, Garrisonian feminists extended the exploration of their ideals from public reform into private life —an extraordinarily difficult matter in a society that provided little systemic support for the equality they envisioned, but one with which they nonetheless struggled nobly.[36] Their views changed over time, but they continued to attract to themselves women and men dissatisfied with the prevailing state of things. Younger women who would be the leaders of American feminism for the remainder of the century—Elizabeth Cady Stanton, Susan B. Anthony, Lucy Stone, and Antoinette Brown Blackwell, among others—acquired concepts and training and courage during their own years of participation in Garrisonian reform in the 1840s and 1850s. Indeed, participants concurred then, as historians do now, that the leading cause of the woman suffrage movement that began in 1848 was this segment of abolitionism.[37]

Feminism and Pacifism in Historical Perspective

Garrisonian perfectionism was one episode in a long history of the association between feminism and pacifism. Among its antecedents was the peace testimony of the Quakers, who also honored the spiritual gifts of women, and it was followed by opposition to war in the early twentieth century on the part of reform-minded suffragists such as Jane Addams, a founder of the Women's International League for Peace and Freedom. "There is no class of persons who have more to hope from a new state of things, which shall not rest upon the foundation of brute force, than women," declared Edmund Quincy in *The Non-Resistant,* articulating an analysis that many later feminists would share in the belief that violence was particularly antithetical to women's interests and common experience.[38]

Even so, the perfectionists' conviction that feminism and pacifism are inseparable did not arise from neglect of issues like those that have been sources of misgiving in contemporary thinking on the relationship between the two causes. Emerging from a culture that emphasized divergence between these sexes, the reformers both drew upon and transformed prevailing images of women. Their insistence that women and men should live by a single moral standard made the supposedly pacific nature of women the standard for both sexes, rather than adapting women's aspirations to the ways of men. But in the hands of these morally strenuous critics of their society, the standard of peace and justice also challenged women as it supported them in a courageous and energetic activism that expanded the range of their experience well beyond the established conventions of the time, accelerating the entry of women into public life in America.

The religious position underlying their radical proposals linked the perfectionists to a long historic tradition and sparked their innovative departures from the conventions of their time. Outside the institutional church but within the tradition of millennial Christianity, avoiding cloistered communitarianism but devising a utopian religious movement nonetheless, these self-proclaimed citizens of the government of God could clearly discern the violence and hierarchy of the governments of men. As with other utopians, social realities often contravened their high standards and great expectations; as a tiny minority in their society, they could hardly overturn the prevailing order so that peace might generally prevail, and they sometimes failed to overturn violence and hierarchy even within themselves.[39] Yet earthly triumph is a poor test for any religious movement. As perfectionists, a small group of women asserted in unmistakable terms their own longings for freedom and often, they believed, found them fulfilled. And with their brothers, they reminded their society of a gospel that calls "ALL . . . to be *gentle.*"

Notes

1. Useful treatments of this relationship include Gerda Lerner, "Black and White Women in Interaction and Confrontation," in *The Majority Finds Its Past: Placing Women in History* (New York: Oxford University Press, 1979), and Nancy F. Cott, "Liberation Politics in Two Eras," *American Quarterly* 32 (1980): 96–105. The latter is a review of three books that are relevant to this topic: Sara Evans, *Personal Politics: The Roots of Women's Liberation in the Civil Rights Movement and the New Left* (New York: Knopf, 1979); Blanche Glassman Hersh, *The Slavery of Sex: Feminist Abolitionists in America* (Urbana, Ill.: University of Illinois Press, 1978); and Ellen Carol DuBois, *Feminism and Suffrage: The Emergence of an Independent Women's Movement in America, 1848–1869* (Ithaca, N.Y.: Cornell University Press, 1978).

2. Mary Pellauer, "War and Sexism in a Nuclear Age," in Charles P. Lutz and Jerry L. Folk, eds., *Peaceways* (Minneapolis: Augsburg, 1983), p. 96.

3. See, for example, Rosemary Radford Ruether, "Feminism and Peace," *The Christian Century* C:25 (1983): 771–776; Pam McAlister, ed., *Reweaving the Web of Life: Feminism and Nonviolence* (Philadelphia: New Society Publishers, 1982); and Cambridge Women's Peace Collective, *My Country Is the Whole World: An Anthology of Women's Work on Peace and War* (London: Pandora Press, 1984).

4. Angelina E. Grimké, *An Appeal to the Christian Women of the South* (New York: American Anti-Slavery Society, 1836), p. 25.

5. Alexis de Tocqueville, *Democracy in America,* vol. 2 (New York: Vintage Books, 1945), p. 223.

6. Nancy F. Cott, *The Bonds of Womanhood: "Woman's Sphere" in New England, 1780–1835* (New Haven, Conn.: Yale University Press, 1977), examines the emergence of the cult of domesticity and its relationship to the social realities of women's lives. Cott's conclusion also lists and assesses other interpretations of the origins and meaning of woman's sphere in this period.

7. Harriet Martineau, *Society in America*, vol. 2 (New York: Saunders and Otley, 1837), p. 233.

8. For a more extensive discussion of women in benevolent societies, see Dorothy C. Bass, " 'Their Prodigious Influence': Women, Religion, and Reform in Antebellum America," in Rosemary Ruether and Eleanor McLaughlin, eds., *Women of Spirit: Female Leadership in the Jewish and Christian Traditions* (New York: Simon and Schuster, 1979). Cott, *Bonds of Womanhood*, pp. 126–159, contains information on the numerical predominance of women as church members and an interpretation of their religious activities.

9. Cott makes this point in "Liberation Politics in Two Eras." See also Hersh, *The Slavery of Sex*, and DuBois, *Feminism and Suffrage*, pp. 21–52. Gerda Lerner has also written about the relationship between feminism and abolitionism in "The Political Activities of Antislavery Women," in *The Majority Finds Its Past*, and in *The Grimké Sisters from South Carolina: Rebels against Slavery* (Boston: Houghton Mifflin, 1967). There were substantial differences in motives, ideas, and experiences between white women and black women opposing slavery. Free black women in the North worked against slavery through the liberation activities of the black community, and occasionally through such predominantly white organizations as the Boston Female Anti-Slavery Society and the Philadelphia Female Anti-Slavery Society. In "Black and White Women," Lerner treats some of the tensions and issues involved. This essay emphasizes the experience of white Northern women, among whom the images of gender under consideration here were most widespread.

10. *The Liberator*, January 7, 1832.

11. Female Anti-Slavery Society of Chatham-Street Chapel, *Constitution and Address* (New York: William S. Dorr, 1834), pp. 8, 14; Chandler in Benjamin Lundy, ed., *The Poetical Works of Elizabeth Margaret Chandler, with a Memoir of Her Life and Character* (Philadelphia: Lemuel Howell, 1836), p. 19.

12. [George Bourne], *The Abrogation of the Seventh Commandment by the American Churches* (New York: D. Ruggles, 1835), p. 17; William Lloyd Garrison to Harriott Plummer et al., March 4, 1833, in Walter M. Merrill, ed., *The Letters of William Lloyd Garrison*, vol. 1 (Cam-

bridge, Mass.: Harvard University Press, 1971), p. 209. Abolitionist women assessed male character in a similar manner: "As *women,* it is incumbent upon us, instantly and always, to labor to increase the knowledge and love of God, that such concentrated hatred of his character and laws may no longer be so intrenched in *men's* business and bosoms" ([Maria Weston Chapman], *Right and Wrong in Boston, in 1836: [Third] Annual Report of the Boston Female Anti-Slavery Society* [Boston: Isaac Knapp, 1836], p. 29).

13. Angelina Grimké to L. L. Dodge, July 14, 1836, in the Theodore Dwight Weld Papers, Library of Congress.

14. Eyewitness accounts of the events of October 21, 1835, may be found in Wendell Phillips Garrison and Francis Jackson Garrison, *William Lloyd Garrison, 1805–1879: The Story of His Life Told by His Children,* vol. 2 (New York: Century, 1885), pp. 9–30; Charles C. Burleigh's account in *The Liberator,* October 24, 1835; and Maria Weston Chapman's account in [Chapman], *Right and Wrong in Boston: Report of the Boston Female Anti-Slavery Society, with a Concise Statement of Events Previous and Subsequent to the Annual Meeting of 1835* (Boston: Boston Female Anti-Slavery Society, 1836), pp. 28–39.

15. For biographical information on Maria Weston Chapman, see Alma Lutz, "Maria Weston Chapman," in Edward T. James, Janet Wilson James, and Paul S. Boyer, eds., *Notable American Women,* vol. 1 (Cambridge, Mass.: Harvard University Press, 1971), pp. 324–325; and William H. Pease and Jane H. Pease, *Bound with Them in Chains: A Biographical History of the Antislavery Movement* (Westport, Conn.: Greenwood Press, 1972), pp. 28–59.

16. Chapman, *Right and Wrong in 1835,* p. 6.

17. "C." quoted in ibid., pp. 12–16.

18. Ibid., p. 47.

19. Ibid., pp. 51, 47, 50–52.

20. Ibid., pp. 47–49.

21. Important works on Garrison and his circle include John L. Thomas, *The Liberator: William Lloyd Garrison: A Biography* (Boston: Little, Brown, 1963), and Aileen S. Kraditor, *Means and Ends in American Abolitionism: Garrison and His Critics on Strategy and Tactics, 1834–1850* (New York: Random House, 1967). A recent work that emphasizes the relationships within "the Boston Clique" is Lawrence J. Friedman, *Gregarious Saints: Self and Community in American Abolitionism, 1830–1870* (Cambridge and New York: Cambridge University Press, 1982).

22. Lewis Perry, *Radical Abolitionism: Anarchy and the Government*

of God in Antislavery Thought (Ithaca, N.Y.: Cornell University Press, 1973), treats the central themes of Garrisonian perfectionism. Other slightly or very different religious positions are also known by this name. Indeed, Timothy L. Smith, "Righteousness and Hope: Christian Holiness and the Millennial Vision in America, 1800–1900," *American Quarterly* 31 (1979): 21–45, discerns what he calls perfectionism in a wide spectrum of American thought. I have been most influenced here by the interpretation of perfectionism in Thomas, *The Liberator,* chap. 12.

23. *Principles of the Non-Resistance Society* (Boston: New England Non-Resistance Society, 1839), p. 7. In this statement, Garrison shows the influence of John Humphrey Noyes, who preached in his newspaper *The Perfectionist* the "ultra" doctrine that the millennium had begun in A.D. 70 and that Jesus Christ was therefore already reigning on "the throne of the world." Noyes and Garrison corresponded during the mid-1830s; later Noyes would found the Oneida Community in upstate New York. John Humphrey Noyes to William Lloyd Garrison, March 22, 1837, in *Life of Garrison,* vol. 2, pp. 145–148.

24. Chapman, *Right and Wrong in 1835,* p. 52.

25. Maria Weston Chapman, "To Female Anti-Slavery Societies throughout New England," June 7, 1837, in Gilbert H. Barnes and Dwight L. Dumond, eds., *Letters of Theodore Dwight Weld, Angelina Grimké Weld, and Sarah Grimké, 1822–1844,* vol. 1 (New York: Appleton-Century, 1934), p. 396.

26. Angelina Grimké is quoted in Lerner, *The Grimké Sisters,* p. 166; Sarah M. Grimké to Theodore D. Weld, June 11, 1837, in Barnes and Dumond, eds., *Letters,* vol. 1, p. 401.

27. Sarah Grimké to Gerrit Smith, June 28, 1837, in Barnes and Dumond, eds., *Letters,* vol. 1, pp. 408–409; Angelina Grimké to Henry C. Wright, August 12, 1837, ibid., pp. 421–422. On Wright, see Lewis Perry, *Childhood, Marriage, and Reform: Henry Clarke Wright, 1797–1870* (Chicago: University of Chicago Press, 1980). The pastoral letter is in [Maria Weston Chapman], *Right and Wrong in Boston: [Fourth] Annual Report of the Boston Female Anti-Slavery Society, with a Sketch of the Obstacles Thrown in the Way of Emancipation by Certain Clerical Abolitionists and Advocates for the Subjection of Woman, in 1837* (Boston: Isaac Knapp, 1837), p. 47.

28. Angelina E. Grimké, *Letters to Catherine E. Beecher* (Boston: Isaac Knapp, 1838), p. 115; Abby Kelley to Elizur Wright, Jr., in *The Liberator,* September 6, 1839.

29. Angelina E. Grimké, *Letters to Catherine E. Beecher,* pp. 115–116. Grimké was writing in response to Catharine E. Beecher, *An Essay*

on *Slavery and Abolitionism, with Reference to the Duty of American Females* (Philadelphia: Henry Perkins, 1837). Beecher's book demonstrates the political implications of her version of the cult of domesticity. On Beecher, an important figure, see Kathryn Kish Sklar, *Catharine Beecher: A Study in American Domesticity* (New Haven, Conn.: Yale University Press, 1973).

30. Sarah M. Grimké, *Letters on the Equality of the Sexes, and the Condition of Woman* (Boston: Isaac Knapp, 1838), p. 122; Angelina Grimké, *Letters to Beecher,* pp. 103–104, 109.

31. Angelina Grimké, *Letters to Beecher,* p. 119; Chapman, *Right and Wrong in 1836,* p. 77; Nathaniel P. Rogers, *An Address Delivered before the Concord Female Anti-Slavery Society, at Its Annual Meeting, December 25, 1837* (Concord, N.H.: William White, 1838), p. 19.

32. New England Non-Resistance Society, *Principles, &c., [and] Declaration of Sentiments, Adopted by the Peace Convention, Held in Boston, September ... 1838* (Boston, 1839). The signatories to the declaration are listed in *The Non-Resistant,* August 3, 1839. *The Non-Resistant* was a biweekly newspaper edited by Maria Weston Chapman and Edmund Quincy, published from 1839 to 1843. In the issue of September 23, 1840, it claimed one thousand subscribers, almost half of them in Massachusetts.

33. Non-Resistance Society, *Principles,* pp. 3–6.

34. The most thorough treatment of Garrisonian nonresistance and its place in the history of Christian pacifism is Peter Brock, *Pacifism in the United States: From the Colonial Era to the First World War* (Princeton: Princeton University Press, 1968).

35. Studies of the schism of 1840 are numerous. A recent reliable source summarizes them thus: "The consensus of historians examining this problem is that all abolitionist factions regarded the women's question as a symbol of more substantial differences" (John R. McKivigan, *The War against Proslavery Religion: Abolitionism and the Northern Churches, 1830–1865* [Ithaca, N.Y.: Cornell University Press, 1984], p. 64).

36. Examples include efforts to build egalitarian marriages on the parts of Angelina Grimké and Theodore Dwight Weld and Abby Kelley and Stephen Foster. For further examples, see Hersh, *The Slavery of Sex.*

37. "Above all other causes of the 'Woman Suffrage Movement,' was the Anti-Slavery struggle in this country," wrote three aging abolitionists, now suffragists, in 1881; Elizabeth Cady Stanton, Susan B. Anthony, and Matilda Joslyn Gage, *History of Woman Suffrage,* vol. 1 (Rochester, N.Y.: Charles Mann, 1889), p. 52. DuBois, *Feminism*

and Suffrage, p. 31, argues that abolitionism provided the "particular framework within which the politics of women's rights developed," and emphasizes the Garrisonian contribution.

38. Edmund Quincy, "Non-Resistance and the Condition of Woman," *The Non-Resistant,* May 11, 1842. Cambridge Women's Peace Collective, *My Country Is the Whole World,* documents the longer history of the association.

39. For example, most Garrisonians finally came to support the Union army during the Civil War, especially after emancipation became a war goal. And shortly thereafter, feminists suffered a division, when Stanton and Anthony determined that an independent women's movement was necessary after some of their former abolitionist colleagues gave woman suffrage a lower priority than black suffrage in their strategy for attaining equality. These events came some decades after the heyday of perfectionism, it should be remembered.

Ten

Images of Women and Jews in Nineteenth- and Twentieth-Century German Theology*

Sheila Briggs

The following study examines the interrelationship between ideas of women and ideas of Jews in German theological ethics. It traces the development of German theological ethics through three major periods. The first comprises the years between the end of the Napoleonic Wars in 1815 and the foundation of the Second Empire in 1871; the second period begins with the proclamation of the Second Empire in 1871 and ends at the beginning of the First World War; the third period extends from the close of the First World War through the Weimar Republic to the early years of the Third Reich.

The interaction between theological image and social reality has particular bearing on the interpretation of the ethical writings of early nineteenth-century Christian male theologians. Nineteenth-century theologians wrote their ethics for a society that did not exist or, at best, was slowly coming into existence; the modern bourgeois liberal society assumed in their ethics was largely unrealized at that time. To use the famous dictum of Karl Marx, the

* The nucleus of this chapter was presented as a paper in the Women and Religion section at the annual meeting of the American Academy of Religion in Dallas, December 1983. I then had the opportunity to revise and expand the original draft for a public lecture and seminar, given at the Pembroke Center for Teaching and Research on Women of Brown University, March 1984. I am grateful to Joan W. Scott, the director of the Pembroke Center, and the other participants in the seminar for the useful discussion and critique of my work. I also must acknowledge my gratitude to Edith Bloch, who extended generous out-of-town hospitality to me and graciously put up with the whims of the researcher.

226

Germans thought what other nations did. Therefore, theological statements by these German Christian males cannot be related to the social phenomena of nineteenth-century Germany. We cannot retrieve from the positive or negative judgments of these theologians an accurate reflection of the lives of nineteenth-century women and Jews, and certainly not of the self-understanding of these two groups.[1] This does not mean that theology performed no social function in nineteeth-century Germany; it means that it did not provide an ideological superstructure for existing social phenomena.

German theological ethics of the nineteenth century was a normative science. Its self-defined task was that of undergirding intellectually what Christian males saw as the actualization of ultimate reality in society. German theological ethics was undertaken in the universities, institutions under the ownership and the tight administration and surveillance of the state. The teachers of theological ethics—university professors—were servants of the state. Their students, like themselves, were Christian males who would hold social responsibility as pastors in a state church or occasionally in some other field, normally under the state's aegis, for example, as teachers in *Gymnasien* (German high schools). Thus, German theologians of the nineteenth century developed their elaborate ethical systems in a Christian male setting as civil servants for an audience of future ecclesiastical and secular civil servants.

What was the role of those who on gender, ethnic, or religious grounds were excluded from the creation and execution of this normative view of social goals? The roles of women and Jews were differently defined but, as we shall see, interlinked.

1815–71: Equality of the Sexes and Female Domesticity

Friedrich Schleiermacher's ethics exercised a profound influence on later thinking. In the earlier part of his intellectual career, when he was part of the early romantic movement, Schleiermacher became friends with several Jewish women. Henriette Herz, Dorothea Veit, and Rahel Levin were among the leaders of the early romantic movement, whose members met in their salons. The prominence of Jewish women resulted from the early romantic protest against the double social constraints placed upon them as Jews and as women. Committed to the theory of *Geselligkeit,* the intimate exchange of thoughts and feelings through a free and close association, the early romantics advocated the natural affinity of all human persons, transcending the barriers of gender, race, and class. The goal was *Bildung,* education that is no less than the spiritual formation of the individuals involved. As an early romantic, Schleiermacher was a critic of the oppression of women, the institution of marriage, and anti-Semitism.

Unlike some other members of the early romantic movement, Schleiermacher did not turn from a revolutionary into a reactionary. Nevertheless, in the period of political repression after the Napoleonic Wars, Schleiermacher adopted a conciliatory stance toward social institutions and saw the possibility of individual and communal self-fulfillment within them. The later Schleiermacher exerted a strong influence on the subsequent development of theological ethics.

In his writings of the romantic period, Schleiermacher emphasized the moral value of love and friendship, since they overcame individual one-sidedness in the process of mutual self-completion. Love and friendship were central to the core ideas of his ethics: *Geselligkeit* and *Bildung.* The early Schleiermacher did not link the complementarity of the sexes with any gender-specific characteristics. Indeed, in the *Catechism of Reason for Noble Women* (1799) women were encouraged to lust after the education and science of men. Yet even in the lectures on ethics Schleiermacher gave as a university professor at Halle in the winter semester of 1805–6, he transposed these romantic views on love between the sexes into the context of a revision of the ethical norms for the institution of marriage.

In the later Schleiermacher's view, marriage was justified as an institution because it healed the split of male and female individuality, and allowed Schleiermacher to posit a gender-specific character for men and women, attributing thought to men and feeling to women.[2] In another writing of the same date, *Christmas Eve,* Schleiermacher took a further step and connected the specifically female capacity for feeling with women's supposed spontaneous and natural religiosity, and the specifically male attribute of intellect with men's supposed struggle between religious faith and doubt.[3] The polarization of sexual stereotypes in nineteenth-century Germany accompanied the split between work and family spheres; the definition of female character in terms of feeling versus male thinking is associated with the designation of domesticity as the proper female role.[4] The resulting dissociation of work and family was advocated by the educated middle classes to which Schleiermacher and most nineteenth-century theologians belonged. In his famous first sermon of 1818, *On Marriage,* Schleiermacher tried to twist the blatantly subordinationist text beginning with Ephesians 5:22 (wives be subject to your husbands as to the Lord) into a declaration of equality of the sexes by arguing that the authority of husband over wife refers only to the husband's sole responsibility of representing the family in the public sphere, an area into which the woman cannot enter with impunity. Otherwise the relation between the sexes is magnificent equality!

A similar gender-based division of character and roles is found in the work of a less well known contemporary of Schleiermacher, Christoph Friedrich von Ammon. In the first edition of his handbook on Christian ethics, published in 1829, von Ammon asserted that women and men have the same needs and duties in marriage. A decade later in a second edition of 1838 he thoroughly revised this opinion in his discussion of adultery. He elaborated sexual stereotypes, ascribing to women a domestic identity that gives them greater culpability for the disruption of the family through marital infidelity, because the family is the area—the sole area—for which they bear responsibility.[5]

The normative description of the man-woman relationship became limited to the institutions of marriage and family. In the 1870s the Erlangen professor, Johann Christian von Hoffmann, criticized an earlier theologian for discussing marriage separately from the family instead of subsuming it properly under the rubric of the family.[6] After Schleiermacher, the ethical progress of society toward perfection was seen as the ultimate realization of social institutions and not primarily of human relationships. Thus, Hegel saw marriage, included within the concept of the family, as the necessary institutionalization of love and explicitly criticized the early Schleiermacher's critique of the institution of marriage.[7]

Women, Jews, and the "Moral Process"

The outstanding midcentury systematization of the developing understanding of male-female relationships can be found in the five-volume work on theological ethics by Richard Rothe, who defined the relationship between the sexes as one of "the particular circles of moral community." [8] Rothe identified the relationship of man and woman with procreation, the first stage of the "moral process." This "moral process" is the forward march of history in its fundamentally ethical character, the male individual's cultivation (*Bildung*) of his universal human function, the basis of moral community. In this process the man-woman relationship was a preliminary stage before the creation of the genuinely central "circles" of moral community: art, science, social life (*Geselligkeit*), and public life.

Because marriage possessed the character of *Bildung,* it was the "moralized relationship of the sexes" and the "morally posited natural relationship." In marriage occurred the transformation of the individual personality (the object of *Bildung*) to universal humanity and moral community.[9] The individual personality remained incomplete unless one entered into a relationship with a person of the opposite sex. "The man," wrote Rothe, "first becomes a complete man through the bond with a woman, and the woman first becomes a complete woman through the bond with a man." [10]

The woman was in greater need of such *Bildung* than the man; her physical and psychic weakness gave her certain disadvantages in the moral process. For Rothe, following Schleiermacher, women had an advantage in their "richness of soul" (*Gemüt*).[11] But this advantage came from their accentuated individuality and hindered them, in contrast to men, in developing universal humanity. Rothe concluded that the individuality of women restricted the sphere of their life and activity to the basic, but also lowest, stage of the moral process, the family.

Rothe's dichotomy between universality and individuality was anchored in his description of human psychology. Sensation, drive, mental sense, and mental strength formed the basic fourfold structure of every human being's psyche. Women possessed more of the qualities of sensation and drive, making them more dependent on the material and natural side of life, whereas men possessed more mental sense and strength, elevating them above material nature. Nonetheless, Rothe regarded men as having more natural vitality than women; his argument for male superordination was predicated on superior male physical and psychic strength. Women's less violently assertive nature did not need to be morally tamed in the same way as men's. Therefore, women remained closer to nature and morally underdeveloped because they did not need to disassociate themselves from the material and natural psychic determination of sensation and drive. The aggressive form of these qualities in men demands that men displace them by the less material and nature-bound characteristics of mental sense and strength.[12]

Women not only suffered from physiological and psychological disadvantages in the moral process; they also lacked a profession or social vocation (*Beruf/Berufung*). For Rothe a profession was the condition for the realization of moral purpose, whereby the interests of the individual and the moral process become identical. Moreover, "there is no social status without a profession," opined Rothe; "the one who has no social status (because he has no profession) has no honour." [13]

The unmarried woman was put in a social and indeed ethical limbo. She could only await the call to enter the moral process, a proposal of marriage from a man. For her, the only possible profession was that of wife and mother. "So marriage is the proper school of *Bildung* for the woman." [14] Even then, marriage did not bring the woman direct access to the higher forms of the moral process; she remained dependent on the mediation of the man.

> The man is in marriage, as the concept of him suggests, the representative of universal humanity, which is the higher and the more authoritative over against individuality, represented by the woman. ... Moreover, the authority of man over woman is founded upon the fact that he indeed lives in the great whole of human community, i.e., he has a public profession. Insofar as the woman lives for her spouse she lives indirectly for the moral community.[15]

Women's sphere, marriage and the family, is in the last analysis the most provisional and most dispensable stage of the moral process. At the apex of the moral process, in the "divine state," "the Kingdom of God," the need for a natural basis in the family will be transcended.

For Rothe, the family was not the only natural community on which the state rested. Alongside and connected with the family was that other natural community, the *Volk*, the people whose national identity was institutionalized in the national state. Schleiermacher and Rothe both saw the *Volk* as a collective personality. The distinguishing mark of a *Volk* was the possession of a common language; a *Volk* is constituted through the intermarriage of families.

Schleiermacher and Rothe did not mention Jews in their discussions of national identity. Language, not race, bound a *Volk* together; its blood ties were familial, not racial.[16] Nevertheless, parallel to the notion that each gender had a distinctive natural character, each state was populated by people with a natural and distinctive national character.

Images of women and Jews coalesced in Schleiermacher and in later theologians' discussions of mixed marriages. Schleiermacher disapproved of marriages between Christians and non-Christians (almost exclusively Jews in Germany during the nineteenth century) because such a union presupposed the religious indifference of the partners. Nonetheless, he defended the introduction of civil marriage, which made it possible for Jews and Christians to marry, although he insisted that the church should not be forced to bless such marriages. Like Catholic-Protestant marriages, Jewish-Christian marriages were, in Schleiermacher's opinion, problematic; it was only a matter of differing degrees of spiritual incompatibility.[17] Christian theologians allowed some latitude for Jewish-Christian marriages. Schleiermacher and Rothe allowed an exception to the rule against intermarriage between Christian and Jew when the Christian partner was convinced that marriage was the only way to convert the non-Christian.

Yet the complementarity of the sexes and gender roles required spiritual compatibility of the marriage partners. Could a Jewish husband represent the interests and sensibilities of his Christian wife in the public sphere? Could a Jewish wife be the moral guardian of the home and educator of the children of her Christian husband? In answer, Rothe quoted Schleiermacher's opinion on mixed marriages as his own, adding the significant observation that

> our Jews are in the majority already in actual fact, though unconsciously, so Christianized in the moral side of their life, and, on the other hand, among Christians in many circles the consciousness of the religious (and hence also of the churchly) side of their Christianity is so weakened.[18]

Since the distinction between Christian and Jew was made on the basis of formal membership in a religious body rather than on individual inner conviction, spiritual incompatibility may not exist in all Jewish-Christian marriages.

This reasoning recurred when Rothe discussed granting the Jews full civil rights. For Rothe, the "moral normality" of the state demanded its "religious normality." It must be a Christian state and all its citizens must be Christian.[19] But Rothe redefined the term *Christian* so that Jews were not excluded from full citizenship. Christian morality or moral Christianity, he explained, can be found among members of a non-Christian religion, namely, Jews. It was the moral, not the religious convictions, of Christianity that were indispensable prerequisites for citizenship.[20] Any ethnic sentiment among Jews was irreconcilable with German national identity and, hence, a barrier to their emancipation. Ethnic identity was the same, for Rothe, as a lack of Christian morality, and could best be overcome by granting Jews full civil rights. Such a measure, in anticipating its goal, would achieve it.[21]

Un-Christianized Jews, like unfeminine women, were signs of the incompleteness of the moral process of society. On the one hand, the separate existence of Jews was seen as the temporary imperfection of the moral process. The assimilation of the Jews and their eventual conversion to Christianity were the goals of the ethical process, since with the increasing perfection of a Christian society religious alternatives to Christianity would become redundant.

On the other hand, the gender differentiation between women and men would increase with the progress of the moral perfection of society. According to Rothe,

> It is a fact of experience that everywhere where individuality is comparatively only little developed (as in the lower classes of the people) the peculiar traits of personal character, through which the sexes differ from one another, are only weakly perceptible. In the lower orders the difference between the personal character of a man and that of a woman is less sharply distinguished than in the educated classes of society. In particular, the women are more unfeminine in the former than in the latter case.[22]

One can surmise that lower-class women were considered unfeminine because they had to work outside the home and, therefore, acted in contradiction to the female "character" assigned to them by theologians.

The difference between male and female roles was considered irreducible; the difference between Christian and Jew was surmountable. Male Christian existence was taken as the norm, and divergence from it was explained in terms either of complementarity or of homogenization. In the period between 1815 and 1871, although the Christian male norm was not fulfilled in reality, there was also little social evidence to challenge it. The three leading Jewish women of the early romantic movement—Henriette Herz, Dorothea Veit, and Rahel Levin—joined the Christian church. Dorothea Veit and Rahel Levin did so in order to marry Christian men. Dorothea Veit, indeed, converted twice, once to Protestantism in order to marry Friedrich Schlegel, and later to Catholicism when he decided to become a Catholic. Her assimilation to Christianity was the epitome of what male Christian theologians envisaged as the outcome of the moral process.

The Moral Turpitude of Emancipation of Women and Jews

An influential theological proponent of antifeminism and anti-Semitism in the nineteenth century, Hans Lassen Martensen, premier bishop of Denmark, was widely read in German translation because of his decidedly German intellectual and cultural outlook. He was immersed in the idealist philosophical and theological tradition, conversant with Hegel and Schleiermacher, and quoted the German poets extensively. Perhaps most important, he was able to express idealist ethics in a down-to-earth and pithy manner, a style that his German readers missed in their own theologians. Martensen was all too willing to leave lofty abstractions for concrete applications. As Denmark's leading churchman he conceived his theological task to be a restatement of the indispensable Christian basis from which all public policy must proceed. From Martensen's vantage point, modern society was only ambiguously on the path to perfection of the Christian ideal. In modern society an "emancipation from Christianity" asserts itself and this must be denied strenuously if the higher reality of society is to be attained.[23]

Martensen opposed the notion of a changeless social order in favor of a constant renewal of a proper relationship between authority and liberty.[24] Authority allowed a relative freedom to those who were subordinate in a hierarchical order: Martensen argued for something

234

resembling the political enfranchisement of male property owners in nineteenth-century constitutional monarchies and thus for certain forms of emancipation. Nevertheless, he favored the subordination of certain groups (women and Jews), not because of the function of those groups in society, but because of their essential characters. Martensen drew a lurid picture of female and Jewish emancipation because their claims to freedom, Martensen believed, cannot exist in any social order and cannot be conceded even a relative legitimacy.

Women's emancipation, he believed, was beneficial neither to women nor to men. North American women grow "pale and faded" from receiving the same education as men.[25] The emancipated woman was a pitiful creature.

> She has torn the veil. There will come hours and seasons in her life when she will experience a deep inward wretchedness, a state of homelessness, and feel herself like a plant torn from its native soil, which can be planted and strike root nowhere; when, from her supposed elevation and fancied freedom, she will long in vain for a quiet unnoticed life, restrained by duty and conscience, within the home and bosom of the family.[26]

Underpinning Martensen's stern rejection of women's emancipation was the view of a polarity of male and female nature that accompanied the separation of the home and the work place, the domestic and the public, in the nineteenth century. Martensen used the classical psychological doctrine of four temperaments—the choleric and phlegmatic, sanguine and melancholic—to account for individual variation in human beings. Male and female natures were a paradigm of the distribution of the four temperaments among human individuals. Martensen's psychic sex stereotypes were particularly rigid. All four temperaments are found in both men and women, but differently balanced. A woman with a predominantly choleric or phlegmatic temperament gives "the impression of unwomanliness, of manliness in the wrong place." [27] This temperamental disequilibrium fit precisely Martensen's description of those emancipated women "who are seen in casinos and coffeehouses in masculine attire, with lighted cigars in their mouth." [28] Isaak August Dorner, a later German theologian, used the same theory, but assigned the temperaments differently to the sexes.

For Martensen as for Rothe, the fundamental expression of the temperamental difference between male and female nature was found in the male orientation toward the universal and the female toward the individual. Martensen expounded at length on what happened when female individuality tried to enter the male sphere of universality. Men were fitted for their role in the public sphere through their adherence to universal moral norms, but women, with their "one-sidedness of feeling," "from want of moral principles," were "unreliable, unsteady, changeable and faithless." Women try to gain power, he wrote, through craft as well as dissimulation, intrigues, tricks, and lying. Woman's individuality made her more prone to corruption than man, "the demoniac, the horrifying, the wild, likewise appear stranger in her than in him." Martensen illustrated this corruption of female nature with reference to powerful women of ancient Israel and Judaism like Jezebel and Herodias and to those prototypes of the radical emancipated woman, the female activists of the French Revolution.[29]

Martensen's view of the corrupting effect of individuality on the realm of power, the public and the universal, pervaded not only his discussion of women and women's emancipation but also his attitudes toward Jews and their emancipation, to which he was vehemently opposed. He repeatedly alleged that the Jews were the leading protagonists of individualism and were in alliance with the liberal parties who promote doctrinaire individualism. Individualism corrupts the public sphere, promotes the dissolution of the Christian state and nation, and undermines Christian morality in society.[30]

Unlike his German peers, Martensen insisted that a distinctive nationality separated Jews from Christians, that this Jewish nationality persisted and was being reinforced in modern Judaism, and that it was in an irreconcilable contradiction with the common interests, attitudes, and sentiments of Christian citizens. Jewish individualism arose out of Jewish character; a predominance of individuality among women arose out of female character. Jewish nationality hence resembled female nature and was subject to the same perversion when it encroached on the public sphere of male Christians. The entrance of Jews into the public sphere, like that of women, allowed an illegitimate access to power. In political life Jews were unable to seek the public good, being only outwardly attached to principles; instead they sought their national self-interest.

The supreme object of all these efforts is the before-mentioned Judaeo-Messianic Kingdom of humanity.... For this object, the entire banishment of Christianity from public life, from legislation and from public institutions, and the snapping of all the ties by which nations are united to Christ, they labour consistently night and day.[31]

Martensen had introduced into the normative reflections of Christian ethics the myth of Jewish ascendancy, which became a foundation of later German theological anti-Semitism. He issued a chilling prophecy on the fate of Jews in the Christian state. Just as the emancipated woman must languish physically and emotionally from trying to be equal to a man, he said, the emancipated Jew will be overwhelmed by persecutions as a result of claiming equality with a Christian.[32] Not surprisingly, Martensen judged that "marriages between Jews and Christians [were], from a religious point of view, monstrous." [33] He gave no reasons for this condemnation, but its unequivocal assertion may be connected with his belief in a distinctive Jewish character. Such unions would be disrupted not only by religious disharmony but also by a permanent incompatibility of national character, expressed as religious disunity.

1871–1914: Gender, Race, and Theology at the Zenith of Christian Male Culture

With the proclamation of the Second Empire in 1871, Germany was politically united. Under the Prussian royal house of Hohenzollern, the Second Empire endured for nearly half a century during which Germany reached a zenith of power and material prosperity. In the eyes of German theologians, the creation of the Second Empire was the result of Germany's cultural and ethical renewal as a Christian nation. German society was undergoing the strains of rapid industrialization and the accompanying urbanization of its population. Political unification also ushered in an age of mass culture, which posed unprecedented problems to the mechanisms of social control exercised by the state and state churches.

The contradictions of the Second Empire were nowhere more apparent than in the status of women and Jews and the attitudes toward these groups. Although Jews were accorded full civil rights under the Second Empire, from the 1870s onward there was an upsurge of virulent anti-Semitism. Adolf Stoecker, court chaplain in Berlin, was chief among the instigators of the anti-Semite movement.[34] He founded the Christian Social party, which aimed at counteracting the growing strength of socialism among the German workers by advocating an extensive social welfare system within an authoritarian political system. Stoecker's Christian Socialism was a precursor of National Socialism in its identification of a composite enemy—liberalism and socialism, capitalism and Judaism—and in its political solution, which was, not the return to feudally governed society, but the creation of an authoritarian state in which social welfare was a means of total social control. In political terms, Stoecker's movement was a dismal failure. Tolerated for a while by the German chancellor, Bismarck, who needed anti-Semite votes in parliament for his struggle against the liberals, Stoecker's bizarre Christian Socialism was mistrusted by the conservatives and described as "nonsense" by the emperor, Wilhelm II. Nevertheless, Stoecker had an enduring influence on Protestant social thinking.

Anti-Semitism in late nineteenth-century Germany was fed by new biological theories of race. These were secular in nature and claimed science rather than religion as their authority. Christian anti-Semites such as Stoecker embraced them cautiously. On the normative level of theological ethics, racial biology had a negligible impact, nor was Stoecker's movement a perceptible influence. Biological theories of race were largely ignored and, if mentioned at all, were met with reserve, even resistance. The Christian ethicist, Isaak August Dorner, had a thoroughgoing and negative appraisal of modern biological race theories. Moreover, Dorner's view of racial difference is structurally dependent on his conception of gender difference.

Dorner, in contrast to Rothe, did not see the intensification of individuality as a handicap in the moral process. On the contrary, the increasing variety of individual existences furthered the development of the moral universe. Crucial to the maintenance and expansion of the moral repertoire of individuality were gender and racial characteristics. They represented permanent states of human difference, and were not simply temporary phases or functional modalities of a homogeneous identity, such as the age or profession of an individual.[35]

Dorner upheld the value of individual human difference but asserted the common humanity of all individuals. He had no time for those who measured the skulls of different races in order to prove major differences among the human species. He also inveighed against the Darwinians, whom he saw as denying the difference between human beings and animals. Such a position, he argued, ignored the spiritual and intellectual nature peculiar to human beings, on which the unity of the species rests. Dorner insisted that all human beings have the same spiritual and intellectual faculties, but these take on an individual form.[36] He used the doctrine of the four temperaments to explain how the individual variations of a common humanity arise. Human personality was constituted in its physiopsychic base through the varying occurrence of phlegmatic, choleric, melancholic, and sanguine temperaments.

The temperaments were rarely to be found in a pure form, but almost invariably in some combination. Furthermore, each individual is influenced by all four temperaments, at least at some point in life. One temperament, however, was dominant in each individual.[37] Which one of the temperaments predominated and how they were synthesized in the individual correlated with the race and sex of the person. Males and whites were in Dorner's scheme undoubtedly favored in terms of what nineteenth-century Germany esteemed most highly. They possessed more of the choleric temperament, which endows them with courage (*Muth*), the capacity to shape actively the external world and produce culture in the areas of the state, art, and science.[38] Women and blacks, on the other hand, tended to the phlegmatic, which bestowed on them equanimity and thus predisposed them to patient endurance.[39]

The polarization of gender and racial characteristics can and should be overcome through marriage and intermarriage.[40] Dorner's moral universe was endlessly polychromatic; each individual and individual group must try to overcome the one-sidedness of its temperament. All temperaments were of equal worth; none is sinful in itself or naturally virtuous; each has its strengths and imperfections. Dorner stressed the advantage of mutual interaction between ethnic groups. Racial purity was an ethical and cultural disability for any nation.

Thus almost all the nations which stand highest in the world came to their national character, as it is now, through the different strata of nations gradually depositing themselves one upon another, and undergoing a process of physical and mental assimilation. This

239

process produced a mutual improvement, and called forth a nationality which did not originally exist of itself, but was the result only of history and of the influence of spiritual forces.[41]

In all of Dorner's discussion of racial differences Jews received no mention. This omission must have been intentional, since Dorner was aware of the racial theories that asserted the biological distinctiveness of Jews. Moreover, the Genesis account of the sons of Noah (Japheth, Ham, and Shem) had long been taken as biblical evidence for three distinct races, Europeans, Africans, and Semites. Dorner was apparently resisting the notion of the Jews as a biologically distinct Semitic race. Even if Dorner had conceived of the Jews as a distinct ethnic element in Germany, he could have evaluated this positively, since in his opinion the multiethnic composition of a nation could help it achieve its highest moral development.

One cannot overlook in Dorner's scheme the contrast between the fluidity of racial types and the rigidity of gender-based traits. Dorner's discussion of gender preceded his general description of the four temperaments as a concrete example of temperamental differences in their purest form. The discussion of race came last and exemplified the tendency of the temperaments to blend in individuals. The sexes, like the races, should endeavor to appropriate the mental excellences of the other. No clear and concrete limits to such appropriation are delineated for the races, but clear limits are given for gender characteristics. Women have no aptitude for politics or scholarship and, hence, women at university and other "attempts at so-called emancipation" did not broaden their personality but only injured their relationship to men.[42] Gender, then, was both the paradigm and the extreme manifestation of human difference. If human difference prescribed distinct roles and spheres for the sexes, it would not be inconsistent to advance the same conclusion for the races. Dorner did not take this step.

Theologians on all points of the political and religious spectrum, from a conservative like F. H. R. Frank to a liberal like Wilhelm Herrmann, did not expound biological theories of race or refer to Jews as a distinct ethnic group. One cannot argue from this silence that they opposed racial biology or anti-Semitism. Yet one can point out that such theories were not seen as ethically normative by late nineteenth-century theologians. But theology was not free of anti-Semitism. An undefined category of race occurs from time to time in the handbooks of theological ethics. Religious-cultural theories of race and anti-Semitism had already in the early nineteenth-century been propagated by the Christian German Table Society, founded by Joseph von Görres and Clemens Brentano, and counting Fichte among its members. The Book of Genesis provided the basis for a religious-cultural racial theory in that the story of the sons of Noah and the table of nations in Genesis 10 were understood as a historical account of the origins of the races. This racial theory (without the violent anti-Semitism) appears in the ethical system of a theologian of minor influence, Karl Werner.[43] There was therefore a recent religious-cultural tradition of anti-Semitism that could be tapped without reference to biological theories of race. Yet it received minimal attention for the purposes of normative Christian ethics throughout the nineteenth century.

Women became visible in the work force during the later years of the nineteenth century. Of course, women had always worked, but their labor had been considered domestic. Seamstresses had worked at home and rural women had often provided the major support of the peasant family by growing crops, yet domestic ideology could describe this activity only as sewing and "gardening." The numbers of women in factories and offices rose steeply in the decades before the First World War. Women demanded and achieved access to university education and to some professions. Such trends flatly contradicted the ethical visions of the theologians, but in general they remained content with the reiteration of the earlier theological position on gender difference and its consequences for male and female nature and roles. Occasionally, theologians discussed on the normative level social roles for women outside the home and family. Their explanation of these roles was that since social conditions prevented some women from marrying, these women must be found a means of livelihood.

Wilhelm Herrmann, the leading liberal Protestant to write a handbook on theological ethics in this period, viewed unmarried women as a potential threat to the family. Unmarried women "out of bitterness for a ruined existence" would easily turn to a sustained effort "to disrupt the peace of the family." To prevent this onslaught against the family, unmarried women must be found occupations, but the "cumbersome objectivity" required by the male professions made them unsuitable for most women. He recom-

241

mended that unmarried women fulfill their thwarted domestic nature in the nurturing professions of social welfare.[44]

On one level, the details of Herrmann's views on women's role
represented the wisdom of the German establishment. On another
level, they were dependent on a shift in the normative social vision
of theological ethics. Ethical meaning, according to Herrmann,
came about through the mastery of nature and its forcible subservience to the moral process. Such human activity led to "the orders that have grown out of history" (*geschichtlich erwachsenden
Ordnungen*).[45] These orders are the family, civilization, and the
state. Society's basic institutions, therefore, were both natural and
the product of human moral effort, which shaped their natural
givenness into systems of personal meaning for individuals and
communities. The concept of orders implied that such institutions
had a normative form and content, and that the norm was present
in certain historical developments of the institutions. Inevitably, an
emphasis on the historical actuality and irreversibility of institutional patterns of human life altered attitudes toward those who
fell outside the norm. For Rothe, women outside the home and
Jews outside Christianity were morally immature, symptomatic of
the moral immaturity of society; for Herrmann women outside the
family were a threat to what had already been won in the history
of human moral endeavor.

Jews were understood to pose a similar threat by their reluctance
to embrace Christianity. An article in the liberal Protestant newspaper *Christian World* in 1893 stated that Jews were not living up
to the expectations of the male Christian norm.

> The Jews have not reached the point of acknowledging Christianity
> as a vital source of culture; they have appropriated Christian cul-
> ture, but have refused to acknowledge that this culture is the
> product of the religious-ethical spirit of Christianity.[46]

It was Christian male moral effort that had produced Western and
German culture. Therefore, it was the responsibility of Christian
males to administer culture and to guard its terrain. Fear of a mis-
appropriation of culture on the part of women and Jews grew.

Throughout the nineteenth century, female and Jewish encroachment on Christian male culture was never explicitly equated
in German theology. Theologians did not construct a concept of
Jewish nature comparable with that of female nature. They did not

wish Jews to exist in a separate sphere: the synagogue was not complementary to the church, as the home was to the public world. On the other hand, the doctrine of the four temperaments, held by several theologians including the conservative Danish Martensen and the more liberal Dorner, underlined that male-female difference could be taken as paradigmatic of all human difference. German theologians of the nineteenth century, from Schleiermacher to Wilhelm Herrmann, gave paramount value to the unfolding of moral personality. Society and its institutions would become more perfect as individuals pursued ethical perfection. On the whole, theologians were loath to translate their theories of personality into prescriptions of social identity—except in the case of gender. Nineteenth-century theological constructions of gender, therefore, were a potential model for the formulation of racial identities.

1918–40: "The Struggle for Christianity"

The real crisis of the male conception of society did not occur until after the First World War. Christian male hopes that women and Jews would find their "proper place"—the family and the Christian church, respectively—were shaken to their foundations by the social and political upheavals that resulted from Germany's defeat in war. Claudia Koonz has shown that the crisis in the family was crucial in gaining support for Hitler.[47] The enormous loss of male life in the First World War left many women, approximately two million, unable to fulfill the female vocation of domesticity. Instead of grasping the necessity of earning a living as an opportunity for independence, many women experienced it as a loss of identity. Being a factory or office worker was not, after all, a particularly fulfilling occupation, and did not offer women an identity that counterbalanced the stigma of being unmarried and childless.

War and defeat radicalized German nationalism. Germany's partial dismemberment by the peace treaties deeply wounded German national identity. *Völkische* ideology, with its racist and anti-Semitic nationalism, made deep inroads into nationalist politics and into church circles. Liberalism, which had been a vehicle of nationalist aspirations in 1870, was deserted by large numbers of the educated middle classes. These groups, including theologians whose origins lay mainly in these social strata, turned to conservative nationalist parties. This shift of middle-class political allegiance can be seen in the individual biographies of Gottfried Traub, a one-time pastor, and of the feminist Käthe Schirmacher. Both were liberals before the First World War, and in 1919 both were elected members of parliament for the conservative nationalist party, the DNVP.

The monarchy of the Second Empire was replaced by the political system of the Weimar Republic. The instability of the Weimar Republic has often been greatly exaggerated. Nevertheless, it did not command the automatic authority of the old monarchy, and the vacuum of perceived authority had two important consequences. First, the "leader principle" and the call for a strong man to guide German destiny paved the way for Hitler's seizure of power. Second, the continuity of German culture and society was broken, giving the middle classes tacit permission to engage in criticism of and experimentation in the political and social order on an unprecedented scale.

In this new situation, a postwar generation of theologians declared an open breach with their predecessors. Theologians on both the right and the left condemned the nineteenth-century attempt at mediation between Christianity and culture. Werner Elert, the conservative Lutheran, no less than his radical opponent, Karl Barth, rejected the synthesis of Christianity and culture. Elert, in his massive work *The Struggle for Christianity,* drew the picture of a nineteenth-century theology that had devoted its energies to coming to terms with modern culture, oblivious to the rejection of Christian ethics and doctrine by modern culture in its search for social emancipation and moral and intellectual autonomy.

The tone of Elert's book was not polemical, but the historical descriptions leave no doubt about the identity of the protagonists of modern culture without Christianity, of the Christian theologians entrapped in the futile task of trying to reconcile Christianity with modern culture, or of the perceptive male Christians who recognized the unbridgeable gulf between Christianity and modern culture. Foremost among those who had demonstrated Christianity's incompatibility with modern philosophy, ethics, social life, and aesthetics were Jews—Heinrich Heine, Karl Marx, the philosopher Hermann Cohen. The secular women's movement had also made demands that conflicted with Christian ethics and yet were met with a dangerous spirit of rapprochement on the part of some Christians. Prominent among those who had at least some appreciation of the hollowness of a Christianity founded on the presuppositions of modern culture were anti-Semites and antifeminists—Hans Lassen Martensen and Adolf Stoecker.

Elert's comparison of Martensen with Richard Rothe reveals the place of Judaism in this interpretation of the nineteenth century. In Elert's judgment, Martensen was still too open toward culture but he refrained from Rothe's identification of Christianity and culture. Hence, Martensen and Rothe proceeded from the same conception of the Christian state but reached divergent conclusions on Jewish emancipation. Martensen's rejection of Jewish emancipation rested, Elert implied, on his resistance to an autonomous human basis for ethics and on his insistence on the abiding validity of the Christian church and a theonomous source of ethics.[48]

Elert's preference for Martensen is to be expected, since Elert's own thesis was a radicalization of Martensen's denunciation of modern culture's "emancipation from Christianity." Elert freely admitted that theology had only become aware of the necessity of a distance between Christianity and culture because the possibility of a synthesis between the two had been so thoroughly undermined by the non-Christian aspects of modern culture. Nor did Elert denounce relative and partial syntheses; he can praise Adolf Stoecker's Christian socialism because it was rooted in Christianity and revised ("moralized") socialist insights for the purposes of a distinctive Christian ethics and social policy. The relationship between Christianity and culture cannot be reciprocal: Christians may shape culture but culture may not mold theological norms. Since the Jewish philosopher Hermann Cohen can argue on the basis of Kant's philosophy that Judaism is the only ethically possible religion, then Christian theologians must exclude Kantian arguments for Christian belief from their systems.[49] Christianity must never allow itself to depend on any foundation of belief and practice outside itself. It may use the philosophy and social ideals of its culture, so long as it maintains exclusive control over their meanings. Christianity must assert its hegemony over culture or repudiate even the relative and contingent points of convergence between itself and culture. The imperative task for Elert is to "extricate Christianity from the knot of a dying culture, so that it is not swept away by the current." [50]

This gloomy prognosis for the future of modern culture reflects Werner Elert's situation as a theologian in the Weimar Republic.

Church and state had been separated, and the state churches had been disestablished, although theology remained in the state universities. Since the state no longer defined itself as Christian or guaranteed Christian morality in society, theology could no longer propound a normative social vision that would be implemented in the social policy of the state. Theology had lost its social function and the state its theological legitimation; the crisis of the identity of theology was thus firmly interlocked with the crisis of the authority of the secular state.

Women and Jews in the "Orders of Creation"

Conservative Lutheran theologians in the decade preceding the establishment of the Third Reich moved away from the notion that social institutions were simply imperfect. Social institutions might be not only retarded in their development but also degenerate from their authentic character, given in the orders instituted in the world by God the creator and preserver of human life. These orders were the natural communities of family, *Volk,* and state, which were identical with the essence of social institutions, though not necessarily with their concrete forms. Thus, the social dislocation that seemed so intractable in the aftermath of war could be assigned a cause in the violation of these orders and the decay of the natural foundations of society: family, *Volk,* and state.

The theology of orders redefined the presence of Jews in German society; Jews were no longer seen as an indication of the moral imperfection of society but as a violation of the "orders of creation." The ethical writings of Paul Althaus, a colleague of Werner Elert on the theological faculty at Erlangen, demonstrate that the sense of crisis in basic social institutions led to the introduction of anti-Semitism into the theological ethics of the 1920s onward. Althaus argued that Jews are an alien element within the German nation. In his *Foundations of Ethics,* published in 1928, he wrote, "To the most difficult questions of national identity for us Germans belongs the Jewish question." Enlightened liberalism, he claimed, was not the answer, since attempts at assimilation had revealed the gulf between Jewishness and Germanness. Jews had allied themselves with the "rational-critical and individualistic spirit of the Enlightenment" against the historical bonds and inherited ideas of the German people. Although at that time Althaus rejected racial anti-Semitism as well as emancipation of the Jews, he called for Jews to recognize their own national identity and, therefore, the necessary limitations on their participation in German life.[51]

Althaus discussed women and the women's question in terms of women's motherly identity and vocation. Motherhood, with its "gift of sympathy and sacrifice," need not, indeed should not, be confined to the domestic sphere. Althaus argued that the life of the *Volk* needs the "extended motherhood and sisterhood" of women in the professional, public, and political spheres.[52] At first glance, the theology of orders does not seem to have produced the same substantive changes in the ethical descriptions of women as it clearly did in the case of Jews. Certainly, male Christian theologians in Germany of the 1920s and 1930s were more absorbed by issues of nationality than by issues of gender. One might even detect a liberalization of their views on women.

A more cogent reason for the apparent continuity in the ethics of gender is that earlier theologians' conceptions of women's nature and roles were accommodated fairly easily into the new normative framework. Earlier understandings of nationality could not be assimilated so readily to a theology of orders. Nineteenth-century theologians had held that the natural character of the sexes prescribed their social roles. The theology of orders substituted marriage and family as an order of creation for marriage and family as a social institution. Both the social institution and female character were seen as derivative from the order of creation. The order of creation determined women for motherhood as both their identity and their role. Women's psychic appropriateness for the role of mother was secondary to and symptomatic of their place in the order of creation. Thus, the theology of orders could dispense with psychological theories of gender difference like the doctrine of the four temperaments. It did not need to explain the origins of female psychic traits, but only to register them as consequences of the vocation of motherhood, the generally observed but not universally necessary psychic component of motherhood.

The link between personal character and social identity and roles, psychic disposition and physical constitution, had been restricted in the nineteenth century to the discussion of gender; the theology of orders made possible the extension of this thesis into the realm of nationality. Gender and ethnic identity and difference became parallel constructs, as can be seen in the formulation of

Althaus: "Out of the reality of the gift of motherhood the conscience of a mother perceives the law of motherly identity. Out of the reality of the bonds of national identity conscience perceives the law of loyalty and sacrifice to the life of the *Volk*." [53] Conversely, the inclusion of marriage and family in the orders of creation endowed them with a public character analogous to that of the *Volk* and the state. Indeed it was the structural interdependence of family and *Volk* that allowed the man-woman relationship to be considered primarily as a concern of the national-public sphere, and only secondarily as a domestic-private one.

In a lecture to the Protestant Alliance in 1940, Werner Elert stressed that the collective We relationship of *Volk* and race precedes all personal I-Thou relationships between marriage partners. Marriage partners are, therefore, "bound to the national estate. Consequently, every marriage is unethical that contradicts the bonds of national identity." [54] Elert felt that it was unnecessary to remind his audience of the "concrete implications" of this sentence. Indeed, Nazi ideology had imbued Germans with doctrines of racial hygiene and of the racial incompatibility of Jew and Aryan. Elert in this passage expressly repudiated Schleiermacher's as well as others' earlier views that marriage was primarily an interpersonal relationship.

"The Bonds of Destiny": *A Conclusion*

Was the theology of orders a radical breach with the preceding generations of theologians, as is so often claimed, or was it the logical successor of that earlier theology under the vastly altered conditions of Germany after the First World War?

Let me address this question by tracing the theological career of Reinhold Seeberg. Born in 1859, Seeberg reached the ranks of the theology professors at the heyday of the Second Empire. He was the epigone of the German idealist philosophy and theology of Hegel and Schleiermacher; at the turn of the century he held the somewhat outmoded belief in the unfolding of the "moral idea" in history. Seeberg's transition from a protagonist of German idealism to a theological sympathizer of National Socialism was marked by the watershed of the First World War.

Seeberg's *System of Ethics in Outline,* published in 1911, was unexceptional in its statements on race and gender. The education of women for an independent profession was permissible as long as it did not conflict with their preparation for the roles of mother and housewife. He even omitted Schleiermacher's, Rothe's, and Dorner's stereotypes of male and female personality. Seeberg included race along with national character (*Volkstum*), language, and ethos as the defining characteristics of a *Volk,* but he left race entirely undefined. A nation for him was a spiritual rather than a biological entity; as elsewhere in nineteenth-century theological ethics, racial categories were not applied to Jews.

The expanded second edition of Seeberg's *Ethics* appeared in 1920 with significant alterations from the 1911 version. He introduced the notion of a polarity of male and female nature, contrasting women's intuition with men's capacity for categorical thought. Although he repeated his earlier position on women's access to education and the professions, he now connected the question of access with the increase in extramarital sex. Seeberg was deeply disturbed by the sexual freedom of the Weimar Republic, which in his estimation was a "waste of physical national strength." [55] The section on nationality in the 1920 edition bristled with resentment at Germany's treatment by the victors of the First World War. Race was defined more closely as the distinctive physical type of a national group, but racial mixing could be beneficial for a nation when it took place between races predisposed to one another. Neither in the discussion of the threat to national identity from defeat in war, nor in the definition of race, was there any mention of Jews.[56]

The substantial changes in Seeberg's understanding of race and gender were undoubtedly caused by the theological upheaval forced upon a German idealist by the experience of war and defeat. Seeberg's collected essays and speeches from the years of the First World War make it obvious that he regarded the war as the means to the ethical fulfillment of Germany's destiny. Germany's defeat, therefore, was the thwarting of Germany's moral destiny, causing a violation of the historical communities of family, nation, and state. These communities had grown out of human striving after the realization of the moral idea; they were, therefore, vulnerable to historical events and trends.

Seeberg placed Germany's defeat in the context of the struggle between idealism and materialism, which decides the turning points and outcome of world history. According to the 1920 ethics, the common cause of the malaise affecting family and nation was materialism. In his *Ethics,* Seeberg gave restrained descriptions of the corrosive effects of materialism on German society and culture. But in lectures and popular articles, his outrage at the materialistic world view and its concomitant individualistic life style was clear. Every social problem, every perceived sign of moral decay, was doggedly traced back to its source in materialism. In lectures and popular articles, Seeberg identified certain groups as the protagonists of materialism. In an essay on the "world-historical crisis" of his day, he numbered women's emancipation among the materialist threats. "In a manner contemptuous of culture and morality," women's emancipation sought equality of women with men, the fulfillment of which would bring about the degradation of woman herself, the collapse of marriage, the destruction of the procreative base of the German *Volk* in the family, and the spread of sexual diseases.[57]

In November 1921 Reinhold Seeberg gave an address to the Central Committee on the *Innere Mission* (Home Mission), the leading social welfare agency of the German Protestant church, entitled "Anti-Semitism, Judaism, and the Church." The basic tenet of his address, hammered home in constant repetition, was that the Jews were engaged in the "undermining of the social cohesion and historical continuity" of the life of the German *Volk* and every nation among whom they dwelt. This subversion was carried out, according to Seeberg, through the "proclamation of the undifferentiated equality of all individuals." [58]

The key passage was that in which Seeberg exposed the materialistic nature of the Jews and associated the formulations of female character by nineteenth-century theologians with Jewish character. He noted that certain racial theoreticians "have perceived the essential Semite character in its leaning toward religion, whereas the Indo-Europeans lean more to critical scholarly thought. The latter would, so to speak, represent the masculine element, the Semites the feminine." [59] Seeberg did not contest this equation of Jewish with female character, but he did dispute the total feminization as Judaization of religion, which the racial theories implied. As he continued with his racial character sketch of the Jews, he unmistakably redefined Jews in terms of the theological understanding of women. The Jews, as depicted by Seeberg, possessed the "simple, elementary type of spirit," which allowed them to grasp the religious more easily and to hold more tenaciously to their religious past. But they lacked the richer and more complex intellectual and spiritual endowment of the Aryans. Whereas the German was lost in reflection, the Jew quickly fixed on what was close at hand, tangible, and material. Thus, the Jews conformed to the female stereotype of spontaneous rather than reflective religiosity, of mental simplicity, and of concern for the material things in their immediate environment. Cognitive thinking remained the prerogative of male Aryans.

Seeberg argued that a combination of childlike stubbornness and belief in their innate superiority had equipped the Jews to be leaders of modern attacks on the idealist culture of Europe. Seeberg did not credit the Jews with the intellectual initiation of modern currents such as rationalism, democracy, and socialism, because in his scheme the Jews did not have the capacity to produce an original thought. Nonetheless, in their receptivity to other people's materialistic notions, and through their lust for power over the nations, Jews had forwarded these movements. Like Martensen in the previous century, Seeberg emphasized individualism as the cardinal sin of the Jews. Individualism was synonymous with the undermining of the idealist tradition and historical bonds of a nation. In this respect also, Jews resembled women. Judaism, like feminism, represented the encroachment of materialist individualism on a public ideal realm, which must remain exclusively male, Christian, and Germanic.

The third edition of Seeberg's *Ethics* was published posthumously in 1936. In an introduction, his son informed the reader of the author's conviction that "a Christian social ethics is better and more correctly developed on a foundation of the orders of creation, shaped by National Socialism, than on the basis of how life is ordered after a democratic or liberal model." [60] Seeberg attempted in his 1936 edition a transfiguration of National Socialism into idealist ethics. In a Hegelian tone Seeberg described the self-realization of the "objective spirit" in the orders of social, historical, and national life. The struggle between materialism and idealism was being resolved under National Socialism in favor of the latter; the orders of the objective spirit had gained a new vitality. There was a return to the optimism of nineteenth-century theological ethics, accompanied by a representation of the nineteenth-century view of the increasing polarity of the sexes and their attributes as the moral process reached higher levels.

> Education (*Bildung*) and self-education of the two sexes should be molded according to this difference in character. As men become more masculine and women more feminine, then human character will have a richer profile, the attraction to one another will be quickened, and the progress of humanity greater.[61]

Yet Seeberg's "objective spirit," clothed in the orders of a National Socialist society, had feet of materialist clay. Spirit no longer transcended nature but was obsessed with it. The ethical fulfillment of society became dependent on racial hygiene, the increase of population, and the decline of birth control. Seeberg, who quoted population statistics and referred to eugenics, was preoccupied with social phenomena as signs or countersigns of the normative moral development of society to an extent unknown in theological ethics of the nineteenth century. Indeed, there was a collapse of a normative ethical social vision into the empirically observable trends of society. Seeberg was incapable of evaluating the divergence between National Socialist theory on family and sexuality and Christian idealist ethics. That National Socialism was the executor of the male Christian norm was sufficiently demonstrated for Seeberg by the fact that women and Jews were no longer in the "wrong place."

Seeberg concluded his section on sexuality and marriage with the portrait of a society on the path to the recovery of its patriarchal health. Women's search for equality with men had faded away. National revival had led to a "more natural view"; marriage was once more accepted as the natural goal of a woman, and if she must work, she chose a profession suitable to her female nature. Women no longer needed to attend university, since enforced spinsterhood and economic impoverishment as well as individualism and egalitarianism had been overcome.[62] In the 1936 work, a section on the "Jewish question" was included for the first time. Racialist theories were applied specifically to Jews, and their German nationality was denied. They were assigned a "pronounced racial character, which conflicts extensively with the German type." The racial and no less the spiritual character of the Jews induced them to attempt "to undermine national consciousness and replace it with individualism." Hence, it was justifiable to exclude them from public life and the professions (as was done in the Third Reich).[63]

The antifeminism and anti-Semitism of the idealist Seeberg were closely akin to those of the theology of orders. Therefore, we must ask whether anti-Semitism, although absent in nineteenth-century ethics, was nonetheless implicit in their normative core. Idealism, in its many schools and variations, had pervaded nineteenth-century Protestant and Roman Catholic theology. Every German theologian of the 1920s and 1930s was an heir to this tradition, however strained or broken the relation was through the official condemnation of Catholic idealist theologians or the experience of war. During the Weimar Republic, there was a reversal of the categories of nineteenth-century theological ethics. German theologians of earlier generations had professed their strong belief in a forward direction of history and in moral progress. They took up a "progressive" ethical stance, placing the accent on the moral transformation of society through the ethical formation (*Bildung*) of the personality of individuals and communities. In the 1920s and 1930s there was a shift to conservative insistence on the unchangeable character of destiny. The community, as it concretely existed in family, nation, and state, came before the individual, limited the individual to the character of that person's sex and *Volk,* and bound him or her unreservedly to its destiny.

The same scheme was proposed from positions antagonistic to the Lutheran theology of orders, from Catholic natural law and from Seeberg's idealism. It was not only Seeberg and the theology of orders who hailed Hitler's rise to power as moral salvation; Protestant theologians such as Emmanuel Hirsch and Friedrich Gogarten and numerous Catholic theologians, among them Karl Adam, Michael Schmaus, and Joseph Lortz, did also. This remarkable consensus of German theologians stemmed from the shared conviction that the Third Reich would renew the "bonds of destiny," as Elert called them, which held individuals in their proper place.

Earlier theological-ethical categories were not abolished in twentieth-century German theology. The bounds of nineteenth-century discourse remained intact to a high degree, especially the construction of gender. Nineteenth-century normative ethics had conceptualized the dialectic between individuality and universality in the moral self. The tension of individuality and universality cre-

253

ated their reconciliation in the mutual fulfillment of individual personality and social obligation, and in the correspondence of private and public spheres.

The moral self was intrinsically the male self. Only men inhabited both private and public realms, only men had to meet the social obligation in a profession outside the home, and only men were universal human beings. Women existed outside the great moral tension between individuality and universality and outside its resolution, from which all human progress flowed. They stood outside the dramas of the struggle for religious faith and the self-surpassing achievements of culture. Woman's one-sided individuality, her confinement to the private sphere, her lack of a profession, were signs of a danger that could afflict even the (male) moral self —individualism. Resignation of one's responsibility in the public realm, cessation from the struggle for religious faith and for a morally perfect society, the negation of one's universality: these were the insidious temptations that threatened to feminize the moral self. No wonder that antifeminism surfaced in German theology long before anti-Semitism.

The theologians of the postwar period no longer saw simply a tension between individuality and universality, but a quite undialectical conflict. They sided with universality against individuality. The category of the universal was posited as absolute. The synthesis of individual and universal was understood as the radical subordination of the former to the latter. Individuality had value only relative to its qualification by the universal, but universality was unqualified by individuality. The private sphere was engulfed in the public, eliminating the strict separation of private and public. The private sphere had no ends or values of itself. It was objectified in an "order," its reality defined in terms of its public functions and goals—the family as the reproductive base of the *Volk.* The universal overpowered the individual to such an extent that it replaced it on one level. The orders of creation and objective spirit were both universal and concrete. This made them total individuals, that is, they were attributed the concreteness of individuals but not the limitations. The nineteenth-century demand for a mediation between individuality and universality was seen as redundant, since the total individuals of family, *Volk,* and state determined everyone's personal identity and the range of thought, feeling, and action. The charge of individualism was now leveled against those who did not accept the "bonds of destiny" placed upon them by the incorporation of their personal individuality into the orders.

The new theoretical construction of individuality and universality had little practical effect on the definition of women in theological ethics. Gender had already prescribed destiny in the nineteenth century; now not only gender but also race and nationality were to determine the identity and roles of individuals. The inherited identification of the feminine with the individual was extended to the Jews; Jewishness was equated with female individualism. Seeberg's 1921 address made explicit the link between Judaism and femininity, Judaism and individualism. But the repeated charge that individualism was not only part of the political stratagem of the Jews but also their national identity indicates that theologians such as Althaus had expanded the paradigm of perverse female character as individualism to Jews. The polarity of male and female nature, which accompanied the dissociation of work and family, was now duplicated in the diametrical opposition of Aryan and Jewish race and the call for the segregation of Jewish life from German culture. Yet the redefinition of Jew in terms of woman was fraught with contradictions.

The discussion of mixed marriages by the theological admirers of the Third Reich exemplifies the inconsistencies of the genderization of race. The earlier religious understanding of Jewish-Christian marriage as that between Christian and non-Christian gave way to seeing such marriage as between Aryan and Jew. This entailed a male Christian redefinition of Jewishness along the lines of Nazi propaganda. There were now Aryan Christians and Jewish Christians, a distinction that earlier would have seemed nonsensical. Such a conception naturally led to the rejection of Jewish assimilation and conversion as advocated in earlier theology, since Jewish national identity and religion were viewed as inextricably linked together. Walther Künneth, also a representative of the Lutheran theology of orders, saw Jewish equality as irreconcilable with German national identity, but was distressed at the fate of those Jewish Christians and those Christian families, consisting of Jewish and Aryan members, that were being pulled apart by Nazi race legislation.[64]

Seeberg, like Althaus, eschewed "racist" anti-Semitism. He described Semitic character as primarily a "type of spirit," and only secondarily as a biological datum. He could envisage the eradica-

255

tion of Semitic character when Jews had intermarried with Germans and adopted Christianity, and yet he rejected further Jewish conversions to Christianity as motivated by opportunism, and not by the desire for spiritual rapprochement with the Aryan. The difference between Jew and Aryan had become as irreducible as that between the sexes.

Nevertheless, the feminization of the Jews had to remain incomplete. The identification of Jewishness with individuality could only be made in the negative sense of the feminine—as individualism, the corruption of the universal. There could be no positive evaluation of Jewish nature because there was no sphere in which Jewish character could legitimately be expressed. The rejection of the conversion of Jews to Christianity was not a plea to recognize that church and synagogue complement one another, as do work and home. Christian theologians could applaud the Third Reich for removing women from paid, nondomestic labor and returning them to the female, domestic sphere. But in which Jewish sphere could they ask Hitler to place the Jews? Women could be absorbed into the total individual of the family, but by definition Jews could not be present within the total individual of the *Volk* without violating the universal in its concrete form—the Germanic race.

In the nineteenth and twentieth century in Germany, women do not appear on the plane of normative theological ethics as historical actors but as images, as building blocks of a male Christian imagination that sought to assert itself as the ethical norm. Women and Jews were ciphers in a theological discourse that used their existence to illustrate the proper relation of individuality and universality, the private and the public. Women as representations of individuality were excluded from the male realm of the public and the universal; they were put in their place, the home and the family. But Jews had no place. To define them as having no part in the male Christian sphere was to exclude them from existence.

Notes

1. Ute Gerhard, *Verhaltnisse und Verhinderungen. Frauenarbeit, Familie und Rechte der Frauen im 19. Jahrhundert mit Dokumenten* (Frankfurt am Main: Suhrkampt, 1978). Gerhard has described the protracted and uneven growth of the conditions of modern industrial

society that placed early nineteenth-century German women in a period of uneasy transition between a feudal and a bourgeois social order in terms of the forms of family and work, of legal regulations and ideological debates.

2. H. J. Birkner, ed., *Brouillon zur Ethik* (Hamburg: Meiner, 1981), pp. 55ff.

3. *Christmas Eve,* trans. Terence T. Rice (Richmond, Va.: John Knox, 1967), pp. 54f., 83.

4. Karin Hausen, "Family and Role Division: The Polarization of Sexual Stereotypes in the Nineteenth Century—An Aspect of the Dissociation of Work and Family," in Richard J. Evans and W. R. Lee, eds., *The German Family: Essays on the Social History of the Family in Nineteenth- and Twentieth-century Germany* (London: Croom Helm, 1981), pp. 51–83.

5. Christoph Friedrich von Ammon, *Handbuch der christlichen Sittenlehre,* 2d ed. (Leipzig): Goschen, 1838), p. 199.

6. Johann Christian von Hoffmann, *Theologische Ethik* (Nordlingen: C. H. Beck, 1878), p. 216.

7. C. W. F. Hegel, *Philosophy of Right,* trans. T. M. Knox (London: Oxford University Press, 1967), p. 263.

8. Richard Rothe, *Theologische Ethik,* 2d ed., vol. 2 (Wittenberg: Zimmermann, 1867), p. 265.

9. Ibid., p. 252.

10. Ibid., p. 256.

11. Ibid., p. 268.

12. Ibid., pp. 267f.

13. Ibid., pp. 215ff.

14. Ibid., p. 299.

15. Ibid., pp. 298f.

16. Schleiermacher, *Die christliche Sitte,* ed. L. Jonas, in *Samtliche Werke,* 2d ed., vol. 12 (Berlin: Reimer, 1884), p. 655; Rothe, *Theologische Ethik,* vol. 2, p. 421.

17. Schleiermacher, *Die christliche Sitte,* pp. 324ff.

18. Rothe, *Theologische Ethik,* 2d ed., vol. 5 (Wittenberg: Koelling, 1871), pp. 49ff.

19. Ibid., pp. 356ff.

20. Ibid., pp. 359f.

21. Ibid., pp. 361f.

22. Rothe, *Theologische Ethik,* vol. 2, p. 281.

23. H. L. Martensen, *Christian Ethics* [Christian Ethics, vol. 1], trans. C. Spence (Edinburgh: T. and T. Clark, 1873), p. 49.

24. Ibid., pp. 457f., 462f.

25. H. L. Martensen, *Christian Ethics. Special Part—Second Division: Social Ethics* [Christian Ethics, vol. 3], trans. William Affleck (Edinburgh: T. and T. Clark, 1882), p. 53.

26. Ibid., p. 56.

27. H. L. Martensen, *Christian Ethics. Special Part—First Division: Individual Ethics* [Christian Ethics, vol. 2], trans. William Affleck (Edinburgh: T. and T. Clark, 1881), p. 12.

28. *Christian Ethics,* vol. 3, p. 48.

29. *Christian Ethics,* vol. 2, p. 18.

30. *Christian Ethics,* vol. 3, pp. 106, 109.

31. Ibid., p. 107.

32. Ibid., p. 114.

33. Ibid., p. 36.

34. P. G. J. Pulzer, *The Rise of Political Antisemitism in Germany and Austria* (New York: John Wiley and Sons, 1964), pp. 88–102.

35. Isaak August Dorner, *System of Christian Ethics,* trans. C. M. Mead and R. T. Cunningham (Edinburgh: T. and T. Clark, 1887), pp. 149f.

36. Ibid., pp. 165–169.

37. Ibid., p. 157.

38. Ibid., pp. 151f., 154, 159, 170.

39. Ibid., pp. 152f., 158, 160, 169.

40. Ibid., pp. 155, 171.

41. Ibid., pp. 171f.

42. Ibid., p. 154.

43. Karl Werner, *System der christlichen Ethik,* vol. 1 (Manz: Regensburg, 1850), pp. 196–200.

44. Wilhelm Herrmann, *Ethik. Grundriss der theologischen Wissenschaften,* 2d ed. (Tübingen: Mohr, 1901), pp. 194f.

45. Ibid., p. 173.

46. Quoted in Uriel Tal, *Christians and Jews in Germany: Religion, Politics, and Ideology, 1870–1914* (Ithaca: Cornell University Press, 1975), p. 164.

47. Claudia Koonz, "Mothers in the Fatherland: Women in Nazi Germany," in Renate Bridenthal and Claudia Koonz, eds., *Becoming Visi-*

ble: Women in European History (Boston: Houghton Mifflin, 1977), pp. 447–473.

48. Werner Elert, *Der Kampf um das Christentum* (Munich: C. H. Beck, 1921), pp. 138f.

49. Ibid., p. 487.

50. Ibid., p. 489.

51. Paul Althaus, *Leitsatze zur Ethik* (Erlangen: Merkel, 1928), pp. 54ff.

52. Ibid., p. 47.

53. Paul Althaus, *Theologie der Ordnungen* (Gutersloh: Bertelsmann, 1935), p. 17.

54. Werner Elert, *Stand und Stande nach luterischer Auffassung* (Berlin: Verlag des Evangelischen Bundes, 1940), pp. 10f.

55. Reinhold Seeberg, *System der Ethik*, 2d ed. (Leipzig: A. Deichert, 1920), pp. 171–175.

56. Ibid., pp. 184f.

57. Reinhold Seeberg, "Die weltgeschichtliche Krisis der Gegenwart und das Christentum," in *Zum Verstandnis der gegenwartigen Krisis in der europaischen Geisteskultur* (Leipzig: A. Deichert, 1923), pp. 61f.

58. Reinhold Seeberg, "Antisemitismus, Judentum und Kirche," in *Zum Verstandnis der gegenwartigen Krisis*, pp. 115ff.

59. Ibid., p. 111.

60. Reinhold Seeberg, *Christliche Ethik* (Stuttgart: W. Kohlhammer, 1936), p. v.

61. Ibid., p. 246.

62. Ibid., p. 253.

63. Ibid., pp. 266f.

64. Walther Künneth, "Das Judenproblem und die Kirche," in *Die Nation vor Gott: Zur Botschaft der Kirche im Dritten Reich* (Berlin: Wichern, 1933), pp. 101, 103f.

Eleven

Simone Weil's Religious Imagery: How Looking Becomes Eating*

Judith Van Herik

"The great trouble in human life is that looking and eating are two different operations. Only beyond the sky, in the country inhabited by God, are they one and the same operation. . . . It may be that vice, depravity and crime are nearly always . . . attempts to eat beauty, to eat what we should only look at. Eve began it. If she caused humanity to be lost by eating the fruit, the opposite attitude, looking at the fruit without eating it, should be what is required to save it."

Simone Weil, *"Forms of the Implicit Love of God"*

The thought and life of French philosopher and mystic Simone Weil (1909–43) have received wide attention in this country since publication in English of her biography (*Simone Weil: A Life*) by Simone Pétrement in 1976 and *The Simone Weil Reader* (edited by George A. Panichas) in 1977. Scholars of religion (particularly of contemporary theology and mysticism), Catholic intellectuals, and political and social philosophers in Europe and America have been aware of her thought since the 1950s. Some have seen her as a saint and her death by starvation as martyrdom. Her writings on history, politics, society, labor, science, God, and the human soul,

* I am grateful to Caroline W. Bynum, the University of Washington, Isabel F. Knight and Emily R. Grosholz, the Pennsylvania State University, Catherine F. Smith, Bucknell University, Jorunn Jacobson Buckley, University of North Carolina at Greensboro, Thomas Buckley, University of Massachusetts at Boston, and the editors of this volume for critically reading and commenting on earlier versions of this essay.

260

assembled from her notebooks, letters, and articles published in small-circulation journals, fill seventeen volumes in the French. Influential thinkers—among them Albert Camus, T. S. Eliot, Czeslaw Milosz, Susan Sontag, Elizabeth Hardwick, Leslie Fiedler, Graham Greene, and Gabriel Marcel—have recognized the importance and brilliance of her ideas.[1]

Weil, an agnostic Jewish intellectual, entered Paris's elite École Normale in 1928 at age nineteen, where she was a student of Alain (Émile Chartier) and a classmate of Simone de Beauvoir. She taught philosophy at girls' *lycées* between 1931 and 1937, after which she was on leave because of illness. While teaching, she was deeply involved in Marxist and syndicalist labor movements, an involvement that sometimes threatened her teaching positions and her reputation with her students' bourgeois parents (one newspaper article referred to her as "the red virgin of the tribe of Levi, bearer of the Muscovite gospels").[2] She also gave free classes and much of her salary to workers and the unemployed. She worked in 1934–35 on factory assembly lines, despite increasing frailty and punishing headaches, to understand the effects of mechanization on the soul. Her well-known *La Condition ouvrière* (1951) was based on this experience, which convinced her that domination induces submissive docility in the dominated rather than revolt.

In 1932 Weil traveled to Germany to understand the rise of Hitler and in 1936 she joined an anarchist group in the Spanish Civil War. Cruelty on both sides in Spain confirmed her conviction that the good could not originate in the social and political realms, which were ruled by necessity and force. In 1938 she experienced the first of many unanticipated presences of Christ, which she wrote about only twice, in two letters in 1942. Her friends, family, and co-workers were unaware of her religious experiences, but her private writings became increasingly dedicated to construction of an "architecture in the soul" and a science of the supernatural.[3] Because this essay focuses on those private writings, it may seem that she withdrew from political life into religious contemplation, but this was not the case. In 1940, after the Nazi occupation, she and her parents left Paris for Marseilles. Increasingly ill and tired, Weil labored in fields and vineyards in the south of France until she and her parents sailed to New York in 1942, via Casablanca. Her best-known religious writings, assembled in *Gravity and Grace* and *Waiting for God,* are from this period.[4] She left France only because she hoped to get to England to undertake dangerous missions for the Resistance and to have her plan for a cadre of self-sacrificial front-line nurses adopted. She did go to London to work for the Resistance, where, to her deep disappointment, she was assigned editing and writing tasks and refused the dangerous work in occupied France that she ardently desired. In the nine months before her death in August 1943, in a tuberculosis sanitarium, she wrote at least fifteen major essays as well as a book-length plan for French polity after the then uncertain liberation, published in English as *The Need for Roots: Prelude to a Declaration of Duties toward Mankind* (1952).

I cannot provide here a comprehensive introduction to Weil's religious, social, or political philosophy. Instead I examine a special but central web of her complex religious imagery: imagery of eating and food, looking and light, and waiting (*attente*) for and on God. I assemble and analyze such images to present Weil's view of the dilemma of the "natural" human condition and its "supernatural" resolution. I then use this view to address an issue that Weil herself ignored: that she experienced the human condition as a woman.

Weil systematically reflected on domination, submission, and affliction, which she defined, not as a psychological state such as suffering or grief, but "a pulverization of the soul by the mechanical brutality of circumstances." Affliction is suffered unwillingly, destroys flesh, soul, and human personality, and is caused by force, "that x that turns anybody who is subjected to it into a *thing*." [5] But she did not consider these issues in terms of gender or adopt a feminist point of view. She considered being born a woman a "great misfortune," referred to herself sometimes in the masculine gender, and signed some youthful letters to her parents as Simon, their "respectful son." [6] Seeing that her parents and the world considered manhood more appropriate to the life tasks she set for herself, she ignored her own womanhood as much as possible in her daily and professional life. In her writings she was indifferent to women as a disadvantaged group, despite her identification with all others experiencing oppression. She seldom mentioned womanhood in public or private writings until after her mystical experiences, and then it was as an image of the human soul rather than a psychological, social, or cultural situation. But by studying her imagery of eating and food, in particular, we can see that she turned women's traditional situation as feeder and nourisher—the situation she saw in her family and society—into images of a stringent spirituality.

Weil's story is unlike the contemporary American feminist journey to self-affirmation, development, and actualization. On this journey, one moves from being an unwilling object of male power and sexuality to autonomous, self-fulfilling subjectivity. Part of this journey is often a quasi-Marxist critique of Christianity and Judaism as legitimators of sexism that leads to agnosticism, atheism, or feminist religious reform or recreation. Simone Weil began her adult life as an agnostic, voluntarist philosopher who fearlessly led workers' strikes, self-confidently argued with political and intellectual leaders (among them, Trotsky), and always placed her intellectual integrity above social pressures or priestly opinion. Her outspoken autonomy never wavered, even when in her late twenties, to her surprise, she became a mystical lover of Christ (never of any man) with a spirituality of self-emptying self-decreation. In her spiritual life, instead of seeking personal power, she sought impersonality and humility. Instead of spontaneous creativity and self-expression, she sought to be an obedient vessel of transcendent, changeless truth. She dedicated herself to destroying obstacles that particularity of self placed between her and truth so that truth might shine through her like light. She wrote that "for glass, there is nothing better than absolute transparency. For a human being there is nothing more than to be nothingness. Every value in a human being is really a negative value. It is like an opaque stain on glass." [7]

To encounter a woman with one of the most powerful minds of her generation who sidestepped the roles of bride, wife, and mother (but not daughter), yet developed a spirituality of selflessness, is challenging and often irritating to the American feminist sensibility. Nevertheless, her story is an excellent example of the until recently frequent disjunction between a woman's religious imagery and her social reality. In Weil's case, the relationship is more complex than either disjunction or conjunction. She did not seem to think about women, but, as a woman, thought about humanity. To understand this perspective, it is necessary to understand some themes of her mature theology and her biography.

Necessity and the Good: Theological Themes

For Weil, there is no principle in this world, including human nature, by which one rises. The good (God's love, grace) that is this principle enters the world from the outside, of its own volition. The source of good is a reality outside the world, "outside space and time, outside man's mental universe," and inaccessible to human faculties.[8] This world is ruled by necessity (force, gravity), which is indifferent to the good. Hence evil is in the world but the world is not itself evil. This view is important to Weil's ethics, for if good were in this world, compassion for affliction would be impossible because affliction would be interpreted as punishment.

Weil interpreted innocent suffering as the working of necessity, over which God is powerless once he created it. God created by abdicating, by consenting to be less than everything to allow a realm that is not-God to exist. This limits God's power. Her self-emptying God is not omnipotent, but is perfect in love: "God gives himself to men either as powerful or perfect—it is for them to choose." [9] Weil chose perfection and sought to imitate it.

This world of necessity is thus God's renunciation, absence, and love. The human task is to love God through it.

> The evil which we see everywhere in the world in the form of affliction and crime is a sign of the distance between us and God [and necessity and the good]. But this distance is love and therefore it should be loved. This does not mean loving evil, but loving God through the evil. When a child in his play breaks something valuable, his mother does not love the breakage. But if later on her son goes far away or dies she thinks of the incident with infinite tenderness because she now sees it only as one of the signs of her child's existence.[10]

For Weil, evil, necessity, force, and affliction as well as beauty are signs of the other reality. Because it is "the unique source of all the good that can exist in this world" and because the good descends from there through the intermediary of "those minds whose attention and love are turned towards that reality," human attention and love are important.[11] Love is expressed by decreating the self, because the self creates illusions that this world is the true reality and that good can originate here, and because the self is between God and God: "God can love in us only this consent to withdraw in order to make way for him, just as he . . . withdrew in order that we might come into being." God loves the "perspective of creation which can only be seen from the point where I am. But I act as a screen. . . . If only I knew how to disappear, there would be a perfect union of love between God and the earth I tread, the sea I hear." [12]

Good does not come through progress, science, politics, or social change; it descends only when the selfless decreated soul makes the supreme effort of loving attention. The descent of good is a transformation. Weil's imagery of eating, looking, and waiting expresses her view of the "mechanics" of this transformation.

Love and Food: Biographical Themes

Some events of Simone Weil's life prefigure her religious imagery. What she and her biographers say about love, food, and family is selected and condensed in this section.

Weil's father, Bernard Weil, was a successful, hard-working physician whom Pétrement described as gentle, humorous, kind, "taciturn," and quiet. He became easily "overwrought and anxious" and suffered migraine headaches, as his daughter did, which at their worst made eating impossible for him.[13] No interpretive commentary on the relationship between father and daughter is available. Her mother, Selma Reinherz Weil, was highly intelligent and energetic. Pétrement describes Mme. Weil as having a passion for life and a great desire for happiness. She seems to have lived to love and nourish her husband and two children. "She could persuade one with so much ardor and so pleasantly that one felt overwhelmed. Extremely generous, she devoted herself unstintingly to her family and her friends. . . . Her affection and her ability to organize were so overpowering that one was tempted to submit to her, to let her take over. But she did not want to take over; she only wanted to serve and be useful. Her authority was felt despite a real desire on her part to be effacing," Pétrement writes.[14] Mme. Weil typed letters and manuscripts for Simone, provided her with food, clothing, and furniture after she left home to teach, and convinced café owners to feed her more than she ordered by giving them money in advance. She attended demonstrations with Simone, helped her smuggle a list of names of Trotskyists out of Germany, and housed and fed a steady stream of refugees whom Simone sent to her parents in the 1930s.

Simone later wrote that her brother, André, who was three years older than she, had a childhood like that of Pascal.[15] André was a mathematical prodigy and many commentators, including Simone, mention her emulation and sense of inferiority to him. When Simone was six and the First World War began, Dr. Weil was called up and Mme. Weil and the children followed him from post to post, despite policy against this. Simone was therefore educated by André and tutors until she was nine and he twelve; she studied to exhaustion. She compared herself unfavorably to André's genius and, like Plato, identified its area, mathematics, as the gate to contemplation of the infinite, the only realm of value. She later wrote of her mental state at age fourteen: "I seriously thought of dying because of the mediocrity of my natural faculties. The exceptional gifts of my brother . . . brought my own inferiority home to me. I did not mind having no visible successes, but what did grieve me was the idea of being excluded from that transcendent kingdom to which only the truly great have access and wherein truth abides. I preferred to die rather than live without that truth." [16] Her decision not to die grew from the conviction that by longing exclusively for truth, by concentrating perpetual attention on it, one could penetrate that realm.

About Simone's relationship to their mother, André Weil told Malcolm Muggeridge, "It would not be wrong to call my mother in some ways a possessive character, rather than dominating, and except where she considered it an essential duty, my sister tried her best to entertain the illusion in her mother that she, my sister, was my mother's thing in a way, and certainly this caused a certain amount of strain on her which, joined with many other strains, eventually led to her death." [17] The only dream of Simone's that I have found (there are no dreams in the notebooks) suggests the tenderly constraining, ambiguous whorl of mother-daughter symbiosis. In a letter to her mother in spring of 1934, Simon wrote, "I had a strange dream this morning. I dreamt that you were saying to me: I love you too much, I can no longer love anyone else. And it was dreadfully painful." [18] She placed herself between her mother's love and its objects just as she was between God's love and the world; in both situations, perhaps, the only solution was removal of self.

When Simone was six months old, her mother, who was nursing her, developed appendicitis, and Simone's health, normal until then, underwent a "precocious decline." At eleven months she was weaned and became seriously ill for nearly a year; her refusal to take food except from a bottle weakened her further. At three and a half she had a severe attack of appendicitis and, four months later, surgery. She suffered intensely and developed a terror of doctors. Later she complained "with a smile" of having been "poisoned in infancy," which made her a failure.[19] In a letter to her parents during her last illness she wrote, "Whatever nostalgia I . . . feel for the yolk of eggs and vegetables and fruit which I didn't eat at five months and which would have imparted today such an accelerated rhythm to my work of covering sheets of paper which no one will ever look at (except you, perhaps, some day . . .), I would rather have had a mother like mine (not to mention the father), in spite of the inadequate milk." [20] Longing, distrust, rage, and pain, always associated with feeding in infancy, might have become particularly tied to nourishment in her earliest years.

Throughout her life eating was problematic for her, as were other things that her parents valued. André Weil said, disputing the common belief that Simone deliberately stopped eating in order to die, that not eating was a habit for her. "It had always been necessary for my mother to be around as much as possible to see to it that she fed herself, even in days when rations were not talked about." [21] Weil had various moral and political rationales for not eating. She would not eat more than the workers, more than her factory wages could provide (after she gave away most of them), more than those on rations in occupied France when she was in New York and London. She could not eat when she was upset by others' affliction or humiliation.

Even when Simone was grown, her parents found it necessary to supervise her, sometimes resorting to subterfuge in their efforts to keep her fed, healthy, and rested. She accepted their efforts with amused affection and then neutralized them. In a letter to her husband, written in December 1931, Mme. Weil expressed rare exasperation. Having found Simone living without heat or food only two months after she had settled her in a comfortable apartment, Mme. Weil wrote, "No, really and truly, I don't think she is marriageable!" Some of the exchanges between health-minded parents and ascetic daughter are humorous, such as when an adult Simone interrupts a detailed and sophisticated letter about politics to ask, "1. How do you cook rice? 2. How do you eat bacon—raw or cooked?" [22] When she worked in a factory and dined at her parents' home, she would leave the cost of the meal on the table, to their horror. Leslie Fiedler described the situation: "Her father and mother came to represent, in an almost archetypal struggle with her, the whole solid bourgeois world, to whom a hair shirt is a scandal, and suffering a blight to be eliminated by science and proper familial care." [23] But the tone of their communication was tender and humorous, never bitter or accusatory. Simone's letters to her parents usually minimized the discomfort and strenuousness of her life and emphasized meals, beauty, and friends. When she was hospitalized and nearing death in England, Simone kept her illness secret and wrote letters to New York that were "one long lie full of tenderness." [24]

Weil was incapable of expressing affection physically except, it appears, with her family. As an adult, "embraces repelled her"; as a child, she once burst into tears when kissed on the hand by a family friend, an elderly doctor. She shouted "Water! Water!" and wanted to wash. Pétrement explains this by noting that the family had an extreme fear of microbes that gave Simone "certain strong feelings of repugnance." [25] She never outgrew these feelings.

Her tender empathy for the afflicted, whom she defined as inspiring horrified aversion in others, apparently contradicted her incapacity for affectionate gestures, but she feared both impurity entering from outside and her own imperfections, which could contaminate others. In her view, only the good was immune to her harmfulness. At perhaps age five, when she was sometimes unable to touch something that had been touched by someone else, she often said that she couldn't do this or that because of her "disgustingness." There are many stories about her disgust for certain kinds and conditions of food. Simone Anthériou, her roommate in 1931–32, remembered that "Simone could only eat absolutely fresh food of the highest quality. For her, eating was more of a chore than a pleasure; she was not greedy and was disgusted by anything that was not absolutely flawless. Just a spot on a piece of fruit was enough to make her lay it aside." [26] Weil's notebooks refer to this. She writes, "my two enemies: *fatigue* and *disgust* (physical disgust for all kinds of things). Both of them wellnigh invincible," and later, "to admit it to oneself and yield to it is to fall. To admit it to oneself and not yield to it is to rise. . . . Disgust, under all its forms, is one of the most precious natural evils that are given to Man as a ladder to rise. (My personal share in this particular favour is a very large one)." [27]

This turn of thought is characteristic. Wryly, here, she refuses to yield to an unconquerable "natural evil" and, contemplating it, makes it a ladder. She more often used the image of a lever applied to the inner life. She loved the image because a lever is a way of "raising while lowering," and "perhaps this is the only way of rising given to us." Its apparent contradiction (a precious evil) is also characteristic. One of Weil's most frequently used methods was this: "As soon as we have thought something, try to see in what way the contrary is true." [28] She saw meditation on contradiction as a path to transcendence, because resolution of contradiction occurs only on a higher level of understanding.

The Value of Hunger

Feeling hunger when food might be tainted and eating painful, feeling love when touching or being touched was horrifying, and longing for truth when seeing it required perpetual attention—these ambivalences illuminate Weil's absolute distinction between energy or desire and its true, as opposed to imaginary, object. The true object is supernatural; the imaginary one, natural. Her spiritual effort was "to go down to the source of our desires in order to tear the energy away from its object. It is there that desires are true, in so far as they are energy. It is the object which is false," she wrote.[29] Hunger and food are preferred images of desire and its natural object: "Hunger; we imagine different foods; but the hunger itself is real; we must seize hold of the hunger." [30] Her comments on mysticism apply this distinction to loving God.

> To reproach mystics with loving God by means of the faculty of sexual love is as though one were to reproach a painter with making pictures by means of colours composed of material substances. We haven't anything else with which to love.... There is a world of difference between the mystic who violently turns toward God the faculty of love and desire the physiological basis of which is sexual energy, and that false imitation of the mystic who, leaving its natural orientation to this faculty, and providing it with an imaginary object, labels this object with the name of God.[31]

Desire must be purified in two steps. The first is analogous to not eating: refusing to replace the supernatural object with a natural one. The second step is turning the "eyes of the soul" in the proper direction, a process analogous to looking.

For Weil, a natural object cannot be good, only necessary. "The

269

difficulty is that the limited forms of good—ways of living, satisfaction of material needs, one's family, friends, etc.—all this is necessary to us; we draw our vital energy from it. All this constitutes food, and where such sustenance is lacking a real hunger is produced. We find it difficult to conceive that what is necessary to us is not automatically good." [32] Instead of accepting natural objects as good, one must accept the absence of all objects and accept the lack of compensation for their absence. Weil calls this accepting "the void," which means expecting no reward, loving hunger rather than food, remaining empty, keeping desire when it has no fulfillment, in short, refusing to eat. What happens then is "supernatural mechanics." She notes that if, doing violence to the need, powerful as gravity, to fill the void, we leave it, "there takes place as it were an inrush of air, and a supernatural reward supervenes." It will not supervene "if we receive any other wages." [33] This may be how she understood her experiences of Christ's presence, which she described as "more personal, more certain, and more real than that of a human being." She wrote that neither senses nor imagination had any part in the experience. It was only a feeling, in the midst of suffering (from migraine), of "the presence of love, like that which one can read in the smile on a beloved face." [34]

The Danger of Eating

For Weil, hunger both purifies desire and spares the food, the desired object. Her imagery probes what psychoanalysts call oral ambivalence: awareness that eating destroys the food one desires. Her earliest notebook entries about the dilemma of desire and destruction, in her early twenties, refer to friendship and love, domination and submission, rather than to eating, but the issues are soon joined. Two notes address domination and submission: "Avoid at all costs any situation in which one is reduced to being completely a puppet," and "It is impossible to be dependent upon human beings without aspiring to tyrannize over them." [35] In a letter to a student, which Weil wrote at twenty-six, she says that "love seems to me to involve . . . the risk, if one is the object of a profound love, of becoming the arbiter of another human existence." [36] Human love makes one a tyrant or puppet; eater or food. Later, God's love and loving God release her from this dilemma.

Similarly, she notes that art symbolizes the "two noblest human efforts: to construct (work), and to refrain from destruction (love overcome). For all love is naturally sadistic; and modesty, respect, reserve, are the mark of the human." [37] In 1942 her metaphor for natural, destructive love changes from sadism to cannibalism. She laments that "instead of loving a human being for his hunger, we love him as food for ourselves. We love like cannibals. To love purely is to love the hunger in a human being." The "wretched limitation of human love" is that "one loves only what one can eat. When a thing is no longer edible one leaves it to anyone else who can still find nourishment in it." [38]

Humans must develop the "supernatural virtue" of not possessing or changing what they love, of refusing power. Friendship, for Weil, "is a miracle by which a person consents to view from a certain distance, and without coming any nearer, the very being who is necessary to him as food. It requires the strength of soul that Eve did not have." [39] Like hunger, "carnal desire" is "so precious that it has not got to be satisfied." She writes that "children display a presentiment of this when they hesitate to eat some dainty whose delicious quality is already clearly visible to the eye. To look at it seems to them better, and though they finally end up by eating it, they have the feeling that in so doing they are lowering themselves a little." [40] To look is to rise, to eat is to fall. Weil wants to reverse what she defined as Eve's crime: If a woman's hunger caused sin, another woman's hunger will save.

The Value of Looking

In Weil's imagery, eyes may touch and taste, but hands and mouth may not. She seems to have taken almost literally Plato's allegory of the cave, which turns on images of eyes, light (sun and fire), and darkness. In the allegory, turning the eyes to the light is knowing the good, the soul's conversion. Weil's objective was to contemplate her way to the point where seeing light (the good) is feeding on it. Her purpose was a supernatural transformative moment, when seeing is as real as eating.

She writes that the trouble with looking is that only extreme attention convinces us that the visible is real. "Children are keenly conscious of this. What is eaten is necessarily destroyed. What is not eaten, the reality of it is not fully grasped." But in the supernatural sphere, the soul "devours truth through contemplation.

Partake of this All through renunciation." [41] Looking is Weil's
sensory image of renunciatory salvation and eating of destructive
satisfaction. These images express the natural dilemma: One either
violates the beloved or remains hungry. The image of supernatural
eating, which *is* looking, resolves the natural dilemma. "Man's great
affliction, which begins with infancy and accompanies him till death,
is that looking and eating are two different operations. Eternal
beatitude ... is a state where to look is to eat." [42]

The context of Weil's first experience of Christ's presence, in
late 1938, suggests that her convictions about the contradiction
between looking and eating on the natural level and their identity
on the supernatural level were important to its occurrence. She
was reciting, with complete attention, George Herbert's poem
"Love," which a young Catholic Englishman had introduced to
her the previous Easter and which her mother had sometimes read
with her when a headache was particularly excruciating, as it was
on this occasion.[43] The poem reads:

> Love bade me welcome: yet my soul drew back,
>   Guiltie of dust and sinne.
> But quick-ey'd Love, observing me grow slack
>   From my first entrance in,
> Drew nearer to me, sweetly questioning,
>   If I lack'd any thing.
>
> A guest, I answer'd, worthy to be here:
>   Love said, You shall be he.
> I the unkind, ungratefull? Ah, my deare,
>   I cannot look on thee.
> Love took my hand, and smiling did reply,
>   Who made the eyes but I?
>
> Truth Lord, but I have marr'd them: let my shame
>   Go where it doth deserve.
> And know you not, sayes Love, who bore the blame?
>   My deare, then I will serve.
> You must sit down, sayes Love, and taste my meat:
>   So I did sit and eat.

The connotations in the first stanza are of a man making love to a
woman, which are overlaid by connotations of the sinner with his
Lord and loving creator. Eyes are important; Love is "quick-ey'd,"
the sinner's eyes are marred. But Christ has borne the blame and

offers meat, so the sinner can both look and eat. The poem heals the split between looking and eating. Seeing, tasting, and loving unite in a synesthetic sacramental meal.

Weil's imagery of eyes receiving light makes clear that the supernaturally edible good is like light, not like natural food. Light, unlike food, is not harmed when we receive it, for we cannot grasp or change it. We can only let it pass through or obstruct it, let it enter our eyes or turn them away. Weil examines relationships between light, eyes, the sun, and food with minute care. If the point is to rise, one must live on light. Plants are an image of salvation because they absorb solar energy and use it to rise. The remedy for the human desire to devour anything edible is to find a mediator analogous to chlorophyll, which confers "the faculty of feeding on light." She takes this further: "There is only one fault: incapacity to feed on light." "Grace represents our chlorophyll." [44] When one refuses to eat, looks and waits, grace comes from above like light to feed the soul. And while the soul that eats natural food falls, the soul that is fed light rises.

The Looking Soul as Food

In Weil's imagery, God is food but so is the soul. If the soul fixes its eyes and waits with attention, grace may feed it *and* God may eat it. In one of her extended metaphors, the world's beauty is the enticing mouth of a labyrinth. The soul walks on and on, "worn out, with nothing to eat or drink, in the dark, separated from his dear ones." Finally, the afflicted soul reaches the center of the labyrinth, where "God is waiting to eat him." When he leaves he is changed by "being eaten and digested by God." [45] Her notebooks are full of ideas about mediation, transformation, and transubstantiation. She reflects on how mechanical energy becomes luminous energy; how light and human energy become matter when they pass into food; how food is living matter that dies and then becomes human energy; how, through attention, something that enters the eyes is translated into muscular action; how in the sacraments matter becomes Christ's flesh and blood; how in the incarnation God has descended into matter. In short, she examines from numerous angles many senses in which humans incorporate God and God incorporates humans.

She tried to make her actual and spiritual hunger count by

becoming sacrificial, sacramental food. After her mystical unions, laboring in fields and vineyards had theological as well as social and political import. A notebook entry made in New York reads: "If I grow thin from labour in the fields, my flesh really becomes wheat. If that wheat is used for the host it becomes Christ's flesh. Anyone who labours with this intention should become a saint." [46] She would transform herself into sacred food.

According to Weil's science of the supernatural, eating the food of this world strengthens precisely what must be killed so that, in the other realm, the looking soul will eat light. Hunger for food is the earthly image of hunger for God, but the two hungers are opposed in action. If one is satisfied, the other cannot be. Weil practiced her conviction of opposition even in her attitude to the sacraments. She understood them as the way God enters food to be eaten, but she gazed at the bread and wine of Holy Communion with rapt attention, without ever touching or taking either. Nor did she ask for or receive baptism, although she longed for it. She believed this was Christ's will for her. She would eat light, not matter; become food, not eat it. She would be consumed to become the host and consumed again as it.

Images of the Waiting Soul

Waiting with eyes fixed on the light is *attente,* waiting for (on) God. For Weil, terrestrial life is impossible. "We are like flies caught inside a bottle, attracted to the light and unable to go towards it. Nevertheless, it is better to remain stuck inside the bottle throughout the whole of time than to turn away from the light for a single moment." [47] *Attente* is Weil's paradigmatic attitude to the supernatural. It is transformational: Natural eating becomes looking and looking becomes supernatural eating and feeding. *Attente,* keeping oneself empty, is the way to give and receive spiritual nourishment without harming the food, the feeder, or the eater. Food, feeder, and eater are now both God and soul, engaged in mutual nourishment.

Weil's images of *attente* emphasize not-touching, not-eating, and looking as ways to receive the soul's food. Three figures frequently represent the waiting soul: the devoted slave (or servant), the hungry child, and the future wife. Here womanhood, absent in Weil's political and social thought, reappears. The slave is obedient in affliction: "Let the slave await the master until his physical strength is totally exhausted." [48] The hungry child is loyal to its hunger: The waiting soul "knows for certain only that it is hungry. The important thing is that it announces its hunger by crying. A child does not stop crying if we suggest to it that perhaps there is no bread. . . . The danger is not lest the soul should doubt whether there is any bread, but lest, by a lie, it should persuade itself that it is not hungry." "May those cries which I raised when I was a week or two old continue incessantly in me for that milk which is the seed of the Father." [49] And the future wife waits with obedient virginity: "Our love for God should be like a woman's love for a man, which does not express itself by making advances but consists only in waiting." [50] The relation between God and the soul resembles the "relation between a bridegroom and a still virgin bride on their wedding night. Marriage is a consented rape. And so is the soul's union with God. The soul feels cold and is not aware of loving God. It does not know, of itself, that unless it loved it would not consent." [51] To be penetrated by God, one must "preserve in oneself *only* that which is passive." The soul should be like a receptacle, the earth, the Great Mother. To receive the sperm of God "the soul must become simply a matrix, a vessel; something plastic and passive, like water." In this way "Christ is born in the soul." [52]

All that Weil forbids here below, between humans, she accepts in relation to God. The earthly evils of slavery, submission, fatigue, tyranny, rape, murder—being eaten and eating—become images of the soul's love of God and God's love of the soul. Many are images of women's vulnerability. Mme. Weil said that Simone "would have killed in no other situation, but perhaps she might have killed to prevent a rape or to defend herself from it," because it was even more frightful than murder.[53] Simone noted that murder and rape are crimes because "they constitute illegitimate imitations of God's action." "God alone has the right to kill, violate, reduce to slavery the souls of men. And it is a violence which is to be desired above all possible forms of good." [54] Her imagery transforms natural oppression, which takes place under the rule of necessity and force, into supernatural contact with God. Her explanation of this method helps explain the harshness of its content. She wrote that "there is a resemblance between the lower and the higher. Hence slavery is an image of obedience to God, humiliation

275

an image of humility, physical necessity an image of the irresistible presence of grace. . . . On this account, it is necessary to seek out what is lowest as an image." [55] God and the soul have both refused power—God in creating the world, the soul in remaining hungry— to make possible their mystical union. But from the soul's point of view, the union is also a violent annihilation.

Religious Image and Social Reality

Weil's images of *attente* contrast both with the demands of her social and political philosophy—the inviolable dignity of every individual soul—and with her actions as an embodied woman. But one theme is found in both life and imagery—remaining hungry oneself and feeding (becoming food for) others.

The imagery of womanhood in Weil's notes on *attente* repeats and intensifies qualities that have become stereotyped as "feminine." Womanhood, in this imagery, is the soul's obedient and suffering reception of the violent planting of God's divine seed. It is flesh and food. Her view of women's situation (which she rejects as incompatible with her values and vocational commitment but later embraces, without changing her behavior, as a purifying image of *attente*) is the traditional view that contemporary feminists find so limiting to living women. But Weil would turn subjection and affliction—symbolized by edibility—into levers to raise the soul. Remaining naturally hungry (refusing power) and becoming spiritual food became her strenuous ways to escape the realm of force.

Weil did not mean that *attente* was how anyone, woman or man, should live the embodied aspects of life. She did not conduct herself with waiting obedience in society or the political world, nor did she urge such conduct on others. More importantly, for her the proper spiritual attitude would indeed appear evil to the natural eye. Nonetheless, rather than recommending a different way of life for living women, Weil made some uncharacteristically commonplace notes on what to preach to them. She wrote, "There are some sayings which refer particularly to them. . . . Compare all pains and afflictions to birth pangs. For young girls, the parable of the wise virgins. Every young girl lives provisionally, in a state of expectancy, ready for a time when she will leave the paternal roof." [56] Weil would perhaps have thought it degrading to dwell on womanhood as a particularly heavy cross in comparison to those of all creatures (if so, she is exceptionally fastidious in this, which says something about women's dilemmas). Insofar as womanhood was a cross, she embraced it by making it an image of the impossible in *attente*. Lowering was the way to rise. Her sense of the purifying power of images of the soul as a violated virgin or suffering mother probably came from her frequent admonitions to herself: "Love what is intolerable. Embrace what is made of iron, press one's flesh against the metallic harshness and chill." [57] Thus she rejected womanhood, understood as flesh and food, for herself in this world, developed no critique of it as a social, cultural, political, or economic situation, embraced it in religious imagery, and, I suggest, drew on it to illuminate the human condition.

Conclusions: Womanhood and the Human Situation

Weil's apparent disinterest in women's social and cultural jeopardy does not require us to duplicate it. Indeed, her disinterest may have been only apparent. I believe she implicitly criticizes women's situation in her reflections on the human situation. Her focus on purity and impurity, domination and subjection, greed and self-control, force and affliction, addressed in imagery of eating and food, suggests that she grappled with dilemmas that may confront many women more inescapably than men because women's bodies represent and provide the original food—nourishing, poisonous, pure, contaminating, longed-for, devouring, and devoured. Weil's thought turns on these ambiguities of our cultural and religious images of womanhood. She splits them into natural (poisonous, contaminating) and supernatural (nourishing, pure) realms, so that at the natural level mutuality of feeding and being fed is impossible. She then restores mutuality on the spiritual level where God and the soul become food for one another.

A second reason to suspect that Weil addresses the human condition through the lens of women's situation is the many parallels between her life and thought and what the American psychiatrist Hilde Bruch has called the "anorexic stance." [58] Weil's convictions about eating and not eating, power and impotence, passivity and activity, and purity and contamination express and, when interpreted, criticize an aspect of human experience with which many women grapple, and which for anorexic women becomes all of experience. I have examined these parallels elsewhere, not to make a clinical diagnosis, but to suggest that Weil's concerns are drawn from an experience of womanhood.[59] Making such a diagnosis adds little to our understanding of Weil's religious thought. On the other hand, Weil's thought raises the question of whether some anorexic women are especially sensitive to women's symbolic edibility and protest it by refusing to treat anything else as food.

If Weil's thought implicitly expresses a particular sensitivity to women's situation, it also criticizes the situation in which women are cultural symbols of the edible, split into vulnerable and devouring, impure and nourishing. This criticism is that the situation is impossible. I suggest that her understanding of the afflicted human situation could be formulated as follows. If, in this world, one collaborates with the laws of force by eating or being edible, one strengthens the rule of force. "Here below," both eating and being eaten are destructive and contaminating; they contaminate both food and eater. Eating and being eaten in this world make one part of the natural system of impurity and force. Then one is inedible to God and unable to eat God, who is the only proper eater and the only proper food. But if one refuses power one may, by looking and waiting, become edible for God. Then God will feed the soul and use it to nourish others in a way that is uncontaminated and uncontaminating, sacramental and salvific. Thus, noteating, looking, and waiting are passages to the absolutely good and real realm. But one reaches it only for a moment, in mystical union or death. In her conviction that God's eating the soul annihilates the person, Weil reiterated her conviction that the eater destroys its loved food. The soul is to be eaten regardless, but Weil chose to be eaten by God.

Attente was a bridge between Simone Weil's natural and supernatural experience. It made the impossibility of life here below into the spiritual possibility of feeding on light. It was a symbolic, conceptual, and real resolution of the natural dilemma as she experienced it. Her imagery of *attente* expresses women's situation of being seen as food, as prey, in universal terms. If giving and receiving, eating and being eaten, loving and being loved, were not mutual in this world of force (and for Simone Weil and many others they are not), then Weil perhaps found mutuality outside the world. Even so, her purpose was not to escape the world but to illumine it with truth.

Notes

1. Albert Camus, "La condition ouvrière de Simone Weil," *L'Express,* December 13, 1955; Preface to Weil, "L'Enracinement," in Camus, *Oeuvres complètes (Essais)* (Paris: Bibliotheque de la Pleiade, 1965), vol. 2, pp. 1700–1702; T. S. Eliot, Preface to Weil, *The Need for Roots: Prelude to a Declaration of Duties toward Mankind,* trans. Arthur Wills (New York: G. P. Putnam, 1952; repr. New York: Harper Colophon, 1971); Czeslaw Milosz, "The Importance of Simone Weil," in *The Emperor of the Earth: Modes of Eccentric Vision* (Berkeley: University of California Press, 1981), chap. 7; Susan Sontag, "Simone Weil," in *Against Interpretation* (New York: Farrar, Straus, and Giroux, 1967), pp. 49–51; Elizabeth Hardwick, "Reflections on Simone Weil," *Signs* 1 (1975): 83–91; Leslie Fiedler, Introduction to Weil, *Waiting for God,* trans. Emma Craufurd (New York: G. P. Putnam, 1951; repr. New York: Harper Colophon, 1973); Graham Greene, "Waiting for God," in *Collected Essays* (London: Bodley Head, 1969), pp. 372–375; Gabriel Marcel, "Simone Weil," *Month,* July 1949, pp. 9–18. Simone Pétrement's biography was published by Plon (Paris, 1973); I use the English translation: *Simone Weil: A Life,* trans. Raymond Rosenthal (New York: Random House, 1976). Panichas's reader is *The Simone Weil Reader* (New York: David McKay, 1977). Recent bibliographies of Weil's works in French and in English translation and of selected secondary sources can be found in Panichas's reader and George Abbott White, "Simone Weil's Bibliography: Some Reflections on Publishing and Criticism," in White, ed., *Simone Weil: Interpretations of a Life* (Amherst: University of Massachusetts Press, 1981), pp. 181–194. Some of the writings that most compelled and influenced her were those of Homer, the Pythagoreans, the Greek tragedians, Plato, the Gospels, aspects of Manichaeism, the Cathars, St. John of the Cross, the Bhagavad Gita and Upanishads, Marx, and, from the Hebrew Bible, the beginning chapters of Genesis, parts of the Psalms and Prophets, and Job and the Song of Songs.

2. Pétrement, *A Life,* p. 114.

3. *First and Last Notebooks,* trans. Richard Rees (London: Oxford University Press, 1970), p. 208. This volume contains her prewar notebook (1933 to (?) 1939), New York notebook (1942), and London notebook (1943). Her notebooks for 1940–42 are in English as *The Notebooks of Simone Weil,* 2 vols., trans. Arthur Wills (London: Routledge and Kegan Paul, 1956; repr. 1976).

4. *Gravity and Grace,* trans. Arthur F. Wills (New York: Putnam's Sons, 1952). On *Waiting for God* see note 1.

5. Weil, *Gateway to God,* ed. David Raper (Glasgow: Collins, Fontana edition, 1974), p. 88; *The Iliad or the Poem of Force,* trans. Mary McCarthy (Wallingford, Pa.: Pendle Hill, pamphlet 91, 1956), p. 3.

6. Pétrement, *A Life,* pp. 26–28. For discussion of Weil's "feminine identity," see Lucy Bregman, "The Barren Fig Tree: Simone Weil and the Problem of Feminine Identity," in Thomas A. Idinopulos and Josephine Zadovsky Knopp, eds., *Mysticism, Nihilism, Feminism: New Critical Essays on the Theology of Simone Weil* (Johnson City, Tenn.: Institute of Social Sciences and Arts, 1984), chap. 4.

7. *First and Last Notebooks,* p. 350.

8. "Draft for a Statement of Human Obligations" (1943), in Weil, *Selected Essays, 1934–1943,* ed. and trans. Richard Rees (London: Oxford University Press, 1962), p. 219.

9. *Gravity and Grace,* p. 144.

10. *Gateway to God,* p. 81.

11. "Draft for a Statement of Human Obligations," p. 219.

12. *Gravity and Grace,* p. 89.

13. Pétrement, *A Life,* p. 5.

14. Ibid., p. 6.

15. "Spiritual Autobiography," in *Waiting for God* (Colophon ed.), p. 64.

16. Ibid.

17. Appendix ("André Weil, a scientist, discusses his sister with Malcolm Muggeridge") to Weil, *Gateway to God,* p. 149.

18. Pétrement, *A Life,* p. 203.

19. Ibid., p. 7.

20. Simone Weil, *Seventy Letters,* trans. Richard Rees (London: Oxford University Press, 1965), p. 195.

21. Appendix to *Gateway to God,* p. 159.

22. Ibid., pp. 93, 85.

23. Introduction to *Waiting for God,* p. 14.

24. Ibid., p. 521.

25. Pétrement, *A Life,* p. 11.

26. Ibid., pp. 11, 81.

27. *The Notebooks of Simone Weil,* vol. 1, pp. 153, 301.

28. Ibid., p. 72, *Gravity and Grace,* p. 156.

29. *The Notebooks of Simone Weil,* vol. 1, p. 203.

30. Ibid., p. 28.

31. Ibid., vol. 2, p. 472.

32. Ibid., p. 492.

33. Ibid., vol. 1, p. 135.

34. Pétrement, *A Life*, p. 340.

35. *First and Last Notebooks*, pp. 17, 27.

36. "Letter to a pupil," in *Seventy Letters*, p. 13.

37. *First and Last Notebooks*, p. 42.

38. Ibid., pp. 284, 322–323.

39. "Forms of the Implicit Love of God," in *Waiting for God*, p. 205.

40. *The Notebooks of Simone Weil*, vol. 2, p. 416.

41. Ibid., p. 461.

42. Ibid., p. 637.

43. Jacques Cabaud, *Simone Weil: A Fellowship in Love* (New York: Channel Press, 1964), p. 169.

44. *The Notebooks of Simone Weil*, vol. 1, p. 223; vol. 2, p. 368.

45. "Forms of the Implicit Love of God," pp. 163–164. Discussing mystics' experience of God as "spiritual sense perceptions," Wolfgang Riehle argues against understanding their use of language of earthly sense perceptions to convey spiritual meaning as ordinary use of metaphor because this language is the one in which the mystical experience itself takes place. "In theological terms the 'spiritual senses' are not just five powers permanently residing in the soul—by analogy with the physical senses—but are temporary spiritual acts" in which "it seems to the soul that it is experiencing a supernatural object which reveals itself as if it were present in some concrete manner" (*The Middle English Mystics*, trans. Bernard Standring [London, Boston, and Henley: Routledge and Kegan Paul, 1981], p. 104). Weil's imagery formulates experiences, not just abstract speculations. Riehle also points out that in Christian Europe until the seventeenth century it was taken for granted that knowing was a sensual experience, that wisdom could be savored (p. 109). Perhaps Weil had to formulate her synesthetic experiences, such as eating good, as absolutely supernatural because by her time the sensual, intellectual, and spiritual were philosophically and experientially split apart. I owe knowledge of Riehle's work to Caroline W. Bynum, whose thorough study of food imagery in the piety of late medieval women provides a historical and theological context for a fuller understanding of Weil's experiences than I have presented here. See Bynum's "Fast, Feast, and Flesh: The Religious Significance of Food to Medieval Women," paper presented to the Bunting Institute Colloquium, Cambridge, Mass., February 14, 1984; forthcoming in *Representations*, no. 11, August 1985.

46. *First and Last Notebooks,* p. 96.

47. Ibid., p. 292.

48. Ibid., p. 177.

49. "Forms of the Implicit Love of God," p. 210; *First and Last Notebooks,* p. 99.

50. *Gateway to God,* p. 84.

51. *First and Last Notebooks,* p. 244.

52. *The Notebooks of Simone Weil,* vol. 1, p. 248; *First and Last Notebooks,* p. 287.

53. Pétrement, *A Life,* p. 193.

54. *The Notebooks of Simone Weil,* vol. 2, pp. 390, 504.

55. *Gravity and Grace,* pp. 80–81.

56. *First and Last Notebooks,* p. 267.

57. *First and Last Notebooks,* p. 260.

58. Hilde Bruch, *The Golden Cage: The Enigma of Anorexia Nervosa* (Cambridge, Mass.: Harvard University Press, 1978).

59. "Looking, Eating, and Waiting in Simone Weil," in Idinopulos and Knopp, eds., *Mysticism, Nihilism, Feminism,* pp. 81–84. Conversations with Caroline W. Bynum and reading her manuscript, "Holy Feast and Holy Fast: Food Motifs in the Piety of Late Medieval Women" (in preparation) have helped me better understand the relationships in Weil between food imagery, sacramental theology, and the experience of womanhood.

Twelve

Sacrifice as Remedy for Having Been Born of Woman

Nancy Jay

Feminist scholars cannot limit themselves to studying the *participation* of women in culture, society, or history, important as this is. Nor can we, like traditional scholars, take for granted the *exclusion* of women from vast areas of cultural life. Rather, we must subject these areas to critical analysis in order to disclose and to demystify the gender relations that underlie them.

This essay examines the gender relations of blood sacrificial ritual as it has been practiced in ancient religions, in contemporary tribal societies, and in symbolic form in Christianity. Almost all of the immense literature on sacrifice either ignores or takes for granted its gender-related features. Consequently, recognizing these features as problematic, in need of explanation, will lead to a radically new understanding of those socially organized contexts within which sacrificial ritual is meaningfully performed. This new understanding of the social relations of sacrificial practice will, in turn, make aspects of the Judeo-Christian sacrificial tradition that have been mystified or obscured both visible and intelligible.

Gender-related Features of Sacrifice

The practice of blood sacrifice has an extraordinary, worldwide distribution. Excluding its Christian form, blood sacrifice either is, or has been, practiced from Ireland to New Zealand, from Siberia to South Africa, and in both North and South America. We call all these rituals sacrifice because, even in wholly unrelated traditions, they share certain features. Some of the most prominent of these features are gender related, such as an opposition between sacrificial purity and the pollution of childbirth, and a rule that only males may perform sacrificial ritual.

In the polarity between blood sacrifice and childbirth, killing receives a positive value and giving birth a negative value. The Aztec sun rose purposefully, accompanied by spirits of human sacrifice victims. Only repeated sacrificing gave it life each morning and enabled it to climb upward, but it sank to its death each evening accompanied by the spirits of women dead in childbirth. The opposition between sacrifice and childbirth may not be dramatized daily across the heavens in other traditions, but a structurally analogous opposition is a regular feature of most sacrificial religions.

Among the Israelites, the pollution of childbirth, and also of menstruation, typified pollution in general. For example, Ezekiel described the Exile as divine punishment for conduct "like the uncleanness of a woman in her impurity" (36:17). The very first illustration in the priestly rules for occasions requiring purifying expiatory sacrifice is after childbirth, when a woman must bring a sin offering and a burnt offering for the priest to sacrifice. If she has given birth to a female child, her uncleanness is exactly double that for a male child's birth. She must wait twice as long before her impurity has faded enough so that the priest can "make atonement for her and she shall be clean" (Lev. 12:8).

The Greeks were not comparably concerned about menstrual blood, but here too the pollution of childbirth appears to have been a paradigm for ritual pollution. The most complete study of the pure and the impure in ancient Greece says of the pollution of childbirth, "Cette souillure n'est pas autre chose que la saleté qui éloigne l'homme des dieux." [1] ("This pollution is none other than the filth that estranges man from the gods.") Here too the pollution of childbirth could be removed only by sacrifice. What is it about childbirth that can only be undone, remedied by sacrifice?

Around the world, ordinarily only adult males (fathers, real and metaphorical) may perform sacrifice. Where women do so it is as virgins or in some other specifically nonchildbearing role. [2] It is not women as such who are regularly prohibited from sacrificing, but women as childbearers or as potential childbearers. [3] Among the West African Ashanti, drawing water is a woman's job, but water to be used in sacrificial ritual must have been drawn by a woman past menopause. [4]

These common gender-related features of sacrificial practice cannot be explained culturally as features of a single religious tradition. Nor are they noncultural, inevitable features of all human societies at a certain level of development; in spite of its wide distribution, the practice of blood sacrifice is not universal.

We can understand gender-related features, along with many other aspects of sacrificial ritual, by recognizing the relation of sacrifice to a particular kind of social organization, itself gender related. That is, we must understand the relation between sacrifice and family structure, taking "family" structure in its wider sense to include the kinship structures in which tribal societies organize themselves.

Sacrifice and Kinship Organization

There is an immense variety of ways in which religious practices serve to order or constitute moral community in family or family-like structures. These range from the ways in which religions of tribal societies work to identify, maintain, and legitimate social structure along kinship lines to the metaphorical recreation of familylike structures in Christianity and other salvation religions. Here, I want to describe an affinity between blood sacrificial religion and those social systems that make the relation between father and son the basis of social order and continuity. These are systems of patrilineal descent, in which continuity is figured through men only, from father to son; in other words in which women give birth to children but have no descendants. Within these systems, blood sacrificial ritual can serve as evidence of patrilineal descent, and in so doing it works to constitute and maintain patrilineal descent systems.

For this discussion I shall draw on ethnography, primarily studies of African societies, as the richest source of description of sacrificial practice and its relation to tribal social organization. In conclusion I shall show some ways in which these ethnographic studies of the social context of sacrifice can illuminate sacrificial features of the Judeo-Christian tradition. In analyzing both ethnographic and Judeo-Christian sacrificial social organization I shall use a few technical kinship terms. For example, in order to show that sacrifice is "at home" in patrilineal descent systems in a way it is not in other forms of social organization, I shall need to contrast patrilineal and matrilineal descent systems. Readers will need to know that although patrilineages are patriarchies, matrilineages are not matriarchies. Men ordinarily hold the major positions of authority in matrilineages as well as in patrilineages. It is the *descent* of authority, and of property, that differs: in patrilineages descent is from father to son, in matrilineages from mother's brother to sister's son, from uncle to nephew.

The affinity between sacrifice and systems of patrilineal descent does not mean that sacrifice is performed only in societies organized exclusively in terms of patrilineal descent. For one thing, descent may be figured in more than one way in any given society. The ancient Romans distinguished between two ways of figuring descent: cognation and agnation. Cognation refers to all descent relationships traced through men and women, between persons descended from a common ancestor, whether male or female. Agnation refers to relation by descent through males only. Agnation (which is patrilineal descent), but not cognation, was inseparable from sacrificial religion.

Some societies, like the West African Yakö, organize themselves in both patrilineal and matrilineal descent groups. Each Yakö, female and male, belongs to a patrilineage and also to a matrilineage. But *only* the patrilineages practice sacrifice.[5]

Even in societies organized primarily in terms of matrilineal descent, sacrifice may be practiced, but it is much rarer, and its relation to the social context differs ordinarily in very important ways from sacrifice performed in patrilineal descent groups. Patrilineages commonly use rights to participate in sacrifices to identify membership; matrilineage membership is not identified in this way. Sometimes sacrifice works in direct opposition to matrilineal structural bonds, a reversal of its role in patrilineal descent groups. There are fathers and sons in every society, and sometimes sacrifice is practiced in relation to secondary patrilineal organization within a primarily matrilineal society. With one exception (see below) sacrifice in matrilineal societies never achieves the central significance it has in patrilineal descent systems. It may have so minor a role that it is overlooked by ethnographers. (The matrilineal Crow, says Lowie, "made no bloody sacrifices."[6] Nevertheless he describes a finger sacrifice—performed with reference to descent from fathers, not from mothers or from mothers' brothers.)[7] In order to understand relations between sacrifice and its social context in matrilineal societies, each case must be examined individually. I will give two illustrations, one fairly typical, one exceptional.

Victor Turner has described ritual acts he identifies as sacrifice among the primarily matrilineal Ndembu of Central Africa. According to Turner, "Ndembu do not have autonomous sacrificial rituals; sacrifice is always encompassed by a sequence of activities which includes many other ritual types." He contrasts this with the practice of two African patrilineal societies "for whom purely sacrificial rites are central in their religious practice." [8] Indeed, in his detailed description of the Chihamba ritual he identifies thirty-two separate procedures in the four-day ritual, only two of which involve killing.[9] These are the symbolic slaughter of a male demi-god, Kavula, involving the actual beheading of a real red cock, and the symbolic beheading of candidates, represented by the actual beheading of white hens.

Turner writes, "Whether this symbolic slaughtering of Kavula and the subsequent symbolic beheading of the candidates are to be defined as 'sacrificial' acts is problematic." But he does identify the killing of the birds as sacrifice even though some expected features are missing. (For example, "the fowls are *not* eaten in a communion meal. There *is* a communion meal but the sacred food eaten is not meat but beans and cassava.") Even if this identification as sacrifice is correct, the purpose of the Chihamba ritual is *not* to align participants with the matrilineal descent system, but *the reverse*. According to Turner, in the Chihamba, candidates are "being separated from" a matrilineal ancestress and dedicated to Kavula, who is not a matrilineal ancestor but is portrayed in the ritual as the husband of the ancestress and therefore in a paternal position. Turner describes this Ndembu sacrifice as freeing participants from the formal social structure and contrasts this with Roman sacrifice offered "to maintain the structured order." "One destructures, the other restructures," he says. He calls these opposed ritual functions "abandonment," which destructures, and "prophylaxis," which restructures.[10]

Ndembu sacrifice of abandonment, according to Turner, acts to release participants from the " 'deadly sins' of social structure . . . that all may be one outside structure and inside communitas." [11] The Roman sacrifice of prophylaxis, in contrast, is not a means of creating structure-free *communitas* but "the very means of maintaining order and structure." [12] Turner does not account for this difference with reference to the contrasting systems of descent, but only as a consequence of the greater development, wealth, and complexity of Roman society. Turner also discusses a number of other sacrificial religions, both of simple and of complex, literate societies (*all* of which are religions of patrilineally organized societies) and suggests that sacrifice in the simpler African societies is more like Ndembu sacrifice. But sacrifice among the patrilineal African groups he cites is never used to "destructure" patrilineal descent structures, but rather to identify and maintain them, and in *all* of them sacrificial ritual is "central in their religious practices" in a way it is not for the Ndembu.

Turner has also discussed sacrifice with reference to Ndembu ritual in *The Drums of Affliction*. He includes here, along with the Chihamba ritual, a Ndembu circumcision ritual that he chooses to identify as sacrifice.[13] But in this ritual it is the father-son relation, not that between mother's brother and sister's son, that is significant both ritually and in terms of social organization. That is, it is performed with reference to patrilineal, not to matrilineal, descent.[14]

The exception mentioned above to the marginal role of sacrifice in matrilineal societies is found in the West African kingdom of Ashanti. To my knowledge, this is the only society organized primarily in terms of matrilineal descent in which traditional religious practice is profoundly and elaborately sacrificial. Even here most sacrifice is performed in contexts organized entirely in terms of patrilineal descent: either that of the secondary patrilineages (less important for social and economic organization than the matrilineal clans), or, in the case of human sacrifice before the British conquest, the patrilineally organized royal bureaucracy. Individuals also sacrifice to the patrilineally organized gods, who are linked to the patrilineages. Sacrifice *is* performed in relation to the matrilineal chiefs, but this office is a political, not a family, institution, and unlike membership in the matrilineages, it is inseparably linked with patrilineal descent. No sacrifice is performed in a context of ordinary membership in the matrilineages, nor is sacrifice offered to matrilineal ancestors as such. This is in sharp contrast to sacrificial practices in the similar, but patrilineally organized, West African kingdoms of Benin and Dahomey.[15]

How can we understand this apparent affinity between sacrifice and patrilineal descent? Why do patrilineage members so commonly insist that sacrifice is absolutely essential for the maintenance and continuity of the social (and even natural) order, while matrilineage members can order their descent systems without need for sacrifice? What differences between the two systems can illuminate this?

Systems of Unilineal Descent

The formation of unilineal descent groups (whether patrilineal or matrilineal) is only one of a number of ways in which people may order social relations in terms of descent.[16] As *descent* systems, they are all ways of ordering the social relations of reproduction. Further, as is true of all forms of social organization, unilineal descent systems are associated with specific kinds of economic production. Lineage structure is particularly efficient for control and transmission (by inheritance) of productive property such as farm land, or certain monopolized skills, including priestly skills. Unilineal descent groups are not of significance among people, such as hunter-gatherers, who have little durable property. Nor do such groups usually survive the introduction of a modern capitalist economy with occupational differentiation and monetary media of exchange. Like blood sacrificial religions, unilineal descent groups are concentrated among precapitalist societies with some degree of technological development in which rights in durable property are highly valued.[17] This middle range has enormous breadth. Both unilineal descent groups and blood sacrifice are found among subsistence farmers, with no central government at all, and in highly sophisticated societies like prerevolutionary China.[18]

Societies organized in corporate lineages are by definition societies in which productive property is controlled by descent groups, and in which, therefore, the control of the means of production is inseparably linked with the control of the means of reproduction, that is, the fertility of women. As Meyer Fortes says, using traditional androcentric language,

> I have several times remarked on the connection generally found between lineage structure and the ownership of the most valued productive property of the society, whether it be land, or cattle, or even the monopoly of a craft like blacksmithing. . . . A similar connection is found between lineage organization and control over reproductive resources and relations.[19]

(For "reproductive resources," read "child-bearing women.")
"Rights over the reproductive powers of women," says Fortes, "are
easily regulated by a descent group system." A lineage head is a
trustee of property and "has a decisive jural role also in the dis-
posal of rights over the fertility of the women of the group." [20]

Presumably this last refers only to patrilineages, for matrilineages may be said to dispose of rights of sexual access to women,
but not of rights over their fertility. In reference to the control of
the means of production, matrilineages and patrilineages are inter-
changeable. But in terms of the control of the means of reproduction they are not, since matrilineages divide men's rights over
women's bodies between brothers and husbands, who are necessarily members of different lineages. In this sense the identity of
the group controlling productive and reproductive property is always imperfect in matrilineages.

Whether descent is figured from father to son or from uncle to
nephew, both systems can be understood as ways of formally connecting men with women as childbearers, that is, ways of organizing
intergenerational continuity between men and men in the face of
the fact that it is women who give birth and with whom the next
generation begins life already in close relation. Both systems are
ways in which men regulate rights over women's reproductive powers, but in matrilineal descent systems these rights are divided: The
man with rights of sexual access and the man and group with rights
in the offspring are not the same.

Although obviously both types of descent, father-son and uncle-
nephew, are equally dependent on women's powers of reproduction
for their continuity, this dependence is structurally recognized in
matrilineal descent, but transcended in patrilineal descent. Rights
of membership in a matrilineage may be determined by birth alone,
providing sure knowledge of maternity. Paternity never has the
same certainty, and birth by itself cannot be the sole criterion for
patrilineage membership. Nor can any enduring social structure be
built only upon the shifting sands of that uncertain relation, biological paternity. Jural paternity (paternity in terms of rights and obligations) and biological paternity may, and often do, coincide, but
it is jural paternity that determines patrilineage membership. Some
sacrificing societies, such as the Romans or the Nuer, distinguish
between biological and jural paternity in their vocabulary, for ex-

ample, the Latin distinction between *genitor* and *pater*. It was the *pater* who was significant sacrificially.

Unilineal descent groups are concerned not merely with an existing social order but also with its continuity through time, generation succeeding generation. When the crucial intergenerational link is between father and son, for which birth itself cannot provide sure evidence, sacrificing may be considered essential for the continuity of the social order. What is needed to provide clear evidence of jural paternity is an act as powerful, definite, and available to the senses as birth. When membership in patrilineal descent groups is identified by rights of participation in blood sacrifice, evidence of "paternity" is created that is as certain as evidence of maternity, but far more flexible.

Consider patrilineal ancestor cults, whose powerful affinity with sacrificial ritual is widely recognized. As Fortes has said, sacrifice is "the crucial ritual institution of ancestor worship." [21] Fortes does not discriminate here between matrilineal and patrilineal ancestor cults; but purely matrilineal ancestor cults, although equally concerned with enduring social continuity, do not depend on blood sacrifice as their "crucial" ritual, even though offerings of food are commonly important. Ancestral sacrifice ritually defines patrilineage boundaries (keeps the difference between members and not-members) by distinguishing between those who have rights to participate and those who do not, and at the same time extends the temporal continuity of the lineage beyond its living members to include the dead, and sometimes the unborn. Patrilineage members (but only as lineage members) may also look forward to transcending their own mortality as future ancestors, sacrificially maintained by lineage descendants.

Sacrificial ancestor cults are commonly features of corporate patrilineal descent groups whose members are tied to a certain locality by inherited farm land, and also often by ancestral graves. Rights of participation in sacrifices can also identify patrilineage membership even when the lineage is not a corporate group and is not clearly defined territorially, but in this case there may not be an ancestor cult, and sacrifice, more "spiritual" as the group is less corporate, is offered to divinities. The Nuer and Dinka are examples. Sacrificing may be the exclusive privilege of only one patrilineal descent group in a society: a hereditary priesthood, who may keep their own lineage boundaries absolutely clear while other, nonsacrificing descent groups in the same society may lose such clearly defined identity. In this case the ideology of eternal genealogical continuity is also centered in the priesthood. The Israelite priesthood is an example.

Because it identifies jural and moral descent, rather than "mere physiological" descent, rights of participation in sacrifices can define membership in groups with only a metaphor of patrilineal descent defining their organization. This is the case with the purely symbolic blood sacrifice of the Eucharist, offered only by members of a "patrilineage" whose descent is similarly symbolic: the formally institutionalized apostolic succession of the clergy. This social organization is a truly perfect "eternal line of patrilineal descent," in which, as it were, authority descends from father to father, through the "one Son made perfect forever," in a line no longer directly dependent on women's reproductive powers for continuity.

Sacrifice as Evidence of Patrilineal Descent

The claim that sacrificing works as evidence of, and therefore as a means of constituting, lines of patrilineal descent is not mine but that of many sacrificers. Among the Nuer, East African cattle herders, the word Evans-Pritchard translates as "agnates" (that is, persons related patrilineally) means literally "people who share the meat of sacrifices." [22] The Tallensi, West African subsistence farmers, repeatedly told Meyer Fortes that their patrilineal "clanship ties are a consequence of sacrificing together." [23] In Dahomey, descendants of powerful kings told Herskovits that patrilineage continuity is dependent on sacrificing.[24] And Durkheim's teacher, Fustel de Coulanges, was only taking the ancient Romans at their word when he said that Roman agnatic family relations were "established" by sacrificial worship.[25] For patrilineage members, it is sacrificing, not giving birth, that maintains lineage continuity as patrilineage.

Social scientists have tended not to believe these claims. For example, Fortes himself dismissed the Tallensi claim as merely "an *a posteriori* argument which is common all over the country." [26] Again, the young Durkheim (who later changed his point of view) criticized his teacher, saying Fustel had "mistaken the cause for the effect." [27] Social scientists' disbelief appears to be sometimes a consequence of their understanding of ritual as purely expressive action, without instrumental power, sometimes a consequence of their taking patrilineal descent for granted as normal. For ethnographers, that women give birth to children but have no descendants was an aspect of an alien reality not requiring explanation. Like the Romans, social scientists can accept the notion *mulier finis familiae est*[28] without asking how this is accomplished. But patrilineal descent systems are always social achievements, transforming biological descent in the interest of social continuity.

When a form of social organization is dependent on sacrifice for its identification and maintenance, it can also be lost by failure to sacrifice or endangered by improper sacrifice. Kinship relations can be restructured, individuals can be adopted, and even subsidiary lineages can be incorporated into a descent group by participation in sacrifice. Conversely, when this is not intended, it is extremely important to exclude from sacrifices persons not in the line of descent, because partaking in those sacrifices will supersede biological paternity and will indeed constitute recognized alliance by descent. The ethnographic literature sometimes contains vivid accounts of bitter arguments between lineage leaders as to who can, and who cannot, participate in a given sacrifice. Irregularities in descent that occurred generations back figure powerfully in the present. Even among the Tallensi, who keep jural and biological paternity very close, Fortes encountered one such struggle over the inclusion of an accessory lineage of slave descent. (There were whispers of strangers being present, and Fortes thought at first that they meant him, but as delays, tensions, and acrimonious debate followed he realized that the presence of members of this accessory lineage was in question.)[29] It is always a serious matter, not just because ancestors may be offended, but because rights of participation in sacrifice can carry with them rights in productive property of the lineage. When sacrifice works in this way, it is what Austin called "performative"[30] or what Thomas Aquinas called an effective sign,[31] one that causes what it signifies: patrilineage membership.

The Logic of Sacrifice

Why, in unrelated traditions, should sacrifice, rather than some other ritual, be used to identify patrilineage membership? Possible psychological reasons could be suggested. Symbolic reasons may

293

also be offered: The only action that is as serious as giving birth, which can act as a counterbalance to it, is killing. This is one way to interpret the common sacrificial metaphors of birth and rebirth, or birth done better, on purpose and on a more spiritual, more exalted level than mothers do it. For example, the man for whose benefit certain Vedic sacrifices were performed dramatically re-enacted being born, but he was reborn as a god, not a helpless infant. The priest, in officiating, in enabling this "birth" to take place, performed a role analogous to that of a mother.[32] Some of these metaphors are astonishingly literal: In the West African city of Benin, on the many occasions of human sacrifice, the priests used to masquerade as pregnant women, having sent all real women out of the city.[33]

Unlike childbirth, sacrificial killing is deliberate, purposeful, "rational" action, under perfect control. Both birth and killing are acts of power, but sacrificial ideology commonly construes childbirth as the quintessence of vulnerability, passivity, and powerless suffering.

Symbolic representation, differing as it does with each unique cultural situation, is not by itself an adequate way to understand features of sacrificial practice that transcend the boundaries of different traditions. From a social structural perspective, the formal logical structure of sacrifice itself may offer the most helpful way of understanding why sacrificial ritual is chosen to identify patrilineage membership in unrelated traditions. Analysis of the two modes of sacrifice, communion and expiation, as well as their interrelation, reveals this logical structure.

Communion sacrifice unites worshipers in relation to the good, whereas expiatory sacrifice separates them from evil. These two forms have often been discussed as if they were wholly separate or separable kinds of action.[34] But like the gender-related features of sacrifice, the interconnection of communion and expiation is a regular feature of sacrificial religions recognizable across unrelated traditions. This is the case even though one mode may be more heavily emphasized than another in any given society at any given historical period. The ethnographic literature may accentuate this imbalance as, according to the interests of the ethnographer, the focus is on one mode to the near exclusion of the other (for example, Meyer Fortes's focus on Tallensi communion sacrifice,[35] or Evans-Pritchard's less restricted focus on Nuer expiatory sacrifice).[36] The secondary literature sometimes treats one mode to the total exclusion of the other, as, for example, M. Detienne's interesting discussion of Greek sacrifice, *Dionysos Slain*.[37] Because this is a structural analysis of Greek alimentary codes, it is concerned exclusively with communion sacrifice (*thusia*), since Greek expiatory sacrifice (*enagismos*) was not eaten. (One kind of Greek expiatory sacrifice was *Holocaust*, meaning "burnt whole.") Sometimes expiatory aspects of sacrifice are ignored for no apparent reason, as in van der Leeuw's phenomenological discussion of sacrifice.[38]

Considered as logical structures, communion and expiation are two aspects of *one* process, no matter how heavily one or the other may be emphasized in particular ritual acts. In a purely formal sense, communion is a kind of integration, and expiation a kind of differentiation, and these are always and everywhere (even in mathematics) two aspects of one inseparable process. Integration, constituting or recognizing the oneness of anything, is not possible without differentiating it from *other* things.[39] And conversely, we cannot differentiate something from the rest of the world without at the same time integrating it, without conceiving it as a recognizable whole. So in sacrifice, as that wonderful English word reveals, all atonement is also always at-one-ment.[40]

The interrelation of communion and expiatory sacrifice may be understood as being or creating a formal logical structure in the following way. Communion sacrifice unites worshipers in one moral community and at the same time differentiates that community from the rest of the world. Expiatory sacrifice integrates by getting rid of countless different moral and organic undesirable conditions: sin, disease, famine, spirit possession, social discord, blood guilt, incest, impurity of descent, pollution of childbirth, and so on, all having in common only that they must be expiated. What is integrated is one. What is differentiated is logically without limit and can be expressed in a single term only negatively, as *not* the integrated whole, as opposed to it as disorder is to order, as unclean is to clean, or in formal logical terms, as Not-A is to A. In the terms of formal logic, the work of sacrifice is the creation and maintenance of contradictory dichotomy.[41]

Recognizing this unity of communion and expiation, as a way of creating both oneness and separateness, makes it possible to understand sacrifice as symbolic action without being stopped short at the boundary of every unique cultural situation by the variety and conventional nature of symbol-referent relations. We can describe the kind of logical structure that is created and maintained by sacrificial integration-and-differentiation as a purely formal empty structure, A versus Not-A, leaving aside the specific contents of this structure, which do indeed vary from culture to culture.

Recognizing the logical structure of sacrifice also helps to understand aspects of sacrificial religion sometimes considered to be "irrational," such as the contagion of pollution. (An Israelite example of the contagion of pollution is that a man who touched a menstruating woman, or anything directly in contact with her, became unclean himself.) Logically, except that it is not A, Not-A is wholly undefined and *undefinable*. This is what logicians mean by the "infinitation of the negative." Whatever is contiguous with Not-A, whatever is not formally separated from it, is logically included in Not-A itself. In this way, the contagion of pollution becomes understandable as a *logically* necessary consequence of this structure of formal logic when it is applied directly to the material world.

Sacrifice may be performed for many reasons. But it is beautifully adapted for integrating patrilineal descent groups, a goal that can only be accomplished by differentiation from all other lines of descent. Sacrifice can both expiate descent from women (along with other dangers) and integrate the "pure and eternal" patrilineage. Exogamous patrilineal descent groups, in which, as it were, A men must marry Not-A women, are dependent on alien women for their continuity. But if descent from these women were given full social recognition, the patrilineage would have no boundaries and no recognizable continuity. As an illustration of how recognizing descent from women can destroy the continuity of the patrilineal line, consider the genealogy of Abraham in Genesis 11. Here the Priestly source, P, far more concerned with purity of patrilineal descent than the other sources, lists nine "begettings" between Noah's son Shem and Abraham. In the tenth ascending generation only the name of Noah is needed for perfect continuity. But had bilateral descent been consistently recognized, for the same perfect continuity one thousand and twenty-four ancestors would have had to be named in Noah's generation—a task beyond even P's ability.

The integration of a unilineal descent group, its continuity through time as the same, as one, can only be accomplished by differentiation from other such lines of descent. There is necessarily an either-or about lineage membership (members must be distinguished from not-members), and for patrilineages this either-or requires transcending descent from women. This is one way to understand why childbearing women must not sacrifice and also why the pollution of childbirth so commonly needs to be expiated sacrificially.

It is a common sacrificial principle that participation in the rule-governed (moral, not biological) relatedness of father and son in a ritually defined social order enduring continuously through time overcomes birth and death (continually changing the membership of the "eternal" lineage) and all other threats of social chaos. Man born of woman may be destined to die, but man integrated into an "eternal" social order to that degree transcends mortality. I use the word *man* advisedly for in sacrificially maintained descent groups, "immortality," which may be no more than the memory of a name in a genealogy, is commonly a masculine privilege: it is through fathers and sons, not through mothers and daughters, that "eternal" social continuity is maintained. Daughters, who will marry out, are not members of the lineage in the same way as are their brothers, nor do mothers ordinarily have full membership in the lineage of their husbands and sons. Where participation in "eternal" social continuity is a paternal inheritance, mortality itself may be understood as a maternal inheritance. (As Job said, "Man that is born of woman is of few days, and full of trouble. . . . Who can bring a clean thing out of an unclean?" 14:1 and 4.) Sacrificially constituted descent, incorporating women's mortal children into an "eternal" (enduring through generations) kin group, in which membership is recognized by sacrificial ritual, not merely by birth, enables a patrilineal descent group to transcend mortality in the same process in which it transcends birth. In this sense, sacrifice is doubly a remedy for having been born of woman.

Sacrifice in the Judeo-Christian Tradition

This analysis of the work of sacrifice can illuminate aspects of Israelite blood sacrifice as well as its Christian derivatives. I have selected two examples of Israelite sacrifice, one mythical, one historical, to illustrate some of the ways in which an understanding of sacrifice as a means of identifying, maintaining, and even constituting social relations in terms of patrilineal descent can offer new interpretations. First consider Jacob's sacrifice (his first) at the time of his covenant with his mother's brother, Laban.

Throughout the stories of the Patriarchs the continuity of patrilineal descent appears precarious. It was a dark moment for patriliny when Isaac (who *never* sacrificed) lost control of his line of descent. All seems lost when Jacob, the sister's son, fleeing his angry father and brother (patrilineal relatives), went to his mother's brother, taking with him the blessing of the heir, gained deceitfully under his *mother's* guidance. Laban (who turns out later to insist on the principle of descent through women) welcomed him, saying (ominously), "Surely you are my bone and my flesh" (Gen. 29:14). And Jacob, entangled in what looks very much like a matrilineal scene (a sister's son working for his mother's brother, married uxorilocally and avunculocally to his mother's brother's daughters)[42] could not escape for twenty years. Finally Jacob fled again, this time back to the home of his father, taking with him his wives and children. Laban, of course, pursued him, claiming, "The daughters are my daughters and the sons are my sons" (Gen. 31:43), these "sons" being the ones everyone else thinks of as Jacob's sons and whose relation to Laban can only be traced through women. Finally Laban was forced to admit defeat, and in making his covenant with Jacob he invoked "the God of Abraham, the God of Nahor, the God of their father" to keep peace between them. Then Jacob sacrificed and invited his "brethren" to eat (Gen. 31:53–54). (The Hebrew word means literally "brothers.")

There is a problem here for translators, for sense requires that Laban must have shared the sacrificial meal, since the covenant was with him, yet as one biblical scholar writes, "Laban is not said to partake, but the 'brethren' of Jacob," and *Jacob did not have any brethren with him.*[43] Scholars have had to choose between literal and sensible translations of this passage. (The word *brethren* is used in the King James Bible, *brothers* in the Jerusalem Bible; more circumspectly, the Revised Standard and New English Bibles use *kinsmen,* and cautiously avoiding all kinship terminology, the Anchor Bible chooses *companions.*) But interpreted in terms of the relation between sacrifice and patrilineal descent, the problem vanishes. Jacob and Laban's resolution of their descent conflict was to rephrase their relationship, by means of sacrifice, in terms of patrilineal descent. This is why the invocation was to "the God of

Abraham, the God of Nahor, the God of their father." Nahor, Abraham's brother, was Laban's patrilineal grandfather, just as Abraham was Jacob's patrilineal grandfather. The father of both Abraham and Nahor was the ancestor who represented the point of patrilineal alliance between Jacob and Laban. (In ancestral cults, the ancestors who are ritually important are precisely those who mark alliances and distinctions between lineages.) In terms of this sacrifice, Laban was no longer Jacob's mother's brother, but one of his "brethren," his patrilineal classificatory brother. Through this sacrifice, Jacob had patrilineally reconstituted (had at-oned) their descent relations. They had become agnates sacrificing together.

Now consider this historical problem facing biblical scholars: during the time of the Monarchy and earlier, the peace offering, a *communion* sacrifice, was common. After the Exile, when the returning Jews established the Second Temple at Jerusalem and Israel became a theocracy, the peace offering was abandoned and the sin offering, an *expiatory* sacrifice, took its place.[44] Why? For over a hundred years, this radical change in Israelite sacrificial practice has been explained psychologically, as a consequence of guilt. According to the great nineteenth-century biblical scholar, Julius Wellhausen, the Exile and the disasters preceding it created such despair that "the whole of the past is regarded as one enormous sin." [45] The changes in sacrificial practice are supposed to follow from this, but they can be explained more adequately in terms of changes in social organization.

As in many traditions, Israelite communion sacrifice was to be eaten, but expiatory sacrifice was not. The rare and most solemn expiatory sacrifices were not eaten at all, but the ordinary sin offering, in actual performance, was almost identical to the peace offering.[46] Identical portions were burnt on the altar and identical portions were to be eaten. But while the meat of the peace offering was shared among all concerned, priests and nonpriests, the meat of the sin offering could be eaten *only* by males of the priestly lineage: an expiatory sacrifice for the general population and a communion sacrifice for priests only. The peace offering could integrate all Israelites, differentiating them from the pagan "nations," but the sin offering identified and integrated only the priestly lineage, sharply differentiating it from the rest of the population. Before the Exile (in the times of the peace offering), when priests were mere royal appointees, it was not nearly as important for them to differentiate their lineage as it was after the Exile when they were the ruling body of the country. (And of course, compared with the post-exilic Priestly source's obsession with the purity and patrilineality of descent, the earlier sources, who provide accounts of peace offerings, were comparatively unconcerned with purity of priestly patrilineal descent.)

This analysis has been concerned with sacrifice, not as divine action, but as a form of human social action; not with relations established by sacrifice between men and divinities, but with relations established by sacrifice between men and men and with the relevance of these relations for women. In turning to Christian sacrificial practices, we are concerned only with "sacrifice" as it is, or has been, practiced by ordinary members of a particular social structure, connecting males with one another in enduring unilineal descent of order: the apostolic succession of the clergy. Just as we can only metaphorically identify the Christian ritual and the form of social organization associated with it as a "blood sacrifice" and a "patrilineal descent system," respectively, so too we can only identify analogies between Christian and tribal use of sacrifice for maintaining social order.

Church historians describe in detail both changes in the social organization of the church and changes in eucharistic practice and theology, but they do not describe these changes as features of one another. Attention to their interrelation shows that eucharistic practice and theology never changed without corresponding changes in social organization. The Eucharist as "blood sacrifice," the Christian clergy as a specific sacrificing priesthood, and the uni-lineal organization of that priesthood as exclusive inheritors of apostolic authority, all came into being together and developed together; and the rejection of one entailed the simultaneous rejection of the others.

The church began with neither "blood sacrificial" practice nor related social structure. Nowhere in the New Testament is the Eucharist described as being itself a sacrifice, nor is there any indication of a special office for celebrating it. The New Testament refers to Jewish and pagan priests, but nowhere to Christian priests (except the universal priesthood of all believers). There is not only no mention of the apostolic succession, but by implication there can be no successors to the apostles as such.[47]

300

Hebrews is the only New Testament book specifically about sacrifice, but it is about the end of all sacrificing. According to Hebrews, the temporal Levitical priesthood, with membership "according to a legal requirement concerning bodily descent" (7:16), dependent on repeated sacrifices, has been superseded. There is no more repeated father-son succession, perfect Father-Son continuity having been achieved for all time. The perfect sacrifice having been offered once for all time, there is neither need nor possibility of any Christian acting as a priest sacrificing for others. The only sacrifices believers are to make are of alms and praise. There is no mention of the Eucharist, nor is there the slightest reference to any formal social structure (except the obsolete Levitical priesthood) that could conceivably depend on repeated sacrifices for its identification and maintenance.

As the Second Coming was delayed, the major problems facing the church became precisely those of temporal continuity and succession of authority: the preservation of the church as *one* against heresy and schism as well as persecution. On the institutional level this was finally achieved by the development of the apostolic succession of the clergy, a purely male unilineal descent of order, and on the ideological level by the intensification, materialization, and centralization of repeated sacrifice.

The process began early. The first explicit description of the Eucharist as sacrifice is in the *Didache* (14:1–3), probably written in the early second century. Here it is already taken for granted that the Eucharist is a sacrifice, although not yet a "blood" sacrifice.[48] Contextually, it is clearly an offering of praise and thanksgiving, made by the bishop for the congregation. Although the bishop was not yet a priest, there was now a special office for celebrating the ritual.

This development was gradual, but especially during its occasional spurts the inseparable relation of sacrificial ideology and social organization is evident. Cyprian was bishop of Carthage for only ten years in the mid-third century. During that brief period he was the first to make the explicit transition from the universal priesthood of all believers to the particular priesthood of the sacrificing bishops, and the first to develop systematically the idea that the apostolic heritage was attached to the office of bishop rather than to the church as a whole. He was the first to use the word *sacerdos* (priest) for the Christian clergy (the episcopate) and he was also the first to make the body and blood of Christ the object of sacrifice by Christian priests, not only by more transcendent powers.[49] Cyprian's central concern was the unity of the church, and he understood this as absolutely dependent on *one* legitimate line of succession. Probably none of these changes appeared as innovations to Cyprian, and taken in their contexts, they appear far less radical, but the contextual situations remained in the past and the innovations endured as eternal tradition.[50]

A century later, Christianity became the established religion. Step by step, with the consequent rapid expansion and development of the clerical hierarchy, came radical changes in eucharistic theology. Ideas of the Eucharist as a literal blood sacrifice appeared and with them sacrificial concerns about ritual purity, pollution of childbirth, and so on. (Remember Jerome's celebration of *non*childbearing women, virgins, and widows.) All kinds of conversionist theories developed to explain how bread and wine actually became body and blood. These questions were not resolved by the doctrine of transubstantiation until the clerical hierarchy reached its ultimate development in the thirteenth century, but along the way, as the hierarchy grew, every major eucharistic controversy was won by the side with the more literal, "blood sacrificial," interpretation.

During this entire period, from Augustine to Thomas, theology of sacrifice, but *not* theology of the church, changed in accord with developments in clerical social organization.[51] The priesthood was specifically identified by its exclusive right to sacrifice, and its other functions receded into the background.[52] As differentiation between clergy and laity increased, just as we would expect, the eucharistic sacrifice became more and more expiatory. The participation of lay persons in the Eucharist correspondingly shrank until they were mere spectators,[53] communicating only once a year and then receiving only bread. Just as with the Israelite priesthood, the sacrifice that identified the Christian priesthood had become a sin offering, eaten by the priests alone, or sometimes not eaten at all.

The Protestant reformers disagreed strongly among themselves on interpretations of the Eucharist, but they were united in rejecting it *as sacrifice,* and with it the sacrificing priesthood and the apostolic succession of the clergy. When Luther said, "In truth, your resacrificing is a most impious recrucifying," he was attacking not merely an interpretation of a ritual but also the social structure that was identified by and depended on that ritual. And in response to the Protestant reformation, the Roman Catholic church, at the Council of Trent, logically reaffirmed its commitment to eucharistic sacrifice and to the exclusive sacrificing power of those ordained in the apostolic succession.

With the partial exception of some radical sects, the Protestant reformers' rejection of ecclesiastical patriliny was not, of course, a rejection of patriarchy itself, but rather a feature of their break with ecclesiastical continuity. Patriliny is only one of many forms of patriarchy. (Consider, for example, the Pastoral Epistles, which are thoroughly patriarchal without either sacrificial or patrilineal imagery.)

Controversy over the Eucharist as sacrifice is alive and well in the twentieth century in a way it has not been since the sixteenth because of renewed ecumenical interest. Particularly in Anglican-Roman Catholic ecumenical discussion,[54] the issue of sacrifice is central, since for the Roman Catholic church, those who are not part of the sacrificial cult are outside the true succession of Christianity. The arguments carried on in ecumenical discussions by the strongest advocates of sacrifice are sometimes uncannily like the equally serious arguments reported in ethnographies between patrilineage leaders about who can and who cannot participate in a certain sacrifice. The immovable barrier to sacrificing together is not theological but a concern for purity of descent. Like tribal leaders, churchmen cite irregularities in descent occurring generations back as insuperable barriers to sacrificing together. As a Jesuit historian writes,

> Roman Catholic apologists do not cease to point out that no matter how nearly Anglicans may advance towards acceptance of the full Catholic doctrine of the priesthood and of the Eucharist, no matter how earnestly they may desire to attribute to their clergy the Catholic sacerdotal power, that cannot restore the loss if, as a consequence of the events of the mid-sixteenth century, the apostolic succession of order was extinguished in the Church of England.[55]

Still today, those churches demanding episcopal ordination on the basis of the exclusive apostolic succession of the clergy are the only churches celebrating the Eucharist as a sacrifice. They still do not ordain women, with the exception of the Anglican and Episcopal churches, which are internally divided on that issue just as they

303

are internally divided on eucharistic theology. In the sacrificing churches, resistance to ordination of women is not just psychological. Those who reject women's ordination do so for reasons as profound as their concern for the preservation of the structure of the church. And conversely, the women who seek ordination in the Catholic church also seek restructuring of the church, calling for a church order faithful to the New Testament, with neither eucharistic sacrifice nor apostolic succession of the clergy.[56] Both sides of the controversy over women's ordination appear to share an understanding with sacrificing patrilineage members around the world: recognition of the power of sacrifice as a ritual instrument for establishing and maintaining an enduring male-dominated social order.

Notes

1. Louis Moulinier, *Le Pur et l'Impure dans la Pensée des Grecs d'Homere à Aristote* (Paris: Librarie C. Klincksieck, 1952), p. 70.

2. An interesting example of women sacrificers whose role is specifically nonchildbearing but neither virginal nor postmenopausal is the Lovedu of Southern Africa. This is the only traditional society I know in which women are reported to be the major sacrificers. Even the idea of a married woman herself performing sacrifice, as Lovedu women do, would be an abomination in most societies. As is common elsewhere, Lovedu sacrifice is ordinarily performed within specific lineages. A Lovedu woman never sacrifices in her husband's and children's lineage, but only in her father's and brother's lineage. This is because she is recognized as the one who enabled the line of descent from father to son to continue—but notice it is not by bearing children that she performs this service. Her children are born for her husband's lineage, in which she *never* sacrifices. She is responsible for lineage continuity because it is her marriage cattle, the bride wealth given by her husband's lineage, that enabled her brother to acquire a wife, who will bear children to perpetuate his lineage. E. Jensen Krige and J. D. Krige, *The Realm of a Rain-Queen: A Study of the Patterns of Lovedu Society* (London and New York: Oxford University Press, 1943). Also, J. D. Krige and E. J. Krige, "The Lovedu of the Transvaal," in Daryll Forde, ed., *African Worlds: Studies of the Cosmological Ideas and Social Values of African Peoples* (London: Oxford University Press, 1954), pp. 55–84.

3. The only exception I know to the rule excluding childbearing women from the practice of sacrifice is contemporary Haiti, where traditional family structure has been doubly dislocated. The first disruption of the West African patrilineal descent systems was a consequence of transporting slaves to the New World. In rural Haiti family structure was partially reconstituted around inheritance of land, but during slave times, when land did not perform that organizing function, although the ideology of patrilineal descent endured, women probably assumed atypical positions in family structure. More recently, in moves to the city, where only women are likely to find employment and inherited land loses its organizing power, family structure is further reorganized. Families with a heritage of patrilineal ideology find themselves organized around women as exclusive economic producers. Today, urban Haitian voodoo priestesses regularly sacrifice small animals, although they will call in a male priest to sacrifice large ones. Women are not sacrificers in the traditional West African religions from which Haitian voodoo takes its roots, nor do they ordinarily sacrifice in rural Haiti (Karen McCarthy Brown, personal communication).

4. Robert Sutherland Rattray, *Ashanti* (Oxford: Clarendon Press, 1923), p. 96.

5. Yakö social organization is called double descent. This is not like our own "bilateral descent" (in which we understand ourselves to be descended from all our ancestors, both female and male), but rather, each Yakö belongs to two distinct corporate lineages, through which quite different kinds of property are inherited, and whose members meet to perform certain rituals. One of these lineages comprises only persons related through their mother, their mother's mother, and so on; the other, persons tracing their descent only through fathers and sons. Any lineage has both male and female members, but a woman cannot hand on to her children membership in her patrilineage, nor a man membership in his matrilineage. The matrilineages do not sacrifice, although when the two meet together, as at a funeral of a member of both, the matrilineage may provide a victim, such as a sheep, for the patrilineage to sacrifice. Daryll Forde, "Death and Succession: An Analysis of Yakö Mortuary Ceremonies," in Max Gluckman, ed., *Essays on the Ritual of Social Relations* (Manchester: Manchester University Press, 1962). Also, Daryll Forde, *Yakö Studies* (London and New York: Oxford University Press, 1964).

6. Robert H. Lowie, *The Crow Indians* (New York: Rinehart, 1956), p. 237.

7. Ibid., pp. 239–240.

8. Victor Turner, "Sacrifice as Quintessential Process: Prophylaxis or Abandonment?", *History of Religions* 16 (February 1977): 189–215.

9. Victor Turner, *Religion and Divination in Ndembu Ritual* (Ithaca and London: Cornell University Press, 1975), pp. 42–44.

10. All quotations in this paragraph are from Turner, "Sacrifice," pp. 193, 194, 199, 212, 215.

11. Ibid., p. 197. Turner uses *communitas* to mean social linking characterized by good will rather than power and formal organization, and opposes this to "structure," meaning formal and powerful social organization.

12. Ibid., p. 202.

13. Victor Turner, *The Drums of Affliction: A Study of Religious Processes among the Ndembu of Zambia* (Oxford: Clarendon Press, 1968), p. 276.

14. Ibid., p. 12.

15. Since space here does not allow examination of the complex and richly developed Ashanti sacrificial practices, I refer interested readers to my dissertation, "Through-out Your Generations Forever: A Sociology of Blood Sacrifice" (Ph.D. diss., Brandeis University, 1981), pp. 176–213.

16. I am using the term *unilineal descent group* as a gloss covering a variety of different unilineal descent structures: clan, sib, lineage (maximal and minimal), and so on.

17. Meyer Fortes, "The Structure of Unilineal Descent Groups," *American Anthropologist* n.s. 55 (1953): 17–41, 24.

18. Modern capitalist corporations have certain resemblances to corporate lineages, in ownership of property, enduring continuity, and so on (as Sir Henry Maine said, "corporations never die"); but when there is no longer even a metaphor of descent in conceptions of legal or moral corporate unity, sacrificial ritual is wholly irrelevant.

19. Fortes, "Structure," p. 35.

20. Ibid., pp. 30, 32.

21. Meyer Fortes, "Some Reflections on Ancestor Worship in Africa," in M. Fortes and G. Dieterlen, eds., *African Systems of Thought* (London and New York: Oxford University Press, 1965), p. 140.

22. E. E. Evans-Pritchard, *Nuer Religion* (New York and Oxford: Oxford University Press, 1956), p. 287.

23. Meyer Fortes, *The Dynamics of Clanship among the Tallensi* (London: Oxford University Press, 1945), p. 197.

24. Melville Jean Herskovits, *Dahomey: An Ancient West African Kingdom* (New York: J. J. Augustin, 1983), p. 228.

25. N. D. Fustel de Coulanges, *The Ancient City* (New York: Anchor Books, Doubleday, n.d.), pp. 58–59.

26. Fortes, *Clanship*, pp. 54–55.

27. Emile Durkheim, *The Division of Labor in Society* (New York: Macmillan, 1933), p. 179.

28. "A woman is the end of a family." See, for example, Fortes, *Clanship*, p. 191.

29. Ibid., pp. 54–64.

30. J. L. Austin, *How to Do Things with Words* (Cambridge, Mass.: Harvard University Press, 1962).

31. Thomas Aquinas, *Summa Theologica*, III, Q 62:1. For Thomas and Austin, as well as for the Tallensi, the effective work of symbolic action is, of course, also reflexively dependent on the existence of other structures (social, religious, linguistic, legal). Social scientists who have analytically split apart "instrumental" and "expressive" action, and have construed ritual as purely "expressive" action without empirical ends, fail to see this reflexive relation.

32. Henri Hubert and Marcel Mauss, *Sacrifice: Its Nature and Function*, trans. W. D. Halls (London: Cohen and West, 1964), pp. 20–21.

33. Robert Elwyn Bradbury, *The Benin Kingdom and the Edo-speaking Peoples of South-western Nigeria* (London: International African Institute, 1957), p. 59.

34. Modern sacrificial literature began with this assumption. For example, Robertson Smith (*The Religion of the Semites*), following historical biblical scholarship, believed that Israelite worship originally consisted *only* of communion sacrifice. Expiatory sacrifice was a late introduction, not even a natural development, but a consequence of historical events. Jane Harrison (*Prolegomena to the Study of Greek Religion*) reversed this chronology, understanding Greek expiatory sacrifice as a survival from an earlier, primitive, pre-Greek society. The arrival of the rational Greeks brought only communion sacrifice. Hubert and Mauss (*Sacrifice*) were the first to recognize the *insepara*-bility of communion and expiation, but this insight appears to have had little effect on the literature.

35. Fortes, *Clanship*. See also *The Web of Kinship among the Tallensi* (London: International African Institute; Oxford University Press, 1949).

36. Evans-Pritchard, *Nuer Religion*. See Evans-Pritchard, *The Nuer*

(Oxford: Clarendon Press, 1940), for more on Nuer communion sacrifice.

37. Marcel Detienne, *Dionysos Slain,* trans. by Mireille Muellner and Leonard Muellner (Baltimore: Johns Hopkins Press, 1979).

38. Gerardus van der Leeuw, *Religion in Essence and Manifestation: A Study in Phenomenology,* trans. J. E. Turner (Gloucester, Mass.: Peter Smith, 1967).

39. In many Christian churches, the ritual commemorating a sacrifice is called specifically communion, never expiation; but this same ritual necessarily puts worshipers in relation to the Lamb of God, which *takes away* the sin of the world.

40. See *Oxford English Dictionary,* s.v. "atone," for the history of this word, originally meaning "to set or make at one."

41. See Jay, "Through-out Your Generations Forever," pp. 79–89, for a more complete discussion of binary opposition and sacrificial logic.

42. These terms are used by anthropologists in reference to matrilineal societies. They mean, respectively, that a husband resides at the home of his wife, and at the home of his mother's brother.

43. R. J. Thompson, *Penitence and Sacrifice in Early Israel outside the Levitical Law: An Examination of the Fellowship Theory of Early Israelite Sacrifice* (Leiden: E. J. Brill, 1963), p. 67.

44. Most early accounts describe burnt and peace offerings performed together; later accounts pair burnt and sin offerings.

45. Julius Wellhausen, *Prolegomena to the History of Israel,* trans. J. Sutherland Black and Allen Menzies (Edinburgh: A. and C. Black, 1885), p. 279. Quoted in Thompson, *Penitence,* p. 5.

46. The only other difference in the formal procedure is that in the sin offering, a little blood is put on the horns of the altar and the choice of victim is slightly more restricted. The blood rite is an expiatory element present even in the peace offering, but it increases in complexity as the expiatory significance of the different kinds of sacrifice increases. For P's account of the different kinds of Israelite sacrifice and how to perform them, see Leviticus 1–7.

47. Raymond E. Brown, S.J., *Priest and Bishop: Biblical Reflections* (London: Geoffrey Chapman, 1979), p. 55.

48. Robert J. Daly, *Christian Sacrifice: The Judaeo-Christian Background before Origen* (Washington, D.C.: Catholic University of America Press, 1978), p. 313.

49. Cyprian, *Ep.* 63:17.

50. His powerful insistence on only *one* line of episcopal succession was in response to the Novatian schism. His statement that "the passion of the Lord is the sacrifice we offer" was made in the context of insisting that a mixture of wine and water be used in the Eucharist, in opposition to a contemporary use of water alone.

51. Adolph Harnack, *History of Dogma,* vol. 6 (New York: Dover, 1961), pp. 127ff.

52. Brown, *Priest and Bishop,* p. 99.

53. The phrase *mere spectators* does not indicate that visual participation is meaningless. On the contrary, only those who are present, but not permitted to partake, can be fully aware of their exclusion. The differentiating work of expiatory sacrifice is associated everywhere with prohibitions, complete or partial, of alimentary participation. In contrast, in all traditions I know of, the integrating work of communion sacrifice as evidence of patrilineage membership requires actual alimentary participation. For a discussion of the power and meaning of visual participation, see Margaret Miles, *Image as Insight* (Boston: Beacon Press, 1984).

54. For a good review of the literature of recent Anglican and Roman Catholic ecumenical positions, see R. W. Franklin, "An Outline of Arguments on *Apostolicae Curae* from 1896 to 1984," a consultation paper given at the Anglican/Roman Catholic Consultation, New York City, December 11, 1984.

55. Francis Clark, S.J., *Eucharistic Sacrifice and the Reformation* (Oxford: Basil Blackwell, 1967), p. 15.

56. See, for example, Anne Elizabeth Carr, "The Church in Process: Engendering the Future," in Anne Marie Gardiner, ed., *Women and Catholic Priesthood: An Expanded Vision: Proceedings of the Detroit Ordination Conference* (New York, Paramus, and Toronto: Paulist Press, 1976).

Index

Abolitionism, *see* Slavery
Acts of the Apostles, *see* New
    Testament, Books and
    Letters of
Adam, Karl, 253
Addams, Jane, 219
Adultery, *see* Marriage
African tribal rituals, *see* Sacrifice
Aladel, Père, 176
Alain (Émile Chartier), 261
Alberti, Leon Battista, 150
Althaus, Paul, 246–48, 255
Ambrose, St., 150
Amores (Pseudo-Lucian), 69
Ancestor worship, 291, 293, 299
Androcentrism, *see* Male-female
    relationship
Anglican Church, 303. *See also*
    Protestantism
Anne, St., 152
Anthériou, Simone, 268
Anthony, Susan B., 218, 225n39
Anti-Semitism, 188; Christianity
    and, 7, 236–37; gender issues
    in, 7, 227; German, 237–38,
    242–43, (criticized) 228, (of
    theologians) 234–37 *passim*,
    240–41, 245, 246–47, 250–56
Aphrodite (Greek goddess), 65,
    70
Apostolic succession, *see*
    Christianity
Art: symbolism of, 270–71. *See*

also Devotional paintings;
    Greek literature and art
Artemidorus, 69, 70
Asceticism, *see* Celibacy
Asclepiades, 65, 70
Association of Christian Mothers
    (Paris), 161
Assumptionists, *see* Roman
    Catholic Church
Assumption of the Virgin, *see*
    Mary
Astrology, 47, 69–70
Atkinson, Clarissa W., 2, 5, 8,
    11, 310
Attente (waiting for and on
    God), 262, 274, 276–77, 278
Augustine, St., 5, 8, 10–11,
    139–51 *passim*, 156–64 *passim*,
    302; and Augustinians, 144,
    148–51 *passim*, 162, 163, 185;
    Confessions, 140, 143, 144,
    147–51 *passim*, 156, 160, 164;
    Dialogues of, 143; *Lives* of,
    144; Order of Hermits of
    (OSA), 148; Rule of, 167n26
Aurelianus, Caelius, 69, 70
Auspiciousness: of female
    sexuality (in Hindu myth),
    46–47, 53, 54; of food, 123; vs.
    impurity, 40, 44–46;
    -inauspiciousness dichotomy,
    55–56
Austin, J. L., 293

Protestantism: vs. Catholicism, 153, 154, 163, 182, 190; and the family, 152–53, 163, 241; feminization of, 193; and gender roles, 204, 241; and idealism, 253; Protestant Reformation, 154, 160, 161, 163, 302–3; and Protestant social thinking, 214, 238, 242, 250; and Second Great Awakening, 204, 211, 212; and worldly vocation, 154

Psalms, see Hebrew Bible, Books of

Pseudo-Lucian, 69, 70

Ptolemy, 70

Purity, see Impurity

Quakers, 204, 211, 219. See also Protestantism

Quélen, Archbishop of Paris, 176

Quincy, Edmund, 211, 216, 219, 224n32

Race, see Ethnicity/race

Rāmāyana (Sanskrit epic), 42

Rationalism: Roman Catholic Church attitude toward, 5, 181–82, 185

Reality, see Social reality

Reformation, Protestant and Catholic, see Protestantism; Roman Catholic Church

Religion: degeneration of tradition of, 130; feminization of, 193, 250. See also Christianity; Hinduism; Islam; Judaism; Protestantism; Roman Catholic Church; Tibetan Buddhism

Religious symbols or imagery, see Symbols

Rémond, René, 185

Renaissance, Italian, 11, 147–52

Revelation, see New Testament, Books and Letters of

Revelations (St. Birgitta), 145–47

Ricoeur, Paul, 41

Right and Wrong in Boston (Chapman), 208, 209

Ritual: blacks' use of, 94, 96; Eucharist as, see Eucharist, the; Greek, 284, 295, 307n34; Hindu, 40, 41, 49–51; at Lourdes, 191–92; mourning (for virginity), 29–30, 32; as "poetry of everyday practice," 13, 41; Tibetan Buddhist, 123, 125, 129. See also Sacrifice

Rogers, Nathaniel Peabody, 216

Roman Catholic Church: Assumptionists of, 185–89, 191; and Catholic Reformation, 153, 154, 174; and Councils of Florence, Trent, 149, 153, 303; French, 153, 159, 160, 161, 164, 173–90, (feminization of) 193; hierarchy of, see Hierarchy (of Christianity); and idealism, 253; and Marian devotion/symbolism, see Mary; misogyny of, 154; and "modernism," struggle against, 5, 158, 160, 164, 181–82, 189, 195; and "ordinary" women, 158–59, 163–64; Protestantism vs., see Protestantism; and role of papacy, 181–84; sacrifice as issue in, 303; and St. Monica, 148. See also Christianity

Romans, ancient, 293; and homosexuality, 78, 79; literature of, 66–70, 71, 80; and sacrifice, see Sacrifice

Romans, Letter to the, see New Testament, Books and Letters of

Rosaldo, Michelle Zimbalist, 18

Rothe, Richard, 229–33, 235, 238, 242, 245, 249

Ruether, Rosemary, 114; quoted, 113

Sacred Heart of Jesus, 183, 184, 186, 191

Contributors

CLARISSA W. ATKINSON is Associate Professor of the History of Christianity at Harvard Divinity School. She was a visiting scholar in the Women's Studies in Religion Program in 1974–75 and 1975–76.

DOROTHY C. BASS is Assistant Professor of Church History at Chicago Theological Seminary. She was a visiting scholar in the Women's Studies in Religion Program in 1977–78 and 1978–79.

SHEILA BRIGGS is Assistant Professor of Religious Studies at the University of Southern California. She was a visiting scholar in the Women's Studies in Religion Program in 1982–83.

BERNADETTE J. BROOTEN is Assistant Professor of New Testament at Harvard Divinity School. She was a visiting scholar in the Women's Studies in Religion Program in 1978–79.

CONSTANCE H. BUCHANAN is Assistant Dean of Harvard Divinity School and has been the Director of the Women's Studies in Religion Program since 1977.

JO ANN HACKETT is a Mellon Fellow in Near Eastern Studies at the Johns Hopkins University. She was a visiting scholar in the Women's Studies in Religion Program in 1981–82.

NANCY JAY is Visiting Lecturer on Social Science and Religion at Harvard Divinity School. She was a visiting scholar in the Women's Studies in Religion Program in 1980–81.

ANNE C. KLEIN is Lecturer in Religious Studies at Stanford University. She was a visiting scholar in the Women's Studies in Religion Program in 1982–83.

FRÉDÉRIQUE APFFEL MARGLIN is Assistant Professor of Sociology and Anthropology at Smith College. She was a visiting scholar in the Women's Studies in Religion Program in 1976–77 and 1977–78.

Contributors

MARGARET R. MILES is Professor of Historical Theology at Harvard Divinity School.

BARBARA CORRADO POPE is Director and Assistant Professor of Women's Studies at the University of Oregon. She was a visiting scholar in the Women's Studies in Religion Program in 1981–82.

JUDITH VAN HERIK is Associate Professor of Religious Studies at the Pennsylvania State University. She was a visiting scholar in the Women's Studies in Religion Program in 1974–75.

DELORES S. WILLIAMS is Instructor in Religion and Literature at Fisk University. She was a visiting scholar in the Women's Studies in Religion Program in 1980–81.